TRANSFORMING CHILD WELFARE

Interdisciplinary Practices, Field Education, and Research

Voices from the Prairies

Previous publications in the Voices from the Prairies series:

Passion for Action in Child and Family Services (2009)

Awakening the Spirit: Moving Forward in Child Welfare (2012)

*Reinvesting in Families: Strengthening Child
Welfare Practice for a Brighter Future* (2014)

TRANSFORMING CHILD WELFARE

Interdisciplinary Practices, Field Education, and Research

Voices from the Prairies

edited by

**H. Monty Montgomery, Dorothy Badry,
Don Fuchs, and Daniel Kikulwe**

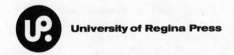 **University of Regina Press**

Transforming Child Welfare: Interdisciplinary Practices, Field Education, and Research may be downloaded free of charge from www.uofrpress.ca or may be reprinted or copied, in whole or in part, *for educational, service, or research purposes* without permission. For all other purposes, written permission to reprint or use is required. Requests for written permission should be sent to the publisher.

Production of *Transforming Child Welfare: Interdisciplinary Practices, Field Education, and Research* has been made possible through funding from the Alberta Centre for Child, Family & Community Research (ACCFCR), the Social Sciences and Humanities Research Council of Canada (Connections Grant Program), and the Saskatchewan Health Research Foundation (Research Connections Program). The views expressed herein do not necessarily represent the views of ACCFCR or those of the editors. Every reasonable effort has been made to secure necessary permissions, but errors or omissions should be brought to the attention of H. Monty Montgomery at H.Monty.Montgomery@uregina.ca.

Suggested Citation: Montgomery, H., Badry, D., Fuchs, D., & Kikulwe, D. (Eds.). (2016). *Transforming Child Welfare: Interdisciplinary Practices, Field Education, and Research.* Regina, SK: University of Regina Press.

Printed and bound in Canada by Friesens. The text of this book is printed on 100% post-consumer recycled paper with earth-friendly vegetable-based inks.

Cover Design: Duncan Campbell, University of Regina Press
Text Design: John van der Woude Designs
Copy editor: Kirsten Craven
Proofreader: Katie Doke Sawatzky
Index: Patricia Furdek
Cover Art: "Silhouette of girl blowing dandelion" by Ulkass / Dreamstime.com

Library and Archives Canada Cataloguing in Publication

Transforming child welfare : interdisciplinary practices, field education, and research : voices from the Prairies / edited by H. Monty Montgomery, Dorothy Badry, Don Fuchs, and Daniel Kikulwe.

Includes bibliographical references and indexes. Issued in print and electronic formats. ISBN 978-0-88977-451-3 (paperback).—ISBN 978-0-88977-452-0 (pdf).—ISBN 978-0-88977-453-7 (html)

1. Child welfare—Canada. 2. Children—Government policy—Canada. 3. Children—Canada—Social conditions. 4. Family policy—Canada. 5. Social work with children—Canada. 6. Social work education—Canada. I. Badry, Dorothy Eleanor, 1958-, author, editor II. Kikulwe, Daniel, author, editor III. Fuchs, Don, 1948-, author, editor IV. Montgomery, H. Monty, 1962-, author, editor

HV745.A6T73 2016   362.70971
C2016-904752-0   C2016-904753-9

10 9 8 7 6 5 4 3 2 1

 University of Regina Press

University of Regina Press,
  University of Regina
Regina, Saskatchewan, Canada, S4S 0A2
TEL: (306) 585-4758 FAX: (306) 585-4699
WEB: www.uofrpress.ca

We acknowledge the support of the Canada Council for the Arts for our publishing program. We acknowledge the financial support of the Government of Canada. / Nous reconnaissons l'appui financier du gouvernement du Canada. This publication was made possible through Creative Saskatchewan's Creative Industries Production Grant Program.

 Canada Council for the Arts   Conseil des Arts du Canada

 Canada   creative SASKATCHEWAN

This book is dedicated to those who care for and work with children. We must go forward with care, community, and compassion in striving for what is best for children and families, keeping in mind human rights and justice. The time for transformation in child welfare is here.

Contents

Part III. Research

Part IV. Teaching

Foreword

Brad McKenzie

"Wicked problems" are problems that are difficult to solve because they have a high degree of complexity, and the circumstances surrounding them are somewhat unique. Each solution gives rise to a new problem; thus, problems must be resolved over and over again without the ability to apply a commonly recognized model or blueprint (Rittel & Webber, 1973). Child abuse and neglect are wicked problems, and in the last national study conducted in Canada in 2008, more than 235,000 allegations of child maltreatment were identified (Public Health Agency of Canada, 2010). The rate of children in care in Canada is among the highest in the developed world (Thoburn, 2007), and the disproportionate rate of Indigenous children in care, particularly in Western Canada (Sinha, Trocmé, Blackstock, MacLaurin, & Fallon, 2011), is a national tragedy. The child welfare system is under intense public and media scrutiny, yet efforts to protect children and support families continue to be confronted by constraints in funding, poorly coordinated service responses, and challenges in training and retaining professionals. An even more important issue is the inadequate systemic response to the structural causes of child maltreatment, including poverty, poor housing, and racial injustice, which in the case of Indigenous children and families are related to the legacy of residential schools and other forms of colonialism. The plethora of special studies and inquiries have, at best, resulted in modest changes in service delivery or funding, and too often these are accompanied by new procedures and requirements for compliance that seem to impede rather than support best practices that both protect children and support families. Meanwhile, our search for a single best practice model in child and family welfare, like the search for the Holy Grail, continues in vain.

If the child welfare system and allied professions like education, health, and justice are really addressing wicked problems, it will be apparent that there is no single best practice model. Instead, we must focus our efforts on creating multiple best practice solutions oriented to the issues presented in different contexts. This is the goal of the chapters selected for this book on *Transforming Child Welfare: Interdisciplinary Practices, Field Education, and Research*, which are based on topics presented at the 2014 symposium of the Prairie Child Welfare Consortium. Reflecting the theme of *transformative change* by building on strengths, engagement through empowering relationships, and the integration of research evidence with practice knowledge and experience, these chapters identify some of the pathways to follow in dealing with the wicked problems found in the child welfare system.

The messages in these chapters resonate with four other developments in the field of child and family welfare that give me cause for "hope and optimism" – to borrow a phrase from the late Jack Layton. First is the report of the Truth and Reconciliation Commission of Canada (2015) on residential schools and its ninety-four recommendations that outline a model for reconciliation between Indigenous and non-Indigenous Canadians. The current Liberal government of Canada has voiced support for these recommendations, and thirty-seven of these recommendations focus on ways to address some of the disparities in the education, child welfare, health, and justice systems affecting many Indigenous people. If implemented, these actions will make a difference. Second is the January 2016 ruling by the Canadian Human Rights Tribunal that the federal government has discriminated against First Nations children in funding for children's services on reserves for decades (Rabson, 2016). We can despair that it took a long legal challenge to overcome resistance from the Harper Government to this basic human right; at the same time, a new-found commitment to address this disparity will also make a difference. Third is the slow but growing realization that a differential or alternate response to working with families receiving child welfare services is required where more emphasis is placed on supportive engagement with families and collaboration with other community services as a first response to allegations of abuse and neglect. This trend is consistent with more attention to other innovations, such as customary care in Indigenous communities. Fourth is evidence that the responses to shortcomings in the child welfare system, which at the most serious level result in the death of a child, have often focused disproportionately on introducing more rules and procedures to ensure increased policy compliance. Too often the result has been to overbureaucratize the service delivery system and divert attention away from professional judgment and the development of more creative service responses (Munroe, 2011). Accountability is important, but Munroe also calls for the need to build a learning culture within service organizations that supports the development of more flexible programs, knowledge based on reflective practice, and collaboration among service providers.

The chapters in this collection are consistent with these general themes but give more specific attention to solutions to various aspects of the wicked problems underlying a number of our responses to child and family welfare in our communities. One chapter gives specific attention to child rights and another describes the experiences of racialized workers' perspectives in working with diverse families. Four chapters highlight the importance of engaging more directly with service users. For example, there are two selections that focus on building client-worker alliances within a harm reduction strategy, another that describes methods of strengthening children's capacities to cope with separation and loss, and a chapter that examines the experiences of women with learning difficulties who have been criminalized. The theme of positive engagement is also evident in several chapters that connect research to collaborative practice across systems. These include chapters that discuss research in and with First Nations communities, community-based research in HIV training for child welfare workers, community-engaged research with youth transitioning from care to emerging adulthood, and the need for continuing collaboration in developing distance education courses that support child welfare practice among partners to the Prairie Child Welfare Consortium. Finally, three chapters focus specifically on developing solutions that support better services for children affected by fetal alcohol spectrum disorder (FASD) in the child welfare system. The high rate of children in care affected by FASD and the high social and economic costs associated with this disability makes this issue one of the most important to address in reducing the disparity in outcomes between children and youth in the child welfare system and those in the general population.

Responding to the wicked problems associated with child maltreatment by building on the four major developments in the field I have summarized, and expanding the implementation of best practice solutions described in this volume will not be easy. Many of these promising solutions remain in their formative stages. Broader application of these approaches and the importance of ongoing collaboration to connect these solutions to structural responses that will more effectively address problems of poverty, marginalization, and racial injustice are required, and this demands a strong and continuing commitment to advocacy both within and beyond the child welfare system. It also requires a special focus on building relationships with partners who will prioritize principles of equity and social justice in programs and services for our most disadvantaged children and families.

References

Munro, E. (2011). *The Munro Review of Child Protection: Final report – A child-centred system*. London, UK: The Stationery Office Limited.

Public Health Agency of Canada. (2010). *Canadian incidence study of child abuse and neglect-2008: Major findings*. Ottawa, ON: Author.

Rabson, M. (2016, January 27). "A victory for children": Canadian Human Rights Tribunal rules federal government's child welfare program discriminated against First Nations kids for decades. *Winnipeg Free Press*, p. A1.

Rittel, H., & Webber, M. (1973). Dilemmas in a general theory of planning. *Policy Sciences, 4*, 155–168.

Sinha, V., Trocmé, N., Blackstock, C., MacLaurin, B., & Fallon, B. (2011). Understanding the overrepresentation of First Nations children in Canada's child welfare system. In K. Kufeldt & B. McKenzie (Eds.), *Connecting research, policy, and practice in child welfare* (2nd ed.) (pp. 307–322). Waterloo, ON: Wilfrid Laurier University Press.

Thoburn, J. (2007). *Globalisation and child welfare: Some lessons from a cross-national study of children in out-of-home care*. Social Work Monograph, School of Social Work, University of East Anglia, UK.

Truth and Reconciliation Commission of Canada. (2015). *Honouring the truth, reconciling for the future: Summary of the final report of the Truth and Reconciliation Commission of Canada*. Ottawa, ON: Author. Retrieved from http://www.trc.ca

From the Editors

We are very delighted to bring you this book, *Transforming Child Welfare: Interdisciplinary Practices, Field Education, and Research*. It is the fifth publication of the Prairie Child Welfare Consortium (PCWC) in our Voices from the Prairies Series. It is strongly supported by the faculties of social work at the University of Calgary, University of Manitoba, and University of Regina, as well as the Saskatchewan Federation of Indigenous Nations, Canada First Nations University Social Work Program, and the Alberta Centre for Child, Family and Community Research.

The chapters in the book represent a selection of some of the outstanding presentations made at the Prairie Child Welfare Consortium's eighth biennial symposium, Celebrating Child Welfare Transformations: Interdisciplinary Practices, Field Education and Research, held in Saskatoon, Saskatchewan, on October 1–3, 2014. Individuals attending previous PCWC symposia (Saskatoon, 2001; Winnipeg, 2003; Edmonton, 2005; Regina, 2007; Winnipeg, 2009; Edmonton, 2012) emphasized the great importance of sharing information about programs, policies, and initiatives found to be supportive and effective when working with at-risk children and families. Also, individuals attending previous symposia have emphasized the urgent need to reawaken the passion for action to reduce the growing rates of child maltreatment and increased number of children coming into care. The past symposia have highlighted the need to reinvest in families to strengthen and support them to provide safe nurturing environments for children.

Previous symposia have identified the need for the development of innovative programs based on Indigenous Knowledge and methods. In addition, they have pointed to the need to develop evidence-based, culturally appropriate, anti-oppressive practice to ensure that well-intentioned policy, programs, and intervention do no harm but continue to evolve to provide effective services to children and families at risk to child maltreatment.

The PCWC symposium in 2014 aimed to create opportunities where child welfare stakeholders could engage with current knowledge and each other to forge partnerships in support of transforming child welfare practice and research. It also aimed to enhance capacities to build effective networks and collaboration across disciplines and jurisdictional boundaries. The symposium organizers believed it was important that the seventh biennial PCWC symposium continue to work toward child welfare transformation by engaging diverse groups of researchers, practitioners, and community representatives in the sharing, analysis, brainstorming, knowledge creation, and application of child welfare best practices. In addition, the symposium provided an opportunity to promote child welfare transformation through knowledge exchange and showcased innovations within the field of child welfare and field education training across disciplinary and jurisdictional boundaries. Further, the symposium provided a mechanism to promote and foster specific cross-sectorial collaboration among child welfare service providers, as well as promote scholarly research and human resource development.

The program for the 2014 PCWC symposium was designed around the main conference theme of Celebrating Child Welfare Transformations: Interdisciplinary Practices, Field Education and Research. This theme reflected a call to keep advancing the progressive changes that are occurring in child welfare and to chart new directions for the future. The selection of this theme built upon the themes of previous symposia so as to encourage stakeholders to recognize the progress that has occurred, especially with regards to interdisciplinary collaboration, field education, and research in child welfare.

Securing a brighter future for children and families requires co-operative and collaborative planning between child welfare and other systems to better serve and support families. This book has attempted to capture the spirit and commitment of the symposium participants to transform the child welfare system through co-operative, collaborative, and innovative interdisciplinary and intersectoral policy, program, and practice initiatives.

Consistent with the mandates of the PCWC, this book is intended to convey the work of presenters who were able to dedicate time and energy to the difficult task of presenting their experiences, ideas, and research in print form for publication purposes. The outstanding contributions that have resulted reflect the dedication, commitment, and passion of the authors to create a child welfare system that effectively helps children and families grow and thrive.

The introduction to the book outlines holistic perspectives that promote co-operative and collaborative interdisciplinary and intersectoral approaches. We maintain that these approaches are necessary for the transformative changes that actually contribute to the welfare of the child and families. The first chapter of this book examines the changes that have been brought about since the United Nations Convention on the Rights of the Child. Marvin Bernstein, the director of UNICEF Canada, concludes, "There is much yet to be done." As the world marks the twenty-fifth anniversary of the adoption of the Convention on the Rights of the Child, we must continue to work toward full implementation of the convention in Canada. Bernstein indicates, "Ultimately, we must find creative and transformational ways to work together in partnerships."

The PCWC is a tri-provincial and northern multisector, cross-cultural child and family services network representing university educators, government, First Nations, and Métis in-service training and service delivery administrators. Members of the network are dedicated to working together collaboratively for the purpose of strengthening and advancing education and training, policy, service delivery, and research in aid of children and families in need across the Prairie provinces. The development of the PCWC has been profoundly influenced by Aboriginal and Métis peoples and agencies deeply concerned with the escalating numbers of their children and youth in the care of the state. This influence permeates the PCWC's vision, mission, and goals, which are directed toward ensuring that child and family services in the Prairie provinces and the North meet the needs of the children, families, and communities they support. Working together across many levels and sectors, the PCWC partners seek to influence, advocate, and change education, training, research, policy, and practice/service delivery through collaboration, innovation, and partnering. Ensuring respect for the needs of Aboriginal communities in the delivery of child welfare services is fundamental. In this quest, the PCWC seeks affiliation with other national child welfare bodies for joint initiatives that would further the PCWC mission and present a Prairie/northern perspective at the national level.

It is the intention of the editors and the authors of this book to help strengthen the child welfare community in Canada by adding to its distinctive body of child welfare knowledge. Further, it is our hope that the perspectives contained within this book will help foster child welfare transformations that lead to effective collaborative and co-operative interdisciplinary and intersectoral policy, programs, and practices that work to strengthen families in a supportive culture and community. As always, the ultimate goal is to provide safe and healthy environments for children to grow and thrive in, free from the risks of maltreatment.

—Monty Montgomery, Dorothy Badry, Don Fuchs, and Daniel Kikulwe

Acknowledgements

This book represents the interprovincial collaboration among the Prairie Child Welfare Consortium partners: the universities of Manitoba, Regina, and Calgary, and the First Nations University of Canada. It would not have been possible without the contribution of many people and, as editors, we would like to thank each of them for their hard work and support. We must begin by acknowledging the outstanding contributions of the chapter authors, whose expertise, wisdom, and patience with the editing process have created a manuscript that will benefit the field of child welfare research and practice. The chapters reflect the breadth of the authors' considerable experiences as social work practitioners in the field of child welfare, and as researchers, program planners, curriculum developers, and academics. Readers can learn more about the chapter authors in the Contributors section of the book.

The following people served as peer reviewers and provided feedback and suggestions on the chapters. Their comments helped sharpen the focus and the key messages emerging in each chapter and we are sincerely grateful for their input: Dorothy Badry, Linda Burnside, Don Fuchs, Deborah Goodman, Yahya El-Lahib, Therese Grant, Les Jerome, Daniel Kikulwe, Kathy Levine, Audrey McFarlane, Denise Milne, H. Monty Montgomery, Nancy Poole, Christine Walsh, Chris Wekerle, and Alex Wright.

We are grateful to Bruce Walsh, director and publisher of University of Regina Press, who agreed to publish and distribute the hard copies of the book. We are greatly indebted to Donna Grant, senior editor at University of Regina Press, for her ongoing support and encouragement. We would also like to acknowledge the fine work of Duncan Campbell on the cover design of this book. Staff members from University of Regina Press meticulously corrected all of the inconsistencies across chapter formats and contributed substantially to the overall quality of the book.

We wish to acknowledge the time and commitment of the planning committee members of the PCWC's seventh biennial symposium held in Regina, Saskatchewan, on October 1–3, 2014. Particularly, we would like to acknowledge Monty Montgomery and his colleagues for their work in organizing the Saskatchewan symposium. We acknowledge that the presentations from the Regina symposium have formed the basis of the chapters contained in this book. We also acknowledge Brad McKenzie for writing the foreword to this fifth book in the PCWC series.

We wish to thank the faculties of Social Work at the University of Calgary, University of Manitoba, and at the University of Regina for providing us with the encouragement and administrative infrastructure support to carry out much of the work of this book. The editors had valuable assistance from a number of people within their universities.

As well, we would like to thank the core partners of the Prairie Child Welfare Consortium and the Centre of Excellence for Child Welfare for their co-operation and support: Faculty of Social Work, University of Manitoba; Faculty of Social Work, University of Calgary; Faculty of Social Work, University of Regina; First Nations University of Canada; Manitoba Family Services; Alberta Human Services; Saskatchewan Child and Family Services; Federation of Saskatchewan Indian Nations; and Métis Association Alberta.

Introduction

H. Monty Montgomery

Opportunities for cross-organizational networking and interdisciplin-ary cross-pollination such as what typically occur at the biennial Prairie Child Welfare Consortium (PCWC) symposia still remain elusive across the field of child welfare across Western Canada, despite increasing calls for interprofessional collaboration, collaborative research, and wrap-around approaches to service delivery. Realizing that opportunities to gather together in person are limited, the organizing committee that planned and coordinated the 7th Biennial Prairie Child Welfare Symposium held in Saskatoon, Saskatchewan, in 2014 sought to create venues for knowledge sharing between a wide range of individuals and organizations that col-lectively hold much interest in the safety, health, and well-being of chil-dren and youth. Presentations at the conference were geared toward an audience of child welfare workers, children's rights activists, academics, program administrators, and substitute caregivers from the child-serving systems across Western Canada. During the October 2014 conference, over 250 registrants from First Nations, governmental, and community-based organizations sat alongside one another in a culturally safe and neutral space where matters of common interest were introduced and discussed with sensitivity, thoughtfulness, and respect.

Based on feedback from previous symposia and the overall objectives of the constituent members of the Prairie Child Welfare Consortium steering committee, the theme of the 2014 PCWC symposium was Celebrating Child Welfare Transformations: Interdisciplinary Practices, Field Education and Research. Although we understood that many people (including some of our colleagues) may not feel that there is much to "celebrate" about child welfare currently, the organizing committee settled upon this title because we knew that positive change *is* happening within child and family services across the Prairies, Canada, and internationally. As individuals holding considerable knowledge and lived experience with the multidimensional nature of child welfare practice, policy, and research, the organizing committee members sought opportunities to spotlight evolving practices and programs that rarely are given opportunities to tell their own stories but instead remain inflexibly cast in widespread public narratives that arise alongside too frequent incidents of tragedy, misfortune, and political miscues. The symposium organizers recognized that at times when the public and elected representatives are demanding change there is always something to criticize. However, the organizing committee also knew that unless purposive steps are taken to recognize the incremental and substantive initiatives that are occurring daily to improve child welfare services, cynicism and disillusionment could easily supplant evidence-based narratives of success.

Following upon the success of the 2014 symposium, the PCWC steering committee collectively agreed to support the development of a fifth volume in the Voices from the Prairies book series that could draw upon the conference's overarching theme of discussing multiple dimensions of transformational change that have been gradually retooling the roles and functions of people and organizations who are touched by child welfare across Western Canada. Conference presentations spoke to the transformational power of healing and truth telling among service users and practitioners alike. Other presentations demonstrated how scholarly research can document evolving social phenomena and provide evidence in support of updated policies and programming. Some presenters spoke to changes in policy directions that have occurred over time, and their visions for future improvements. And still others spoke to the possibilities for transformation that can occur through well-designed training, professional development, and higher education. These four dimensions of transformative change were identified as the main thematic tracks for the 2014 PCWC symposium.

The variability of transformations that are occurring within social policy, interpersonal relationships, scholarly research, and adult education is also used as a guiding framework for this book. The four conference thematic tracks established for the 2014 symposium organically replicated themselves in the submissions that were received in response to the invitations that the co-editors of this volume distributed to the conference presenters following the conclusion of the event in 2014. Accordingly, the chapters of this book have been grouped together into four sections: policy, practice, research, and teaching.

Each section is comprised of two or more complementary chapters that introduce and discuss varying dimensions of contemporary research and thinking taking place within the child welfare domain. Individually, the chapters articulate the distinct author's subjective positioning with, knowledge of, and philosophical orientation toward the subject matter. Although separate chapters have been grouped together for presentation in this book, each chapter is the author's own scholarly exploration of a topic related to transformational change within child welfare. Academic peers who possess subject matter expertise on the topic have reviewed each chapter. Each chapter therefore stands on its own and should not be read as either an endorsement of, or critique of, any other chapter presented in the same section or elsewhere in the book. Every vision of transformation – like beauty – is in the eye of the beholder, and we ask readers to bear this in mind as you engage with the diverse portraits of transformation that are presented throughout this volume.

The first section of this book comprises three chapters that focus generally on transformational change at the organizational and policy levels. Chapter 1 was written by Marvin Bernstein as an adaptation of a keynote speech he gave to the 2014 PCWC symposium audience. The broad focus of this chapter relates to the need to increase the integration of children's rights within child welfare legislation, policy, and practice. Drawing our attention to the twenty-fifth anniversary of the 1989 endorsement of the United Nations Convention on the Rights of the Child, Bernstein presents a synopsis of the social policy shifts that the convention initiated within Canadian legislation and jurisprudence over the intervening years. Much has changed for the better, but much more still remains to be done if child welfare systems and practice in Canada are to be transformed to better respect children's rights.

Judy Gillespie, who identifies issues with and opportunities for increased interprofessional and interdisciplinary collaboration within the field of child welfare services, wrote Chapter 2. To what extent, Gillespie asks, are common understandings of child welfare actually commonly held and understood? The chapter details and decries the dearth of literature regarding how university-trained professionals work with, communicate, and understand their complementary functions across the complex and interrelated client-serving systems that comprise modern child welfare services. New pathways for transforming interprofessional relationships can be opened by generating and disseminating more research into "core" child welfare knowledge, and the methods by which it is acquired. The development of common knowledge among professionals working with children and families involved with child welfare systems must occur across all disciplines, organizations, and sectors.

Chapter 3 was co-created by an Indigenous author group who presented as a plenary panel to the 2014 symposium. The co-writers of this chapter—H. Monty Montgomery, Margaret Kovach, and Shelley Thomas Prokop—speak to their collectively held thoughts on transforming relationships between scholarly researchers and Aboriginal communities. Drawing upon the spoken words of Elders A. J. and Patsy Felix, the co-author group present key factors that ought to be taken into consideration by people interested in research study design, research ethics, data collection, and authentic representation of Indigenous voice in child welfare research. This chapter provides an overview of the contemporary relationship that many First Nations have with social science research, the role that an Indigenous Research Advisory Committee can take in guiding ethical research activities, and Elder teachings that speak to the steps that individuals can take to initiate and conduct research in a respectful and good way.

The second section of this book presents three chapters that aim to foster transformational change in the actions of child welfare practitioners, managers, and administrators. Chapter 4 discusses the observations of author Peter Choate on the sensitive topic of publicized child death reviews. Choate's extensive research examines numerous reports that have generated significant public attention and outrage. In an effort to apply the findings of practice reviews toward improving child protection practice, the author systematically identifies a set of recurring themes that have been articulated in reports that found that preventable practice errors had occurred. The chapter concludes with recommendations for remedial action that aim to address systemic public policy and educational gaps within existing child welfare policy. This chapter prompts calls for practice transformation via a series of recommendations directed at social work educators, practice professionals, and policy-makers.

In Chapter 5, author Sharon McKay calls attention to the everyday discourse of child welfare practitioners as they interact with children who have come into care. She asserts the importance of paying careful atten-tion to the language being used when interacting with younger people who rarely have any substantial say over their living circumstances. McKay's writing acknowledges the significance of roles enacted by front-line prac-tice teams, and the need for careful scripting of face-to-face interactions with the young people with whom they interact. Caseworkers, assigned foster/group home parents, agency supervisors, and others in immediate contact with children in care should be conscious that the language they use is crucial to helping children in temporary or permanent care to main-tain strong senses of identity and connectedness to family members.

Chapter 6 explores theoretical and pragmatic implications for trans-forming child welfare practice with high-risk children and youth. In ask-ing readers to consider shifting current casework practice toward a model founded upon harm reduction principles that suit this vulnerable popu-lation, author Peter Smyth presents a compelling argument for change. Smyth draws upon contemporary harm reduction literature and real prac-tice scenarios in order to illustrate a vision of youth work that utilizes proven strength-based methods to enhance relationship building and trust between workers and young people. Informed by principles of social jus-tice and a sincere motivation to recalibrate relationships that are frequently strained, Smyth enunciates a heartfelt model for transformed practice that resonates with potential and hope for both workers and youth alike.

The overarching theme of the third section of this book draws attention to contemporary research associated with the broad range of phenom-ena, practices, and experiences that comprise the field of child welfare. Disciplined research—whether applied, experimental, confirmatory, or exploratory—has much to say about the past, present, and future of child welfare across the Prairie provinces, nationally, and internationally. The information obtained through the structured sampling, data collection, and analytic practices of researchers, analysts, adjudicators, and evalu-ators frequently shapes government and community-based organization programming and policy decisions. Thus, in turn, research conducted today may create significant impacts for current and prospective child wel-fare service users in the future. Clearly, ethically based and well-designed quantitative, qualitative, and mixed-method studies create evidence that can be a catalyst for transformational change for individuals and social service organizations.

Chapter 7 presents the findings of a study undertaken by Don Fuchs and Linda Burnside, who examined the prevalence of fetal alcohol spectrum disorder (FASD) and in utero exposure to alcohol among children in care. This study adds to the established history and proven utility of quantitative research designs that can generate new knowledge in support of change within the field of child welfare. The authors' findings are based on their secondary analysis of data held within child welfare administrative databases. These findings provide a clear illustration of the usefulness and reliability of accurate and consistent electronic information as a source of evidence upon which to guide quality-improvement initiatives and programmatic decision making. Such administrative databases are vital to contemporary child welfare practice, and this chapter provides a clear illustration of the importance of accurate data entry, coding, and data integrity procedures. This study documents existing challenges and illuminates significant and practical opportunities for improving the outcomes for children with persistent disabilities who receive services from child welfare systems across Canada.

The research that underpins the content of Chapter 8 demonstrates the contribution that well-designed and respectfully enacted qualitative research can make to the field of child welfare. Consistent with many studies that utilize community-based research methods, this chapter presents an example of one tangible output of research methodologies that anticipates the co-creation of knowledge. Co-authors Saara Greene, Doe O'Brien-Teengs, Gary Dumbrill, Allyson Ion, Kerrigan Beaver, Megan Porter, and Marisol Desbiens describe persistent and particular impacts of HIV on women and mothers living in Canada and draw attention to the intersection of HIV and child welfare. In a pragmatic effort to address clearly articulated and commonly held issues, the chapter's co-authors describe their motivation to build upon the strengths, interests, and capabilities of a local population of HIV-infected women in order to inform students and helping professionals on how to better meet these women's unique needs. By building upon the expertise of those most affected, the authors demonstrate the transformational potential that may be activated within human beings when their lived experiences are heard, valued, and translated into purposive action.

Chapter 9 underscores the capacity of qualitative research methods to mobilize individual curiosity as a means of exploring and documenting emergent social phenomena that may otherwise remain marginalized within established scholarly and professional discourse. The content of this chapter is based upon graduate research conducted by Daniel Kikulwe for his social work doctoral degree that he received in 2014. Kikulwe's qualitative study explored the experiences of Canadian-born and foreign racialized workers who are increasingly finding employment within the child welfare systems across Canada, while within other domains of their lives they find themselves and their own families experiencing marginalization due to their physical characteristics, accents, and surnames. Points raised within the chapter speak to many rarely voiced dimensions of professional practice, including issues of identity, insider/outsider dilemmas, stereotypifying reification, and the erasure of difference. In creating a platform from which the embodied truths of marginalized workers/people may be expressed, Kikulwe offers hope for transformation within Canada's helping systems in directions that simply may not have even been considered by previous generations of activists, policy-makers, and administrators.

In Chapter 10, co-authors Marie Lovrod, Darlene Domshy, and Stephanie Bustamante give voice to a population that is especially impacted by child welfare policy and practice: youth who are transitioning out of government care. Drawing upon their thematic analysis of conversations with Saskatchewan-based young people who are particularly vulnerable to the arbitrary decision making of adults unrelated to them, the authors of this chapter identify ten domains within which helping professionals could benefit from increased awareness and professional development. By designing and conducting research in ways that provide safety for youth to voice their experiences of lives lived in transition and that empower youth in care to share their visions of better practice, the researchers created conditions conducive to the emergence of substantive new knowledge. As described in the chapter, this collaboration has led to the development of curricular materials intended to assist current and future youth workers with transition planning and follow-through with young adults as they exit the child welfare system.

Chapter 11, as with the other chapters in this section, documents an altogether different set of perspectives than those presented elsewhere in this book. In their chapter entitled "Narrative Threads in the Accounts of Women with Learning Difficulties Who Have Been Criminalized," co-authors Elly Park, David McConnell, Vera Caine, and Joanne Minaker draw upon the self-voiced experiences of participants involved in an eight-een-month narrative inquiry study into the lives of women with learning disabilities who had become involved in the criminal justice system. The wealth of experiences expressed in the words of the participants provides insights into the lives of individuals whose lives are frequently marked by uncertainty, stigma, and social exclusion. Collectively viewed, the powerful narratives referenced in this chapter call attention to the need for a retooling of contemporary programming of service models that are capable of and willing to foster individualized support plans tailored to each service user's unique challenges and obstacles. Such planning is especially important when working with women in their childbearing years, and those who have already become mothers, whose life paths will see them returning to risk-filled social environments where helpful supports may not be as readily available or as trustingly accepted.

The final section of this book focuses broadly on the transformative potential of education (teaching) within child welfare. In keeping with one of the key purposes of the Prairie Child Welfare Consortium—i.e., preprofessional education and practitioner training—the co-editors have designated the concluding section of this volume to author groups whose writing speaks to the pedagogic domains of child welfare service delivery. When practitioners and instructors engage with each other and purposively selected curricular resources, practice can indeed shift. It is no surprise that many calls to action and recommendations arising from external child welfare practice and program reviews call explicitly for more/better training of helping professionals. This concluding section presents two chapters that detail the critical necessity of creating and utilizing accurate and timely curricular materials and pedagogic methods as catalysts for individual learning and organizational change.

Chapter 12 details the development and efficacy of a set of publicly available curricular resources produced to address issues related to and emerging from in utero exposure to alcohol. Co-authored by Dorothy Badry, Deborah Goodman, and Jamie Hickey, the chapter documents the development and implementation of an online public education curriculum funded by the Public Health Agency of Canada. The online curriculum is directed toward altering public misperceptions of alcohol use during pregnancy and ameliorating the social impacts upon children who exhibit symptoms of FASD. Many of the resources were designed to provide accurate and practical information to caregivers who may not otherwise have ready access to opportunities to systematically improve their knowledge, understandings, and skills relating to young people with whom they regularly interact. This chapter describes the content and target audiences of the self-directed Caregiver Curriculum on FASD, the method by which resources are being delivered, and the growing usage of the materials since the resources were published online in 2014.

Jim Mulvale, the author of Chapter 13, brings a faculty administrator's perspective to the final chapter in this book. As a contributor to the scholarship of teaching and learning, Mulvale draws upon established social justice principles that anticipate emancipatory and transformational change as students and instructors interact with each other and curricular resources in classroom and field-based settings. In this chapter, the utility and effectiveness of distance-learning pedagogy and technology as a means of educating child welfare professionals is discussed. The chapter recognizes and examines the work done to date by the e-learning committee of the Prairie Child Welfare Consortium; proposes extending and enhancing this work to reach more students, practitioners, and researchers; and maps out challenges facing administrators, curriculum developers, and instructors involved with the delivery of the PCWC's e-learning courses that are offered between universities in the provinces of Alberta, Saskatchewan, and Manitoba.

Collectively, the thirteen chapters in this book provide significant insight into some of the most pressing issues for child welfare research, policy, practice, and training across Canada. The work of the co-editors and the contributing authors has documented a range of significant dimensions and innovative practices that may well shape the child welfare theories, practices, and services of tomorrow. It is not a road map for change that is presented here but rather a digital snapshot of where child welfare scholarship currently stands. Much like the sepia-toned photographs created using technology of yore, such time-stamped snapshots create important documentary evidence against which change—both incremental and transformative—may be measured by future generations of children, families, policy-makers, scholars, and practitioners. Change is a great teacher.

PART I

Policy

Honouring the Twenty-Fifth Anniversary of the United Nations Convention on the Rights of the Child: Transforming Child Welfare in Canada into a Stronger Child Rights-Based System

Marvin M. Bernstein

This chapter is based on the Prairie Child Welfare Consortium (PCWC) symposium keynote presentation I gave in October 2014, on the topic of honouring the twenty-fifth anniversary of the United Nations Convention on the Rights of the Child, hereinafter referred to simply as "the Convention" or the UNCRC. My position as the chief policy advisor for UNICEF Canada has provided me with access to scholarly research into this topic area. Although UNICEF Canada is based in Ontario, it transcends provincial boundaries and geographic regions of Canada. UNICEF Canada engages with all levels of government and with other partners to promote the rights of children everywhere in Canada and to advocate for the implementation of the principles set out in the Convention. UNICEF is the only organization named in the UNCRC as a source of expertise for governments.

Suggested Citation: Bernstein, M. (2016). Honouring the twenty-fifth anniversary of the United Nations Convention on the Rights of the Child: Transforming child welfare in Canada into a stronger child rights-based system. In H. Montgomery, D. Badry, D. Fuchs, & D. Kikulwe (Eds.), *Transforming Child Welfare: Interdisciplinary Practices, Field Education, and Research* (pp. 3–26). Regina, SK: University of Regina Press.

In keeping with the theme of the 2014 PCWC Symposium — Celebrating Transformations in Child Welfare — this chapter describes the role that the UNCRC has played in transforming child welfare across Canada, especially with respect to strengthening the rights of children. The five key themes of this chapter are as follows:

1. the important functions of the UNCRC in advancing children's rights;
2. the progress made within Canada since adoption of the Convention twenty-five years ago;
3. an overview of the current state of Canada's children;
4. the current challenges impeding full implementation of the UNCRC across Canada; and
5. what action steps still need to be taken to fulfill the original vision of the Convention.

What Is the United Nations Convention on the Rights of the Child?

Before moving ahead with the discussion on the state of children's rights within Canada, it is useful to first refamiliarize readers with some background information on the Convention itself. The UNCRC was adopted by the United Nations General Assembly on November 20, 1989. Canada became a signatory to the Convention in 1990 and ratified it in 1991. The UNCRC is the most widely and rapidly ratified international human rights treaty in history, and, as of 2016, it has been ratified by 196 nations. Only the United States has failed to ratify it. It was once described by the late Nelson Mandela (2000) as "that luminous living document that enshrines the rights of every child without exception to a life of dignity and self-fulfillment."

The UNCRC is comprised of fifty-four separate articles, forty-two of which are substantive. These articles bring together civil, political, economic, social, and cultural rights for children. Children's rights are often clustered for descriptive purposes under different themes, such as rights of provision, protection, and participation. The Convention aims to protect and support children in all areas of their lives and provides a comprehensive framework for the basic conditions of good childhood. With respect to age parameters, the Convention covers the rights of children from birth to age eighteen.

There are four guiding or general principles enshrined in the UNCRC that are meant to assist with the interpretation of the Convention as a whole and thereby guide national programs of implementation. These four principles are formulated in Article 2 (the right to nondiscrimination); Article 3 (the best interests of the child); Article 6 (the child's right to life, survival, and development); and Article 12 (the child's right to be heard). The influence of the adoption of the Convention has been widespread since 1989; however, much work remains to be undertaken in creating a rights-respecting culture for children in Canada.

What Progress Has Occurred with Respect to Advancing Children's Rights within Canada within the Past Twenty-five years?

UNICEF Canada is not alone in working to advance the rights of children and youth. Across Canada, dozens of prominent Canadian organizations and institutions, parliamentarians of different parties, committed individuals, and talented and thoughtful children and youth have taken much action and inspired numerous positive changes since the UNCRC was adopted in 1989.

Drawing strength from individual and collective initiatives, substantial progress on advancing children's rights has been made in a number of areas. Federal and provincial laws have been enacted to better protect children. Legislative amendments have established the best interests of the child principle (Article 3) as a paramount or primary consideration within provincial child welfare, adoption, and child custody legislation. Numerous statutes have been developed to enable children to become actual or deemed parties who are capable of participating in court proceedings on matters relating to them (e.g., provincial/territorial child welfare legislation). Canadian courts have drawn upon the Convention for guidance in interpreting domestic legislation, including the Canadian Charter of Rights and Freedoms. To assist with the operationalization of the Convention, independent child and youth advocate/representative offices have been created in nine provinces and two territories. Finally, but not of least importance, since the 1989 adoption of the UNCRC, numerous Canadian civil society groups focusing on promoting children's rights have emerged and have taken an active role in policy formation and evaluation through preparing and disseminating shadow or alternative reports (i.e., 2011, 2012) to the UN Committee on the Rights of the Child in Geneva.

Upon recognition of the twenty-fifth anniversary of the Convention, there is much to celebrate within Canada. However, there is also much to challenge and confront in the mission that many individuals and organizations share as we seek to advance the health, well-being, and potential of each new generation.

What Is the Current State of Canada's Children?

Clearly, much progress has been made over the past twenty-five years on advancing children's rights within Canada. Despite these advances, the work to make the vision of the Convention a reality for every Canadian child is far from finished. Although it is tempting to look only at the successes that have been achieved since 1989, it is only when the current state of well-being of our children is compared with that of other industrialized countries that a more fulsome picture of Canada's progress can be determined. This message was made clear to me when I returned to Toronto from Saskatchewan in 2010 to take up the role of chief policy advisor at UNICEF Canada. At that time, I was expecting to find a positive picture at the national level. However, I was surprised and disappointed to find that on the international stage, Canada was stuck in mediocrity in terms of the overall state of well-being of our children. Although I understood that there would be some challenges in promoting the implementation of the UNCRC, I must say that the evidence of Canada's performance has been decidedly underwhelming.

This evidence is captured in UNICEF's (2013) *Report Card 11* that ranks child well-being across twenty-nine affluent nations. The child well-being ranking presents comparative averages of twenty-six indicators across five dimensions, including material well-being; health and safety; education; behaviours and risks; and housing and environment. In *Report Card 11*, Canada ranked seventeenth out of the twenty-nine nations measured with respect to child well-being. This is a position that had not budged since UNICEF's research arm had last measured child well-being this broadly in *Report Card 7* in 2007. In *Report Card 11*, the top five performing countries were the Netherlands, Norway, Iceland, Finland, and Sweden. This is surprising to most Canadians, who believe that Canada is the "best place to grow up." But the index shows that nations with similar economic means achieve widely different outcomes for children. Since Canada signed onto the UNCRC, economic progress has outpaced progress in advancing child well-being. In fact, among the twenty-nine countries in this index, Canada is among a group of five countries with the least improvement and most regression. The children we are leaving furthest behind are Indigenous. This is an uncomfortable truth but not an inevitable situation.

Areas where Canadian children are doing better than their peers in most other countries include the low smoking rate (third) and the high achievement of children age fifteen and under in math, reading, and science (second). Overall, Canada's education system does a comparatively good job in the early years of equipping our children with functional skills. We also know that Canada has made progress on a number of other fronts. For example, breastfeeding rates are increasing across Canada. Additionally, there has been a demonstrated commitment to improve the mental health of children and adults since 1989. Finally, it is also important to note that considerable advances in federal and provincial legislation that better protect children from injury and exploitation have been made.

But in some fundamental aspects of survival and health, the state of Canada's children is alarming. This is especially disconcerting when considering that Canada has the technology, the information, and the resources to ensure the highest possible state of health for its children. Yet, in the domain of health and safety, Canada ranks as low as twenty-seventh among the twenty-nine industrialized countries measured. Among the greatest areas of concern are the high rate of unhealthy weight (twenty-seventh), the high rate of bullying (twenty-first), the lower rate of children aged 15–19 participating in further education (twenty-fourth), and the high rate of cannabis use among youth (twenty-ninth). Disappointingly, Canada's children are among the unhappiest, ranking twenty-fourth within the twenty-nine countries when children's views of their own life satisfaction are measured (when taking into account their views of their relationships with their peers, mothers, and fathers). The indicators for healthy relationships in *Report Card 11* suggest that Canadians need to pay more attention to the development of healthy relationships at home and with peers, including the role of social media, and families squeezed for time. When factoring in the size and health of Canada's economy among the twenty-nine nations measured, UNICEF's *Report Card 11* clearly shows that the overall well-being of Canadian children could be much better.

Every child born into this nation holds enormous potential and possibility, for surely they will shape the future of our society. Societies can only develop in a sustainable manner when all children, particularly the poorest and most deprived, are nurtured and cared for and receive the education and protection they deserve. The state of Canadian children's well-being isn't predetermined or inevitable. It can be positively affected by progressive and inclusive policy development that is child-centred and dedicated to building strong families and communities.

What Current Challenges Are Impeding the Full Implementation of the UNCRC across Canada?

Unfortunately, there are a great deal of children's rights challenges still facing Canadians. In 2007, in its final report, *Children: The Silenced Citizens*, the Standing Senate Committee on Human Rights noted: "At the ground level, children's rights are being pushed to the side and even violated in a variety of situations....The Convention has been effectively marginalized when it comes to its direct impact on children's lives" (p. ix).

In 2016, nine years after this Senate report was released, little has changed to ameliorate the degree of marginalization facing the UNCRC across Canada. For a variety of reasons, persistent factors have impacted efforts to achieve full implementation of the Convention. Some of the challenges to full implementation include an absence of political will, factors related to Canadian federalism, governance issues, communications procedures, and technical inflexibility in interpretation.

With respect to political will, it is clear to me that there is an absence of a systematic, comprehensive approach to establishing children's rights as a political priority within Canada. The political structure seems at times to place more value on our natural resources, as opposed to our most precious human resources. Although seven million children make up about a quarter of the Canadian population, and constitute the future of our society, their concerns are seldom given top priority in the political sphere. The lack of voting status among children seems to diminish the leverage that this group of vulnerable citizens might otherwise possess.

The disenfranchisement of Canada's children is further compounded by the structural limitations of federalism that counteract aspirational efforts to implement initiatives of national importance. In Canada, the federal government has responsibility for compliance with the Convention within its sphere of jurisdiction (i.e., immigration, youth justice, on-reserve health, education and child welfare services, tax benefits, divorce law). However, many of the matters covered by the UNCRC fall under provincial jurisdiction (e.g., social services, health, education, and child welfare) in the Canadian federal system of government. This division of jurisdictional responsibility creates a significant challenge in terms of coordinating, implementing, and monitoring progress in the area of children's rights. Stalemates are frequent, wherein federal officials maintain they cannot do more to advance children's rights as a result of the subject matter being under provincial jurisdiction. Provinces, as well, are sometimes reluctant to assume any direct responsibility for meeting international commitments undertaken by Canada at the federal level.

As a compounding factor, there has been a failure to fully institute good governance measures with respect to children's rights in any part of Canada. This is despite the presence of Article 4 of the UNCRC (1989), which obliges all ratifying nations to "undertake all appropriate, legislative, administrative and other measures for the implementation of the rights recognized in the present convention." Further guidance in the area of governance was provided to ratifying nations in General Comment No. 5 (2003), where a series of General Measures of Implementation were enumerated to assist state parties in fulfilling UNCRC rights within legislation, policy, and practice. Specific recommendations of General Comment No. 5 articulated efforts necessary to create national action plans and strategies for implementation of the Convention, to establish national mechanisms for coordinating implementation, and to undertake law reform and judicial enforcement of the rights of children. Further recommendations aimed at enhancing awareness raising, training and education, encouraging civil society participation, and fostering international co-operation. The establishment of statutory children's rights institutions, monitoring and data-collection regimes, and mechanisms to explicitly make children visible in budgets were also identified in General Comment No. 5.

Despite being recommended by Canada's Standing Senate Committee on Human Rights, Canada has fallen behind other nations in implementing the accountability mechanisms established in General Comment No. 5. Such governance measures have been successfully implemented with considerable effect by many other governments, including those in the United Kingdom, the European Union, Australia, and New Zealand.

Across Canada, it is clear that an absence of effective complaints mechanisms have created a challenge to the full implementation of the Convention. When the UNCRC was adopted in 1989, it was the only core international human rights treaty that did not have a complaints procedure. This significant gap was addressed when the *Optional Protocol to the Convention on the Rights of the Child on a communications procedure* came into effect in April 2014. The UNCRC Optional Protocol #3 allows individual children or their advocates to submit complaints when state parties have violated or failed to protect their rights under the Convention and its first two optional protocols.

The *Optional Protocol to the Convention on the Rights of the Child on a communications procedure* establishes an international communications or complaints procedure with two mechanisms for children to challenge violations of their rights alleged to have been committed by ratifying nations. Article 5 creates a procedure that enables children to bring individual complaints about violations of their rights to the United Nations Committee on the Rights of the Child if they have not been fully resolved in national dispute resolution processes, and Article 13 establishes an inquiry procedure for the same committee to consider grave and systematic violations of children's rights. To date, Canada has yet to express an intention to ratify UNCRC Optional Protocol #3. There has been some speculation that the delay in ratification may be as a result of concern over Aboriginal children or their representatives using this instrument to initiate inquiries alleging grave and systematic violations of the rights of Aboriginal children or youth.

In the absence of complaints mechanisms within the UNCRC as it was originally worded in 1989, Canada's former federal government (as of the time of writing in 2016) appears to have taken an overly technical approach to issues relating to equitable treatment of Aboriginal children. Not only has this overly rigid approach been taken to the UNCRC but also to the United Nations Declaration on the Rights of Indigenous Peoples and the Canadian Charter of Rights and Freedoms. Examples of interpretational rigidity can be found in the positions that Canada has taken on the provision of equitable funding for on-reserve child welfare services for prevention and early intervention services and in the implementation of Jordan's Principle.

With respect to matters relating to equitable funding for on-reserve child welfare services, the federal government at the time initially objected to the Canadian Human Rights Tribunal having jurisdiction to hear a complaint lodged in 2007 by the First Nations Child and Family Caring Society and the Assembly of First Nations on the basis of the absence of a technical comparator group. The federal government initially asserted that because different service recipient groups were receiving services from different levels of government, no standard of reasonable comparability had been established. It was not until 2014 that evidence relating to the actual merits of the inequitable funding complaint was concluded after several intervening appeals on jurisdictional grounds, notwithstanding that the initial complaint had been filed in 2007.

It was not until January of 2016 (nine years later) that the Canadian Human Rights Tribunal was finally able to render its decision (*First Nations Child and Family Caring Society of Canada et al. v Attorney General of Canada*), where it found discrimination against First Nations children living on-reserve and ordered the federal Department of Indigenous and Northern Affairs Canada to remedy that discrimination immediately by reforming and ceasing discrimination under the First Nations Child and Family Services Program and by taking measures to immediately implement the full meaning and scope of Jordan's Principle.

What Big and Small Action Steps Need to Be Taken to Fulfill the Vision of the Convention?

While the federal government is the primary duty bearer when it comes to implementing the Convention rights of Canadian children, the well-being of our children should be everyone's concern. Serious-minded Canadians simply cannot rely upon government exclusively to carry out the tasks of promoting and protecting children's rights. We need to encourage more work to be done at the civil society level. In order to facilitate conversation and movement among concerned individuals and civil society, the concluding sections of this chapter introduce a series of action steps that individuals—alone or within organizations—can consider taking to make a real difference in the lives of children who come into contact with the child welfare system. It is my belief that the following ten activities can assist individuals in advancing the rights of all children within Canada and internationally.

1. Learn More about Children's Rights and the
Convention on the Rights of the Child

In its *Concluding Observations* to Canada, the United Nations Committee on the Rights of the Child (2012) urged Canada

> to develop an integrated strategy for training on children's rights for all professionals, including government officials, judicial authorities, and professionals who work with children in health and social services. In developing such training programmes, the Committee urges the State party to focus the training on the use of the Convention *in legislation and public policy, programme devel-opment, advocacy, and decision making processes and account-ability. (para. 27)*

Part of the problem is that the Convention is not well publicized as a piv-otal human rights treaty and training on the Convention for profession-als, especially those working with or for children, is rare. While there are training courses on child rights and human rights for some professionals, they are often of a voluntary, rather than an obligatory, nature. It is my observation that practising social workers, lawyers, and psychologists generally know very little about the principles set out in the UNCRC. In the case of the legal profession, while there is a great deal of legal education about the Charter of Rights and Freedoms, there is very little emphasis placed on the role of the UNCRC as an advocacy tool.

There are a number of actions that child welfare professionals can take to familiarize themselves with children's rights, including obtain-ing and reading through the provisions of the Convention and the United Nations Declaration on the Rights of Indigenous Peoples. Youth-friendly versions of posters of the UNCRC, such as those prepared by the Office of the Ontario Provincial Advocate for Children and Youth and UNICEF Canada, can be displayed in places frequented by children and their caregivers. Individuals can also read over the wide range of General Comments on a variety of topics issued by the UN Committee on the Rights of the Child and that committee's most recent *Concluding Observations* delivered to Canada in December 2012. Such reports can be searched by theme, and the recommendations found can open oppor-tunities to establish a series of working committees (by theme) with experts, researchers, government officials, and children and youth to advance the progressive implementation of the committee's recommendations. This can be done on a provincial level with time-sensitive work plans and public reporting, regardless of the degree of participation of the federal government.

Further, individuals can also request a child rights training workshop to be presented by UNICEF Canada to governmental departments or organizations. Such workshops allow participants to learn the fundamentals of the UNCRC and the child rights-based approach, including the application of these important resources to legislation, policies, programs, and practices, as well as advocacy and administrative decisions affecting children. The UNICEF Canada workshop curriculum promotes learning to assess the impacts of legislation, policies, and programs on children to ensure that their best interests are considered in decision-making processes.

2. Bring Child Welfare Out from the Shadows and the Children In from the Margins

Child welfare has operated in the shadows for far too long. While issues of confidentiality and publication bans on using identifying information are important considerations, there has also been resistance to letting others into the inner sanctum of child welfare out of a sense of mistrust and a fear of piling on further complaints to a system that many people within the system already feel is unfairly criticized and under-resourced. In my opinion, much more could be done by practising professionals to become more trusting and transparent in encouraging public debate about the state of child welfare across all jurisdictions. Child protection is everyone's business, and if we want the public to invest more heavily in the effectiveness of the child welfare system, we should be more inclusive and provide the public with opportunities to engage in dialogue and express their views through the vehicles of town halls, newsletters, public consultations, and surveys.

In dealing with the media, the days of saying "no comment," or "the matter is before the courts" should be long gone. While child welfare practitioners cannot refer to individuals by name or refer to specific facts in individual cases that could identify clients, media inquiries can be seen as opportunities to speak about general practices of governmental departments and/or Aboriginal agencies. Such opportunities can be used to inform the public about the particular circumstances of child-serving organizations, the challenges that are currently being faced, and what kinds of solutions would produce better service delivery and outcomes for children, families, and their communities.

3. Attend Crossover Conferences and Develop Relationships that Harmonize Child Welfare and Children's Rights

On far too many occasions, child welfare and child rights appear to oper-ate in separate spheres, with no clear intersection or integration. Perhaps this may arise from misperceptions that the Convention does not suf-ficiently respect the role of family, but it does, in fact, envision that the optimal environment for the fulfillment of a child's rights is within his or her own family. Regardless of the source of underlying misconceptions, it is clear that tensions between child welfare and children's rights have impeded harmonization and unity. Such tensions have kept people inter-ested in the well-being of children apart in many ways. For example, it is not uncommon for one group to attend child welfare conferences while another group of different people attends child rights conferences. Having personally attended many conferences and symposia on both of these themes, it is clear to me that there is frequently very little overlap between the attendees and presenters who attend such conferences.

In order to foster cross-disciplinary relationship building and knowl-edge sharing, it is important for child welfare workers to participate in child rights conferences and to speak about the innovative things their organizations are doing to respect children's human rights. For example, I have presented at the International Summer Course on Children's Rights at the University of Moncton annually for several years now. Every sum-mer, a different Convention Article and theme are profiled in this course. In 2012, it was the child's right to be protected from all forms of violence under Article 19 and, in 2013, it was Article 12 (i.e., the child's right to be heard). I have attempted to inform colleagues within the child welfare community that the course may have some value for them and that they may even wish to profile some of their innovative initiatives at such sum-mer session offerings, but there has been little participation from my child welfare colleagues. Missed opportunities to speak with students and pro-fessionals thwart information sharing on the positive messages about the many achievements that are happening within child welfare generally.

Harmonizing child welfare and child rights—even in such a minor way as crossover participation at each other's conferences—can offer many opportunities. Collaboration can create a stronger child welfare system—in both process and outcomes. It can transform children from objects of protection to full rights holders, build their self-esteem, and enable child participation in decision making affecting their lives. Harmonized collaboration among professionals can create opportunities to introduce child rights principles within child welfare legislation, policy, and programming, and place children involved in child welfare at the centre of all child-serving systems.

As the adults in their lives strive to emphasize an integrated approach to problem solving for children who cross over into different service sectors, it can lead to more sustainable outcomes for children and youth and highlight the importance of family and community in the lives of children. Emphasizing the importance of equitable treatment and the right to nondiscrimination of all children will bring into sharper focus the many underlying causes of rights violations and broaden partnerships for children beyond their traditional counterparts.

4. Be Honest with Children Having Contact with the Child Welfare Sector and Respect Their Right to Be Treated as the CEO in Relation to Their Life Circumstances

It is important to be honest with children and not sugar-coat their life circumstances. They have a right to know what is going on. Article 13 of the UNCRC (1989) sets out the right of the child to freedom of expression, which "shall include freedom to seek, receive and impart information and ideas of all kinds, regardless of frontiers, either orally, in writing or in print, in the form of art, or through any other media of the child's choice." The Convention recognizes the role that information plays in the child's physical, mental, spiritual, moral, and social development, as children first have to gather information before they can form their own views. Accordingly, the adults who care for children and youth must keep them informed. For children in care, being informed must mean that they are informed about their parentage, their family history, and significant events in their lives, in a language suited to their developmental stages.

Unfortunately, the demands of child welfare are such that, at times, the need to ensure that the child understands what is going on is lost in the host of other casework demands. This dynamic was addressed in the 2010 report of the Ontario-based Sparrow Lake Alliance Children in Limbo Task Force. This report underscored that in child welfare, as far as information is concerned, children should be considered to be their own chief executive officer (CEO). Such a position means that children, while not being given the burden of decision making, should—whenever feasible—be adequately consulted and should know and understand, as far as possible, the circumstances behind the realities and decisions that affect their lives.

There is naturally no perfect time to impart difficult information to a child, but postponing the truth-telling process can often lead to negative consequences for uninformed children. This is especially the case when a child hears the information in an inappropriate or inadvertent way from peers or learns about it online. As we all know, it is even more difficult to keep secrets in the digital age.

5. Modernize Child Welfare Language and Avoid the Use of Stigmatizing Terminology

Given that children and youth coming into contact with the child welfare system, or who are already in care, have often been victimized or even traumatized due to circumstances for which they were not responsible, it is all the more essential that they be protected from further harm. No matter how complex and arduous the process, it is essential to change the demeaning and stigmatizing terminology used in relevant legislation and in child welfare practice. We must eliminate hurtful words that have seeped into everyday language that apply to children and youth for whom our society is responsible.

The various provincial child welfare statutes across Canada contain archaic and discriminatory terms that dehumanize and confuse youth and even imply criminality. Too often legislative phrasing persists with objectionable language, despite many worthwhile submissions over the past decade that criticize the terms applied to young citizens who fall into the temporary or permanent care of the child welfare system. Some examples of the use of criminal law language are the term "apprehension" in Ontario and other provincial legislation to denote a nonconsensual removal from parental care, or "adoption probation" to mean the first period of an adoption placement. The term "custody" also implies punishment and control rather than simply referring to "care." The term "runaway" continues to appear in

Ontario legislation, which automatically labels youth in care as delinquent when they may be running away from a dangerous situation involving physical or sexual abuse. In addition, terms in the Ontario child protection legislation like "Society and Crown Wardship" represent outmoded language and are not used anywhere else in provincial child welfare legislation.

Postmodern theorists (e.g., Jean-François Lyotard, Michel Foucault) remind educated people that words are important and a change in language can lead to a change in culture. All of us have a role to play in avoiding the use of disempowering and stigmatizing language. We must change the child welfare lexicon. Children in contact with the child welfare system are not offenders, victims, or the property of others, but, rather, they are individuals full of potential for achievement and success. Taking a nondiscriminatory approach contributes to the conditions for youth in care that will promote their inner strength and resiliency.

Children in contact with the child welfare system, or in care, have a right not to be subjected to discriminatory or stigmatizing language. This right to nondiscrimination is upheld in the Convention. Article 2 establishes that all children have a right to protection from "discrimination of any kind," including on the basis of his or her "status." This definition encompasses discriminatory or stigmatizing language or other such offensive treatment of those children. Article 3 of the UNCRC also guarantees to children the right to have their best interests treated as "a primary consideration" in all actions concerning them. Accordingly, it is inappropriate and disrespectful to use language that conjures up notions of penal or mental health institutionalization.

Current and former children in care should be consulted to obtain their views and suggestions for alternative language that they see as nonstigmatizing and nondiscriminatory. In Ontario, for example, a subcommittee of the Children in Limbo Task Force worked with the Office of the Provincial Advocate for Children and Youth to consult with a group of young people with a view to contributing a report for the five-year review of Ontario's child welfare legislation. This process was important because it recognized that young people may not view the same terms as being demeaning, or may have problems with other terms considered benign by adults. Such consultative processes can also create venues to introduce alternative terminology that youth have at their disposal but which may otherwise elude many adults.

6. Provide Children with the Right to Be Heard
in Meaningful and Innovative Ways

In its *Concluding Observations* to Canada, the United Nations Committee on the Rights of the Child (2012) recommended the following:

> *[That Canada] continue to ensure the implementation of the right of the child to be heard in accordance with article 12 of the Convention. In doing so, it recommends that the State party promote the meaningful and empowered participation of all children, within the family, community, and schools, and develop and share good practices. Specifically, the Committee recommends that the views of the child be a requirement for all official decision-making processes that relate to children, including custody cases, child welfare decisions, criminal justice, immigration, and the environment. The Committee also urges the State party to ensure that children have the possibility to voice their complaints if their right to be heard is violated with regard to judicial and administrative proceedings, and that children have access to an appeals procedure. (para. 37)*

Reflecting on this point reminds me of many interactions I have had with children and youth who have been in care. For example, shortly after my having been appointed as the provincial children's advocate in Saskatchewan, I had a conversation with a senior child welfare government official who—with the best of intentions—assured me that youth would be consulted later on in the child welfare policy development process. I suggested, however, that youth should be involved much earlier in the process. I also recall hearing from many young people in care who stated they weren't active participants in developing their plans of care. Many weren't certain of the reasons why they came into care and had little notion of what it would take for them to leave care. Others had no plan for where they would go or who would support them after they left care. This is not to cast blame but to emphasize that we cannot make assumptions about what we think youth in care actually know. Without providing venues for listening to youth perspectives of their own life experiences, the range of options under consideration becomes narrower.

One meaningful forum that recently enabled greater youth participation in the child welfare context is described in Ontario's (2013) *Final Report of the Youth Leaving Care Working Group.* The report describes the Our Voice, Our Turn: Youth Leaving Care Hearings forum organized by current and former wards of the province of Ontario. The hearings shed light on the challenges faced by permanent wards in Ontario. The process made it clear that more must be done to support and recognize these young people at all times, but particularly when they are transitioning into independence. These hearings were convened and chaired by young people and took place in the Ontario Legislative Assembly with the support of the Office of the Provincial Advocate for Children and Youth. Many informed professionals testified and filed submissions with the young people, but the title of "expert" was reserved for the experiential youth who testified about their life experiences and the changes they believed could improve life conditions for youth in similar circumstances. Members of Provincial Parliament, ministry staff, service providers, and members of the public attended at different times to listen and learn. The participation by these young people in these youth-led hearings resulted in May 14 being proclaimed in legislation as "Children and Youth in Care Day" in 2014. Ontario now annually recognizes the strength, courage, and resilience of children and youth in care, and acknowledges the contributions they have made to the province.

The participation of these young people didn't end with the conclusion of the Youth Leaving Care hearings. After the process concluded, several youth participants read and analyzed all of the submissions and wrote a report. Their report, entitled *My Real Life Book*, was presented to the Ontario Legislature on May 14, 2012. This report has since led to the preparation and release of a final government report, called *Blueprint for Fundamental Change to Ontario's Child Welfare System.* Among other things, this process was successful in obtaining more government-funded educational assistance for youth when transitioning out of care. A similar model for youth-in-care engagement has since been developed for the province of New Brunswick.

7. Develop and Apply a Child Rights Impact
Assessment (CRIA) Framework
Child rights impact assessments (CRIAs) are not new and have been used in a variety of policy domains in Canada, such as environmental protection, health, and privacy. In particular, a CRIA is a tool for assessing the potential impacts of a proposed policy, law, program, or particular decision on children and their rights. The UNCRC is the framework used to

assess these impacts. The impacts revealed can be positive or negative, intended or unintended, direct or indirect, and short-term or long-term. The focus of a CRIA is to understand how matters under consideration will contribute to or undermine the fulfillment of children's rights and well-being. A CRIA process can maximize positive impacts and avoid or mitigate unintended negative impacts. CRIAS are mostly used within government policy-making processes; however, they can also be carried out by agencies or people outside of government.

In the hands of committed individuals, CRIAS are tools to advocate for children's rights in relation to specific issues (e.g., the rights of children in care to access appropriate health supports or their ability to gain age-appropriate access to justice). A CRIA is one method that can ensure that those concerned with the well-being of children remain on track. As Cheryl Milne (2014), the chair of the Canadian Coalition on the Rights of the Child, recently pointed out, CRIAS are not meant to be an additional burden, not more paperwork or another level of scrutiny that can lead to delay. CRIAS can help to ensure that we keep our eye on the ball and not be distracted by factors that take us away from acting in the best interests of children.

Some groundbreaking work is happening in Canada to assess government legislation, policies, and actions through the lens of child rights. In New Brunswick and Saskatchewan, children's rights are being considered as a framework for reforming child welfare and adoption legislation. In New Brunswick, there is an all-of-province commitment to using CRIAS. Since February 2013, it has been mandatory for all New Brunswick government departments to complete a CRIA and attach it to a memorandum to executive council whenever a proposed law or policy is being forwarded to Cabinet for its consideration and approval.

8. Elevate the Maximum Age for Child
Protection to Eighteen Years of Age

From the standpoint of equitable treatment for all Canadian children who may be in need of protection, there should be a uniform maximum age of at least eighteen for purposes of providing child protection intervention. Article 1 of the Convention on the Rights of the Child defines a "child" as a human being up to the age of eighteen. Yet there are different maximum ages for child protection intervention across Canada's provinces—ranging from age sixteen to nineteen. It is important to amend the definition of "child" in provincial child welfare statutes in order to provide for the possibility of child welfare intervention and court-ordered findings of need for protection and best interests dispositions up to the age of eighteen. In this way, all sixteen- and seventeen-year-olds can be protected from harm and violence and be better supported.

There are situations, where sixteen- and seventeen-year-old youth are homeless and living on the streets because of abuse or neglect in their family homes. Many of these young people would like to come into care, but many provincial child welfare statutes preclude this possibility simply on the basis of age discrimination. There may also be situations where sixteen- and seventeen-year-old youth have delayed their disclosures of parental maltreatment for fear of retaliation and further punishment, or because of repressed memories of traumatic events. Aside from the question of parental maltreatment, there may also be situations where sixteen- and seventeen-year-olds are living on the street because of problems of family poverty and homelessness. There are also situations where families support their sixteen- and seventeen-year-olds entering care temporarily because of the child's health or addiction issues. And, of course, a finding of need for protection doesn't equate to an automatic admission to care. It may simply mean that child protection authorities can offer supportive services, with or without a supervision order, with the sixteen- or seventeen-year-old continuing to reside in the family home.

The degree to which children should be able to exercise their right to be protected from violence under Article 19 of the Convention should not turn on the child's place of birth or current residence. Article 19 of the UNCRC (1989) states: "State Parties shall take all appropriate legislative, administrative, social and educational measures to protect the child from all forms of physical or mental violence, injury or abuse, neglect or negligent treatment, maltreatment or exploitation, including sexual abuse, while in the care of parent(s), legal guardian(s) or any other person who has care of the child." Further, the United Nations Committee on the Rights of the Child (2012) also addressed this point in its *Concluding Observations* to Canada, where it urged Canada "to ensure the full compliance of all national provisions on the definition of the child with article 1 of the Convention, in particular to ensure that...all children under 18 who are victims of sexual exploitation receive appropriate protection" (para. 31).

9. Promote Fair and Equitable Treatment for
Indigenous Children and Other Minority Groups

Based on the relevant provisions of the Convention on the Rights of the Child, it is important to respect the rights of Indigenous children and other minority groups. It is clear the Convention can contribute to a child welfare infrastructure of cultural competency. The UN Committee on the Rights of the Child (2012), in its *Concluding Observations*, recommended that Canada's actions to address disparities in the treatment of Aboriginal children should include taking "urgent measures to address the overrepresentation of Aboriginal and African-Canadian children in the criminal justice system and out-of-home care," and taking "immediate steps to ensure that in law and practice, Aboriginal children have full access to all government services and receive resources without discrimination" (para. 33[a], [d]).

UNICEF Canada's position is that Aboriginal children are not being treated equitably or fairly in this country. They should not be compelled to wait for years while the wheels of litigation grind slowly. Instead, they should be able to exercise their full constellation of rights under the Convention on the Rights of the Child, which are not being sufficiently implemented. For example, Aboriginal children have equal rights to non-discrimination (Article 2); to have their best interests treated as a primary consideration in all decisions affecting them (Article 3); to life, survival, and development (Article 6); and to enjoy their own culture and language (Article 30). Having ratified the UNCRC in 1991, the government of Canada has an obligation to ensure the laws, policies, funding, and services that provide for these rights do so equitably. Provisions set out in the United Nations Declaration on the Rights of Indigenous Peoples and the Charter of Rights and Freedoms further reinforce the right to fair and equal treatment.

UNICEF Canada recommends that some important steps be taken by our governments and institutions to fulfill their commitments to Indigenous children and to put their interests above others, as outlined in the UNCRC. A foremost priority should be the appointment of a national children's commissioner. Such an appointment should be made by an all-party process, in consultation with Aboriginal peoples. This important function would help ensure that Aboriginal children don't become the innocent casualties of jurisdictional, political, and funding disputes. It also would ensure that their voices are heard through the process of crafting long-term solutions to very serious systemic problems. A national children's commissioner should have the power to investigate and mediate interjurisdictional disputes that so often envelop First Nations children on-reserve.

A second recommendation relating to the equitable treatment of Aboriginal children entails making children visible in the budgeting process. By doing so, a clearer picture of investments being made in children will be evident. Governments at all levels should provide more information on the amount of money being spent on children and the levels of disparity where the spending is disproportionate for certain groups of children. Such openness will establish fair and transparent funding mechanisms to ensure a level of equity in the funding of services and programs for Aboriginal children. The government of Canada can use a budget analysis to reallocate funding to close the child welfare service gap.

Finally, as stated previously in this chapter, a consistent and liberal interpretation of Jordan's Principle should be implemented. Such consistency will enable Jordan's Principle to truly function as a "child first" approach to resolving jurisdictional disputes. Jordan's Principle should be seen as simply a means to an end—applying core human rights principles fairly—in order to advance the best interests of Aboriginal children.

It is also vital to develop a child welfare infrastructure that is more culturally competent when it comes to the rights and interests of Aboriginal children. Pivotal players within the child welfare sector (e.g., front-line child protection workers, foster parents, and caregivers at residential and institutional facilities) must be free to educate themselves on Aboriginal values. It should not be the responsibility of Aboriginal children and youth to insist upon services being provided in a culturally competent manner. I recall travelling to an Aboriginal community in northern Saskatchewan and having made the mistake of saying that I was advocating for more culturally sensitive services in all parts of the province. An Aboriginal woman in attendance confronted me by saying that there has been enough cultural sensitivity espoused by well-meaning, but inept, professionals. She stated that what is now required is cultural competency to be practised by child welfare professionals who know what they are doing.

10. Establish a Principled Basis for Child Welfare Service Delivery and Avoid Extreme Pendulum Shifts

Child welfare is frequently subject to extreme pendulum shifts in ideology, often moving between family preservation and child protection. In the past, different theories would come and go, and with them, the latest child welfare guru who espoused them. It is important to anchor good child welfare practice in evidence-based research and understandings of the outcomes generated by certain "best practice" clinical approaches and interventions. However, it is also important to solidify child-centred human rights principles (e.g., those enunciated in the UNCRC) into policy and practice. Saskatchewan's *Children and Youth First* principles offer a promising approach to incorporating rights-based principles.

In order to address the needs and rights of children and youth more effectively, and to place the interests of children and youth first in Saskatchewan, the Children's Advocate Office developed a set of principles to establish a vision for all children and youth in Saskatchewan in 2007. The Children and Youth First Principles were founded on the most critical and relevant provisions of the United Nations Convention on the Rights of the Child. After seeking internal and external feedback from organizations and youth focus groups, discussions took place with the various child-serving ministries to incorporate the identified principles into proposed and existing legislation, policy, programming, and practice applicable to children and youth in receipt of government services. A Children and Youth First Action Plan was adopted by the Saskatchewan government in 2009 and subsequently renamed the Saskatchewan Children and Youth First Principles (Saskatchewan, 2009; Bernstein & Schury, 2009).

This set of principles states that all children and youth in Saskatchewan are entitled to rights defined by the United Nations Convention on the Rights of the Child, including their rights to participate and be heard before any decision is made. To have their "best interests" be given paramount consideration in any action or decision involving them, Saskatchewan children and youth are entitled to receive an equal standard of care, protection, and services and the highest standard of health and education possible. They are entitled to safety and protection from all forms of physical, emotional, and sexual harm while in the care of parents, governments, legal guardians, or any person and must be treated as the primary client, and at the centre, of all child-serving systems. Finally, Saskatchewan children and youth merit due consideration being given to the importance of their unique life histories and their spiritual traditions and practices, in accordance with their stated views and preferences.

It is my belief that the Saskatchewan Child and Youth First Principles—a bill of rights for children as it were—could be enshrined in provincial child welfare legislation across Canada as part of a declaration of principles. Creating a consistent set of trans-jurisdictional principles would fit well into a rich and well-considered CRIA process.

Conclusion

As the world marks the twenty-fifth anniversary of the adoption of the Convention on the Rights of the Child, it is critically important that we do more than engage in lofty rhetoric and simply take account of our successes and failures. In order to fulfill the true promise of the Convention, we must continue to work toward its full implementation in Canada. The General Measures of Implementation can assist us greatly in this task. Over and above the larger implementation steps that fall predominantly to governments, policy-makers, and legislators, there are many attainable action steps that can be undertaken by child welfare professionals.

Ultimately, we must find creative and transformational ways to work together in partnerships. We cannot afford to continue at the same pace for the next twenty-five years. We know that children in this country are too often stuck in the middle and there has been no improvement in over nearly a decade. Unless efforts are stepped up, the rights of too many children in Canada will continue to be violated or go unnoticed. The time has come to act with passion and a sense of urgency in raising the bar on children's rights and child well-being in this country. It is up to each of us to take action!

References

Bernstein, M. M., & Schury, R. A. (2009). Passion, action, strength and innovative change: The experience of the Saskatchewan Children's Advocate's Office in establishing rights-based "children and youth first" principles. In S. McKay, D. Fuchs, & I. Brown (Eds.), *Passion for action in child and family services: Voices from the Prairies* (pp. 15–47). Regina, SK: Canadian Plains Research Center.

Canada. (2007). *Children: The silenced citizens* (Final Report of the Standing Senate Committee on Human Rights). Retrieved from http://www.parl.gc.ca/Content/SEN/Committee/391/huma/rep/rep10apr07-e.pdf

First Nations Child and Family Caring Society of Canada et al. v Attorney General of Canada, 2016 CHRT 2. Retrieved from http://www.afn.ca/uploads/files/2016_chrt_2.pdf

Mandela, N. (2000). *Statement on building a global partnership for children.*
    Retrieved from www.oneworldonepeople.org/articles/mandela_children.htm

Milne, C. (2014, May 7). Keynote address. *Working Together for the Best Interest of
    the Child.* Symposium conducted at the Johnson Shoyama Graduate School of
    Public Policy, Saskatoon, SK.

Ontario. (2013). *Final report of the Youth Leaving Care Working Group.* Retrieved
    from http://www.children.gov.on.ca/htdocs/English/documents/topics/
    childrensaid/youthleavingcare.pdf

Saskatchewan Ministry of Social Services. (2009). *Putting children first:
    Addressing the challenge: Response to the Saskatchewan Children's Advocate
    report on foster home overcrowding in the centre region.* Retrieved from http://
    www.gov.sk.ca/adx/aspx/adxgetmedia.aspx?mediaid=722&pn=shared

Sparrow Lake Alliance Children in Limbo Task Force. (2010). *There are no
    wizards: The child welfare conundrum.* Retrieved from https://ovot.files.
    wordpress.com/2014/05/no-wizard-revised-april-25-2014.pdf

UNICEF. (2007). *Child poverty in perspective: An overview of child well-being in rich
    countries* (Innocenti Report Card 7). Florence, Italy: UNICEF Innocenti Research
    Centre. Retrieved from http://www.unicef-irc.org/publications/pdf/rc7_eng.pdf

UNICEF. (2013). *Child well-being in rich countries: A comparative overview. UNICEF
    Report Card 11.* Florence, Italy: UNICEF Innocenti Research Centre. Retrieved
    from http://www.unicef-irc.org/publications/pdf/rc11_eng.pdf

UNICEF Canada. (2013). *Stuck in the middle: A Canadian companion to Report
    Card 11 — Child well-being in rich countries: A comparative overview.* Retrieved
    from http://www.unicef.ca/sites/default/files/imce_uploads/DISCOVER/
    OUR%20WORK/ADVOCACY/DOMESTIC/POLICY%20ADVOCACY/DOCS/
    unicef_rc_11_canadian_companion.pdf

United Nations. (1989, November 20). *Convention on the Rights of the Child* (A/
    RES/44/25). New York, NY: Author. Retrieved from http://www.ohchr.org/en/
    professionalinterest/pages/crc.aspx

United Nations. (2011). *Optional Protocol to the Convention on the Rights of the
    Child on a communications procedure* (adopted December 19, 2011, entered
    into force April 14, 2014). Retrieved from http://daccess-ods.un.org/access.nsf/
    Get?Open&DS=A/RES/66/138&Lang=E

United Nations Committee on the Rights of the Child. (2003, November). *General
    Comment No. 5, General Measures of Implementation of the Convention*
    (Document CRC/GC/2003/5). Retrieved from https://www.unicef-irc.org/
    portfolios/general_comments/GC5_en.doc.html

United Nations Committee on the Rights of the Child. (2012, December
    6). *Concluding observations on the combined third and fourth periodic
    report of Canada* (Document CRC/C/CAN/CO3-4). Retrieved from
    http://tbinternet.ohchr.org/_layouts/treatybodyexternal/Download.
    aspx?symbolno=CRC%2fCAN%2fCO%2f3-4&Lang=en

CHAPTER 2

Forms and Strategies for Integrated Working in Child Welfare

Judy Gillespie

Introduction

In the majority of developed countries, a cadre of disciplines, professions, agencies, and organizations are implicated in the well-being of children, from universal education and health care programs, to targeted supports for vulnerable or "at risk" children and families, to statutory interventions to protect children considered at risk of maltreatment. And while in Canada there are calls for greater integration between and among them, there is limited theoretical discussion of the forms through which integration occurs, the reasons for it, as well as the skills and strategies that promote integration. This chapter discusses three processes in integrated working: coordination, co-operation, and collaboration; and three forms through which these occur to address child well-being: child and family casework, interagency/interorganizational partnerships, and multi-sector collaborations. Key challenges for each of these are discussed, as well as the skills and strategies required for their success. The chapter begins with a closer look at the terms "coordination," "co-operation,"

Suggested Citation: Gillespie, J. (2016). Forms and strategies for integrated working in child welfare. In H. Montgomery, D. Badry, D. Fuchs, & D. Kikulwe (Eds.), *Transforming Child Welfare: Interdisciplinary Practices, Field Education, and Research* (pp. 27–41). Regina, SK: University of Regina Press.

and "collaboration," as well as the concept of "integration," situating it in relation to the differentiation that characterizes the provision of services and supports to address child and family well-being. The chapter concludes with implications for professional education and areas for further research.

Differentiation and Integration in Child Welfare

The language used to identify forms and strategies of integrated working in child welfare has been viewed as a "terminological quagmire," with words such as "coordination," "co-operation," "partnerships," "alliances," "coalitions," and "collaborations" sometimes viewed as interchangeable and sometimes as highly distinct (Lloyd, Stead, & Kendrick, 2001). It has been pointed out that the abundance of terms obscures the simple fact that what is being talked about are the processes by which people work and learn together (Leathard, 2003). Yet "working and learning together" is perhaps too simplistic a way of understanding the myriad of approaches and forms through which integration is occurring; some distinctions are needed in order to understand these differences, as well as the challenges they entail (Horwath & Morrison, 2007; Wright, 2012).

Theorizing interprofessional and interorganizational working in child welfare, Willumsen (2008) suggests that it constitutes a balance between differentiation and integration: *differentiation* refers to the distinct roles, responsibilities, resources, perspectives, and knowledge bases that the many individuals and agencies/organizations involved bring to child well-being, while *integration* refers to ways in which they come together: sharing information or tasks, defining common goals, or pooling resources. Understanding this balance, how integration occurs in relation to differentiation, is critical for theorizing the ways in which various disciplines, professions, agencies, organizations, and sectors all contribute to child and family well-being. Differentiation and integration constitute a continuum of practice within child welfare, taking place in forms that encompass child and family casework, interagency or interorganizational partnerships, or multisectoral collaborations. Striking the "right" balance along this continuum of differentiation and integration depends on understanding the particular task at hand, as well as the skills needed within various approaches to integration. This chapter examines three approaches that fall along this continuum of differentiation and integration: coordination, co-operation, and collaboration.

Coordination is characterized by the greatest degree of differentiation and the least degree of integration. It occurs when the distinct roles or responsibilities of two or more independent individuals, groups, or organizations involved in child welfare entail some degree of overlap. For example, despite working largely independently within their respective roles and mandates, police officers and child protection workers often coordinate their efforts in cases of child physical or sexual assault. Cooperation involves a stronger degree of integration; it entails some exchange of the unique resources that individuals, groups, or organizations have access to in order to assist one another in meeting their goals. For example, schools may provide space to child care programs, which, in turn, may provide meal programs for students. Collaboration requires the strongest commitment of all as it entails the greatest degree of integration. Individuals, groups, or organizations work together from a shared understanding of a problem toward mutually identified goals, pooling resources and efforts to achieve these goals. For example, a street outreach team comprised of health and social workers from various organizations might collaborate in assisting persons who are homeless.

Child and Family-Centred Casework

Child and family-centred casework is perhaps the most common form through which differentiation and integration are balanced to promote the welfare of children, youth, and families. It is characterized by a host of day-to-day interactions between those working directly with children, youth, and their caregivers. It occurs when a teacher notices a troubling difference in a student's day-to-day demeanour and shares this with a school social worker, who, through meeting with the parent, learns of a health issue and provides a referral to a local clinic, where a nurse arranges for the necessary care. It occurs when a physician reports their suspicion of a nonaccidental injury to a child protection social worker, who then gathers information from the child's teacher and makes a police referral. It occurs when a mental health social worker convenes a multidisciplinary case conference to develop a plan to support a vulnerable youth.

The interprofessional or interdisciplinary child welfare "team" is viewed as the most common structure for integration. In some instances, this

consists of a group of professionals working together within or coordinated through a single organization such as a specialized child abuse team
in a large hospital. Much more common, however, is a team of professionals brought together from a range of organizations on an ad hoc basis to
identify and address needs around a specific child or family (as in the
third example above). Most common of all are the fleeting interactions of
professionals whose roles briefly overlap through referrals or information
sharing (as in the first and second examples above).

Research suggests practitioners across a variety of domains often find
child and family-centred casework to be a source of major stress and conflict, and one for which they feel poorly prepared (Goldman & Grimbeek,
2014; Raman, Holdgate, & Torrens, 2012; Rowse, 2009). Issues of complexity are at the heart of the challenges experienced and expressed by most
professionals. These include the ambiguity, unpredictability, and volatility
of child welfare situations and their highly emotional and value-laden content, compounded by the dynamics of the interprofessional, interorganizational, and often cross-cultural practice required to identify and address
the needs of vulnerable children (Bunting, Lazenbatt, & Wallace, 2010;
Hood, 2014; Thompson, 2013). The teacher must decide if their concern
warrants breaching the child's privacy in a discussion with a school counsellor, and the school counsellor must decide if and how to approach the
parent. In this case, coordination is fairly straightforward; pass on information and leave the action up to another. For the physician, coordination is perhaps more complex — they must decide whether their suspicions
warrant action and, if so, how to best proceed, as well as the potential
consequences to the child and family of any action taken or not taken,
and perhaps the ramifications of such action/inaction for their own professional practice and reputation. This professional uncertainty is at the
heart of both under-reporting and over-reporting to child protection systems (Mathews & Kenny, 2008; Webster, O'Toole, O'Toole, & Lucal, 2005).

A multidisciplinary case conference to develop a plan for a vulnerable
youth may move beyond coordination; in addition to sharing information
or clarifying roles, participants may be asked to co-operate or collaborate
in the provision of specific services or resources, or to collectively advocate
for the youth with their own or other systems. Yet participants may have
very different views of problems and needs, and different understandings
of their own and others' roles (Thompson, 2013).

Interagency or Interorganizational Initiatives

Integration at interagency/interorganizational levels may range from simple interagency teams to coordinate service provision, to co-location of services in multiagency neighbourhood centres or family hubs, to collaborations that develop and deliver programs and services (Graham & Barter, 1999). Such integration may be initiated and driven from the "top-down" (i.e., government legislation or policies that require integration of services or service providers), or it may be initiated and driven from the "bottom-up" (i.e., the service providers themselves come together to develop and deliver services). Jones, Crook, and Reid Webb (2007) discuss the "collaborative pathway" of interagency or interorganizational initiatives that follows certain steps, beginning with environmental circumstances identified as a public problem. A method of resolution is then developed that involves coordination of services and takes into account purpose/context, membership, structure, process, and resources. Mediating variables (e.g., cultural and social, philosophical, economic, political, and environmental) affect the accomplishment of interim successes. Successes increase stakeholders' willingness to remain collaborative. The attainment of the identified goals leads to the resolution of the public problem and possibly a shift to broader goals. For example, one bottom-up interagency initiative began with an identified concern that certain community groups were unsure of how to respond to situations of domestic violence. The agencies that came together to address this issue included child protection, police, and mental health services. A number of in-service workshops were planned and conducted within the community, targeting faith-based organizations and nonprofit service providers. The workshops were well attended and the goal of increased public awareness was deemed to have been met. However, the workshops identified a broader concern for supports for families impacted by violence, which led to a new and broader interagency initiative.

As Willumsen (2008) notes, interagency and interorganizational forms of integrated working, while impacted by interpersonal and interprofessional dynamics, are highly dependent on the structural and functional qualities of participating agencies and organizations that come together. These encompass internal as well as external structures and functions, including division of labour; information flow; degree of formalization; availability; distribution of resources, leadership, and governance; and relationship to the state, to the market, and to society. Like interprofessional practices, interorganizational integration is impacted by dynamics within the processes of coordination, co-operation, or collaboration, including issues of conflict, power, trust, and commitment. An example is school-community teams that meet on a regular basis: the nature and quality of the work done by these teams is impacted not only by the skills, knowledge, and resources that each member brings to the team, and the dynamics between the various team members, but also by the different mandates, rules, and resources of the various agencies, as well as the dynamics between them; this includes their organizational commitment to integration.

Multisector Integration

The idea of community "sectors" is the notion that, within a community, various groups play specific roles (i.e., the "business" sector, the "health" sector, or the "education" sector). Each of these sectors brings different resources and provides different functions within a community. Yet it is increasingly recognized that complex social problems cut across sectoral boundaries. An example is homelessness, which typically cuts across issues of employment (business), addictions and mental health (health), and school achievement (education). Multisector integration refers to balancing differentiation and integration across multiple sectoral boundaries. The concept of "collective impact" has been given to multisector collaborations geared toward addressing complex social problems that result from an interplay of multiple factors that cut across sectoral boundaries: "No single organization is responsible for any major social problem, nor can any single organization cure it" (Kania & Kramer, 2011, pp. 38–39). As the broadest form of integrated working, it addresses issues, problems, or needs that cannot be effectively addressed by any one sector in isolation. United Way campaigns are one example of such integration; they typically involve businesses, government, nonprofit organizations, schools, health care, and others coordinating, and often co-operating, in fundraising efforts for a range of community-based organizations. Saint John, New Brunswick's YMCA Early Childhood Education Employment Initiative brought together government, education, social service, and business sectors to address employment for women living in poverty and facing multiple barriers (Caledon Institute, n.d.), while the Peace River Aboriginal Interagency Committee, a ten-plus-year initiative aimed at improving Aboriginal well-being in north-western Alberta, has brought together sectors of health, education, social services, child welfare, justice, municipal and First Nations governance, and more (Gillespie, Supernault, & Abel, 2014).

Balancing Differentiation and Integration in Child Welfare

As noted above, working across disciplinary and professional boundaries to address the needs of vulnerable children, youth, and families, through processes of coordination, co-operation, or collaboration, is a matter of balancing differentiation and integration. Figure 2.1 identifies strategies necessary for achieving this balance within each of these processes and illustrates the increased levels of commitment to integration encompassing required strategies from the previous level, as well as strategies required for that specific level of commitment. The concept of differentiation refers to the distinct roles and responsibilities, resources, perspectives, and knowledge bases that various individuals and agencies/organizations bring to child well-being. At the most basic level of integration, that of coordination, the understanding of and respect for differentiation is key. Research has shown that many of the problems in interprofessional and interdisciplinary working stem from misconceptions of roles and responsibilities, or from not understanding or respecting the different resources, knowledge, or perspectives that others bring to the process (Thompson, 2013).

A second and related requirement of coordination is effective communication. In noting the communication problems that "haunt" child welfare, Reder and Duncan (2003) suggest that communication is "far more complex than has ever been envisaged" (p. 84). Effective communication requires both effective *transmission* of information and its meaning, as well as effective *interpretation* of information and its meaning. This is challenging enough during direct communication between those from different disciplines, professions, agencies, or organizations, with their different training, knowledge, professional or disciplinary codes, perspectives, mandates, policies, and procedures. Indirect communication, such as fax, voice mail, email, written case notes, and information passed on by others, introduces additional complexities since the meta-communicative cues (such as facial expressions and tone of voice) are not available to assist in transmission and interpretation. Territorialism;

perceptions of role, status, power, or areas of expertise; professional and organizational policies; values and beliefs about children and families; stereotypes of one another; and past working relationships also impact effective communication.

Co-operation encompasses but goes beyond the level of integration required for coordination. Consequently, the requirements for successful co-operation encompass but go beyond those for coordination. Roles and responsibilities must be clear and there must be effective communication. Co-operation also requires mutually reinforcing activities and sharing of resources. In order to reinforce one another's activities, diverse stakeholders must understand their different goals and determine how they can support and facilitate the success of another stakeholder's goals. The focus of co-operation is on action, albeit action informed by understanding and communication. Co-operation also entails commitment to sharing resources. If differentiation is the value that each player brings to the co-operative process, integration is the process through which this value is realized as others gain access to knowledge, skills, or other resources that are needed to enhance the success of their efforts but are lacking within their own systems. Yet co-operation is challenging in contexts where needs are multifaceted and resources are scarce. The current system of competition between agencies for government contracts sets up rivalries that mitigate against co-operation. Moreover, co-operative partnerships and alliances are often the first casualties of government cutbacks (Provan, Veazie, Staten, & Teufel-Shone, 2005).

Collaboration requires the strongest commitment, and numerous elements are necessary for successful collaboration. These encompass the conditions required for coordination and co-operation: understanding of different roles and responsibilities, effective communication, mutually reinforcing activities, and sharing of resources. However, it also includes development of a common understanding of the problem to be addressed, as well as shared goals and measures of success.

> *Collective impact requires all participants to have a shared vision for change, one that includes a common understanding of the problem and a joint approach to solving it through agreed upon actions.... Every participant need not agree with every other participant on all dimensions of the problem....All participants must agree, however,*

on the primary goals for the collective impact initiative as a whole.
(Kania & Kramer, 2011, p. 39)

Also, shared vision and collective goals must go beyond vague aspirations; specificity is needed regarding what is to be achieved, as well as how, and this should include clarity regarding the roles of the various participants (Jones et al., 2007; Auspos & Kubisch, 2012). And shared vision and common goals must be supplemented with agreement on the ways success will be measured and reported. Shared measures of success provide a form of action research that enables collaborative efforts to remain aligned, holding participants accountable to one another and facilitating processes of feedback on successes and failures within the various strategies.

Strong leadership is an additional condition required for successful collaboration, whether this takes the form of a single champion that initiates support and maintains commitment during difficult times or if it is characterized by a team of leaders that responds to the numerous challenges entailed in collaboration. This leadership must be complemented by a supporting infrastructure that includes communicative and administrative support; lack of supporting infrastructure is one of the most frequent reasons why collaborative efforts fail (Jones et al., 2007; Kania & Kramer, 2011).

Figure 2.1. Conditions for Success in Integrated Working in Child Welfare

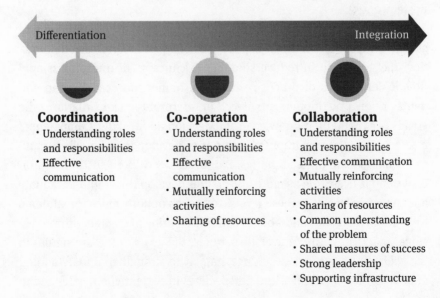

Coordination
* Understanding roles and responsibilities
* Effective communication

Co-operation
* Understanding roles and responsibilities
* Effective communication
* Mutually reinforcing activities
* Sharing of resources

Collaboration
* Understanding roles and responsibilities
* Effective communication
* Mutually reinforcing activities
* Sharing of resources
* Common understanding of the problem
* Shared measures of success
* Strong leadership
* Supporting infrastructure

Implications for Education and Professional Development

Development of the knowledge and skills to effectively balance differentiation and integration in child welfare is almost impossible within dominant approaches to professional education and development. While coordination, co-operation, and collaboration in child and family-centred casework require understanding of and respect for different roles and mandates, the majority of professional groups receive minimal education or training in child welfare, and the modal form of training is uniprofessional (Nayda, 2005; Goldman & Grimbeek, 2014; Polnay, 2000; Rowse, 2009).

Interprofessional education (IPE) has been defined as situations where two or more professions come together to learn with, from, and about each other to improve their capacity for integrated working (Barr, Koppel, Reeves, Hammick, & Freeth, 2005; Centre for the Advancement of Interprofessional Education, 2002; Oandasan & Reeves, 2005). The goals of IPE include strengthening understanding of the roles, responsibilities, knowledge base, and unique perspectives of other disciplines and professions, as well as one's own role in relation to these (Clark, 2006). Research suggests that IPE results in positive interactions that engender mutual trust and support and promote respect and collaboration between professions. IPE has been associated with reduced stress, increased job satisfaction, and better recruitment and retention (Barr et al., 2005; Lalayants & Epstein, 2005).

IPE is often viewed as a continuum ranging from exposure to immersion to competence/mastery. Exposure occurs prior to professional practice; the goal is to introduce students to concepts of interprofessional practice and types of practice situations. Immersion occurs when students or new practitioners are placed in interprofessional situations; the goal is to expand their knowledge and develop initial skills. Competence/mastery occurs as practitioners continue to develop their knowledge and skills and to train others (Charles, Bainbridge, & Gilbert, 2010). A significant trend is occurring as more universities develop IPE at undergraduate and graduate levels. At these levels, IPE offers opportunities for students to learn "with, from, and about each other" prior to engaging in professional practice. Within university settings, the goals of IPE are similar to the goals of IPE in practice settings, namely to strengthen understanding of other professional roles and perspectives in patient/client care, and to promote the capacity for reflective practice that can capitalize on opportunities for integration across professional and disciplinary boundaries.

Assisting those new to the field of child welfare to understand the nature of their role in child and family-centred casework and to appreciate the role of others would seem to be an important area for IPE. Consequently, it would seem logical that IPE with a specific child welfare focus would be fairly widespread. Curiously, this does not appear to be the case. Despite the recent surge in IPE in Canada, current initiatives are heavily focused in the area of health care—there is little evidence of a specific child welfare focus. Given the nature and complexity of child welfare, it is inappropriate to assume that health-focused IPE can generate the knowledge and skills needed for interprofessional/interdisciplinary practice in child welfare. An exception is occurring in the United Kingdom, where the government has emphasized integrated working and learning in basic or "core" child protection among and across various professional bodies through a variety of expectations, protocols, and procedures, and where post-secondary institutions, agencies, and organizations are implementing programs and strategies to promote stronger integrated working (Crokett et al., 2013; Davies, 2014; Department for Education, 2013; Glennie, 2007).

Implications for Research

In relation to child and family-centred casework, there is a dearth of research regarding interdisciplinary and interprofessional knowledge and skills needed for integrated working in child welfare and how these are acquired and developed. At the interagency and interorganizational level, there have been numerous case studies, however there is limited empirical examination of the roles of differentiation and integration in relation to the sustainability of co-operative and collaborative efforts. How do different resources, mandates, perspectives, and goals contribute to or detract from these efforts? And what organizational structures and strategies are most useful in meeting the challenges of sustainability? In relation to multisectoral initiatives, considerable work is occurring around methods to evaluate their impacts and outcomes (Abel & Gillespie, 2015). Given the increasing emphasis on evidence-based policy, this work is laudable; however, an important but underdeveloped area concerns child welfare-related measurement of impacts and outcomes.

The value of cross-jurisdictional research in child welfare systems has long been recognized; comparisons allow policy and practice in one or more jurisdictions to be benchmarked against others, assisting in illuminating particular strengths and weaknesses and identifying promising practices and alternative strategies to promote children's well-being (Gilbert, Parton, & Skivenes, 2011; Mathews & Kenny, 2008). The growth of integrated learning and practice in child welfare in the United Kingdom and the many interagency and multisectoral initiatives in the United States and other countries all offer opportunities for comparative research with Canadian initiatives regarding the knowledge, skills, and strategies for effective integrated working, while maintaining a focus on our own unique contexts and needs.

Conclusion

The lack of effective integration between disciplines, professionals, agencies, organizations, and sectors within our society is blamed for a host of problems from the tragic and "preventable" deaths of children to the challenges of navigating services, to the inability to address our most complex and entrenched social problems. Much of this criticism is warranted, and efforts to foster stronger integration are clearly needed. However, in promoting stronger integration, we need to maintain respect for the role that differentiation plays in promoting the well-being of children and families. As stated earlier, the key is understanding the balance needed between the two in order to effectively address the task at hand, as well as understanding the strategies and skills required to maximize the effectiveness of the approach being used. Fostering this understanding requires commitment to, and strategies for, interdisciplinary and interprofessional education in our universities, as well as in our agencies and organizations. Finally, we need research that assists in developing a better understanding of effective integrated working in all its forms and approaches, and the skills and strategies that help to achieve this. A major step forward would involve the development of comparative cross-jurisdictional research that assists us to understand how this is occurring within diverse contexts and needs, while enabling us to shape our own unique approaches.

References

Abel, M., & Gillespie, J. (2015). Network analysis in co-productive research with a multi-sector community network. *Community Development Journal, 50*(2), 327–344. doi:10.1093/cdj/bsu040

Auspos, P., & Kubisch, A. (2012). *Performance management in complex, place-based work: What it is, what it isn't, and why it matters.* Washington, DC: The Aspen Institute. Retrieved from http://www.aspeninstitute.org/sites/default/files/content/images/rcc/Aspen_Performance_Management.pdf

Barr, H., Koppel, I., Reeves, S., Hammick, M., & Freeth, D., (2005). *Effective interprofessional education: argument, assumption & evidence.* Oxford, United Kingdom: Blackwell Publishing.

Bunting, L., Lazenbatt, A., & Wallace, I. (2010). Information sharing and reporting systems in the UK and Ireland: Professional barriers to reporting child maltreatment concerns. *Child Abuse Review, 19*(3), 187–202.

Caledon Institute. (n.d.). *Vibrant communities 2002–2011: Early childhood education program seeing success in Saint John.* Retrieved from http://www.vibrantcommunities.ca/

Centre for the Advancement of Interprofessional Education. (2002). The definition and principles of interprofessional education. Retrieved from http://caipe.org.uk/about-us/the-definition-and-principles-of-interprofessional-education/

Charles, G., Bainbridge, L., & Gilbert, J. (2010). The University of British Columbia model of interprofessional education. *Journal of Interprofessional Care, 24*(1), 9–18.

Clark, P. (2006). What would a theory of interprofessional education look like? Some suggestions for developing a theoretical framework for teamwork training. *Journal of Interprofessional Care, 20*(6), 577–589.

Crockett, R., Gilchrist, G., Davies, J., Henshall, A., Hoggart, L., Chandler, V.,... Webb, J. (2013). *Assessing the early impact of Multi Agency Safeguarding Hubs (MASH) in London: Project Report.* London, United Kingdom: London Councils.

Davies, J. (2014). Maritime City: Using serious gaming to deliver child protection training. *Advances in Dual Diagnosis, 7*(1), 34–42.

Department for Education. (2013). *Working together to safeguard children: A guide to interagency working to safeguard and promote the welfare of children.* London, United Kingdom: The Stationary Office.

Gilbert, N., Parton, N., & Skivenes, M. (Eds.). (2011). *Child protection systems: International trends and orientations.* New York, NY: Oxford University Press.

Gillespie, J., Supernault, G., & Abel, M. (2014). Community networking: A promising practice for Aboriginal child welfare. In D. Badry, M. Montgomery, D. Fuchs, & S. McKay (Eds.), *Reinvesting in families, securing a brighter future: Voices from the Prairies* (pp. 201–219). Edmonton, AB: Prairie Child Welfare Consortium/Alberta Centre for Child, Family and Community Research.

Glennie, S. (2007). Developing interprofessional relationships: Tapping the potential of inter-agency training. *Child Abuse Review, 16,* 171–183.

Goldman, J., & Grimbeek, P. (2014). Bridging the gaps in child sexual abuse reporting and disclosure: Child sexual abuse and mandatory reporting intervention preservice content preferred by student teachers. *Journal of Child Sexual Abuse, 23,* 1–16.

Graham, J., & Barter, K. (1999). Collaboration: A social work practice method, families in society. *The Journal of Contemporary Human Services, 80,* 6–13.

Hood, R. (2014). Complexity and integrated working in Children's Services. *British Journal of Social Work, 44,* 27–43. doi:10.1093/bjsw/bcs091

Horwath, J., & Morrison, T. (2007). Collaboration, integration and change in children's services: Critical issues and key ingredients. *Child Abuse & Neglect, 33*(1), 55–69. doi:10.1016/j.chiabu.2006.01.007

Jones, J., Crook, W., & Reid Webb, J. (2007). Collaboration for the provision of services: A review of the literature. *Journal of Community Practice, 15*(4), 41–71. doi:10.1300/J125v15n04_03

Kania, J., & Kramer, M. (2011, Winter). Collective impact. *Stanford Social Innovation Review,* 36–41. Retrieved from http://www.ssireview.org/articles/entry/collective_impact

Lalayants, M., & Epstein, I. (2005). Evaluating multidisciplinary child abuse and neglect teams: A research agenda. *Child Welfare, 84*(4), 433–458.

Leathard, A. (2003). Introduction. In A. Leathard (Ed.), *Interprofessional collaboration: From policy to practice in health and social care* (pp. 2–10). New York, NY: Routledge.

Lloyd, G., Stead, J., & Kendrick, A. (2001). *Hanging on in there: A study of inter-agency work to prevent school exclusion in three local authorities.* London, United Kingdom: National Children's Bureau.

Mathews, B., & Kenny, M. (2008). Mandatory reporting legislation in the United States, Canada and Australia: A cross-jurisdictional review of key features, differences and issues. *Child Maltreatment, 13,* 50–63.

Nayda, R. (2005). Australian nurses and child protection: Practices and pitfalls. *Collegian, 12*(1), 25–28.

Oandasan, I., & Reeves, S. (2005). Key elements of interprofessional education. Part 2: Factors, processes and outcomes. *Journal of Interprofessional Care (Supp), 1,* 39–48.

Polnay, J. (2000). General practitioners and child protection case conference participation: Reasons for non-attendance and proposals for a way forward. *Child Abuse Review, 9,* 108–123. doi:10.1002/car.1099-0852

Provan, K., Veazie, M., Staten, L., & Teufel-Shone, N. (2005). The use of network analysis to strengthen community partnerships. *Public Administration Review, 65*(5), 603–613.

Raman, S., Holdgate, A., & Torrens, R. (2012). Are our frontline clinicians equipped with the ability and confidence to address child abuse and neglect? *Child Abuse Review, 21,* 114–130. doi:10.1002/car.1180

Reder, P., & Duncan, S. (2003). Understanding communication in child protection networks. *Child Abuse Review, 12,* 82–100. doi:10.1002/car.787

Rowse, V. (2009). Support needs of children's nurses involved in child protection cases. *Journal of Nursing Management, 17,* 659–666. doi:10.1111/j.1365-2834.2009.00987.x

Thompson, K. (2013). Multi-agency information practices in children's services: The metaphorical "jigsaw" and professionals quest for a "full" picture. *Child and Family Social Work, 18,* 189–197. doi:10.1111/j.1365-2206.2011.00821.x

Webster, S., O'Toole, R., O'Toole, A., & Lucal, B. (2005). Overreporting and underreporting of child abuse: Teachers' use of professional discretion. *Child Abuse & Neglect, 29,* 1281–1296.

Willumsen, E. (2008). Interprofessional collaboration — A matter of differentiation and integration? Theoretical reflections based in the context of Norwegian childcare. *Journal of Interprofessional Care, 22*(4), 352–363.

Wright, A. (2012). A conceptual framework for child welfare service coordination, collaboration, and integration. In D. Fuchs, S. McKay, & I. Brown (Eds.), *Awakening the spirit: Moving forward in child welfare: Voices from the prairies* (pp. 117–133). Regina, SK: Canadian Plains Research Center.

CHAPTER 3

Saskatchewan First Nations:
Researching Ourselves Back to Life

H. Monty Montgomery, A. J. Felix, Patsy Felix, Margaret Kovach, and Shelley Thomas Prokop

> *"I love my Indigenous Knowledges. I know that way is a sure way."*
> —*Elder A. J. Felix, 2015*

This chapter endeavours to transcend some of the historic mistrust and missteps that have taken place with respect to child, family, and community research with Indigenous peoples across the Numbered Treaty areas of Canada. In a spirit of openness to the transforming of relationships between social science researchers and their participants, the co-authors of this chapter present our thoughts on the importance of conducting research with First Nations peoples in a good way. Drawing upon the spoken words of Elders A. J. and Patsy Felix (Sturgeon Lake First Nation), the writers of this chapter present key factors that should be taken into consideration by people interested in research study design, research ethics, data collection, and authentic representation of Indigenous voice in child welfare research. This chapter provides an overview of the contemporary relationship that many First Nations have with social science research, the role that

Suggested Citation: Montgomery, H. M., Felix, A.J., Felix, P., Kovach, M., & Thomas Prokop, S. (2016). Saskatchewan First Nations: Researching ourselves back to life. In H. Montgomery, D. Badry, D. Fuchs, & D. Kikulwe (Eds.), *Transforming Child Welfare: Interdisciplinary Practices, Field Education, and Research* (pp. 43–58). Regina, SK: University of Regina Press.

an Indigenous Research Advisory Committee can take in guiding ethical research activities, and Elder teachings that speak to the steps that individuals can take to initiate and conduct research in a respectful good way.

Together, the listed co-authors of this chapter have contributed decades of effort in support of First Nations-administered child and family services agencies as cultural advisors, staff trainers, policy developers, program evaluators, and researchers. All of the co-authors have Indigenous ancestry, two are Elders, and several have earned graduate degrees. As Indigenous people who are interested in improving relationships among people who serve the children of our communities, we present this information in a spirit of generosity and with no aim of casting aspersions among those who are truly interested in helping, healing, and decolonizing child welfare across Canada.

> *"First Nations have been researched to death. Now we're researching ourselves back to life."*
>
> —*Mary Teegee, 2014*

This chapter advances some of the concepts that were introduced at an invited plenary panel presentation the co-author group gave at the 2014 Prairie Child Welfare Consortium (PCWC) symposium entitled Coming Together as a First Nation Child, Family and Community Research Advisory Committee. The panel was comprised of key members of the Saskatchewan First Nations Family and Community Institute's Research Advisory Committee (RAC) at the time, including Warren Seesequasis. Warren was unfortunately unavailable to assist with the writing of this chapter. The panel was asked to speak to the importance of contextualizing research involving First Nations children and families in ways that recognize the strengths of communities and downplay the typifying representations of data in pathologizing terms. The presentation ended the first day of the general session of the 2014 PCWC conference, and was preceded by an earlier presentation that provided a venue for several First Nations child and family service directors to discuss transformational change initiatives that they had borne witness to over the past decades in their jurisdictions. It was at that earlier session that many audience members heard the inspirational words (cited above) of Mary Teegee of Carrier Sekani Family Services in British Columbia as she spoke of the self-determining stance that her organization's member Bands had taken in reaction to the numerous self-serving offers of help that had been extended to them as they sought to develop their own capacity to serve First Nations children and families in north central British Columbia in culturally appropriate ways. Bearing in mind much respect for Mary's powerful words, we, too, were inspired to consider how First Nations people in Saskatchewan can best begin the work of researching ourselves back to life.

Researched to Death

In 2003, Maori scholar Linda Tuhiwai-Smith succinctly described the way that many Indigenous peoples globally have come to view a range of activities that have been imposed on their members and communities, purportedly in the name of scientific research, medicine, or progress. "Research," she wrote, "...is probably one of the dirtiest words in the Indigenous world's vocabulary" (p. 1). This dynamic has since been expanded upon by an emergent group of Indigenous scholars (e.g., Wilson, 2008; Kovach, 2010; Chilisa, 2012) who have detailed the dearth—and importance—of respect, reciprocity, and relationality within health, education, and social science research on, for, and with Indigenous peoples within Canada and across the world. Over the past twenty years, the coherent critique of Western thought and culture articulated by Indigenous scholarly writers (e.g., Little Bear, 2000; Bubar, 2013; Cisneros, 2014) has gathered strength as Indigenous and non-Indigenous researchers (e.g., Debassige, 2010; Absolon & Willett, 2005; Thomas, 2014) have taken up the inquiry-based tools that legitimize knowledge and create evidence for much needed change. The field of child welfare has not been a central focus of study within the critical discourse to date, but the findings that have begun to be documented elsewhere within the social sciences are now also beginning to shape academic and professional discourse and policy making. In order to build the context for the inevitable philosophical change that is building as we begin researching ourselves back to life, it may help to first explain how it is that First Nations have come to be researched to death.

Since the age of worldwide imperialism began, Indigenous people have freely shared their intellectual, genetic, and cultural birthrights with newcomers and visitors, only to have found the process has often left them powerless, voiceless, economically disadvantaged, and socially marginalized.

Colonialism has normalized the Western world's appropriation of the products of Indigenous Knowledges for individual gain by seeking out elements that may easily be stolen, patented, rebranded, and packaged for commercial use. Initially, the raw materials (e.g., minerals, plants, fish, animals) found on Indigenous peoples' lands were the targets of exploitation, the extraction of which fit into capitalist narratives of hinterlands, economic development, and robber baron heroes (Churchill, 1983). As agricultural pastoralism supplanted and complemented first-wave raw material extraction, Indigenous people came to be seen as impediments to progress in any way other than contributing their manual labour to the wealth building of others (Duff, 1969; Daschuk, 2013). Rather than looking to how Indigenous peoples could contribute to advancing society and solving pressing concerns, Western-educated seekers of knowledge looked more to empirical science for legitimate solutions to emerging social, medical, and economic problems (Bishop, 1999).

Over time, relational narratives changed from those of partnership (e.g., treaties) to pathologizing tales of Indigenous peoples destined to live out their devalued days on the social and geographic margins of Western progress (Borrows, 2005). Early social science researchers sought evidence for theories to support myths of the vanishing Indians, racial inferiority, and social deviance, and too often their research efforts highlighted the deficits of Indigenous peoples, who themselves were struggling to adapt to massive social, economic, and political change (Francis, 1992). Many social reformers and academics began to view Indigenous peoples' languages, practices, and traditions (e.g., ceremonies that marked the natural transformations of people's lives) as anachronisms with no practical future in a rapidly modernizing world. Early knowledge dissemination practices (e.g., journalism, memoirs, public lectures) provided "evidence" of emergent and expedient theories upon which to support race-based, proreligious, and economically disadvantageous social engineering programs (Blaut, 1993). Soon thereafter, social policy based upon popularly held Victorian-era beliefs was passed by the legislative, executive, and judicial branches of the Dominion of Canada (i.e., the Crown—federal, provincial, and territorial governments of all political stripes). Having enacted enabling policy, funding authorities were established to bankroll social control mechanisms such as the residential schools, Indian hospitals and sanatoriums, and eugenics programs (e.g., forced sterilizations) implemented across many Canadian jurisdictions (Kelm, 1998). Enforcement provisions of civil law were enacted to enable the paramilitary branches of government (e.g., magistrates, police, child protection) to pursue "peace, order and good government" in the "best interests" of all Canadian citizens. Research became a handmaiden to Canadian nationalism as publicly visible groups, who were then considered to be living deviant lifestyles (e.g., Indigenous peoples, homosexual people, non-Caucasian immigrants) (Boldt, 1993), became the targets of scholarly informed social injustice. It was not until the United Nations was formed in 1949, after which a number of international conventions on human rights were agreed to, that things began to change and the more egregious aspects of oppressive federal and provincial social policy became less fashionable (Miller, 2000).

Following hard upon the adoption of the 1949 United Nations Convention on Universal Human Rights, Canada amended the Indian Act in 1951 to enable provincial laws of general application to have effect on federal lands (e.g., military bases, Indian reserves) (Miller, 2000). Advocacy groups had pushed for this extension of authority to broaden the reach of provincial social programs to reserve residents with little advance consultation with the people who would be most affected by this legislative revision. Whatever critiques that may have been raised by Indigenous peoples themselves and social scientists (e.g., anthropology, religious studies), who decried the loss of traditional Indigenous lifestyles and cultural practices, were given short shrift among other social scientists (e.g., commerce, home economics, political science), who looked to Victorian-era, "scientific" explanations of and social justifications for racial inequality (McKillop, 2013) as the best way to advance political and financial freedom for a generic population they described as "mankind." Individuals employed to work on the front lines of social programming (e.g., social workers, nurses, teachers, police) were empowered to enforce the quotidian necessities of assimilation by withholding benefits and enforcing penalties upon those individuals and families who would not or could not comply with, or were absolutely unaware of, the macrosystemic factors that had foreclosed their cultural freedoms (Satzewich & Liodakis, 2013).

During the latter half of the twentieth century, many reserve residents witnessed the systematic apprehension of their community's children, the institutionalization of their sick and aged, the deliberate flunking out of their youth, the imprisonment of their neighbours, and the chronic underinvestigation of acts of victimization. Many of the perpetrators of these injustices purported to be acting in "the best interests" of children and communities, and/or in a manner that was purported to be supported by social science research and "best practice" (Kline, 1992). For many Indigenous people who lived through these times, their witnessing of decades of past bad practice remains strong in their individual memories and the collective narratives of their communities. It matters little whether the research methods that informed the various historic practices of oppression took the form of comprehensive risk assessments, medical experiments, standardized tests, or criminal jurisprudence — there is clear evidence that First Nations have experienced oversurveillance and have been underserved by social science researchers. When research is undertaken and cited as the evidence base for past and continuing oppression, it is easy to see how the very idea of such research can come to be seen as a very dirty word indeed in many First Nations families and communities.

Not Quite Dead Yet

One outcome of all the research/data collection/testing activities undertaken by health researchers during the twentieth century is that it is now clear that Indigenous people are not disappearing. The Darwinian theorizing that predicted Indigenous people as being "the last of his race" has not come to pass. Disease has not killed us all off. Starvation is no longer a threat. Mandatory involuntary sterilization is no longer legal. Widespread immunization has saved the lives of countless people, and the efforts underway to develop additional treatments for chronic conditions such as HIV infection, diabetes, and rheumatoid arthritis hold much promise to further improve the well-being of future generations of Indigenous peoples. International agreements such as the 1951 United Nations Convention on the Prevention and Punishment of the Crime of Genocide and the 2007 United Nations Declaration on the Rights of Indigenous Peoples have given Indigenous peoples of North America fighting chances to keep our bodies strong, although our cultural and spiritual practices have suffered significantly from the colonial onslaught that was purportedly undertaken as a means to protect, save, and civilize Indigenous people. Decades of bench research, normative analysis, and clinical trials have generated evidence related to the health and social outcomes of Indigenous peoples, albeit frequently as a comparator to other societal populations. Health research (Wade, 1995) has chronicled the resiliency of Indigenous peoples and the fact that we are indeed not a vanishing race. The body of evidence is something to celebrate.

Although scholarly inquiries aimed at giving validity to sociological race-based theorizing and rationalizing the unethical practices espoused by researchers who sought to prove the alleged inferiority of Indigenous people have long been discredited, much of the social science data gathering related to Indigenous children, families, and communities has still not yet led to increased well-being for Indigenous people. By considering Indigenous peoples as being incapable of participating in data collection in any manner other than as a research subject or service user, little consideration was given to Indigenous peoples who sought to use scholarly research methods to tell our own stories. Largely due to historic social policies (e.g., residential schooling, segregation, economic dependency), many Indigenous people never had opportunities to graduate from high school or attend university before the 1970s (Merasty, Bouvier, & Hoium, 2013). Indigenous people were not being trained to develop hypotheses, conduct research, undertake analyses, or write up and disseminate findings on matters that sparked their own curiosities. We could become teachers, social workers, accountants, and lawyers, but Indigenous people holding these professional designations were more likely to follow policy than to generate evidence in support of better policy and programs.

Because of this history, few Indigenous communities had access to the sociological information that was being collected about us, our ancestors, our children, and our families. Indigenous people were unable to correct the many errors that were captured in research project datasets and governmental databases, and the collectors of that information became used to not sharing datasets they considered to be their own. No pathways were created to enable Indigenous researchers to query data related to their relatives, or to offer differing analyses than were being presented as incontrovertible facts in reports produced using that data. There was no way to check for and correct data-entry errors, insufficient coding categorizations, and personal biases that may have systematically corrupted the data upon which purported findings were being justified and presented in scholarly or trade publications. Indeed, if few Indigenous people had been given opportunities to apprentice and practise as disciplined social science researchers, how, then, could people of Indigenous ancestry ever hope to be considered peers capable of participating in collegial peer reviews of scholarship?

Saskatchewan First Nations Responses to Toxic Research

Indigenous peoples across Canada did not simply acquiesce and capitulate to the forces of Western social science. Some insightful Aboriginal leaders recognized that science was being used against them, and they advocated for educational programs (e.g., tuition support, scholarships, bursaries) that could enable bright young Indigenous minds to learn how to become researchers capable of telling more nuanced stories of their communities. Indian control of Indian education was not envisioned as being solely limited to K–12 schooling (Richardson & Blanchet-Cohen, 2000) but was also seen as the opening of a pathway to university, where students could learn to conduct research and generate alternative evidence that was then being presented by non-Indigenous social science researchers. As control for educational and social service programming transferred over to First Nations administration, in the 1970s–1980s, Indigenous people began generating and tracking their own utilization data regarding First Nations reserve-based programming (Modeste et. al, 1993). Initially, the impetus for much of the data-collection activity was driven by externally mandated reporting requirements, wherein there was little recognition that the information itself should remain under the care and control of the Indigenous people who had contributed to it or collected it.

However, as years passed and First Nations developed their capacity for developing, delivering, and administering an increasingly sophisti-cated range of social programs, many First Nations became more proac-tive in their use of data management and analysis tools to assist them in tracking emergent patterns. For example, in 1996 the Cowichan Tribes on Vancouver Island initiated the development of a robust Structured Query Language (SQL) database electronic file management system that ensured that the information being entered into the system would remain in the care and control of the First Nation that purchased the system (About CFS Best Practices, 2008). Initial modules of this program were designed to facilitate the administration of the Band's financial assistance program, and as other First Nations heard of the utility of the technology in facilitating report generation, demand for the data management system increased across Western Canada. Subsequent additional modules were developed to collect and administer data germane to First Nations child and family service programming, and those First Nations who were early adopters of the technology—including First Nations in Alberta and Saskatchewan—found themselves in a much better position to utilize data to generate reports capable of demonstrating robust and reliable evidence in support of their programs.

Since the 1980s, the practice capacity of First Nations has strengthened through recruitment and training of individuals interested in practising and administering child and family services in a culturally competent manner. Technological advances in communications and data management also encouraged First Nations to begin sharing information among themselves, and a degree of unity that was tied to matters of collective interest (e.g., legislative reform, standards development, training) emerged among some regional First Nations child and family service providers. Such shared interest has led to calls for shared child welfare advocacy among First Nations, regardless of the linguistic, cultural, and historic differences between Bands. Commonality of interest in the areas of research and knowledge mobilization has led to the establishment of Indigenous entities that have been mandated by First Nations specifically for such purposes. The Saskatchewan First Nations Family and Community Institute is one such organization that aims to advance the interests of Indigenous peoples and programming across the treaty areas of the lands now known as Saskatchewan.

After years of sitting together in council and planning, the leaders and chiefs of many of Saskatchewan's seventy-three First Nations demonstrated unity in the area of child and family services by successfully incorporating the Saskatchewan First Nations Family and Community Institute (SFNFCI) in 2007. The founding principles guiding the creation of the SFN-FCI give direction to permanent staff and qualified contractors who focus on the three core business areas:

1. research, policy, and standards development;
2. training and professional development;
3. strategic partnerships and collaboration.

Clearly, Indigenous research interests underpin much of the work being undertaken by the SFNFCI. In order to guide planned activities and ensure that the SFNFCI's work is undertaken in a manner that is sensitive to Indigenous Knowledges, practices, and methodologies, the visionary leaders of the SFNFCI installed its Research Advisory Committee (RAC) in 2010. Comprised of Indigenous male and female volunteers who are acknowledged to possess in-depth understandings of both academic and traditional knowledge processes, the RAC members serve the SFNFCI members (i.e., Saskatchewan First Nations child and family service agencies) by developing, implementing, and monitoring the organizational research program. To assist with the undertaking of SFNFCI projects, the RAC's input has assisted the development of a draft ethical framework to better understand and guide the expectations of research activities. This Indigenous ethical framework ensures that all research projects are based on implementing meaningful awareness and change within the child welfare organizations participating in the projects. Ultimately, the intention of the SFNFCI ethical framework is to improve and increase the capacity of First Nation child welfare organizations to provide relevant programs and services to their community clientele. This guiding ethical framework was created to complement university and/or Indigenous research ethics review processes that may also have interests in the specific projects being considered or delivered by the SFNFCI.

The Elders Speak: Researching Our Families and Communities Back to Life

In an effort to demonstrate how First Nations are taking steps to restore Indigenous Knowledges and reclaim the manner in which the content we provide to researchers gets told, the SFNFCI Research Advisory Committee members came together one afternoon in the fall of 2015 to discuss important considerations for Indigenous child and family research. SFNFCI Elders A. J. and Patsy Felix agreed to share their knowledge with us about this topic. As with all meetings of the RAC, we showed honour and respect for the cultural traditions of the Indigenous peoples upon whose lands we had gathered. We all shared a meal organized by SFNFCI staff policy analyst Shelley Thomas Prokop, our host. University of Saskatchewan, Faculty of Education faculty member Dr. Margaret Kovach and University of Regina, Faculty of Social Work faculty member Dr. H. Monty Montgomery were present, bore witness, and agreed to represent the conversation in text. Prior to the session, we had identified that we were planning to discuss issues relating to First Nations child and family services, so each person present had time to process their thoughts appropriately beforehand. Protocol was followed with the presentation of tobacco to appropriate members and the offering of prayer as a precursor, readying our thoughts for the conversation.

The discussion started off by looking at the current state of affairs within reserve-based child and family service programming in Saskatchewan. Our general consensus recognized that contemporary First Nations child welfare service programs had been mined, cast, and polished using a borrowed recipe and a melting pot of stale-dated scientific evidence that sought to rescue Indigenous children and punish negligent parents. Elders A. J. and Patsy both commented that the consequences of having to deal with decades of policies aimed at crushing Indigenous people and undermining our traditional ways has had devastating impacts on children and families. We recognized that if the current child welfare system had been built upon a system that honoured Indigenous Knowledges, young mothers and fathers—and those in positions to support them—would now also recognize what Elder A. J. explained:

> *Everything starts with the home. Each of us has our own fireplace, and we have to respect that fire. When the fire dies out, we need to keep it alive. Teachings tell us that it's wrong to hit your wife, wrong to drink and wrong to leave God out of your life. We're spiritual people; our actions have consequences in the here and now, not when you're in heaven. If you're looking for short cuts to end your pain, you will just create more pain. So, we need to keep on encouraging our young ones. They are having a tough time trying to make their little cheques last. We have to keep on encouraging them.*

It was said by the Elders, "We were forced to accept another culture's concepts of raising our children." We jointly recognized that the contemporary child welfare programs that operate on reserves across Canada had not started out from a foundation based in Indigenous Law. Love, care, kindness, respect, and honesty are Indigenous Laws that Indigenous

Knowledge holders know are supposed to guide the raising of children. However, because there is no legally recognized authority or oversight role granted to culturally informed Indigenous peoples over our own children, there is no mechanism for Indigenous Laws and forms of justice to influence the upbringing of children. As an example of a form of justice that is based in Indigenous Law, Elder A. J. Felix spoke of his understanding of consequential justice as a way of guiding people to live their lives in harmony with one another:

> *Consequential justice means that what goes around, comes around. When you do something good, something good will come of it. If you look after them as kids, they will look after you; and when kids look after elders, they will grow to have grey hair someday. Even at my age, I know that my actions have consequences. So I watch the road I walk and how I walk it. If I want a sense of security when I lay down at night, I must have gratitude when I wake up in the morning.*

A. J. clearly differentiated the concept of consequential justice from mainstream notions of justice that are founded in principles of confession, forgiveness, and repayment of debts to society. Mainstream justice has led to so many young people being in care where they are being raised by people who do not value Indigenous Law. If they are not being properly educated by their caregivers, they will eventually graduate from one institution to another. Too often, that means the penitentiary. But sometimes that can also mean the university. In either of those places, they won't find Indigenous Law. Western institutions do not run on love, care, kindness, respect, or honesty, so when young knowledge seekers are coerced into living in accordance with the formal and informal rules of such institutions in order to survive, they find that Indigenous Law's pathways to Indigenous Knowledges appear to be sealed off.

Elder Patsy Felix commented on the situation facing young knowledge seekers by raising the following observations:

> *The young people always come looking after they turn 18. They graduate from foster care or high school. What little they have, they want more. They shouldn't be scared; they didn't know it was open to them all this time. It's not just for elders—kokums and moshoms.*

If they want to become leaders, we need to invite them in. Come on in. Listen to us. It's not just for chiefs and councils and the big wheels. Hear us now.

After reflecting on these words for awhile, A. J. proceeded to link the concepts that both he and Patsy had been describing into a message that both prospective leaders and knowledge seekers (or researchers) alike might benefit from. A. J. stated:

Go and tobacco an old man, an old woman. Ask them "What do you think—what can I do." Seek advice. Be respectful. Do more listening than talking. Go and be with your people—know them, see them, talk with them. Eat with them. Feel with them. Cry with them. Don't think you're their saviour. You have to be humble. Do ceremony. Seek a name. Honour your name. Be a praying man. Be a smudging man. Be a church man. Learn how to keep your own home fire first. Stay healthy—if you can't keep your own fire going, don't bother. You can't help others if they see that you're not looking after your own little fire, or if you've let your home fire go out.

Offering these important thoughts on Indigenous Knowledges, practices, and attitudes can help First Nations people reawaken the curiosity that was forced into hibernation by the onslaught of Western research. These words were offered in a spirit of generosity and caring to those who would aim to apply their intellectual gifts to solving the multitude of social problems that are facing so many young Indigenous people and their families.

Conclusion

Through referencing both the accumulated wisdom found within academic scholarship and that of traditional Indigenous Knowledge systems, this chapter has shown that Indigenous people are indeed capable of reawakening ourselves and motivating evidence-based transformative change within First Nations communities. Clearly, the pace could be much greater if sufficient financial, human, and intellectual resources were contributed to the development of First Nations research centres, as has been recommended in research generated for the Royal Commission on Aboriginal Peoples in 1996 and the national policy review on the funding of First Nations child and family services in 2005 (Canada, 1996; Blackstock, Prakash, Loxley, & Wien, 2005).

Regardless of the research design, individuals involved, or analytic frames utilized to generate evidence in support of new intervention strategies, programmatic approaches, or funding models, within First Nations child welfare, one point must remain clear. Indigenous child welfare must align with Indigenous Law if transformative change is ever going to return to the lives of Indigenous children, families, and communities. What would child welfare look like if the field and workplace truly modelled a practice based on love, care, kindness, respect, and honesty? Indigenous Law tells us that these principles drive all possibility for harmony and well-being among Indigenous peoples and all others with whom we share the world. They are more than aspirational, they are Law, and in the words of Elder A. J. Felix: "Take that route, and the results will be long-lasting."

Tapwe

References

About CFS Best Practices. (2008). *CFS Best Practices*. Retrieved from http://www.cfsbestpractice.com/about.htm

Absolon, K., & Willett, C. (2005). Putting ourselves forward: Location in Aboriginal research. In L. Brown & S. Strega (Eds.), *Research as resistance* (pp. 97–126). Toronto, ON: Canadian Scholars' Press.

Bishop, R. (1999). Kaupapa Maori research: An Indigenous approach to creating knowledge. In N. Robertson (Ed.), *Maori and psychology: Research and practice* (pp.1–6). Hamilton, New Zealand: Māori and Psychology Research Unit, University of Waikato.

Blackstock, C., Prakash, T., Loxley, J., & Wien, F. (2005). *Wen:de: We are coming to the light of day*. Ottawa, ON: First Nations Child and Family Caring Society of Canada.

Blaut, J. (1993). *The colonizer's model of the world: Geographical diffusionism and Eurocentric history*. New York, NY: Guilford Press.

Boldt, M. (1993). *Surviving as Indians: The challenge of self-government in Canada*. Toronto, ON: University of Toronto Press.

Borrows, J. (2005). Crown and Aboriginal occupations of land: A historical comparison. Toronto, ON: Attorney General of Ontario, Ipperwash Inquiry.

Bubar, R. (2013). Decolonizing sexual violence: Professional Indigenous women shape the research. *International Review of Qualitative Research, 6*(4), 526–543.

Canada. (1996). *Report of the Royal Commission on Aboriginal peoples. Volume 4: Perspectives and realities.* Ottawa, ON: Minister of Supply and Services Canada.

Chilisa, B. (2012). *Indigenous research methodologies.* Thousand Oaks, CA: Sage Publishing.

Churchill, W. (1983). *Marxism and Native Americans.* Boston, MA: South End Publishing.

Cisneros Puebla, C. A. (2014). Indigenous researchers and epistemic violence. In N. Denzin & D. Giardina (Eds.), *Qualitative research outside the academy* (pp. 164–178). Walnut Creek, CA: Left Coast Press Inc.

Daschuk, J. (2013). *Clearing the plains: Disease, politics of starvation, and the loss of Aboriginal life.* Regina, SK: University of Regina Press.

Debassige, B. (2010). Re-conceptualizing Anshinaabe mino-bimaadiziwin (the good life) as research methodology: A spirit centred way in Anishinaabe research. *Canadian Journal of Native Education, 33*(1), 11–28.

Duff, W. (1969). *The Indian history of British Columbia: Volume 1—The impact of the white man.* Victoria, BC: Royal British Columbia Museum.

Francis, D. (1992). *The imaginary Indian: The image of the Indian in Canadian culture.* Vancouver, BC: Arsenal Pulp Press.

Indian Act, RSC 1985, c I–5.

Kelm, M. E. (1998). *Colonizing bodies: Aboriginal health and healing in British Columbia, 1900–1950.* Vancouver, BC: UBC Press.

Kline, M. (1992). Child welfare law, "best interests of the child" ideology, and First Nations. *Osgoode Hall Law Journal, 30*(2), 376–425.

Kovach, M. (2010). *Indigenous methodologies—Characteristics, conversations, and contexts.* Toronto, ON: University of Toronto Press.

Little Bear, L. (2000). Jagged worldviews colliding. In M. Battiste (Ed.), *Reclaiming Indigenous voices and vision* (pp. 77–85). Vancouver, BC: UBC Press.

McKillop, A. Brian. (2013). Social Darwinism. *The Canadian Encyclopedia.* Retrieved from http://www.thecanadianencyclopedia.ca/en/article/social-darwinism/

Merasty, G., Bouvier, R., & Hoium, D. (2013). *The Joint Task Force on Improving Education and Employment Outcomes in Saskatchewan.* Saskatoon, SK: Saskatchewan Educational Leadership Unit.

Miller, J. (2000). *Skyscrapers hide the heavens: A history of Indian–white relations in Canada.* Toronto, ON: University of Toronto.

Modeste, D., Elliott, D., Gendron, C., Greenwell, B., Johnny, D., Payne, H.,... Williams, C. (1993). S'huli'utl Quw'itsun: The spirit of Cowichan. A journey through the Tsewultun health centre. In P. Stephenson, S. Elliott, L. Foster, & J. Harris (Eds.), *A persistent spirit: Towards understanding of Aboriginal health in British Columbia* (pp. 331–356) (Canadian Western Geographic Series 31). Victoria, BC: University of Victoria.

Richardson, C., & Blanchet-Cohen, N. (2000). Postsecondary education programs for Aboriginal peoples: Achievements and issues. *Canadian Journal of Native Education, 24*(2), 169–184.

Satzewich, V., & Liodakis, N. (2013). *"Race" and ethnicity in Canada: A critical introduction* (3rd ed.). Don Mills, ON: Oxford University Press.

Thomas, R. (2014). Honoring the oral traditions of my ancestors through storytelling. In S. Strega & L. Brown (Eds.), *Research as resistance: Revisiting critical, Indigenous and anti-oppressive approaches to research* (2nd ed.) (pp. 177–198). Toronto, ON: Canadian Scholars Press.

Tuhiwai-Smith, L. (2003). *Decolonizing methodologies—Research and Indigenous peoples*. London, United Kingdom: Zed Books.

Wade, A. (1995). Resistance knowledges: Therapy with Aboriginal peoples who have experienced violence. In P. Stephenson, S. Elliott, L. Foster, & J. Harris (Eds.), *A persistent spirit: Towards understanding of Aboriginal health in British Columbia* (pp. 167–202) (Canadian Western Geographic Series 31). Victoria, BC: University of Victoria.

Wilson, S. (2008). *Research is ceremony—Indigenous research methods*. Winnipeg, MB: Fernwood Publishing.

PART II

Practice

CHAPTER 4

Child Protection Inquiries: What Are They Teaching Us? A Canadian Perspective

Peter Choate

"Parents of boy killed in foster care suing Sask. government"
  —*CTV News* headline, August 21, 2015

Introduction

Child protection services (CPS) tend not to be in the public's mind unless things go wrong. Then they are reminded of CPS via media stories, such as the one noted above, that will speak about yet another failure resulting in the death or serious harm of a child. This can lead to a weakening in the public mind about the effectiveness of CPS and those who are charged with protecting children (Parton, 2014). A loss of faith in CPS can arise from one case that goes wrong and becomes the focus of intense media coverage. This skews public perception of CPS and deters social workers from doing this work (Brandon et al., 2009; Early, 2000; Jones, 2014).

Suggested Citation: Choate, P. (2016). Child protection inquiries: What are they teaching us? A Canadian perspective. In H. Montgomery, D. Badry, D. Fuchs, & D. Kikulwe (Eds.), *Transforming Child Welfare: Interdisciplinary Practices, Field Education, and Research* (pp. 61–85). Regina, SK: University of Regina Press.

It is often lost that the vast majority of children are safe in the care or oversight of child protection in Canada. The reports that are the subject of the study discussed in this chapter represent insights into when things go quite wrong but equally offer lessons that practitioners can use to establish a sense of both good and concerning practice. It needs to be remembered that the cases reviewed in this research are the exception as opposed to the norm.

Canada has a long history of public inquiries crossing many areas of concern (d'Ombrain, 1997). Canada is about to examine the concerns arising from dead and missing Aboriginal women using a public inquiry method. Another recent example is the Truth and Reconciliation Commission (2015). This chapter focuses on inquiries directed by provincial and territorial governments in whose jurisdictions child protection falls.

When cases become very high profile, engaging politicians charged with child protection portfolios, a public inquiry might be called. This assuages the public while also being seen to do something in response to public outcry. This delays the need to directly face the issues around the administration of CPS. However, the higher the profile issues being addressed, the less likely that the story will fade from public view (Stutz, 2008).

The responsible politician may announce the inquiry with the stated intent of ensuring that there will never be another similar death. It is a promise they cannot fulfill, as child protection is a challenging occupation where it is impossible to predict with certainty those caregivers who are likely to harm or kill a child [1][1] (Taylor & Lazenbatt, 2014). Following the release of the inquiry report, there will be some form of agreement with the recommendations, with a statement adopting most, while studying others. Examples of this can be seen with the Phoenix Sinclair Inquiry, which followed the death of a five-year-old Aboriginal girl killed by her mother and stepfather. Justice Ted Hughes, who led the inquiry, challenged Manitoba to reform CPS and address deeply rooted problems [59]. These included funding, information management, and improvement in foster care and child safety, as well as strengthened accountability for agencies serving children (Government of Manitoba, 2014).

The details of these inquiries can be salacious enough that the media will follow the hearings in excruciating detail, which occurred with the

---

1   Numbers in square brackets refer to a specific inquiry, all of which are listed in Appendix A.

Sinclair case [59]. Winnipeg media, where the inquiry was based, had live online feeds and daily reports. The public could hardly be blamed for feeling that the social workers must border on incompetent, as these daily reports fed a steady diet of details suggesting that it was incredibly obvious this toddler was maltreated and at risk. This is not the first child death inquiry to receive intense media coverage, but this is one of the first to occur with both social media and real-time media coverage.

Inquiries elsewhere have been noted to take a real toll on social workers (Jones, 2014; Laming, 2003; Ruddock, 1991). Examples include the Maria Colwell Inquiry (Field-Fisher, 1974), Kimberley Carlile (Ruddock, 1991), and more recently the reports into the deaths of Victoria Climbie (Laming, 2003) and Baby Peter (Jones, 2014). In these United Kingdom cases, the social workers involved were subject to intense scrutiny in the media that would lead to a frenzied view of the remarkable inability of child protection to get it right (Parton, 2014). The media drove the story in unanticipated directions that focused on blaming the social workers (Jones, 2014).

The media can play a powerful role in bringing cases to the forefront. The PBS program, *Frontline*, for example, ran a story into the death of Logan Marr that named the various workers involved (Dretzen & Goodman, 2008). In 2012, the *Denver Post* ran a series of stories under the banner "Failed to death — an eight part Denver Post Investigative Series" (Brown, Osjer, & Steffen, 2013) that was based largely on fatality reviews done by state officials. In Canada, the media contributed to a national awareness of the death of Jeffrey Baldwin through ongoing coverage of the criminal trials and coroner's inquest (Blatchford, 2014, 2013a, 2013b).

Approaches to the Review of Child Protection Cases

There are at least six common methods a province or territory may choose from for a review of child protection cases:

1. Large-scale inquiries that occur over a lengthy period, in public, and with a series of witnesses. Examples are the Gove Inquiry [30] and the Phoenix Sinclair Inquiry [59]. Reports in these cases tend to be quite long, with a multitude of recommendations. One of the earliest, the judicial inquiry into the care of Kim Anne Popen, ran to a staggering 1,827 pages. There were forty-six days of

hearings, 182 exhibits, and sixty-two witnesses with eighty-seven recommendations [79].

2. Reviews by an agency charged with the responsibility for this task, such as the Office of the Child and Youth Advocate in Alberta (OCYA) and in Saskatchewan (SCYA) and the Representative for Children and Youth (RCY) in British Columbia. They focus on case-specific reviews [e.g., 3, 34, 50] but may also take a look at larger policy issues [8]. The role of these types of reviews is set out in legislation.

3. Coroner's reviews or inquest hearings, although they tend not to offer lengthy reports but may yield quite a number of recommendations.

4. Fatality inquiries are used in some provinces that typically see a provincial court judge hearing evidence and writing a short judgment [e.g., 46, 57]. Like coroner's reviews, fatality inquiries fail to provide enough data in their reports to truly understand what went on in the case.

5. Internal reviews by child protection or other authorities that are rarely made public. In Manitoba, for example, the children's advocate performs such a function, submitting the report to the minister charged with child protection as well as the ombudsman and the chief medical examiner.

6. Aggregate overviews such as the Pediatric Death Review Committee reports seen in Ontario [69–74].

Child and youth advocate reviews permit external, ongoing inquiry into child protection. How they go about it impacts the public view, which is something they are sensitive to, as noted by the Alberta advocate: "The intent...[is] not to find fault with specific individuals, but to identify key issues along with meaningful recommendations which: are prepared in such a way that they address systemic issue(s); and specific enough that progress made on recommendations can be evaluated; yet, not so prescriptive to direct the practice of Alberta government ministries" [39] (Office of the Child and Youth Advocate of Alberta, 2014, p. 9). In British Columbia, the RCY has expressed a similar view [22].

The media may focus upon a specific case or a series of concerns. They can be quite impactful. Alberta recently discontinued a publication ban on the names of children who die in the CPS system (Alberta, 2014) after a series of articles appearing in the Calgary and Edmonton newspapers highlighted stories of child deaths (Kleiss & Henton, 2013). This intense coverage was followed by the minister responsible for CPS holding a public round table that was later followed by the change in policy. Not surprisingly, the *Calgary Herald* and *Edmonton Journal* then ran a series of photographs with the names of the children they had written about in their earlier stories.

In the CPS cases, it is often a very young child who dies. There is a lack of tolerance for such fatalities. CPS is seen as failing to protect the child, whereas the focus is less evidently directed to the caregivers at fault, the ones who actually killed the child (Parton, 2014).

Discussions in Inquiries in Child Death Cases

Some form of public inquiry, when truly systemically focused, can create a sense that the system has checks and balances. A blame-focused approach deeply erodes the confidence in the system, whether that blame is aimed at specific workers or the system at large, such as in Paige [3]. Too often, the review processes are entirely deficit-focused. Admittedly, there are some cases where strengths seem hard to find, but the majority of cases can likely offer insights into good practice if they are sought out.

Inquiries can take at least a couple of different perspectives. There are those that look at the evidence that was available to the workers and then there are those that may seek out new information that might have been available to the workers. Alberta, for example, will review the files but may also seek out interviews or data from other sources [40]. This is taken to a higher level in large-scale public inquiries, such as was seen in the Phoenix Sinclair case [59], where much new information is gathered through formal testimony at inquiry hearings.

Inquiries start with a very different understanding of the case, as they know how the story ends (Jones, 2014). In addition, the inquiry can second-guess workers with no worry regarding the accountability arising from case decisions.

Inquiries where the family members are named are not benign. The family reads about the details of what might have been done to prevent the tragedy. Thus, the child and youth advocate in Alberta chooses not to name the child or the family. They also offer the family an opportunity to be involved in the investigative review process should they choose to do so. There are practice implications arising from inquiries, including an increased reticence by workers to take risks (Fitzgibbon, 2011; Stanley & Manthorpe, 2004). Inquiries can take the form of rethinking how child protection is done. Rather than focus on the specific case, an effort is made to determine what might be done systemically to improve the present system. This can lead to legislative changes [28, 54, 78]. There have been several prior aggregate reviews of lessons learned from inquiries. These have been principally in the United Kingdom (see, for example, Brandon et al., 2012). Such attention has not been previously brought to the collective view of the Canadian work.

Method

There were ninety-one published reports from 1982 to 2015 that were focused upon the death of a child or on systemic errors that were seen to lead to inordinate risk to a child or a group of children. There were two main criteria for inclusion in the study.

1. The report needed to focus on errors that led to the death of, or serious injury to, a child while in the care of, or involved with, CPS.
2. The report existed in the public forum. This could be in the form of a report from a provincial oversight body, such as an ombudsman or an office charged with advocacy for children and youth. The report could be in the form of a court decision that outlined the details of a case (such as the criminal decision convicting the grandparents in the Jeffrey Baldwin case) along with additional data (such as the coroner's report).

The reports acted as the prime source of data, even though some cases may have had significant media attention as well [30, 59].

The reports were entered into NVivo for thematic analysis. Grounded Theory was utilized as an approach to this research given its potential to generate theory through analysis that includes systematically reviewing the reports for themes and factors related to the phenomenon of child death reviews (Charmaz, 2014). While ninety-one reports were included for analysis, there remain a number of inquests and court decisions not identified and internal reviews by various authorities that have not been made public.

Results

The data yields high-level systemic themes, along with quite specific practice error themes. A read-through of the reports shows many repeating themes across inquiries. The inquiries do not seem to get to the more serious question of drilling down into the data to determine what factors appear to exist within systems that allow for the repeated errors. The question of why we continue to see the same errors over time remains unanswered in these inquiries.

Emerging Themes

The Worker as Target
It is the reflections of British social worker Martin Ruddock, who had been involved in the Kimberley Carlile case in the United Kingdom, who has so poignantly written about the impact of inquiry:

> *Before Kimberley was brutally murdered, my imagined social work terror was to be involved in a case where a child's death occurred and I could be held partially responsible. In part that terror related to a fear of being pursued by, and then pilloried by the press. In practice the experience of being involved with Kimberley was very true to the nightmare, except in one clear and painful way. I had been involved in a child's death and, although frightened by the enormity of the potential public outcry, I was also faced with a personal crisis relating to my part in a child's death. (1991, pp.107–108)*

Judge Thomas Gove [30] is very specific about the failings of those involved with Matthew Vaudreuil. He is clear about assigning blame, although he spends a great deal of time addressing systemic issues. One social worker, for example, was noted by Gove to have no second thoughts about her action. He named that person, creating a public guilt about her actions. There were echoes of Gove in a recent British Columbia Supreme Court decision in the case of JP [1]. While this did not involve the death of a child, the workers were chastised for holding onto a view of the case, despite evidence the court believed should have changed the interventions. The echoes continued with the Plecas report, which, like Gove, argued for a major overhaul of British Columbia's child protection system [2].

In the Gove Inquiry, there is little doubt that the worker was seen as having failed in her duty and that Judge Gove was incredulous that she did not see the error of her ways [30]. Such a view can cause the public to wonder about not only the competence of the system but those who manage it. The public is left to ask the clear question of how the worker could not have remorse and wish to do it differently. The media can place specific individuals within the frame of criticism. CBC television's *The Fifth Estate*, with the episode "Failing Jeffrey," looked at the death of Jeffrey Baldwin (Caloz & Anderson, 2006). Viewers were left with no doubt that the Catholic Children's Aid Society of Toronto and its workers were incompetent in how they managed the file. This would be a theme that newspaper columnist Christie Blatchford returned to in her extensive coverage of the case. In her more recent coverage of the inquest in 2013, her readers would have the image created by the *Fifth Estate* affirmed (Blatchford, 2013a, 2013b, 2014). The media coverage in the Baldwin inquest [68] vilified the efforts of specific workers and the supervisor (Blatchford, 2013a, 2013b).

Workers can remain targets after inquiries are completed (Early, 2000). As Armitage and Murray (2007) note, after the Gove Inquiry there was the death of Katie Lyn Baker, a ten-year-old child with Rett syndrome who was allowed to die by the mother and without interference by child welfare: "This time, the social workers, supervisors, and regional manager were suspended pending inquiry, and they were later disciplined" (p. 143). Such actions can be seen as ways to assure the public that government has learned its lesson from the prior inquiry.

Following Paige [3], a new step has emerged. As a result of that report, the Royal Canadian Mounted Police (RCMP) are investigating various professionals to determine if charges should be laid under section 13 of British Columbia's Child, Family and Community Services Act. The province's representative for children and youth, under whose authority Paige's case was investigated, notes that should charges occur, "This may be a turning point," as no such prosecutions have occurred before (Proctor, 2015).

Legislation, Policy, and Procedures

Inquiries can influence legislation, social policy, and the administration of child welfare in positive ways. For example, Judge Gove had an impact on the legislation in British Columbia, forcing a view that child protection should have a child-centred approach [30].

In the Phoenix Sinclair report, Justice Hughes made sixty-two recommendations following a high-profile, three-phased inquiry. He took a systemic approach. Some of the most significant recommendations considered the ways in which child protection is delivered and by whom. For example, he recommended that child welfare workers should hold degrees and also belong to the Manitoba provincial social work regulatory association. He also highlighted the impact of intergenerational public policy on First Nations and the impact that has on bringing disproportionate numbers of Aboriginal children into care [59].

Justice Hughes entered into the core debate that exists in child protection legislation throughout most of the Western nations as to when and how to protect children while also sustaining the superiority of the family as the principle unit for children. Hughes suggested that child welfare should keep as many children at home as possible. But it is this balance between safety of the child and the parental rights to raise children that front-line social workers must manage. Errors in either direction will result in criticism about over- or underzealous social workers. None of the inquiries reviewed offered insight into how, on a day-to-day basis, a social worker must manage this juggling act.

The Phoenix Sinclair Inquiry [59] is reminiscent of the conclusions of a 1987 inquiry, also in Manitoba, that followed the deaths of six children in care the previous year [66]. It is an area for further research.

Systemic Interconnection

Many of the reports talk about the links between child protection and health care, education, justice, and community social service agencies. A common theme is that they do not communicate well or work well together [e.g., 24, 30, 59]. The notion is that social workers are hampered in the assessment of risk and delivery of services when information is not effectively shared with them.

Alberta has attempted to address this through the Children First Act. On its website, the government describes the legislation.

The legislation will define the "tent" within which this information could be shared including government departments, educational bodies, health care bodies, police services, parents or guardians or others as defined elsewhere in legislation. Changes to the Health Information Act and Freedom of Information and Protection of Privacy Act *will promote the sharing of information for the purposes of enhancing a child's well-being, safety, security, education or health, while retaining the ability of individuals and bodies to use professional discretion in assessing when the sharing of information is most appropriate. (Alberta Human Services, n.d.)*

Yet, with information that is accessible, it is critical for professionals to exercise critical thinking and judgment about what should be shared. Gove was unimpressed with how such discretion was exercised [30].

The Cornwall Inquiry in Ontario focused upon the failures of systems to address the sexual abuse of children. Commissioner G. Norman Glaude stated when releasing his report: "Some institutions, such as the Children's Aid Society, had better understanding of these matters than others, but in situations where interagency consultation would have helped, local institutions were rarely on the same page, much less on the same team" [75] (Glaude, 2009, pp. 6–7). There were ninety-seven recommendations arising, with much emphasis on communication between agencies. As a result of Gove and other inquiries, many efforts have been made to allow better information sharing such as the Alberta example noted above.

In Manitoba, the Aboriginal Justice Implementation Commission (Chartrand, Whitecloud, McKay, & Young, 2001) saw that there could be an inherent sociological link between systems with child protection and justice issues within First Nations communities having common roots. Addressing one system without looking at the other was insufficient. How one system deals with a child or family directly impacts the ability of another system to work effectively with the same client.

This Is Human Work

Child protection work is, by its very nature, human work conducted by human beings. It is relational. This means that, like any other relationally based activity, there will be errors in how the relationship evolves. Clients will often find themselves challenged with trusting the worker; workers will often wonder about the degree to which the client is telling the truth. The power differential that exists between worker and family creates inherent strain in the relationship.

In this human endeavour, workers are asked to enter family patterns that have an entrenched history that may cross generations. Yet the worker enters their lives for a relatively short period, seeking to effect change sufficient for the parent to be deemed good enough (Choate & Engstrom, 2014). Research tells us that the best child protection work is done in the context of a respectful working relationship between worker and client (Gladstone et al., 2013; Maiter, Palmer, & Manj, 2006). These reports speak of broken relationships between child, parents, and workers resulting in children not seen [e.g., 1, 59]. Workers can justify gaps in contact as a result of youth being hard to engage [3], parents being uncooperative [1, 3, 59], or difficult to connect with [43].

There is little true focus on just how difficult this work is and the true human toll on the workers. The Plecas report also addressed this by suggesting that few people would want to take on the daunting tasks required of a CPS worker [2]. This rather negative status is one of the significant factors related to experiencing traumatic stress in this work (Sprang, Clark, & Craig, 2011). When workers are vilified in these reports, public confidence deteriorates, as does the status of the work (Sanders, Colton, & Roberts, 1999). As Regehr, Chau, Leslie, and Howe (2002) reported, the inquiries impact the workers personally, their agency, as well as the community's confidence in the work. Reports do not address the toll of child welfare work but instead stay focused on what went wrong. In fact, challenges and true underlying reasons in CPS include high caseloads, high turnover, challenging work, and the frailty of human judgment (Fitzgibbon, 2011; Parton, 2014).

Child Protection Is Always Balancing
Between Family Rights and Child Rights

There is a balance that is struck between the rights of a parent to raise their child as they see fit and the right of society to intervene when the safety of a child is at risk. The definitions have waxed and waned over time. These inquiries make it clear that the worker ought to have understood the nature of the risks and the steps necessary to protect. The Gove Inquiry in British Columbia raised the notion that child protection walked a line between supporting families and protecting children (Hall, 1998). Judge Gove went further, indicating these activities were not synonymous and may even be competitive. He determined that too much effort had been made to support the family while missing the real risks to the child [30].

The Generalist within the World of Specialty

Child welfare workers are expected to address a multitude of complex issues. In the case of Phoenix Sinclair, for example, workers were faced with addictions, mental health, domestic violence, and cultural issues related to the Indigenous reality in Canada [59]. Each of these topics is an area of specialty. The day-to-day interactions between a worker and a client with any or all of these issues require a complex understanding about what might be going on, what might be the best way to intervene, and what might be the indicators of engagement and progress. When the reports are looked at collectively, these complex specialty areas of practice are thematically represented in virtually all reports in some manner. Social work education should emphasize these topics.

Child protection is also expected to understand normative and abnormal child development, including signs of abuse, maltreatment, mental health, and socialization. As workers are seen as failing in these specialty areas, inquiries recommend training to respond to these educational gaps. Such a recommendation begs the question of how a generalist is expected to truly manage specialty issues. The Plecas report suggests that child protection should receive the same level of post-degree training as seen for police forces [2].

Practice Errors That Run through the Reports

There are a series of practice concerns that are found in the majority of the reports. They reflect behaviours that act as barriers to protecting children. Most importantly, they have been found again and again but are quite preventable. One of the most important areas of practice relates to assessments that include both the parent and the child and include risk, mental health, addictions, and domestic violence through to parenting capacity. Concerns with assessments have been flagged as early as the Popen report [79]. Concerns have also been expressed that the standards against which parents and children are to be assessed are often poorly determined [89] (Choate & Engstrom, 2014).

In addition, reports identified that assessments, when done, may be done quite poorly. The problems can be numerous and include:

- credibility of data not questioned;
- people missing from the process;
- perspective of the child missing;
- role of new players (such as new partners or new children) not considered; and
- the threshold of concern or acceptability poorly defined [81, 82].

Further, there is a failure to appreciate that assessments are a view at a point in time. Families are fluid and dynamic and often change quickly [34].

The reports further note that assessments can be deficient as they fail to access needed information, including records of prior involvement with CPS [68]. Such data speaks to the history of risk or harm, as well as efforts to change, whether successful or not. Other sources of data would include information held by police, health care, and other social service providers. As there is no federal CPS, what happens in one province is not necessarily known to another province when families move between provinces. There is some suggestion that workers may also suffer from "start over syndrome," where they do not believe that history matters but rely only upon present concerns. This can result in minimizing what may have been a pattern of risk that has existed over time.

The Office for Standards in Education, Children's Services and Skills (Ofsted) (2015) in the United Kingdom has recently noted that assessment serves vital purposes that are central to protecting children. Without it, workers do not really know what is happening and what interventions are needed. This is a common area of concern in the Canadian reports.

There are a number of other common themes that run through the reports:

- *Information silos*: This refers to valuable data held by various systems that are not made available to child protection for an integrated view. It was Judge Gove [30] who dramatically documented how many saw young Matthew Vaudreuil, but his risks were not amalgamated into a meaningful picture from which case planning and intervention could be achieved. Gove recommended interdisciplinary training, something also seen in Turner [89]. Information sharing is a theme that has persisted over time from Popen [79] on through to current reports.

- *Risks not appreciated*: As noted above, a good deal of child protection work involves complex issues that are quite specialized. As a result, a generalist CPS worker can fail to appreciate the nature of risks identified by other professionals who may have assumed that the CPS worker would understand. There is a need to clearly articulate risks, as is often noted in the reports. A further challenge is when the CPS worker is gathering data but lacks the skills to interpret and understand the meaning of the data.

- *Case conferences*: One way to address the value of the data, or to dig out previously unknown or poorly identified data is through bringing together those who are working with or have worked with the family. The danger of such efforts, however, is willful blindness, which can creep in as the group seeks to have a unified view. There is value in ensuring that these conferences include room for dissenting opinions. A recent British Columbia Supreme Court decision strongly criticized CPS for holding onto a view of the case and not addressing the changing data or competing theories [1]. Case conferences also act as a way for interdisciplinary coordination [81, 82] but might have even more success when overt attempts are made to seek out contrary opinions allowing for reflective critical thinking of the data [2].

- *The unseen child*: This has come up in a multitude of cases both in Canada and other countries (see, for example, Laming, 2003). This concern is reflected in cases where the child has either been kept from the view of the worker, the worker has not developed a relationship with the child, or the caregiver has carefully orchestrated access. CPS workers are well advised, according to these reports, to ensure that the child is seen face-to-face regularly, including and, as appropriate, away from the caregiver.

- *The child not at the focus of the case*: This occurs when the child is lost from view and the focus shifts to the caregivers. Even well-intentioned efforts to make things better can cause workers to focus on what the adults need to do and not on the best interests of the child. When the child no longer occupies centre stage, the reports have noted that the reason for CPS to be involved often slides from its intended focus. The Phoenix Sinclair case [59] shows how a child can be lost from the centre of attention when CPS lacks an active, ongoing relationship with the child.

- *Weak supervision*: As many reports note, workers are often inexperienced or working with high, complex caseloads. Supervision is the opportunity for reflective critical thinking by a more experienced mentor who may have some distance from the case. Several cases have noted weak supervision, such as Baldwin [68], Sinclair [59], and Beaumont [81, 82], for example. Supervision is described as being a unique skill set that is clinically based but also one of leadership. It has its own training requirements.

- *Record keeping*: Records were found to be incomplete, poorly done, or, in a few cases, absent. Through the years, there have also been calls for improvements in systemic record keeping. It was an issue in the Popen Inquiry [79] and comes out often, as recently as the Baldwin Inquest [68].

- *Not seeing what was there*: Although no report specifically identified this in this way, in essence, some reports, such as the Kaufman Inquiry (85), identified that those involved failed to appreciate what they were seeing perhaps due to not really believing what might be occurring. This can also include not believing the reporter, whether it is the child who reports on an authority [89] or a parent who repeatedly tells of abuse but does so in a way that suggests the parent is "hysterical" [1].

- *Failure to provide stability*: This was a dominant theme with Paige [3], a child who was noted to have moved forty times by age sixteen. In Alberta, the report on Makayla saw the negative outcomes arising from many moves. In her case, there were twenty by age seventeen [31].

The Aboriginal Story

The residential schools and the Sixties Scoop are explored in the reports in various ways, although no report articulates the impact of the trauma as the Truth and Reconciliation Commission (2015) has done. Yet the inadequate ways in which Aboriginal peoples have been engaged by child protection can be seen in many reports. Justice Hughes [28] raises the concern that there needs to be a common vision for work with Aboriginal people. The RCY and the Plecas report raised similar concerns [2, 3, 25]. Issues around CPS involvement with Aboriginal people were strong themes in the Phoenix Sinclair Inquiry in Manitoba [59], as well as others, such as the inquiry into the death of Karen Rose Quill in Saskatchewan [56]. The importance of truly addressing the Aboriginal issues in child welfare is a Canadian theme in inquiries that beg broader, urgent action, as the inquiries keep noting. This is hardly a new issue and is strongly linked to the overrepresentation of Aboriginal children in Canadian child welfare systems (Sinha et al., 2011). The reports simply keep raising the concern of how child protection is not managing this well, but efforts are needed to address the systemic issues (Fallon et al., 2015).

That Which Child Protection Cannot Solve

Child protection exists in a context. Poverty is often at the heart of many cases. This is a larger social issue about how society supports those whose economic position leaves them struggling for survival. This is not an issue that child protection can fix but often leads to CPS involvement. Other issues that child protection cannot resolve include funding, legislation, and governmental policies and priorities.

Cases Are Unique: The Need to Also Consider What Went Well

No read-through of these various reports can fail to see that, despite the commonness of many themes, cases are tremendously unique. Each of the reports grappled with what case managers had to understand and manage. Thus, each report includes a variety of recommendations that reflect the specific case.

Some, although not many, of the reports also considered what went well. The few that did pondered where the successes lay and used those as lessons to be understood as well. Many reports failed to see strengths, perhaps because they were overwhelmed with poor practice. The Gove report [30] stands as an example of a case where the negatives were predominant. Yet that report and others may also fail to consider the complex environmental reality in which cases exist. Newer reviews seem more attuned to that. Even though the report on Paige by the representative in British

Columbia [3] was harshly critical, considerable effort was evidently made to consider these environmental influences that were so poorly managed.

Discussion

A concern with the inquiry and review process is that themes are being continually repeated but not much is changing. A reading of the Popen report [79] bears many similarities to the concerns raised in recent reports such as Phoenix Sinclair [59]. Professor Eileen Munro, who authored an extensive report on child protection in the United Kingdom, has suggested that little new learning is coming from ongoing inquiries (personal communication, May 2014). When one looks at the trail of recommendations that have run through these reports, one would be hard pressed to disagree.

In reading research looking at lessons available from reviews, one is struck immediately by the continuing legacy of patterns over time, starting with Reder and Duncan (1993) and on to more recent work such as Brandon et al., (2012). This begs the question that, if the errors continue to be seen from inquiry to inquiry, as the present research indicates, then it may well be that inquiries are looking at the wrong issues. Greater attention needs to be paid to how child protection is structured and how environments are created for decision making. Munro (1999) notes that we need to pay attention to how workers make the decisions they make. From that, we can begin to understand the reasoning process that leads to the practice errors. The reports in this study persistently talk about the judgment errors that have been made but do not ask about how the workers got to the point of believing that what they were doing at the time was the best thing to do. Understanding how workers get to that point will better serve child protection reform. As Munro (2005a, 2005b) has noted, there is a necessity for inquiries to think systemically. There were instances where this occurred, such as in the Hughes Inquiry in British Columbia [28], and is also seen in some of the inquiries by provincial advocates [40, 51]. Popen [79] also considered systemic issues. Munro (2005a) sees human error as the starting point, not the conclusion, of a good inquiry. She suggests that a good review should ask "why the mistake was made, by studying interacting factors in the practitioners, the resources available, and the organizational context" (p. 531). Inquiries are not focusing on how was it that the conditions came together for the worker to make that decision (Munro, 2005b).

Inquiries offer insight into the practice errors that get made repeatedly and should form part of good supervision. By recognizing that these are common areas of concern, care can be taken to look out for them. In supervision, questions can be routinely asked about these risk areas while ensuring that cases stay focused on the child and are ecologically considered. CPS workers are also faced with pressures over which they have no control, such as budgets, caseloads, policy aims of politicians, and the pressures to manage caseloads in accordance with priorities that may have less to do with clinical needs and more to do with these other demands.

There are some harsh realities. Deaths will occur, but there are systemic realties as well. If there are too few social workers available, then the thresholds for opening a case may rise. If community-based supports are too limited, then supporting families is more challenging. If an inquiry has been harshly critical of workers, then workers develop risk aversion and may take more children into care. If workers are too burdened and develop vicarious traumas, then their decision making will be impacted. Inquiries that consider these issues better serve the system, even when the system has badly failed, such as in the case of Paige [3]. The real lessons to be learned are how the system can be effective as opposed to just seeing the practice errors.

There is worry about the emerging trend of vilifying workers whose errors may be more reflective of systemic issues than a level of neglect in their duties, such as seen now in Paige [3]. But such vilification has also been seen in Baldwin (see Blatchford, 2013a, 2013b), as well as in cases in the United Kingdom, such as Baby Peter (Jones, 2014). If we pursue the workers, we create a chill that risks leading to professionals avoiding and leaving the work, while others will err toward caution by bringing children into care. The real questions that need to constantly be asked are these: What can be learned from these inquiries for meaningful change? Why does the system allow the conditions that lead to errors?

Author's Note

This research was funded in part by a grant from Mount Royal University. The work of research assistant Meaghan Reid was vital to the success of this project.

References

Alberta. (2014). Alberta lifts publication ban on children who die in care [Press Release]. Retrieved from http://alberta.ca/release. cfm?xID=368841AFFC12D-EFBD-9BEA-2C0D896DEBC036A7

Alberta Human Services. (n.d.). Children First Act: Enhancing supports and protection for Alberta children. Retrieved from http://www.humanservices. alberta.ca/16594.html

Armitage, A., & Murray, E. (2007). Thomas Gove: A commission of inquiry puts children first and proposes community governance and integration of services. In L. T. Foster & B. Wharf (Eds.), *People, politics and child welfare in British Columbia* (pp. 139–157). Vancouver, BC: UBC Press.

Blatchford, C. (2013a, October 23). Social worker tells inquiry grandmother who starved Jeffrey Baldwin to death seemed "very caring." *National Post*. Retrieved from http://news.nationalpost.com/2013/10/23/christie-blatchford-social-worker-tells-inquiry-grandmother-who-starved-jeffrey-baldwin-to-death-was-very-caring/

Blatchford, C. (2013b, October 24). Social workers closed Jeffrey Baldwin case as soon as his grandmother told them they were "not needed." *National Post*. Retrieved from http://news.nationalpost.com/2013/10/24/christie-blatchford-social-workers-closed-jeffrey-baldwin-case-as-soon-as-his-grandmother-told-them-they-were-not-needed/

Blatchford, C. (2014, February 14). Inquests make problems behind deaths seem more impossibly complex than they are. *National Post*. Retrieved from http://news.nationalpost.com/2014/02/14/christie-blatchford-inquests-make-problems-seem-more-impossibly-complex-than-they-really-are/

Brandon, M., Bailey, S., Belderson, P., Gardner, R., Sidebotham, P., Dodsworth, J.,...Black, J. (2009). *Understanding serious case reviews and their impact: A biennial analysis of serious case reviews 2005–07*. East Anglia, United Kingdom: University of East Anglia.

Brandon, M., Sidebotham, P., Bailey, S., Belderson, P., Hawley, C., Ellis, C., & Megson, M. (2012). *New learning from serious case reviews: A two-year report for 2009–2011* (Research Report DFE-RR226). London, United Kingdom: Department of Education.

British Columbia. *Child, Family and Community Services Act*, RSBC 1996 c. 46. Retrieved from http://www.bclaws.ca/EPLibraries/bclaws_new/document/ID/freeside/00_96046_01

Brown, J., Osjer, C. N., & Steffen, J. (2013). Failed to death: An eight part *Denver Post* investigative series. *Denver Post*. Retrieved from http://www.denverpost.com/failedtodeath

Caloz, M., & Anderson, S. (Producers). (2006, April 12). Failing Jeffrey [Television documentary series episode]. In *The Fifth Estate*. Toronto, ON: Canadian Broadcasting Corporation.

Charmaz, K. (2014). *Constructing grounded theory* (2nd. ed.). Los Angeles, CA: Sage.

Chartrand, P. C., Whitecloud, W. J., McKay, E., & Young, D. (2001). *Aboriginal Justice Implementation Commission*. Winnipeg, MB: Author. Retrieved from http://www.ajic.mb.ca/reports/final_toc.html

Children First Act, SA 2013, c C-12.5.

Choate, P. W., & Engstrom, S. (2014). The "good enough" parent: Implications for child protection. *Child Care in Practice, 20*(4), 368–382. doi:10.1080/13575279.2014.915794

D'Ombrian, N. (1997). Public inquiries in Canada. *Canadian Public Administration, 40*(1), 86–107. doi:10.1111/j.1754-7121.1997.tb01498.x

Dretzen, R., & Goodman, B. (Producers). (2008). Failure to protect: The taking of Logan Marr [Television documentary series episode]. In *Frontline*. Boston, MA: WGBH Educational Foundation.

Early, M. (2000). *Fear of blame: Post Gove child protection in B.C.* (Unpublished master's thesis). University of British Columbia, Vancouver, BC.

Fallon, B., Chabot, M., Fluke, J., Blackstock, C., Sinha, V., Allan, K., & MacLaurin, B. (2015). Exploring alternate specifications to explain agency-level effects in placement decisions regarding Aboriginal children: Further analysis of the Canadian Incidence Study of Reported Child Abuse and Neglect Part C. *Child Abuse & Neglect, 49*, 97–106. doi:10.1016/j.chiabu.2015.04.012

Field-Fisher, T. G. (1974). *Report of the Committee of Inquiry into the care and supervision provided by local authorities and other agencies in relation to Maria Colwell and the co-ordination between them*. London, United Kingdom: Her Majesty's Stationary Office.

Fitzgibbon, W. (2011). *Probation and social work on trial: Violent offenders and child abusers*. London, United Kingdom: Palgrave MacMillan.

Gladstone, J., Dumbrill, G., Leslie, B., Koster, A., Young, M., & Ismalia, A. (2013). Looking at engagement and outcome from the perspectives of child protection workers and parents. *Children and Youth Services Review, 34*(1), 112–118. doi:10.1016/j.childyouth.2011.09.003

Glaude, G. N. (2009). *Report of the Cornwall inquiry* (Vols. 1–4). Cornwall, ON: Author.

Government of Manitoba. (2014). Phoenix Sinclair report released: Province offers apology for failure of child welfare system, acts on recommendations [Press Release]. Retrieved from http://news.gov.mb.ca/news/index.html?archive=&item=20250

Hall, M. I. (1998). *The child at the centre: Rethinking child protection* (Unpublished master's thesis). Faculty of Law, University of British Columbia, Vancouver, BC. Retrieved from file:///Users/pchoate/Documents/ubc_1998-0240.pdf

Jones, R. (2014). *The story of baby P: Setting the record straight*. Bristol, United Kingdom: Policy Press.

Kleiss, K., & Henton, D. (2013). Fatal care. *Calgary Herald*. Retrieved from http://www.calgaryherald.com/news/children-in-care/index.html

Laming, H. (2003). *The Victoria Climbié Inquiry*. London, United Kingdom: Houses of Parliament.

Maiter, S., Palmer, S., & Manj, S. (2006). Strengthening social worker-client relationships in child protective services: Addressing power imbalances and "ruptured" relationships. *Qualitative Social Work, 5*(2), 161–186. doi:10.1177/1473325006064255

Munro, E. (1999). Common errors of reasoning in child protection work. *Child Abuse and Neglect, 23*(8), 745–758. doi:10.1016/S0145-2134(99)00053-8

Munro, E. (2005a). A systems approach to investigating child abuse deaths. *British Journal of Social Work, 35*(4), 531–546. doi:10.1093/bjsw/bch194

Munro, E. (2005b). Improving practice: Child protection as a systems problem. *Children and Youth Services Review, 27*(4), 375–391. doi:10.1016/j. childyouth.2004.11.006

Office for Standards in Education, Children's Services and Skills (Ofsted). (2015). *The quality of assessment for children in need of help.* Manchester, United Kingdom: Author.

Office of the Child and Youth Advocate of Alberta. (2014). *7 year old Jack: An investigative review.* Edmonton, AB: Author.

Parton, N. (2014). *The politics of child protection: Contemporary developments and future directions.* London, United Kingdom: Palgrave Macmillan.

Proctor, J. (2015, September 18). Death of B.C. aboriginal teen Paige under RCMP investigation. *CBC News.* Retrieved from http://www.cbc.ca/news/canada/british-columbia/death-of-b-c-aboriginal-teen-paige-under-rcmp-investigation-1.3234158

Reder, P., & Duncan, S. (1993). *Beyond blame: Child abuse tragedies revisited.* London, United Kingdom: Routledge.

Regehr, C., Chau, S., Leslie, B., & Howe, P. (2002). Inquiries into deaths of children in care: The impact on child welfare workers and their organization. *Children and Youth Services Review, 24*(11), 641–644. doi:10.1016/s0190-7409(02)00250-5

Ruddock, M. (1991). A receptacle for public anger. In B. Franklin & N. Parton (Eds.), *Social work, the media and public relations* (pp. 107–115). London, United Kingdom: Routledge.

Sanders, R., Colton, M., & Roberts, S. (1999). Child abuse fatalities and cases of extreme concern: Lessons from reviews. *Child Abuse & Neglect, 23*(3), 257–268. doi:10.1016/S0145-2134(98)00123-9

Sinha, V., Trocmé, N., Fallon, B., MacLaurin, B., Fast, E., Prokop, S. T.,... Petti, T. (2011). *Kiskisik Awasisak: Remember the children: Understanding the overrepresentation of First Nations children in the child welfare system.* Ontario: Assembly of First Nations.

Sprang, G., Clark, C., & Craig, J. (2011). Secondary traumatic stress and burnout in child welfare workers: A comparative analysis of occupational distress across professional groups. *Child Welfare, 90*(6), 149–168.

Stanley, N., & Manthorpe, J. (2004). *The age of inquiry: Learning and blaming in health and social care.* London, United Kingdom: Routledge.

Stutz, J. R. (2008). What gets done and why: Implementing the recommendations
    of public inquiries. *Canadian Public Administration, 51*(3), 501–521.
    doi:10.1111/j.1754-7121.2008.00035.x

Taylor, J., & Lazenbatt, A. (2014). *Child maltreatment and high risk families.*
    Edinburgh, Scotland: Dunedin.

Truth and Reconciliation Commission of Canada. (2015). *Honouring the
    truth, reconciling the future: Summary of the final report of the Truth and
    Reconciliation Commission.* Ottawa, ON: Author.

Appendix A: Reports Considered

British Columbia

[1] JP as litigant and BTG, KG, PG (Supreme Court of British Columbia)   2015

[2] *Plecas Review, Part One: Decision Time—A Review of Policy, Practice
    and Legislation of Child Welfare in BC in Relation to a Judicial
    Decision in the J. P. case*   2015

[3] *Paige's Story: Abuse, Indifference and a Young Life Discarded*   2015

[4] *Lost in the Shadows: How a Lack of Help Meant a Loss of Hope for
    One*   2014

[5] *Who Cares? B.C. Children with Complex Medical, Psychological and
    Developmental Needs and Their Families Deserve Better*   2014

[6] *Out of Sight: How One Aboriginal Child's Best Interests Were Lost
    between Two Provinces*   2013

[7] *Who Protected Him? How B.C.'s Child Welfare System Failed One of Its
    Most Vulnerable Children*   2013

[8] *Trauma, Turmoil and Tragedy: Understanding the Needs of Children
    and Youth at Risk of Suicide and Self-Harm*   2012

[9] *Honouring Kaitlynne, Max and Cordon: Make Their Voices Heard Now*   2012

[10] *Isolated and Invisible: When Children with Special Needs Are Seen
    but Not Seen*   2012

[11–18] *Summary: A Comprehensive Review into the Death of a Youth
    Known to the Ministry* (Reference 209319; 209325; 209327; 201328;
    209322; 209330; 209328; 209329) (Eight Reports)   2012

[19] *Fragile Lives—Aggregate Review*   2011

[20] *So Many Plans, So Little Stability*   2011

[21] *Isolated and Invisible*   2011

[22] *Fragile Lives, Fragmented Systems: Strengthening Supports for
    Vulnerable Infants*   2011

[23] *K. A. K. v British Columbia*, 2011 BCSC 1391.   2011

Saskatchewan

Manitoba

Ontario

CHAPTER 5

Strengthening Children's Capacity to Cope with Separation, Loss, and Uncertain Futures: Action Steps for Front-Line Child Welfare Practice

Sharon McKay

Introduction

Children and youth deemed to be in need of support and protection beyond what can be provided by their parents and extended family are caught in situations that, however well-mitigated, inevitably trigger emotions of immense fear, confusion, and, possibly, relief or despair. In the midst of overwhelming emotions, the child is wholly dependent upon a wide network of strangers for their safety and well-being, and for their prospects for a productive and healthy future. Yet unrecognized barriers seriously impede the work of individuals and groups, the "network of strangers" involved in a variety of ways in the child's care, making the child's situation even more difficult. Front-line practitioners, foster parents and resident staff, supervisory and administrative personnel, and policy-makers and legislators far removed from the child's personal living situation comprise the network of strangers, a complex mix of influential

Suggested Citation: McKay, S. (2016). Strengthening children's capacity to cope with separation, loss, and uncertain futures: Action steps for front-line child welfare practice. In H. Montgomery, D. Badry, D. Fuchs, & D. Kikulwe (Eds.), *Transforming Child Welfare: Interdisciplinary Practices, Field Education, and Research* (pp. 87–105). Regina, SK: University of Regina Press.

actors, most of whom will never meet the child. Decisions made at one level can have intentional and unintentional consequences for decision making at other levels not infrequently impeding, or at best, delaying necessary actions important to helping the child understand what is happening to their family and why, and helping the child understand who is making decisions, and how the child can express their own opinion. In the midst of this complexity, this chapter underscores the point that the actions taken and the behaviour of members of the front-line protection team directly influence how the child copes with the trauma associated with separation and placement, and aids or deters the child from building the resilience necessary to successfully manage the challenges the child faces in this and future life experiences. The chapter is written for front-line social work practitioners, but the points made apply to all who work individually with the child or youth placed in the care of the state. The known realities as told by children and youth in care and those "aged out of care" provide a context for the chapter.

As foreground, the chapter provides an overview of children's rights as laid out in the 1989 United Nations Convention on the Rights of the Child (UNCRC), to which Canada is a signatory (1990), and briefly discusses issues and impediments to fully acting on the Convention in the fields of policy and practice. To overcome unrecognized barriers, a significant broadening of policy-maker and practitioner mindsets, or "critical thinking lens," is in order. Key to this potentially transformative broadening of the lens is a thorough understanding of children as rights holders: citizens with their own claims to care and protection and to active participation in decisions made affecting their own health and well-being and their future opportunities and choices. However, expanding one's knowledge base or critical thinking lens is helpful only if one has tools to help one act on new insights. Cultural, societal, organizational, and practitioner blinders impeding an expanded view of child and youth policy and practice need to be understood, as these blinders can prevent or impede recognition of children's rights at these levels. The chapter briefly discusses identified blinders such as issues arising during the development of the UNCRC. These blinders need to be understood so that they do not unduly influence the actions of the network of strangers who make policy and practice decisions affecting the well-being of children in the care of the state.

Descriptions of "life in care" told by children and youth in care, and those aged out of care are recorded in several research studies and government reports as identified below. These known realities provide a context for the chapter. The chapter concludes with action steps essential for effective front-line practice.

The United Nations Convention on the Rights of the Child: Development, Guiding Principles, and Challenges

As a member nation, Canada played a role in the development of the United Nations Convention on the Rights of the Child, hailed as a transformative instrument inspiring social change with respect to the care and protection of children around the world. The Convention guides nations, legislators, human rights activists, politicians, governments, and private agencies in understanding and implementing legislation, policies, regulations, and practices upholding children's rights as specified in the Convention's fifty-four articles (United Nations, 1989). As signatory to the Convention, Canada has committed its governments at all levels to being responsible for the provision and protection of the basic rights of children, which are summarized by the United Nations Children's Fund (UNICEF) as the right to protection (from abuse, exploitation, and harmful substances); the right to provision of (education, health care, and an adequate standard of living); and the right to participation (right to "voice" — to express their views and opinions and to participate in decisions affecting their well-being) (UNICEF, n.d.).

Signatory governments are required to prepare an initial report on their progress in advancing children's rights two years after signing the Convention and every five years following. The progress reports are to be filed through the Committee on the Rights of the Child, an independent body of international experts charged with monitoring and evaluating the reports and reporting back to countries with advice and recommendations pertinent to advancing rights in their nation (Child Rights International Network, n.d.). Yet the idea of children as rights holders is not without contention. Rights to nurturance and protection are self-evident, whereas children's rights to self-determination — including the freedom of thought, conscience, and religion; to freely express views, to be heard, to be informed, and to make choices — are not so readily acknowledged or necessarily acted upon within daily practice (McGillivray, 1998; Munro, 2001; Cashmore, 2002; Stasiulis, 2002; Moosa-Mitha, 2005; Lundy, 2007; McGillivray, 2011). Dominant notions of children as "innocents" and adults as authority figures are well ingrained in Canadian society and subtly influence how children are dealt with at home, at school, and in front-line practice. In this context, children's rights to voice and to participate in decisions affecting their well-being can inadvertently be overlooked. Practitioners need to be conscious of the subtle influence of societal resistance, and, in some instances, active backlash against the idea of children's rights to be informed, to voice their opinions, and to be listened to. Such resistance includes strongly held cultural beliefs about children's duties and the rights of the parents or family (McGillivray, 2011; Bunge, 2012).

Article 12 of the UNCRC, titled "The child's right to freely express views and to be heard," states that "States [are to] assure to the child...who is capable of forming his or her own views the right to express those views freely in all matters affecting the child...and...the views of the child are to be given due weight in accordance with the age and maturity of the child." Further to this, Article 17 of the UNCRC, titled "The child's right to be informed," states that "States Parties...shall ensure that the child has access to information and material from a diversity of national and international sources, especially those aimed at the promotion of his or her social, spiritual and moral well-being and physical and mental health" (United Nations, 1989). Yet skepticism about the child's capacity to understand rights and use them appropriately creates barriers to ensuring that children have access to essential information, including basic explanations informing the child of the reasons for being removed from their home, what will happen next, and what has happened to the child's parents and/or siblings and other significant people in the child's life. Prevailing notions of childhood innocence, while important to stimulating action respecting children's safety and protection, can inversely impede the child's right of access to information in the false belief that the child might not understand or might be further harmed. The notion of childhood innocence can also impede efforts to help children express their views, and, importantly, to take the time and space needed to truly listen to them as they try to communicate their thoughts and emotional responses to their personal situations.

Practitioners need to be mindful that all children, even small infants, are capable of expressing themselves through their behaviours, as well as their words. An effort must be made to understand what is being conveyed. Small children's brains have been described as being "like sponges" — new information is gathered and absorbed at rapid speed. How this information is interpreted when the new information is frightening, traumatic, and possibly violent should be of primary concern to all caregivers (National Scientific Council on the Developing Child, 2008–2012). Helping the child express themselves in a safe and caring environment is critical to developing healthy coping skills and attaining resilience to adverse life experiences. Michael Ungar makes a direct link between the role played by front-line workers and the child's resilience. Drawing from Leadbeater, Dodgen, and Solarz (2005), Ungar (2007) states that "resilience is more than a trait of the child. It results from the interaction between the child and his or her environment. When social workers and other helping professionals shape that environment, resilience is more likely to result" (p. 2).

Lived Experience as Told by Youth in Care and Youth "Aged out of Care"

Youth exiting from state care do not often experience the gradual home-leaving experience of most North American adolescents. In numerous studies, youth exiting or having exited from the child welfare system have reported feeling fearful, insecure, and uncertain of their futures: Who is in charge of what happens to me? Who do I speak to? What is going to happen to me, to my brothers and sisters, to my parents? Where do I go for medical care? How do I pay for dental and medical bills? Young people speak of numerous placements over many years, with each move experienced as a further disruption to relationships with their parents, siblings, and social network. Fear of loss of contact with siblings is frequently expressed (Butler, 1994; Aitken, Granofsky, Langer, Palmer, & Mankiewicz Smith, 2005; Jones & Kruk, 2005; Scannapieco, Connell-Carrick, & Painter, 2007; Ungar 2007; Reimer, 2010; Havlicek, 2011; Cunningham & Diversi, 2013).

In many ways, these youth are deprived of knowledge as to how to think about and plan for the "next steps" in their lives. Their futures too often include extended periods of unemployment, inadequate housing and/or homelessness, gravitation to criminal lifestyles and gangs, experiences of mental illness, and, for young women, the actuality of becoming a single parent with few supports. Not surprisingly, a good number of former foster children become long-term users of social welfare. Cunningham and Diversi (2013) note that many of these young people suffer enduring "relational wounds," including a prevailing sense of impermanence and loss (p. 589).

Approximately eight hundred young people in and from care, accompanied by professionals, families, and friends, gathered for the Ontario Youth Leaving Care Hearings at the provincial legislature. Initiated by youth raising their concerns with the provincial advocate for children and youth, this event was designed by and for youth for the purpose of holding public hearings about youth experiences in care and exiting care. The voices heard on these two days, and the subsequent report of the gathering, echoed much of the concerns raised in the aforementioned research (Ontario Provincial Advocate, 2012).

A minority of youth spoke positively of their experiences in care, emphasizing they had the good fortune of having been placed in loving, caring foster homes; that their caregivers, social workers, and other significant adults supported them unconditionally, helping them steer safely through turbulent times to ensure that they completed their education and were well prepared for living independently. These were young people who maintained strong links to their foster families, although they no longer lived in the foster home.

However, the experiences of most presenters were significantly bleaker, characterized by multiple losses, pervasive feelings of loneliness, and high anxiety about their futures. Young people spoke of feeling vulnerable, isolated, and that no one cared for their well-being. As one participant at the hearings noted, "No other relationship begins with an expiry date" (Ontario Provincial Advocate, 2012, p. 11). Youth who had left care spoke of their fears of becoming homeless (some had spent time living under bridges or in shelters), of inadequate housing, of not knowing how to handle finances or how to cook for themselves. Most struggled to find employment, while others did their best to continue their education, even when burdened by not knowing where to look for financial and/or academic support. Finding a healthy peer network was a challenge, in part because of the difficulty of trusting others, based upon too many disappointing experiences. A common theme from the hearings was "being left out of our lives," of being the subject of many meetings in which they did not participate, of watching others plan their lives. One young person asked, "Do you know how it feels to have your life typed and filed?" (Ontario Provincial Advocate, 2012 , p. 12). Another prevailing theme was the longing for at least one "solid support person" to mentor the young person when Crown wardship ends (p. 27). In the words of another young person: "There's no place like a spot in someone's heart" (p. 10).

Younger Children (Pre-Puberty)

One can extrapolate from the experiences reported in the several studies noted above and at the provincial hearing by young people in and aged out of care that the younger the child, the more frightening the experience of removal from the parental home may be, especially for children removed as part of an emergency call to a child protection agency. In addition to the trauma of the situation necessitating removal, the child faces numerous strangers, each of who may be only peripherally involved at the time. Emergency calls to child protection agencies generally involve social workers, police, and others such as teachers and/or mobile emergency-unit responders. The child may be placed in an emergency home overnight or for several days until the authorities are able to determine what will be in the child's best interests. Siblings may or may not accompany the child. None of the individuals encountered in the early days may continue as a primary contact for the child. All may be dependent on the agency "duty roster" at the time of the emergency call and the days following.

Transitions are difficult for young children. Readers will know from experiences with young children of their own that unfamiliar situations and people can trigger alarming reactions. Children will run for their parents, hide behind their legs, or cry uncontrollably if approached. Multiply this experience one hundredfold for the child in care — the child who cannot run to their parents' arms for safety. Reimer (2010) points to the "culture shock" of moving to a stranger's home, where the family culture — the "web of habits and symbols" that form a network of meaning and practices — may be quite different from the home culture. Having meals together may not have been a normal experience in the family of origin. Food may be strange, table rules or manners may be different. Children are placed in a state of "not knowing" — a state that may be perpetuated by subsequent moves to new homes. Language and cultural barriers become heightened for Aboriginal children and children of minority ethnic groups. Children with special needs due to health problems, disability, or sexual identity issues and homeless children and youth living their lives "on the street" are especially vulnerable (Fuchs, Burnside, Marchenski, & Mudry, 2007; Smyth & Eaton-Erickson, 2009).

Expanding the Front-Line Practitioner "Mindset" in Light of the UNCRC

Much of what has been said so far will be sadly familiar to front-line practitioners who frequently encounter the stories of children and youth removed from their homes due to protection concerns. We cannot imagine having to cope with the grief, loss, and confusion faced by children placed in the care of the state—who does that child turn to for comfort? Practitioners who have parented teenagers know first-hand about the not infrequent challenges of communicating with adolescents who have grown up in the security and comfort of their own homes. How can we as front-line protection "strangers" communicate meaningfully with young people whose lives have been so turbulent? The primary "lesson learned" from the foregoing section is that transformative change in practice and policy necessitates a determined effort to incorporate knowledge of the UNCRC and critical thinking about the rights of children in all that we do. We need to be highly conscious of the tendency in our society to think of children and youth, in the words of University of Victoria researcher Mehmoona Moosa-Mitha (2005), as "not-yet-citizens" with full rights to participate in decisions affecting their lives and with the right to express their views as to what they consider to be in their best interest (p. 369).

Adopting a social justice and advocacy stance alongside one's role of ensuring a young person's safety and protection at all levels of care will surely help. Founding this stance clearly on the guiding principles of the UNCRC is essential to alleviating young people's feelings of being left out of their own lives. Embedding the Convention principles into the practitioner's mindset means that front-line practitioners, whatever role they may play respecting the young person's entry into care, life in care, and exiting from care, must diligently pay heed to the child's voice. Doing so requires time and patience. Children and youth often have difficulty expressing themselves and even more so in traumatizing situations.

Matters of child welfare, care and protection, and voice and participation are equally matters of justice. The enormous demands and pressures placed on front-line staff cannot be an excuse for not taking the time to listen to the child. Practitioners need to do their best to keep the child informed, to listen carefully to their thoughts, anxieties, and concerns, and to advocate for the child to ensure they have adequate opportunity to speak to decisions that will affect their care, both in the immediate situation and with respect to future well-being.

Strengthening Front-Line Social Work Practice: A Plan of Action

This section of the chapter recommends seven practice action steps for embedding knowledge of children's rights into key areas of front-line social work practice:

1. agency role assignments;
2. personal self-awareness;
3. preparation for contact with the child;
4. provide information;
5. promote the child's involvement;
6. handle transitions with care; and
7. respect meaningful relationships with parents, siblings, and significant others.

These recommendations flow from the research base noted in this chapter, from my experiences throughout a social work career spanning over forty years, from numerous Prairie Child Welfare Consortium discussions with colleagues practising in the field and/or engaged in child welfare research, and from more recent experience as a member of the Ontario Children in Limbo Task Force (childreninlimbotaskforce.ca). The steps outlined relate directly to the UNCRC, with particular attention to Articles 12, 13, and 14: children's rights to be informed, to freely express views, to be heard, and to participate in decisions made affecting the child. The action steps are mindful of the relational lives of the child and the practitioner's position as a "stranger" with a potentially far-reaching role to play in the life of the child and youth entering care, in care, or exiting care—a stranger with a specific purpose and an urgent imperative to do what one can to help forge long-lasting supportive and caring connections for the child.

These recommendations are made in the full knowledge that front-line practice working conditions fall far short of the ideal. The challenges and complexities of large caseloads, limited time, insufficient supervision, perceived lack of support from senior administrators, and relentless attention of the media when things go wrong are well known (Herbert, 2007). Yet in the midst of these conditions, as reported in the Ontario Youth Leaving Care Hearings, much very fine casework is being done. The steps outlined are intended to augment and strengthen this good work.

Agency Role Assignments

A strong recommendation is that each child/youth served be assigned a personal advocate upon admission to care. The advocate's role will be to oversee arrangements made for the child's care; to follow progress or lack thereof; and to ensure that the child's needs are met for safety, security, health, nutrition, schooling, dental care, sibling and family contact, and cultural identity. The advocate ensures that the child is kept well-informed; is asked for their opinions, ideas, and thoughts on the matters affecting the child; and that the child's voice is seriously considered as decisions are made. The advocate will serve as the primary contact for the child, the child's family, the foster parents, the school, agency personnel, and representatives of the court.

This recommendation is made recognizing that most children and youth entering the child welfare system are assigned a social worker who carries out much of the role outlined. Bell (2002) recommends that the advocate role and the social worker role be viewed separately. She sees the advocate role as additional to, not a substitute for, the social worker, who needs to serve as a "secondary attachment figure along with the child's own parent" (p. 6). Bearing in mind that hiring additional staff to serve as "in-house" children's advocates will be difficult, if not impossible, for most Canadian child protection agencies, I recommend as an interim strategy that the role become that of "social worker/advocate." The change in wording from "social worker" or "caseworker" is deliberate. The term "advocate" adds strength to the social worker role and has implications for agency structure, processes, and funding. The point here is that role assignments must ensure that children's rights, as outlined in the UNCRC, are adhered to and that the child's voice is heard in all aspects of the child's care. The advocate role places the agency squarely in the midst of the UNCRC recommendations.

Personal Self-Awareness

What is important here is for front-line practitioners to increase awareness of the varied ways that one's thinking and personal attitudes have been influenced with respect to children's needs and children's rights. What are our personal "blinders" as noted in the introduction to this chapter? How do these influence our practice? It is important that practitioners understand and respond sensitively to the vulnerability of children and young people caught in circumstances largely beyond their control. It is equally important that the idea of "children as citizens and rights holders" be burned into one's mindset about child protection work, and that we do our best to incorporate a children's rights perspective into all that we do as practitioners with respect to the children and youth we are serving.

It is critical that we are sensitive to the fact that we are yet one more stranger in the child's life. As much as we may want the child or young person to consider us a friend, we are, in fact, an unknown "agent of power" in the child's life. Yet, within this context, we are in a position to serve as a trusted advocate alongside the child (Cashmore, 2002).

Preparation for Contact with the Child

Sensitizing oneself to the emotional and cognitive needs of the child/youth prior to contact is an essential step, even when time constraints are such that the practitioner has only a few minutes to prepare. Two useful resources are helpful here: anticipatory empathy and cultural safety. The two concepts appear in the social work literature and are described below.

Anticipatory Empathy

In their classic text, *The Life Model of Social Work Practice*, Gitterman and Germain (2008) describe the four steps of anticipatory empathy as a preparatory tool by which practitioners can hope to achieve "empathic feeling and thinking within another's frame of reference" (p. 140). As applied to children and youth, the steps would be the following: 1) *identification*, through which the practitioner imagines and tries to experience what the child or youth is thinking and feeling; 2) *incorporation*, through which the practitioner tries to feel the child's experiences as if they were personal; 3) *reverberation*, through which the worker tries to call up personal life experiences that may facilitate understanding those of the child or youth; and 4) *detachment*, "through which the worker engages in logical, objective analysis" (p. 140).

Cultural Safety

Milliken (2012) introduces the concept of cultural safety as particularly relevant to child welfare work, especially with Indigenous children, youth,
and families and with oppressed and marginalized populations. The
concept is far-reaching in its import as it goes beyond terms familiar to
social workers, such as "cross-cultural," "cultural sensitivity," and "cultural competence." The joining together of the two terms "cultural" and
"safety" is intentional. Drawing from Ramsden (1997) in Fulcher (1998),
Milliken (2012) provides a definition of cultural safety as "that state of
being in which the individual knows emotionally that her/his personal
wellbeing, as well as her/his social and cultural frames of reference, are
acknowledged, even if not fully understood. Furthermore, she/he is given
active reason to feel hopeful that her/his needs and those of her/his family
member and kin will be accorded dignity and respect" (p. 95).

Further to this, Milliken (2012) points to three ways that the concept
of cultural safety goes beyond previously used terms. The concept calls
upon the practitioner "to actively support the choices of the other within
the context of the latter's culture" (p. 102); "to acknowledge reasons why
oppressed others might be nervous about trusting social workers" (p.
103); to "make a commitment" to someone's safety within the social work/
client/agency relationship; and to ensure that the client, not the worker,
determines whether or not they feel safe (p. 104). The concept of cultural
safety integrates well with the four steps of anticipatory empathy and is
particularly relevant for the fourth step, detachment.

The two concepts of anticipatory empathy and cultural safety are
suggested as aids to developing a deeper understanding of the child's
experiences and to help support critical thinking and consideration of
positioning oneself as a protective ally of the child. Drawing upon the
foregoing descriptions of the two concepts, the practitioner preparing for
contact with a child placed in foster care for the first time would engage in
the following process.

1. Identification: try to imagine the child's fears and worries arising
    from the incident(s) that led to being placed in care and those that
    arise from being placed in an unfamiliar home with people who
    are strangers.

2. Incorporation: try to "be" the child in one's own psyche. That is, try to identify with the child by taking on the fears and worries as though they were one's own.

3. Reverberation: try to recall experiences in one's own life when an unexpected separation from one's family or close friends or some other traumatic, unanticipated event has occurred. If the practitioner cannot recall experiences in their own life, then one is encouraged to imagine such experiences (e.g., the practitioner may not have personally experienced the trauma the child may have experienced, such as sexual abuse or violence, but most have experienced fear of the unknown).

4. Detachment: recognize that what has been considered may not be at all what the child or youth is feeling and thinking at the moment of contact. The importance of this step is to recognize that no one can assume what another may be thinking or feeling. It is essential to prepare for the meeting in a way that leaves one open to hearing the child's voice and not only the practitioner's own perspectives. As part of this step, the practitioner draws upon their knowledge base and critical thinking skills. Drawing upon the concept of cultural safety, what do we know about the cultural background of the child or youth we will be meeting? What do we know of the developmental life stage the child or youth is going through and how this stage might be handled within their cultural milieu? What do we understand of our role in the situation? What resources are available to the child in the agency and/or community? Recall the importance of helping the youth express their own voice, while recognizing the need for cultural safety. Consider how one might address actual and potential barriers to the child feeling safe and secure. Milliken (2012) suggests asking the client directly: "Are you feeling safe?" "Can you think of anything that would help you feel safer?" (p. 107). She notes that the social worker must understand that "silence does not mean agreement." Rather, silence can mean confusion, not understanding the question, or fear or helplessness due to the power imbalance between the social worker/agency and the client (p. 108).

Provide Information

Identify yourself and explain your role to the child. Be conscious that the child does not know you and may well be confused and fearful of you—always act in accordance with the profession's values and code of ethics. Respect confidentiality and privacy. It is also important for the practitioner to ensure that others in contact with the child or youth do the same (introduce oneself and role and respect confidentiality and privacy). For example, police, emergency workers, health care workers, and foster parents need to identify themselves, as do others such as volunteer drivers, who are occasionally used by agencies to transport children to and from appointments. Giving your name and explaining your role may have to be repeated a number of times. Providing this information conveys the message that the child has the right to know the name and role of each of the strangers involved in their direct care.

Children and youth have a "right to know" why they have been removed from home; what plans are being made for them, their siblings, and their parents; who is making decisions; who they can talk to about their situation; and so on. Helping the child understand their situation means the practitioner must do their best to learn what the child does and does not know, what the child is thinking, and what are the child's worries and fears. Misconceptions and misunderstandings need to be corrected using the clearest language possible in a caring manner. Explanations may need to be given several times—one cannot expect traumatized children and youth to fully understand their situation, especially given the number of strangers encountered.

Promote the Child's Involvement

In her research interviewing twenty-seven children about their involvement in child protection investigations, Bell (2002) examined four areas in which the child's involvement can be promoted: providing information, providing choice, ensuring consultation, and ensuring representation. In each of these areas, children's rights in protection work are best promoted through a trusting relationship developed with a key professional in their network. "It is only within the context and security of a trusting relationship that children can assimilate information, make informed choices as to what their views are and how they are best represented and be enabled to exercise their rights to participation and service provision" (Bell, 2002,

p. 3). Most children in Bell's study reported a positive experience with a social worker and several of the children reported improvements at home, at school, and in their health and behaviour. The qualities listed as being important to the child were that the social worker was "available, reliable and concerned" (p. 5). Children felt listened to when they observed that their social workers were kind and nonjudgmental. Practical help, such as arranging contact with siblings, was valued, as was career guidance and help with life skills. Qualities found unhelpful included being asked questions experienced as threatening or invasive.

Handle Transitions with Care

Children need to be prepared for changes in the roster of adults responsible for their care. Sudden, unanticipated changes due to worker reassignments within the agency or worker departures from the agency need to be minimized. The point is made in several studies that children often see themselves as the "cause" of the troubles that led to removal from their homes. Agencies need to ensure that they do not compound this tendency of children to blame themselves for these changes by their own inattention to transitions that inevitably occur within the child-caring agency itself. Sudden changes of front-line staff due to change of roles and/or circumstances out of anyone's control need to be explained to the child, along with reassurances that the child will not be left on their own and that concern for their well-being remains utmost in the agency's mind. The child needs someone to closely "walk with him" during such times.

Respect Meaningful Relationships with
Parents, Siblings, and Significant Others

What children and youth in care want and need most, of course, is a loving family; a lifelong relationship with committed, reliable adults who will provide guidance and support and care and attention as the child grows and develops. Separation from parents, siblings, familiar surroundings, and culture, no matter how frightening and/or unsafe the home environment is, may cause great anxiety for the child in care. Multiple placements and frequent changes of social workers, foster parents, teachers, and schools can escalate initial anxiety to the point where the child/youth withdraws or acts out in ways that create serious barriers to becoming emotionally close to new caretakers, social workers, or others who may be in a position to help the child deal with their anxiety and fear. For these reasons, an urgent task for the social worker advocate at the point of intake, and throughout the child's stay in care, is to take all possible steps to learn about the nature of the child's relationship with their family of origin, siblings, and significant others and to do what is necessary to maintain and continue connections that are meaningful to the child. Schmied and Walsh (2010) interviewed child protection caseworkers in one state in Australia as a means of collecting information about effective practice with adolescents in the child protection system. In their study, practitioners spoke of "walking it together" as being central to their work with adolescents; of serving as the "common denominator" between the young person and their siblings and other family members, keeping each informed about the other (p. 169).

Planning for the child's return to the parental home, or for a long-term safer home such as a kinship or an adoptive home, should also begin at the point of intake. Where it is impossible for the child to return home, due to the parents' inability to care for the child, the child's rights to maintain personal relations and direct contact with their parents must be adhered to, except where it is contrary to the child's best interests (Article 20, UNCRC). On this point, Coupet (2007) calls for paying attention to the meaningful relationships in children's lives, which may reside outside of parents and kin. She states:

> *Too often, professionals, particularly legal advocates working with children, fail to appreciate the richness of relationships that defy conventional norms and those that, although central to children, have a subordinated place in a rights-based discourse....In its current state, the rights-based regulation of children's relational lives... is insufficiently keyed to children's psychological, emotional, and developmental needs. It remains indeed more attuned to a hierarchy of adult rights of access to children. (pp. 79, 80)*

Coupet argues that it is necessary in many instances to "give legal recognition to those meaningful relationships formed by the child with any adult who, in the immediately preceding period, was most responsible for the child's daily care and supervision, fulfilled the role of good steward, or has been found to have a significant attachment relationship with the child" (p. 85).

In their study of family relationships of youth in care in British Columbia, Jones and Kruk (2005) argue that child welfare systems need to "put more effort into helping foster parents and birth parents develop cooperative and shared parenting relationships" (p. 419). They refer to the success of a Share the Care program initiated in Scotland as a potential model for a shared family responsibility framework.

Final Words

Threaded throughout this chapter is the strong assertion that practitioners at all levels clearly incorporate the principles of the UNCRC in all aspects of their work, and that the centrality of a meaningful relationship with children and youth—a relationship built on commitment, continuity of care, and trust—be foremost in the practitioner's mind. While recognizing the significant influence of policy and administration, the primary emphasis of this chapter is on front-line practice. The front-line practitioner plays a significant role in helping the traumatized child find stability, develop coping skills, and work through their feelings of loss and grief. The critical importance of this work cannot be understated. Seven practice action steps have been outlined to assist in this regard. Raising one's consciousness regarding actual and potential blinders to recognizing, promoting, and advocating the rights of the child is essential to good practice. Practitioners are urged to walk alongside the child in their journey through state care.

References

Aitken, G., Granofsky, B., Langer, R., Palmer, S., & Mankiewicz Smith, J. (2005). Learning from focus groups with former and current Crown wards. *Ontario Association of Children's Aid Societies Journal, 49*(3), 2–17.

Bell, M. (2002). Promoting children's rights through the use of relationship. *Child and Family Social Work, 7*(1), 1–11.

Bunge, M. J. (2012). *Children, adults, and shared responsibilities: Jewish, Christian, and Muslim perspectives.* Cambridge, United Kingdom: Cambridge University Press.

Butler, I. (1994). *Children speak: Children, trauma and social work.* London, United Kingdom: Longman.

Cashmore, J. (2002). Promoting the participation of children and young people in care. *Child Abuse and Neglect, 26*, 837–847.

Child Rights International Network. (n.d.). Committee on the Rights of the Child. Retrieved from https://www.crin.org/en/guides/un-international-system/committee-rights-child

Coupet, S. M. (2007, Fall). Neither dyad nor triad: Children's relationship interests within kinship caregiving families. *University of Michigan Journal of Law Reform, 41*(1), 77–87.

Cunningham, M., & Diversi, M. (2013). Aging out: Youths' perspectives on foster care and the transition to independence. *Qualitative Social Work, 12*(5), 587–602.

Fuchs, D., Burnside, L., Marchenski, S., & Mudry, A. (2007). Children with disabilities involved with the child welfare system in Manitoba: Current and future challenges. In I. Brown, F. Chaze, D. Fuchs, J. Lafrance, S. McKay, & S. Thomas Prokop (Eds.), *Putting a human face on child welfare: Voices from the Prairies* (pp. 127–145). Toronto, ON: Prairie Child Welfare Consortium/Centre of Excellence for Child Welfare.

Fulcher, L. (1998). Acknowledging culture in child and youth practices. *Social Work Education, 17*(3), 321–338.

Gitterman, A., & Germain, C. B. (2008). *The life model of social work practice: Advances in theory & practice.* New York, NY: Columbia University Press.

Havlicek, J. (2011). Lives in motion: A review of former foster youth in the context of their experiences in the child welfare system. *Children and Youth Services Review, 33,* 1090–1100.

Herbert, M. (2007). Creating conditions for good practice: A child welfare project sponsored by the Canadian Association of Social Workers. In I. Brown, F. Chaze, D. Fuchs, J. Lafrance, S. McKay, & S. Thomas Prokop (Eds.), *Putting a human face on child welfare: Voices from the Prairies* (pp. 223–250). Toronto, ON: Prairie Child Welfare Consortium/Centre of Excellence for Child Welfare.

Jones, L., & Kruk, E. (2005). Life in government care: The connection of youth to family. *Child and Youth Care Forum, 34*(6), 405–421.

Leadbeater, B., Dodgen, D., & Solarz, A. (2005). The resilience revolution: A paradigm shift for research and policy. In R. D. Peters, B. Leadbeater, & E. J. McMahon (Eds.), *Resilience in children, families and communities: Linking context to practice and policy* (pp. 47–63). New York, NY: Kluwer.

Lundy, L. (2007). "Voice" is not enough: Conceptualising Article 12 of the United Nations Convention on the Rights of the Child. *British Educational Research Journal, 33*(6), 927–942.

McGillivray, A. (1998). The moral status of children: Essays on the rights of the child. *The Journal of Social Welfare & Family Law, 20*(4), 482–485.

McGillivray, A. (2011). Children's rights, paternal power and fiduciary duty: From Roman law to the Supreme Court of Canada. *International Journal of Children's Rights, 19*(1), 21–54.

Milliken, E. (2012). Cultural safety and child welfare systems. In D. Fuchs, S. McKay, & S. Brown (Eds.), *Awakening the spirit: Moving forward in child welfare: Voices from the Prairies* (pp. 93–116). Regina, SK: Canadian Plains Research Center.

Moosa-Mitha, M. (2005). A difference-centred alternative to theorization of children's citizenship rights. *Citizenship Studies, 9,* 369–388.

Munro, E. (2001). Empowering looked after children. *Child & Family Social Work, 6,* 129–137.

National Scientific Council on the Developing Child. (2008–2012). Establishing a level foundation for life: Mental health begins in early childhood (Working Paper 6, Updated Edition). Retrieved from http://www.developingchild. harvard.edu

Ontario Provincial Advocate. (2012). *My real life book: Report from the Youth Leaving Care Hearings.* Retrieved from http://www.provincialadvocate.on.ca/ documents/en/ylc/YLC_REPORT_ENG.pdf

Ramsden, I. (1997). Cultural safety: Implementing the concept. In P. T. Whaiti, M. McCarthy, & A. Durie (Eds.), *Mai i rangiātea: Māori wellbeing and development* (pp. 113–125). Auckland, New Zealand: Auckland University Press.

Reimer, D. (2010). "Everything was strange and different": Young adults' recollection of transitioning into foster care. *Adoption & Fostering, 34*(2), 14–22.

Scannapieco, M., Connell-Carrick, K., & Painter, K. (2007). In their own words: Challenges facing youth aging out of foster care. *Child and Adolescent Social Work Journal, 24*(5), 423–435.

Schmied, V., & Walsh, P. W. (2010). Effective casework practice with adolescents: Perspectives of statutory child protection practitioners. *Child & Family Social Work, 15*(2), 165–175.

Smyth, P., & Eaton-Erickson, A. (2009). Making the connecton: Strategies for working with high risk youth. In S. McKay, D. Fuchs, & I. Brown (Eds.), *Passion for action in child and family services: Voices from the Prairies* (pp. 119–142). Regina, SK: Canadian Plains Research Center.

Stasiulis, D. (2002). The active child citizen: Lessons from Canadian policy and the Children's Movement. *Citizenship Studies, 6*(4), 507–538.

Ungar, M. (2007). Contextual and cultural aspects of resilience in child welfare settings. In I. Brown, F. Chaze, D. Fuchs, J. Lafrance, S. McKay, & S. Thomas Prokop (Eds.), *Putting a human face on child welfare: Voices from the Prairies* (pp. 1–24). Toronto, ON: Prairie Child Welfare Consortium/Centre of Excellence for Child Welfare.

UNICEF. (n.d.). About the Convention on the Rights of the Child. Retrieved from http://www.unicef.ca/en/policy-advocacy-for-children/ about-the-convention-on-the-rights-of-the-child

United Nations. (1989). Convention on the Rights of the Child. Retrieved from http://www.ohchr.org/en/professionalinterest/pages/crc.aspx

Aligning Practice, Ethics, and Policy: Adopting a Harm Reduction Approach in Working with High-Risk Children and Youth

Peter Smyth

> *"Harm reduction has been conceptualized as a peace movement and is aligned with humanistic values around which social work is organized."*
>
> —Brocato and Wagner, 2003

In the traditional risk-management world of child welfare, one might wonder where there might be room for harm reduction strategies to be applied. As healthy discussions about shifting more toward relationship-based practice continue, the harm reduction perspective can help caseworkers who have very challenging youth on their caseloads to think differently and to actively engage this population in the provision of services. Incorporating harm reduction approaches builds relationship. It opens up communication and demonstrates caring. It opens the door for youth who have experienced much loss and trauma to take the risk of making a connection with somebody. As in the High Risk Youth Initiative (HRYI) in

Suggested Citation: Smyth, P. (2016). Aligning practice, ethics, and policy: Adopting a harm reduction approach in working with high-risk children and youth. In H. Montgomery, D. Badry, D. Fuchs, & D. Kikulwe (Eds.), *Transforming Child Welfare: Interdisciplinary Practices, Field Education, and Research* (pp. 107–131). Regina, SK: University of Regina Press.

Edmonton, Alberta, harm reduction strategies can and *should* intersect with child welfare practice to move away from punishment-consequence interventions and help narrow the power gap, reduce alienation and the marginalization of youth, and promote an anti-oppressive stance. This can also help youth see value in accepting services either voluntarily or involuntarily (as wards of the government) and give them an alternative perspective of how they may view "the system" and how they perceive their relationships with caseworkers and community support staff.

This chapter will examine the application of a harm reduction approach to child welfare practice with high-risk children and youth. It will address the questions about how and why this approach can help engage and empower such a challenging population. The chapter defines harm reduction and it examines the unique application of a harm reduc- tion approach to a traditionally risk-averse system. While there have been questions raised with respect to its use with children and youth, the fit with relationship-based practice and social work values is presented and discussed.

Sarah's story (below) initially illustrates the more traditional approach to working with a youth with many challenges, and then highlights the potential offered by incorporating harm reduction strategies. The initial traditional focus is not unusual as often workers come from a deficit-based perspective and insist on compliance even before building rapport and developing a working relationship. I have heard many accounts from youth over the years relating to their strained connections to their case- workers, the threats of being cut off from services if not complying, being denied access to programs, not being understood, not having a say in their case plans, and feeling their workers are trying to control their lives. As doors are being closed when a youth feels estranged from his/her worker, harm reduction serves to not only open those doors but invites the youth to walk through.

"Sarah"

A caseworker within a government child-intervention department tells "Sarah," a youth on his caseload, that she must stay in her group home, follow the rules, meet curfew, attend school, and see her addictions coun- sellor. The sixteen-year-old youth came into care at age three after many attempts to work with her parents, who genuinely wanted to raise Sarah. After numerous attempts to quit using drugs, and after many visits by the police due to domestic violence, they consented to their daughter being placed in care. Sarah's mother and father loved her but were completely overwhelmed with their own problems, having also been born into chaos and traumatized as children. When Sarah was age five, the state filed an application to be her permanent guardian. A judge granted the order after Sarah's parents failed to show up at court for the third time.

Sarah was in four foster homes from age three to thirteen. She was hard to manage, and the foster parents felt they could not cope with her behaviours and/or they feared for the safety of their own children and other foster children. When she started running away and getting drunk at age thirteen, it was decided that Sarah would be placed in group care. She was influenced by older youth and she started using drugs and staying on the streets for days at a time. Thus began the group home revolving door, as her bed in various places would be closed due to lack of use or because she would show up drunk, get into conflicts with peers, or be verbally abusive to staff. Sarah was good at keeping people at an emotional distance. It was safe, kept workers out of her face, maintained her sense of freedom, and gave her control over her own life.

With Sarah now at age sixteen, the caseworker not only expected compliance from her, he threatened to withdraw the chance for her to move into a supported independent living program, to withhold her bus pass, and to deny her recreation funding to go on a hiking trip to the mountains with a local youth outreach agency where Sarah hangs out and engages in art projects. He even vowed to place her in a secure[1] environment if she was seen to be a danger to herself. Sarah escalated quickly. She told him it's her life and she would do what she wanted.

---

1   "Secure services" is a nonvoluntary, nonhospital setting under Alberta's Child, Youth and Family Enhancement Act. It requires court involvement to either place or justify why a child or youth has been placed in secure services. It is time-limited, but further confinement can be requested to complete an assessment or if it is determined through an assessment that more time is warranted to address the safety concerns. As laid out in section 44(2), the criteria for using this part of the act are: "a) the child is in a condition presenting an immediate danger to the child or others; (b) it is necessary to confine the child in order to stabilize and assess the child; and (c) less intrusive measures are not adequate to sufficiently reduce the danger."

She denied she had a substance abuse problem. Sarah added that if her worker would not help her, she would stay at her boyfriend's apartment, a solution her worker had warned her against given he is thirty years old, abusive, and possibly grooming Sarah for sexual exploitation. Her final words to her worker were, "go fuck yourself," as she stormed out of the office, slamming the door.

While many risk factors are evident, the caseworker was of limited capacity to help as Sarah was angry at him, avoided him, and, given the lack of relationship, she did not believe he would worry about her or that he cared for her. For Sarah, this was not surprising, as she had had many social workers throughout her childhood. She was desperate for a connection with a healthy adult, but risking such a connection was not worth it, as in the end there was always more rejection and abandonment. Close to being an adult, Sarah did not see the child welfare system as relevant in meeting her needs. As she had experienced throughout most of her short life, she was on her own, could not trust anyone else, and would have to survive with minimal supports and resources. She recognized that her boyfriend could be an "asshole," but at least it was a place to shower and sleep, and, after all, he bought her clothes and makeup once in awhile.

Alternatively, the caseworker could recognize that after many attempts at formal group care with all of the rules, the "three strikes" and "zero tolerance" mentality, and the traditional punishment-consequence approach, it is not working for Sarah. Rather, he could ask her what she wants; what might work from her perspective. He could offer alternatives, such as agreeing to meet with a youth shelter program to see if this might offer a more flexible option better suited to her unique needs. If she is not ready, and is likely to run to her boyfriend, Sarah and the caseworker could develop a safety plan together. The caseworker could ensure she has food, transportation, adequate clothing, and a cell phone to help increase the level of safety given her high-risk lifestyle with her boyfriend and her drug and alcohol use. He could help her feel supported and empowered to have a say in the decisions being made about her future. They could work together and start building a relationship.

Adopting a Harm Reduction Approach in the High Risk Youth Initiative

In 1999, in what is now called Edmonton & Area Child and Family Services, a specialized caseload was developed, targeting the most needy and vulnerable youth in the Old Strathcona neighbourhood in Edmonton, Alberta. This became known as the "high-risk youth caseload." The project adopted a harm reduction approach to engaging youth, as well as building community partnerships to maximize the potential of appropriate service provision. At the time, the harm reduction approach was not taken seriously by other caseworkers within child welfare, with comments reflecting that this thinking was not real social work, that it allowed youth to take control ("soft-on-teens unit"; "you allow the youth to walk all over you"), and that the project was for bleeding hearts. However, in November 2005, this project was legitimized as a program in the form of the High Risk Youth Initiative[2] on a regional level. The harm reduction philosophy remained one of the cornerstones of the initiative, although conversations with senior managers within the Edmonton region indicated some trepidation given the departure from the traditional risk-management structure within child welfare services (Lonne, Parton, Thomson & Harries, 2009; Smyth & Eaton-Erickson, 2009).[3] Over the years, the harm reduction approach has

---

2   The original criteria for accepting youth into the High Risk Youth Initiative included a minimum of fourteen years of age; drugs and/or alcohol interferes with their day-to-day functioning; their choice of where they are living or who they are associating with puts their safety in jeopardy; they cannot identify a healthy adult in their lives outside of the professional community; they have spent time in multiple placements, including locked facilities (jail or mental health services); they struggle with authority and have few, if any, people they can trust; they typically have mental health issues and are living an unpredictable day-to-day existence; and their involvement with child welfare services is multigenerational. A vast majority of the youth have also experienced childhood trauma that has impacted their ability to make significant connections with others (Smyth & Eaton-Erickson, 2009).

3   In recent history, other regions within Alberta Human Services, Child and Family Services would not endorse a harm reduction approach to working with high-risk youth, and, in fact, were surprised the Edmonton region had endorsed such an approach. In provincial meetings, staff from other regions were not given permission to even use the words "harm reduction." Fortunately, this has somewhat shifted.

become more accepted and now is being supported in all areas of service delivery. While policy has yet to be formally developed with regard to the HRYI, there is an acceptance that current general practice policies within intervention services can be flexible and adapted if they present as barriers to best meeting the needs of this challenging population.

The practice framework and philosophy within the HRYI, in addition to the harm reduction and community collaboration aspects, incorporates a resiliency/strength-based approach, draws from attachment theory, and incorporates trauma-informed practice, while adopting an anti-oppressive perspective. The key activity focuses on building relationships through increased face-to-face contact. While very little research literature can be found relating to evaluations of policies and programs targeting the population of high-risk youth,[4] most of the youth who have been involved with the HRYI—many who recount negative experiences with previous child welfare involvement—have generally responded well to the practice framework. They maintain regular contact with the caseworkers, they can identify having a support network (of government and agency workers, as well as community supports), and they start to believe that they are valued. My insight in talking with youth over the years is that experiencing a feeling of being valued, and accepting that someone cares about them, reduces their sense of isolation and marginalization and enhances a belief in themselves that they can make positive changes in their lives.[5]

---

4   A harm reduction approach to working with children in a child welfare setting is a new area of practice and there is little or no research on the subject. However, there is plenty of research addressing the theories and principles incorporated into harm reduction practice, including the importance of relationship (Batmanghelidjh, 2006; Brendtro, Brokenleg, & Van Bockern, 1990; Brendtro & du Toit, 2005; Brendtro, Mitchell, & McCall, 2009; Howe, 2011; Kagan, 2004; Lonne et al., 2009; Luckock & Lefevre, 2008; Maté, 2008; Neufeld & Maté, 2004; Perry, 2006, 2009; Szalavitz & Perry, 2010); resiliency and strength-based practice (Blundo, 2001; Madsen, 2007; Saleebey, 1997; Ungar, 2004, 2005, 2006); attachment, trauma, and brain development (Howe, 2005, 2008, 2011; Kagan, 2004; Levine, 1997; Levy & Orlans, 1998; Maté, 1999, 2008; Perry 2006, 2009; Solomon & Siegel, 2003); anti-oppressive practice (Baines, 2007; Bishop, 2002; Strega & Esquao (Carrière), 2009); harm reduction and social work practice (Bigler, 2005; Brocato & Wagner, 2003); and community collaboration (Brown & Hannis, 2008; Goldblatt, 2007; Wharf, 2002).

5   Two internal studies have been done to gauge how youth are responding to the alternative approach to service provision in the HRYI. In 2007, a number of youth

High-Risk Children

In 2010, members of the High Risk Youth Operations Committee (made up of staff from government ministries and community agencies and organizations involved in working with this population of youth) brought forward a concern that a higher number of younger youth were appearing on the streets and were appearing at agencies to request services or hang out with friends. Given the 11–13 age range of these children, a position paper was drafted to bring wider attention to the issue. Committee members indicated that these youth had been engaging in behaviours that were historically observed in older youth: school truancy/nonattendance; "couch surfing" or living on the streets (i.e., lack of stable placements); use of alcohol/drugs to the point of addiction, criminal activity, and/or being sexually exploited (often to meet basic needs).

The document called for adopting the harm reduction approach for these "high-risk children," knowing this would be controversial given the general hesitancy of government services to incorporate a harm reduction philosophy into service delivery for older youth. When the HRYI started in 2005, the minimum age for accepting youth into the program was fourteen years. At the time, there were fewer street-involved children, and there were ethical challenges around working in a harm reduction paradigm when youth may not be able to comprehend what this means. However, this emerging trend of high-risk children called for a review of this informal policy given the challenges in meeting the needs of this younger group and keeping them safe. This population has proven to be particularly hard to engage. They are also developmentally very young and are less adept at identifying when they may be in danger. Alienating these already damaged and angry children by using traditional approaches was not helping, so new ideas and approaches were needed.

---

forums took place, comparing youth who had open files within the HRYI, youth with open files outside of the HRYI, and youth who identified needs but had no status with Alberta Human Services, Child and Youth Services. The report was called *More Words on the Street: A Follow-up Report on How Youth View Services Aimed at Them* (Steering Committee, HRYI, 2007). This followed a previous report, *The Word on the Street: How Youth View Services Aimed at Them* (Smyth et al., 2005), which looked at how youth viewed the services they were receiving through child welfare services, and which helped launch the HRYI. The second report was the result of a youth forum held with youth directly receiving services through the HRYI and conducted by independent facilitators in May 2009.

The Evolution of Harm Reduction Practices and
the *Positive* Fit for Working with Youth

> *"Harm Reduction is anything that reduces the risk of injury whether*
> *or not the individual is able to abstain from the risky behavior."*
> —David Ostrow, M.D., Ph.D.[6]

Although the term "harm reduction" was not coined until 1984 (Duncan, n.d.),[7] harm reduction strategies started in the early twentieth century when British doctors prescribed heroin and morphine to patients dependent on opioids (Collins et al., 2012; Taylor, 2010). In the 1970s and early 1980s, European countries initiated new concepts in harm reduction with the emerging threat of AIDS (Collins et al., 2012; Taylor, 2010). A number of countries included harm reduction in their official drug policy, given their position that AIDS represented a greater threat to public health than did drug use. Over time, this expanded further to include heroin prescriptions, needle exchange programs, counselling, employment, and housing, especially since police supported harm reduction strategies given they felt that they could not be the solution to society's drug issues. However, the United States and Canada (the latter taking more of a middle ground) did not accept the harm reduction philosophy. In 1971, President Richard Nixon declared the "war on drugs," identifying drug abuse as "public enemy No. 1." In 1984, Nancy Reagan launched the Just Say No anti-drug program (Taylor, 2010). The Canadian government, under Stephen Harper, did not support the harm reduction philosophy. Despite the evidence of lives being saved, the government challenged the right of the Insite supervised injection site in Vancouver's Downtown Eastside to provide services due to public safety concerns.

---

6   This quote is taken from the article, "Harm Reduction History and Definitions" (no date), posted online by AddictionInfo: Alternative to 12-Step Treatment. While the quote is attributed Dr. David Ostrow, there is no author listed for the article.

7   Duncan (n.d.) states that the new direction in drug abuse prevention was given the name "harm reduction" in a report put out by the British Home Office in 1984. The report described "two alternate goals for drug abuse prevention—either reducing drug use or reducing harms associated with drug use" (p. 1). The article can be found at AddictionInfo: Alternatives to 12-Step Treatment (http://www.addictioninfo.org/articles/226/1/A-New-Direction-Harm-Reduction/Page1.html).

However, a Supreme Court decision in September 2011 has supported the right of Insite to operate, as not doing so would be a violation of the Charter of Rights and Freedoms (*CBC News*, 2011). Now, with the election of a Liberal government under Justin Trudeau in October 2015, such opposition is not anticipated and could result in the opening of more supervised injection sites (Kietltyka, 2015) in Montreal (Valiante, 2015), Toronto (Lunn & Zimonjic, 2016), and Edmonton (French, 2016), where the concept is being explored. Health and legal experts are optimistic that roadblocks can be cleared for more harm reduction programs to be introduced (Woo, 2015). At present, harm reduction remains more in the realm of the addictions field, though it does incorporate more mainstream ideas, such as safe grads, designated driver programs, smoking-cessation aids, and safer-sex campaigns.

The HRYI adapted the harm reduction philosophy to the field of human services, particularly child intervention. While there is very little literature in this area, Bigler (2005), in his article, "Harm Reduction as a Practice and Prevention Model for Social Work," states, "In more recent years, the harm reduction model has gained a great deal of attention and support outside of the addictions arena and in other areas of health and human services" (p. 73). In the HRYI, harm reduction is defined as a set of strategies and principles that aims to provide or enhance the skills, knowledge, resources, and support people need to be safer and healthier. The aim is to work to the strengths of the service users. It is empowering, noncoercive, nonjudgmental, builds rapport, sees people as experts in their own lives, and builds on the quality of life for individuals based on their own perceptions and values (Taylor, 2010). Bigler (2005) defines the overriding principle as "reducing the harm associated with specific high-risk behavior" (p. 73), while Maté (2008) tells us "harm reduction means making the lives of afflicted human beings more bearable, more worth living" (p. 312).

Practising under a harm reduction philosophy with high-risk youth is less threatening to the youth, who often react negatively to authority figures who tell them what to do and how to do it (Luckock & Lefevre, 2008; Howe, 2005, 2008; Perry, 2006). The aim should be to draw the youth in, not push them away (Szalavitz & Perry, 2010), and to work in partnership with the youth (power with), rather than as the expert in their lives (power over) (Baines, 2007; Bishop, 2002; Strega, 2007). Speaking to outcomes, Marliss

Taylor (2010), a recognized expert in harm reduction in Edmonton, Alberta,[8] states that this approach restores dignity, self-esteem, and a sense of value for clients. It increases their sense of control and reaffirms that people have a choice. Further, it fosters a sense of partnership and restores hope and a vision for the future, giving individuals a voice. Harm reduction accepts that risk is a natural part of life and that change is incremental. Interventions cannot be rigid, and creativity is required (Elovich & Cowing, 1993). Harm reduction incorporates a strength-based approach, which is also critical in working with high-risk youth, especially when their experiences within child welfare have typically been problem-focused (Blundo, 2001).

Ungar (2004, 2005) argues that troubled youth, despite a lack of positive and healthy resources, demonstrate a remarkable resiliency in trying to forge their own strong and individual identities. He (2005) adds that negative behaviours can actually signal a pathway to hidden resilience and are still a search for health. There is a tendency when working with children and youth to want to change their behaviours, overlooking how those very behaviours make sense to the youth themselves. Ungar (2006) writes, "[T]hey will not heed our words of advice until they are confident we understand they are already doing the best they can with what they have" (p. 3). Ungar (2005) also points out that until we better understand children's and youth's strategies for resilience, we will take their efforts for survival to be signs of "dangerous, delinquent, deviant or disordered behaviour" (p. 1). These hidden pathways to resilience are typically not seen as health-enhancing because the actions of the youth may fall outside of social norms. Rather than suppress their negative behaviours, we are encouraged to search for positive substitutions that are nonthreatening and still maintain their need to attain power (Ungar, 2004, 2006).

---

8   Marliss Taylor is the program manager for the Streetworks program in Edmonton, Alberta (located in Boyle Street Community Services), and sits on the steering committee for the Canadian Drug Policy Coalition. Marliss has a nursing background and spent time working in the remote Nunavut hamlets of Kugluktuk and Gjoa Haven. Marliss, who has won a number of awards for her work, has been immersed in harm reduction approaches for the past twenty years and has been involved with health promotion/harm reduction initiatives in Siberia and Guyana, as well as a multitude of local, provincial, and national research projects. In October 2015, Marliss was appointed to the newly created board of Alberta Health Services.

Ungar (2004) writes: "High-risk teens who were interviewed...showed that experiences that enhance capacities, promote self-determination, increase participation, and distribute power and justice, carry the greatest potential for a positive impact on a teenager's discursive power leading to well-being. These types of experiences allow hopefulness to replace help-lessness...and contribute to psychological growth" (p. 285).

Madsen (1999) echoes Ungar's thoughts when talking of the shift from emphasizing problems to emphasizing competence, a shift from the role of expert—which can invite an authoritarian stance—to the role of account-able ally, and a shift from teaching clients to learning from them. To avoid resistance and demoralization, "recognizing strengths and resources invites hope and possibilities" (Madsen, 1999, p. 27). This is supported by Blundo (2001), who cautions that "traditional practice is disempow-ering as workers use technical skills such as confrontation, overcoming resistance, and managing the manipulative client, while at the same time manipulating the relationship to enhance compliance with professional decisions" (p. 6).

A Resiliency and Strength-Based Focus Helps Create Hope

While Saleebey (1997) reminds us that using resilience as the knowledge base for practice creates a sense of optimism and hope, child welfare still tends to focus on traditional medical model thinking that emphasizes the pathology over individual strengths and personal resources (Bigler, 2005). This practitioner-as-the-expert and paternalistic approach runs contrary to harm reduction values, relies on punishment, and results in judgments being made to determine if the youth is worthy of receiving services (Batmanghelidjh, 2006; Lonne et al., 2009).

Lonne et al. (2009) argue that "many child protection systems are puni-tive to everyone involved in them" (p. 9), while the harm reduction model promotes nonpunitive responses where mutual support and account-ability exist (Bigler, 2005, p. 74). In dismissing the punishment model when working with high-risk children and youth, psychologist Camila Batmanghelidjh (2006) explains:

For this type of child, punishment is not an effective learning tool. The terrorized child has had experiences of extreme violation and horror. There is nothing more one can do to them which would frighten them into behaving better....The violated child is emotionally too disorganized to make the necessary connections and learn from the infliction of punishment. The violated child lives in a different emotional universe from the rest of us. Their sense of personal damage is so profound that mild threats of damage like punishment do not register with them....Punishment is experienced as rejection, which deepens the child's resentment. The only hope is to find love for this child....Once these children feel contained and consistent love, they will not want to lose it. (pp. 101, 103)

The shift to harm reduction approaches is made difficult within traditional child welfare settings, as the focus is on risk management rather than meeting the emotional and safety needs of the child. Lonne et al. (2009) are critical of the approach to current child welfare practices:

What has emerged from the social angst and panic are systems of risk-averse child protection, many of which are driven by pseudo-scientific risk-assessment models and a preoccupation with procedures rather than meaningful and practical assistance. We argue the current narrow theoretical discourse of child protection is largely failing children and young people, and has embraced a commitment to technocratic risk assessment and a forensic approach....In essence, relationship-based social work has been supplanted by case management-driven proceduralism which is devoid of meaningful and respectful engagement with children and parents, instead treating them as the "Other." (p. 8)

Eileen Munro (2011), in reviewing the child protection system in the United Kingdom, makes similar comments referring to a "defensive system that puts so much emphasis on procedures and recording that insufficient attention is given to developing and supporting the expertise to work effectively with children, young people and families" (p. 6). Again, this is contrary to the principles of the harm reduction philosophy, which values making connections and empowering service users. As risk is viewed as part of life in a harm reduction world, approaches that accept and work with risk are required (Bigler, 2005; Lonne et al., 2009; Taylor,

2010). Thus, there is a call for an end to the preoccupation with social control policies that are preventing the provision of social care, and a shift to focusing on "relationship-based practice, respect, and genuine partnerships," which value the "wisdom and expertise that sits with the people who experience the problems that we are trying to resolve" (Lonne et al., 2009, pp. 6–11).

The experience within the HRYI has been that building relationships actually reduces risk. The traditional paradigm of control and punishment often results in noncompliance by the youth, as well as avoiding those who are supposed to be helping them (as in Sarah's situation above). This means that neither the caseworker nor the service provider knows where the youth is or the risks to which they may be exposing themselves. Taking a harm reduction approach, and allowing the youth to be involved in the decisions impacting their lives, typically means they engage rather than avoid, and this open communication allows the workers to know where the youth is and the dangers they may be confronting (see Table 6.1 for a comparison of traditional and harm reduction approaches to working with youth in the child welfare system).

Table 6.1: Contrast between Traditional and Harm Reduction Approaches to Casework in Child Welfare

Traditional Approach to Casework	Harm Reduction Approach to Casework
• focus is on risk management—through legislation and policy, risk is minimized or eliminated	• focus in on building relationship—risk is a part of life, but through establishing relationships, risk can be reduced
• use of deficit-based language	• use of strength-based language
• initial focus of casework is outlining expectations	• initial focus of casework is engagement and safety planning
• service plan focuses on worker's expectations (worker as expert)	• service plan is negotiated with youth identifying goals (youth are experts in their own lives)
• placement needs based on assessments by caseworker	• placement needs based on where youth is willing to stay and safety needs

continued...

Traditional Approach to Casework	Harm Reduction Approach to Casework
• caseworker comes from a *doing to* or *doing for* perspective (power over)	• caseworker comes from a *doing with* perspective (partnership)
• long-term goal is to reduce or eliminate the risky behaviours preventing the youth from meeting their goals	• long-term goal is to change risky behaviours through reducing harm, empowering the youth, and building resiliency by expanding their formal and informal support network*
• face-to-face contact is typically when problems arise ("when I screw up")	• face-to-face contact is based on what is needed to engage the youth and what meets their emotional needs—negotiating together
• addictions: encouraged to attend substance abuse programs, but using drugs and/or alcohol tied to punishment (being asked to leave programs or denied programs due to use)	• addictions: reducing harm, promoting safety, and offering resources; while destructive, recognizing alcohol and drugs can play a role in coping with trauma, so engaging the youth in coming up with alternative ways of coping
• reporting youth to police and probation officers when there are outstanding warrants and/or breaches	• negotiating with police, probation officers, and the youth as to how best to manage warrants and/or breaches
• attending school becomes condition of getting into or staying in programs (even beyond the legal expectation to attend school up to age sixteen)	• ensuring the basic and emotional needs of the youth are met, and walking the youth through the process of registering and attending school based on the level of readiness and ability to cope, rather than reinforcing a sense of failure (regardless of age)
• secure environment obtained for youth if they are a danger to themselves or others; typically imposed on the youth to reduce risk given there is no less intrusive option to keep youth safe	• secure environment obtained for youth if they are a danger to themselves or others; typically negotiated, but, on the harm reduction continuum, imposed if there is no less intrusive option to keep youth safe

*See Ungar (2004, 2005, 2006, 2015).

Criticisms of Harm Reduction

Not surprisingly, the harm reduction paradigm does not come without its critics. Again, there is little evidence of any critical literature with respect to harm reduction and working with high-risk children and youth, but the general philosophy has been denounced for condoning or even encouraging risky behaviour. This perspective is a socially destabilizing force, as the message implies that antisocial behaviour is acceptable. Harm reduction practice has been criticized for maintaining self-destructive behaviours, for not encouraging personal responsibility, for coddling people, and as a way of allowing service users to avoid dealing with their issues (Brocato & Wagner, 2003; Canadian Nursing Association, 2011; Maté, 2008; Taylor, 2010). Harm reduction is also seen as squandering resources on those who are undeserving and who make poor choices, leaving others to pay the costs (Maté, 2008).

While referring to addicts, Maté (2008) challenges such thinking:

> *If the guiding principle is that a person who makes their own bed ought to lie in it, we should immediately dismantle our health care system. Many of our diseases and conditions arise from self-chosen habits or circumstances that could have been prevented. The issue is not whether the addict would be better off without his habit—of course he would—but whether we are going to abandon him if he is unable to give it up....There is, for now, too much pain in their lives and too few internal and external resources available to them. In practicing harm reduction we do not give up on abstinence—on the contrary, we may hope to encourage that possibility by helping people feel better, bringing them into therapeutic relationships...offering them a sense of trust, removing judgment from our interactions with them, and giving them a sense of acceptance. (pp. 316–318)*

Another issue for detractors, which impacts service delivery within the child welfare system, is the perception that children or youth are being left in risky situations instead of removing them and preventing them from returning. It has already been articulated that coercive interventions are not effective, and that there are steps along the harm reduction continuum if the child or youth is a danger to themselves or others, and that risk surrounding us can never be eliminated altogether. As Lonne et al. (2009) and Munro (1999) point out, child protection systems have been strongly reacting to public pressures and are preoccupied with managing and trying to eliminate risk to the point that intervention may actually be doing more harm than good. A reduction in harm may or may not be sufficient for a client, but at least it's a starting point to building rapport, encouraging change, and supporting efficacy (Logan & Marlatt, 2010). After all, harm reduction is based on principles of "compassionate pragmatism rather than moralistic idealism" (Bigler, 2005, p. 79). In addition, Munro (1999) states, "[T]he simplistic view that children can be rescued from harm and live happily ever after needs to be replaced by an understanding that the work usually involves choosing between two undesirable options and hoping to pick the one that does the least damage" (p. 126).

Moving Past Resistance and Engaging Youth

To build a relationship, and to shift away from the punishment paradigm, takes time and patience and an understanding about these children and youth in relation to their life experiences and how they have been impacted. This has been important in developing strategies to engage with and work with high-risk youth and high-risk children (as discussed previously with respect to the position paper and the need to expand the harm reduction principles to this latter population). From a brain development, or "neuroscientific" perspective,[9] some light can be shed on the underlying reasons for the challenging behaviours presented by this population of children and youth, and their resistance to accepting help that would increase their well-being and safety.

Perry (2006) discusses how brain development is critically impacted by early trauma and neglect, resulting in abnormal organization and functioning of important neural systems in the brain. Therefore, in order for children to develop healthy functioning, psychologically and socially, they depend on healthy attachments modelled in early caregiver-child relationships (Howe, 2005; Kagan, 2004; Neufeld & Maté, 2004). It is not

---

9   The neurodevelopment or neuroscientific perspective is explained in detail in the readings of Dr. Bruce Perry (Perry, 2006, 2009; Perry & Szalavitz, 2006; Szalavitz & Perry, 2010), as well as in Solomon and Siegel (2003), Howe (2005, 2008, 2011), Kagan (2004), and Maté (1999, 2008).

surprising that youth exposed to violence, instability of early attachments, and caregiver neglect struggle with high-risk behaviours. This is a profoundly important insight when working with these young persons. Appreciating that unattached children and youth live in a world of heightened sensitivity due to fear and rejection, and that they are unable to self-regulate their emotions (Howe, 2005, 2008), becomes crucial insofar as how to approach them in order to build connections with any measure of success. These insights steer our assessments of needs and intervention strategies. Any repeated traumatic experiences (perceived or real) only serve to reinforce critically impacted brain development caused by early trauma and neglect, increasing fears that adults, and ultimately all others, are not to be trusted (Howe, 2005).

Control and punishment policies typically do not incorporate neuro-developmental knowledge (Smyth & Eaton-Erickson, 2009). Perry emphasizes that clinical interventions should help children and youth regulate their emotions and create safety first (Szalavitz & Perry, 2010; Perry, 2009). In fact, Perry (2006) states that "without an appreciation of how the brain is organized, and how it changes, therapeutic interventions are likely to be inefficient, or sadly ineffective" (p. 30). Fortunately, the brain is malleable during development and, once organized, it is still capable of being influenced, modified, and changed. Thus, the damage done by early trauma and neglect can be mitigated through the power of healthy relationships (Howe, 2005; Perry, 2009). As Howe (2008) points out, "If poor relationships are where emotionally things go wrong, then healthy relationships are where things can get put right" (p. 161). In short, the principals of neurodevelopment can improve child and youth care practice and shape policy (Perry, 2006).

Szalavitz and Perry (2010) also discuss the importance of interventions that bring children closer rather than reject them (such as the punishment-consequence-based "tough love" philosophy). A traditional approach would typically involve immediate intrusive intervention, placing a child/youth in a placement in which it is obvious they will not stay, demanding they follow rules and comply with expectations, or locking them up repeatedly (again, not unlike Sarah). The youth would have minimal input into the decisions being made, and it would appear to the youth they are being punished (Ungar, 2004). Consequently, they do not see their worker as an ally (Bishop, 2002), and their defiance toward authority is reinforced (Howe, 2008). They avoid any contact, thus making it difficult to engage in any kind of safety planning. Such intervention can cause the youth to relive trauma or remain in unsafe situations because they feel they have no control over their lives. And, given they have already experienced a lack of nurturing and have often been exposed to traumatic violence, "they are predisposed to being more impulsive, reactive and violent" (Perry, 1997, p. 131, as cited in Howe, 2008, p. 78).

For these youth, the world is viewed as threatening, unsafe, and frightening. They learn that the only person they can rely on to meet their needs are themselves. While there is a lot of insecurity, they need to survive. Therefore, they will take advantage of others and do what it takes to control their own destiny. Their experience leads them to believe that no one can be trusted (Howe, 2008; Kagan, 2004; Perry & Szalavitz, 2006). When their expectation is re-experiencing more of the same neglect, loss of control, loneliness, and pain (i.e., rejection and abandonment), it is understandable why they will not risk letting anyone into their world (Smyth & Eaton-Erickson, 2009). This strategic behaviour has been adapted and refined over many years, so by the time these children reach adolescence, they are very skilled at keeping people at a distance and creating chaos in an effort to take focus off of themselves.

The walls these children and youth have built around themselves can be very thick, even when they are only eleven, twelve, or thirteen years old. The goal for people working with high-risk children and youth is to find a way through or around these walls. Practitioners must challenge the way these children and youth see their world by inviting them into authentic, trusting relationships, and by demonstrating that there are people who genuinely want to help them and keep them safe (Smyth & Eaton-Erickson, 2009). However, this approach takes time and, unfortunately, caution and resistance expressed by youth is often labelled as oppositional rather than discerning. Constructive reframing of this survival strategy suggests that when they are approached by a stranger and told what to do, it is not simply about being oppositional but it is experienced as a threat to their control, autonomy, and, therefore, to their survival (Howe, 2008). Such stress can result in escalated conflicts with persons in authority, as noted by Howe (2008): "This weakened neurological linkage between thought and feeling, cognition and emotion, means that many abused and traumatized individuals have neither the language nor the emotional management skills to understand and handle themselves and others well at times of stress and anxiety. As a result, their interpersonal and relationship skills are often poor" (p. 89). As the high-risk children and youth have so much investment in the way they act, caregivers and workers cannot take the defensive behaviour personally. This is most often not random, impulsive behaviour but is a reaction to the way they perceive their personal safety, to their survival being threatened, and to avoid the risk of further rejection and abandonment. In fact, from a strength-based and resiliency perspective, these strategies (as limiting as they can be to growth and development) have served the youth (Ungar, 2006).

The challenges these youth very often face with attachment, trauma, and brain development speak, once again, to the need for finding non-traditional ways to engage and make connections. The harm reduction approach highlights anti-oppressive methods, reducing the need for high-risk children and youth to rely on survival and self-protection strategies. As has been demonstrated within the HRYI, defences drop when the interaction is noncoercive, empowering, and nonjudgmental, when children and youth are valued as being experts in their own lives, and when they are encouraged to have a say in decisions being made about their future.

According to caseworkers and services providers connected to the HRYI, the high-risk children, in particular, have proven difficult to engage. They have little fear about being out of the home, do not tend to recognize when they are in dangerous situations, and are vulnerable to being sexually exploited. They are angry, trust no one, and appear unable to make sense of their lives. If traditional approaches are ineffective in making connections and keeping them safe, then there is a responsibility to look at alternative ways to reach the youth and at least create the potential for safety. This requires new ways of thinking and taking risks that benefit the youth rather than system (Lonne et al., 2009; Madsen, 2007; Turnell & Edwards, 1999). (Refer to Table 6.1, comparing traditional approaches to harm reduction processes.) This requires a change in policy, as well as a message, and an acknowledgement, that traditional methods of intervention are not effective when working with high-risk populations. Indeed, the focus must be on building relationships, and these are best facilitated through a harm reduction approach.

Workers must be challenged to make face-to-face contact with these high-risk children a priority, rather than relying on traditional "case management-driven proceduralism" (Lonne et al., 2009, p. 8). Policies must change to reflect such a priority. Workers face high caseloads and administrative duties that can leave them feeling powerless and frustrated and disengaged from children and youth on their caseload, while also feeling unable to speak out and challenge the system (Ruch, 2010). This is simply not good enough if we are to create helping and supportive relationships with this population of children who are lost, traumatized, have little sense of safety, and who see the world as a dark and hostile place. Room must be made to allow caseworkers to spend time with the youth, not just to respond to crisis and mandated purposes but also to build a relationship and get to know each other informally as well. While this takes time, it can improve the outcomes for youth and help them be more open to receiving help and making changes in their lives. If the status quo is maintained, and harm reduction approaches continue to be resisted in the larger child welfare system, the poor outcomes for children who grow up in the system will be maintained as well (Lonne et al., 2009; Batmanghelidjh, 2006).

Conclusion

> *"Harm reduction is as much an attitude and way of being as it is a set of policies and methods."*
> —Gabor Maté, *In the Realm of Hungry Ghosts*, 2008

Part of my role as a social worker is a commitment to social justice, the right to self-determination consistent with that person's capacity, and the right to be protected from oppression and coercion (Canadian Association of Social Workers, 2005). These are certainly compatible with the principles of harm reduction, particularly in relation to empowering marginalized and vulnerable people (Bigler, 2005). In fact, Bigler (2005) goes on to write, "the marriage of social work as a professional discipline and harm reduction as a model to guide practice is a natural one, with the potential for a long and positive relationship" (p. 81). The author further states: "Social workers understand that many of today's problems require new and innovative thinking. Unfortunately, these insights are often gained on the frontline level where workers seem to apply harm reduction principles and strategies in their work almost intuitively because this model is so consistent with their core personal and professional beliefs" (2005, p. 80).

Indeed, social workers—and non-social workers practising in the child welfare system who are motivated by a sense of justice and are drawn to the human services field to make a difference in the lives of others—must take this intuitive work and, in their roles as planners and policy developers, create and advocate for policies, practices, and programs that empower individuals and promote social justice, while eliminating those that are ineffective, inappropriate, or harmful to those who, in particular, have been oppressed and marginalized (Bigler, 2005).

This is particularly true in the area of child protection, given the intense focus on risk management and traditional, punitive, and compliance-based practices that are ineffective in engaging, supporting, and working with high-risk children and youth, most of whom have experienced much loss and trauma in their short lives. It is not good enough to simply tinker with the current system, given the vulnerability to realign with old pressures that have shaped it up to now. The final option of radically altering the social context of child protection seems the only viable alternative (Munro, 1999). Accepting harm reduction as a preferable option to traditional approaches to intervention is overdue, and high-risk children and youth will remain disengaged, disconnected, and unsafe as long as we continue to debate rather than act. It is time that policies reflect the change in thinking and practice so that punishment-consequence perspectives are replaced by caring and connection. As Munro (2011) concluded, with respect to the child protection system in the United Kingdom, "[I]nstead of 'doing things right' (i.e., following procedures) the system needed to be focused on doing the right thing" (p. 6).

References

Baines, D. (2007). Anti-oppressive social work practice: Fighting for space, fighting for change. In D. Baines (Ed.), *Doing anti-oppressive practice: Building transformative politicized social work* (pp. 1–30). Black Point, NS: Fernwood Publishing.

Batmanghelidjh, C. (2006). *Shattered lives: Children who live with courage and dignity*. London, United Kingdom: Jessica Kingsley Publishers.

Bigler, M. O. (2005). Harm reduction as a practice and prevention model for social work. *The Journal of Baccalaureate Social Work, 10*(2), 69–86.

Bishop, A. (2002). *Becoming an ally: Breaking the cycle of oppression in people* (2nd ed.). Black Point, NS: Fernwood Publishing.

Blundo, R. (2001, May/June). Learning strengths-based practice: Challenging our personal and professional frames. *Families in Society, 296–302.*

Brendtro, L., Brokenleg, M., & Van Bockern, S. (1990). *Reclaiming youth at risk: Our hope for the future* (revised edition). Bloomington, IN: National Education Service.

Brendtro, L ., & du Toit, L. (2005). *Response ability pathways: Restoring bonds of respect.* Claremont, South Africa: Pretext Publishers.

Brendtro, L., Mitchell, M., & McCall, H. (2009). *Deep brain learning: Pathways to potential with challenging youth.* Albion, MI: Starr Commonwealth.

Brocato, J., & Wagner E. F. (2003). Harm reduction: A social work practice model and social justice agenda. *Health and Social Work, 28*(2), 117–125.

Brown, J. D., & Hannis, D. (2008). *Community development in Canada.* Toronto, ON: Pearson Education Canada.

Canadian Association of Social Workers. (2005). *Code of Ethics.* Retrieved from http://www.casw-acts.ca/en/what-social-work/casw-code-ethics/

Canadian Nursing Association. (2011). *Harm reduction and currently illegal drugs: Implications for nursing policy, practice, education and research* (discussion paper). Retrieved from http://www2.cna-aiic.ca/CNA/documents/

CBC News. (2011, September 30). Vancouver's Insite drug injection clinic will stay open. *CBC News.* Retrieved from http://www.cbc.ca/news/canada/british-columbia/story/2011/09/29/bc-insite-supreme-court-ruling-advancer

Child, Youth and Family Enhancement Act, RSA 2000, c C-12.

Collins, S. E., Seema, C. L., Logan, D. E., Samples, L. S., Somers, J. M., & Marlatt, G. A. (2012). Current status, historical highlights, and basic principles of harm reduction. In G. A. Marlatt, M. E. Larimer, & K. Witkiewitz (Eds.), *Harm reduction: Pragmatic strategies for managing high-risk behaviors* (2nd ed.) (pp. 3–35). New York, NY: The Guilford Press.

Duncan, D. F. (n.d.). A new direction: Harm reduction. *AddictionInfo: Alternatives to 12-Step Treatment.* Retrieved from http://www.addictioninfo.org/articles/226/1/A-New-Direction-Harm-Reduction/Page1.html

Elovich, R., & Cowing, M. (1993, October 21–23). Recovery readiness: Strategies that bring treatment to addicts where they are. Meeting of the National Harm Reduction Working Group (Location unknown).

French, J. (2016, March 20). Edmonton group pushing for city's first safe injection site. *Edmonton Journal.* Retrieved from http://edmontonjournal.com/news/local-news/edmonton-group-pushing-for-citys-first-safe-injection-site

Goldblatt, A. (2007). *Should we dance: A resource for effective partnering.* Based on discussions of the Partnership Dialogue, sponsored by Inner City Connections, Community Partnership Enhancement Fund, Edmonton, Alberta.

Howe, D. (2005). *Child abuse and neglect: Attachment, development and intervention.* New York, NY: Palgrave, McMillan.

Howe, D. (2008). *The emotionally intelligent social worker.* New York, NY: Palgrave, McMillan.

Howe, D. (2011). *Attachment across the lifecourse: A brief introduction.* New York, NY: Palgrave, McMillan.

Kagan, R. (2004). *Rebuilding attachments with traumatized children: Healing from losses, violence, abuse, and neglect.* Binghamton, NY: The Haworth Maltreatment & Trauma Press.

Kietltyka, M. (2015, October 19). Harm reduction "back on table" with Trudeau win. *Vancouver Metro.* Retrieved from http://www.metronews.ca/news/vancouver/2015/10/20/harm-reduction-back-on-table-with-trudeau-win.html

Levine, P. (1997). *Waking the tiger: Healing trauma.* Berkeley, CA: North Atlantic Books.

Levy, T. M., & Orlans, M. (1998). *Attachment, trauma and healing: Understanding and treating attachment disorder in children and families.* Washington, DC: CWLA Press.

Logan, D., & Marlatt, A. (2010). Harm reduction therapy: A practice-friendly review of research. *Journal of clinical psychology, 66*(2), 201–212. doi:10.1002/jclp.20669

Lonne, B., Parton, N., Thomson, J., & Harries, M. (2009). *Reforming child protection.* New York, NY: Routledge.

Luckock, B., & Lefevre, M. (Eds.). (2008). *Direct work: Social work with children and young people in care.* London, United Kingdom: British Association for Adopting & Fostering.

Lunn, S., & Zimonjic, P. (2016, March 16). Safe injection sites have potential to save lives, says Jane Philpott. *CBC News.* Retrieved from http://www.cbc.ca/news/politics/save-injection-sites-toronto-1.3491134

Madsen, W. C. (1999). *Collaborative therapy with multi-stressed families: From old problems to new futures.* New York, NY: Guilford Press.

Madsen, W. C. (2007). *Collaborative therapy with multi-stressed families: From old problems to new futures.* New York, NY: The Guilford Press.

Maté, G. (1999). *Scattered minds: A new look at the origins and healing of attention deficit disorder.* Toronto, ON: Vintage Canada.

Maté, G. (2008). *In the realm of hungry ghosts: Close encounters with addiction.* Toronto, ON: Alfred K. Knopf.

Munro, E. (1999). Protecting children in an anxious society. *Health, Risk & Society, 1*(1), 117–127.

Munro, E. (2011). *The Munro review of child protection: A child-centred system.* London, United Kingdom: Department for Education, the Stationary Office Limited. Retrieved from http://www.official-documents.gov.uk/document/cm80/8062/8062.pdf

Neufeld, G., & Maté, G. (2004). *Hold on to your kids: Why parents matter.* Toronto, ON: Alfred K. Knopf.

Perry, B. D. (1997). Incubated in Terror: Neurodevelopmental factors in the "cycle of violence." In J. Osofsky (Ed.), *Children in a violent society* (pp. 124–149). New York, NY: Guilford Press.

Perry, B. D. (2006). Applying principles of neurodevelopment to clinical work with maltreated and traumatized children. In N. Boyd Webb (Ed.), *Working with traumatized youth in child welfare* (pp. 27–52). New York, NY: The Guilford Press.

Perry, B. D. (2009). Examining child and maltreatment through a neurodevelopmental lens: Clinical application of the neurosequential model of therapeutics. *Journal of Loss and Trauma, 14,* 240–255.

Perry, B. D., & Szalavitz, M. (2006). *The boy who was raised as a dog and other stories from a child psychiatrist's notebook.* New York, NY: Basic Books.

Ruch, G. (2010). The contemporary context of relationship-based practice. In, G. Ruch, D. Turney, & A. Ward, (Eds.) *Relationship-based social work: Getting to the heart of practice* (pp. 13-28). London, UK: Jessica Kingsley Publishers.

Saleebey, D. (Ed.). (1997). *The strengths perspective in social work practice* (2nd ed.). New York, NY: Longman Publishers.

Smyth, P., & Eaton-Erickson, A. (2009). Making the connection: Strategies for working with high-risk youth. In S. McKay, D. Fuchs, & I. Brown (Eds.), *Passion for action in child and family services: Voices from the prairies* (pp. 119–142). Regina, SK: Canadian Plains Research Center.

Smyth, P., Eaton-Erickson, A., Slessor, J., & Pasma, R. (2005). *The word on the street: How youth view services aimed at them.* Edmonton High Risk Youth Task Force, Edmonton and Area Child and Family Services, Region 6 (Unpublished report).

Solomon, M., & Siegel, D. (2003). *Healing trauma: Attachment, mind, body, and brain.* New York, NY: W. W. Norton & Company, Inc.

Steering Committee, High Risk Youth Initiative, Edmonton and Area Child and Family Services, Region 6. (2007). *More words on the street: A follow-up report on how youth view services aimed at them* (Unpublished report).

Strega, S. (2007). Anti-oppressive practice in child welfare. In D. Baines (Ed.), *Doing anti-oppressive practice: Building transformative politicized social work.* Black Point, NS: Fernwood Publishing.

Strega, S., & Sohki Aski Esquao (Carrière, J.) (Eds.). (2009). *Walking this path together: Anti-racist and anti-oppressive child welfare practice.* Black Point, NS: Fernwood Publishing.

Szalavitz, M., & Perry, B. D. (2010). *Born for love: Why empathy is essential—and endangered.* New York, NY: William Morrow, Harper Collins.

Taylor, M. (2010). *Essentials of harm reduction* (Unpublished PowerPoint presentation). Edmonton, AB: Streetworks.

Turnell, A., & Edwards, S. (1999). *Signs of safety: A solution and safety oriented approach to child protection.* New York, NY: W. W. Norton & Company, Inc.

Ungar, M. (2004). *Nurturing hidden resilience in troubled youth.* Toronto, ON: University of Toronto Press.

Ungar, M. (2005). Delinquent or simply resilient: How "problem" behaviour can be a child's hidden path to resilience. *Voices for Children.* Retrieved from http://www.voicesforchildren.ca

Ungar, M. (2006). *Strengths-based counselling with at-risk youth*. Thousand Oaks, CA: Corwin Press.

Ungar, M. (2015). *Working with children and youth with complex needs: 20 skills that build resilience*. New York, NY: Routledge.

Valiante, G. (2015, November 15). Supervised injection sites: Quebec expects federal approval. *CBC News*. Retrieved from http://www.cbc.ca/news/canada/montreal/safe-injection-sites-supervised-trudeau-canada-government-quebec-1.3319725

Wharf, B. (Ed.). (2002). *Community work approaches to child welfare*. Peterborough, ON: Broadview Press.

Woo, A. (2015, October 20). Harm-reduction drug programs may get OK under new Liberal government. *Globe and Mail*. Retrieved from http://www.theglobeandmail.com/news/british-columbia/harm-reduction-drug-programs-may-get-ok-under-new-liberal-government/article26899895/

PART III

Research

CHAPTER 7

Prioritizing Children in Care with FASD: Why Prevalence Matters

Don Fuchs and Linda Burnside

Introduction

Fetal alcohol spectrum disorder (FASD) is a serious social and health issue for the child welfare, health care, and education sectors in North America, with significant social and economic costs (Fuchs et al., 2009). Current research suggests that the numbers of children with FASD (a preventable condition) are increasing, which reflects a major public health concern (Lange, Shield, Rehm, & Popova, 2013). There is considerable variation by region, jurisdiction, and availability of diagnostic resources. However, even with regional variability, the numbers of children with FASD are increasing, as are the related social and economic costs to Canadian society. Recent studies suggest that one-quarter to half of the children in care may have FASD, and, for Canada's Aboriginal people, it may be a significantly higher proportion (Badry, Pelech, & Norman, 2005; Goodman, 2007; Health Canada, 1998). With this increase, there is a great need to know more about the prevalence of children coming into and transitioning out of care (Lange et al., 2013).

Suggested Citation: Fuchs, D., & Burnside, L. (2016). Prioritizing children in care with FASD: Why prevalence matters. In H. Montgomery, D. Badry, D. Fuchs, & D. Kikulwe (Eds.), *Transforming Child Welfare: Interdisciplinary Practices, Field Education, and Research* (pp. 135–161). Regina, SK: University of Regina Press.

Children and youth with a diagnosis of FASD present in child welfare agencies with an array of complex and variable needs as a consequence of a range of neurodevelopmental disorders. The recognition that FASD is a contributing factor to the increasing social and economic costs is helping to advance research on this important issue. There is growing evidence that these costs are increasing (Popova, Lange, Burd, & Rehm, 2013). However, there is limited Canadian research that investigates the economic impact of FASD in the child welfare, health care, and education sectors (Fuchs, Burnside, Marchenski, & Mudry, 2005, 2007; Fuchs, Burnside, Marchenski, Mudry, & DeRiviere, 2008b).

This chapter will define what prevalence is and discuss why it is important to study the prevalence of children and youth with FASD in the care of the child welfare system. To illustrate the benefits of studying prevalence of children in care with FASD, this chapter presents the major findings of a tri-provincial study of the prevalence of FASD among children in care in Alberta, Manitoba, and Ontario. It will examine the implications of these findings for policy, programming, and training in the Prairie provinces. In addition, it will illustrate the importance of using administrative databases for FASD prevalence research. Finally, it identifies some important directions for further research using data gathered regularly and consistently from administrative databases for evidence-based approaches to the examination of the outcomes of prevention and intervention programs.

What Is Prevalence?

Prevalence refers to the rate of a condition (in this case, FASD) within a population, capturing both new and existing cases during a particular time period, across all age ranges (May & Gossage, 2001). Despite the growing body of literature on FASD as a condition that merits greater understanding and appropriate intervention by schools, health care systems, and social services, most of the professional literature acknowledges that the actual prevalence of FASD is still unknown. It is accepted that FASD is underdiagnosed around the world. The prevalence of FASD worldwide, estimated at 0.33 per 1,000 (Nesbit, Philpott, Jeffery, & Cahill, 2004) is viewed to be an underestimation.

Why Study Prevalence?

Increasingly, prenatal alcohol exposure is acknowledged as a leading cause of preventable developmental disabilities that have serious detrimental outcomes for individuals throughout their lifespans (Health Canada, 2000). FASD results in a wide range of impairments on a continuum from mild to severe, with considerable variation in its impact on individual functioning as a result of the complex teratogenic effects of alcohol (Abel & Hannigan, 1995; Barr & Streissguth, 2001; Coles, 1994; Guerri, 1998; Thomas, Warren, & Hewitt, 2010; Uban et al., 2011).

A high proportion of children in care are likely to have been prenatally exposed to alcohol due to the frequency that parental substance abuse brings families to the attention of child welfare systems, estimated to be from 40 to 80 per cent of families involved with child welfare (Besinger, Garland, Litrownik, & Landsverk, 1999; Curtis & McCullough, 1993; Dore, Doris, & Wright, 1995; McNichol & Tash, 2001; Semidei, Radel, & Nolan, 2001; Young, Gardner, & Dennis, 1998). Spohr, Willms, and Steinhausen (1994) report that numerous alcohol-exposed children are not raised by their biological mothers and often spend their lives growing up in child welfare care. Besharov (1994) estimated that between 65 and 80 per cent of children with FASD were raised by someone other than their birth parents. Therefore, determining the number of children with FASD who are in care, and learning about the needs of these children, as well as their families and caregivers, ought to be a paramount concern of child welfare jurisdictions all over Canada.

In addition, there is great need to establish accurate estimates of the number of alcohol-exposed children in care, including those with diagnoses and those awaiting assessment, to develop effective policies and programs that are aimed at reducing the social and economic impact of the growing numbers of children coming into care with FASD.

Why Is Measuring FASD Prevalence of Children and Youth in Care Important?

Unsurprisingly, the nature of alcohol addiction and adverse life circumstances associated with maternal binge drinking (and therefore the occurrence of FASD) are also strongly associated with children needing child welfare intervention. However, the actual prevalence of FASD-affected children in care in Canada is currently unknown. To date, Fuchs et al. (2005) conducted the only study that captured case-level data about the number of children in care with FASD. This study found that 11 per cent of children in care in Canada had been diagnosed with FASD (following stringent criteria for how diagnoses had been made), and a further 6 per cent were in the process of being assessed for FASD (defined as "suspected FASD").

To add to the challenge, Aronson (2000) observes that information confirming maternal alcohol use in pregnancy (which is necessary for an FASD diagnosis) is often not well documented for children in care, particularly those who have become permanent wards and where no contact occurs between the biological family and the child welfare authority to make inquiries about the child's prenatal history. Additionally, Nanson (2003) and Chasnoff (2011) each caution that it can be difficult to isolate FASD as the cause of many issues facing children in care, given the extensive literature on the effects of out-of-home placement on children and the consequences of adverse life experiences, such as abuse, that may have precipitated the child's admission to care.

In Canada, it is well documented that Aboriginal children are significantly overrepresented in child-in-care populations across the country, especially in the western Canadian provinces (Blackstock, 2007; Blackstock, Prakash, Loxley, & Wien, 2005; Blackstock, Trocmé, & Bennett, 2004). They come into care more frequently partly as a result of the presence of multiple risk factors, such as poverty, oppression, compromised parenting abilities as a result of the impact of the residential school system, and other social, economic, and cultural variables (Fluke, Chabot, Fallon, MacLaurin, & Blackstock, 2010). Therefore, there is an increased likelihood that Aboriginal children in care will have been exposed to alcohol during pregnancy because of these social and environmental factors that contribute to high-risk substance use (Fluke et al., 2010). Given the very real possibility of cultural overrepresentation, the active case ascertainment approach to prevalence estimation can perpetuate the perception that FASD is an Aboriginal issue or a child welfare issue alone, and that children in the overall population are not affected.

While these erroneous assumptions about the prevalence of FASD and the demographics of alcohol-affected children in care must be challenged, it is still important to focus prevalence measurement strategies on high-risk populations such as children in care. Knowing how many children in care are affected by FASD allows child welfare authorities to determine:

- how many children in care need specialized supports;
- what kinds of services they may need to assist them in coping with their disability (for example, according to age and stage of development);
- how many foster parents with knowledge of FASD are required to deliver specialized care;
- how many staff need training in FASD and available services;
- what kinds of agency policies are needed to guide specialized services;
- what kind of funding is required to meet the needs of the population;
- what additional resources are needed due to the size of the population in need; and
- what strategies are required to ensure that children suspected of having FASD actually receive assessments and medical diagnoses.

Estimating Prevalence of FASD

There are three main approaches to measuring the prevalence of FASD: passive surveillance studies, clinic-based studies, and active case/population-based studies. Varying methodologies make it difficult to compare prevalence rates across studies or even determine which study might approximate the actual occurrence of fetal alcohol syndrome (FAS) (May & Gossage, 2001; Ospina & Dennett, 2013).

Passive Surveillance Studies
This approach utilizes existing records in a particular geographic area or with a particular population. Typical records reviewed under this approach include birth certificates, registries of children with disabilities or birth defects, and medical records from diagnostic clinics or hospitals. Assuming that a common definition and diagnostic approach to the confirmation of FASD can be established, this approach can be advantageous, as it accesses existing records, making data collection relatively inexpensive and time-efficient. A frequently cited report by Burd, Martsolf, and

Klug (1996) of birth records in North Dakota identified a prevalence rate of
FAS as 1.1—2.0 per 1,000.

Clinic-Based Studies

Clinic-based studies are conducted in health care facilities (e.g., hospitals, prenatal clinics) and focus on collecting information about mothers' prenatal health and maternal behaviours (e.g., substance use during pregnancy) using screening questionnaires. As the most common method of estimating FASD prevalence, a key advantage of this approach is the opportunity to gather detailed information from women throughout their pregnancies and/or after birth in a standardized way. It is also possible to identify control or comparison groups to analyze differences between jurisdictions or within a clinic's own population.

A longitudinal study by Sampson et al. (1997), based on clinical data gathered in Seattle, Washington (Streissguth et al., 1991; Streissguth et al., 1994), estimated the rate of FAS and alcohol-related neurodevelopment disorder (ARND) combined to be 9.1 per 1,000, a figure that is often quoted but still considered to be a conservative rate.

Active Case Ascertainment Methods

Active case ascertainment methods focus on small, specific populations or groups (often those who are considered at high risk for prenatal alcohol exposure) and assess for characteristics of FASD. This approach tends to yield the highest number of cases and rates of FASD for a particular population. High-risk groups are often those most affected by poverty and adverse life circumstances, often resulting in a higher representation of Indigenous populations in FASD prevalence reports. However, active case ascertainment approaches are time- and labour-intensive and, as a result, can be costly. An active case ascertainment study by Robinson, Conry, and Conry (1987) examined every child living in an isolated British Columbia reserve (102 children) and found a prevalence rate of 190 per 1,000.

———

Each approach to estimating prevalence discussed above has its strengths and limitations, which must be understood to appreciate the interpretation of reported prevalence rates. To date, no universally accepted methodology has been identified that would help to determine the actual rate of

FASD. May et al. (2009) found that the highest rates of FASD were reported by clinic-based and active case ascertainment approaches, especially the latter, which has tended to study high-risk populations. The high prevalence rates associated with a particular high-risk population can also be misinterpreted to mean that FASD is specific to that group, often denoted by cultural origin or geographic location, rather than recognizing the characteristics of poverty, oppression, and adverse life experiences as the main factors that contribute to high alcohol use and the increased risk of FASD.

Challenges

There are numerous challenges in measuring the prevalence of FASD. Estimating prevalence is compromised by inconsistent diagnostic criteria, definitions, and diagnostic assessment processes used across studies. Such inconsistencies affect which cases are included or excluded in a given prevalence query (Pacey, 2009). Estimating the prevalence of other types of FASD—such as partial FAS (pFAS), fetal alcohol effects (FAE), or ARND—is even more challenging due to greater variability in defining diagnostic symptoms compared to the diagnosis of FAS. As noted by May et al. (2009), "although key diagnostic features of FAS are generally well established, the specific assessment techniques and statistical measurements used to make the definitive diagnosis of FAS and other FASD are still debated" (p. 176). Additionally, FASD is often underdiagnosed due to researchers/clinicians' inability to confirm maternal substance misuse, one of the key criteria in diagnosis (Aase, 1994; Thomas et al., 2010).

Clarren and Lutke (2008) assert that estimating the true prevalence of FAS/FASD is more complicated than for most other health conditions. Evidence of brain damage is often not evident until the child has reached the school-age years, making early diagnosis difficult, and there are fewer diagnostic resources available for youth and adults, often leaving their functional challenges undiagnosed. Other barriers in determining the occurrence of FASD include reluctance to diagnose due to the stigmatization of the condition (Nesbit et al., 2004), a lack of training in making FASD diagnoses (Clarke, Tough, Hicks, & Clarren, 2005), belief that the condition can be treated effectively without the FASD label (Gardner, 1997), and the lack of diagnostic services in general (Elliott, Payne, Morris, Haan, & Bower, 2008).

The occurrence of FASD in children and youth is also associated with various environmental and social circumstances. Studies tracking drinking patterns note that young women of child-bearing age are drinking more alcohol than in previous generations, and are particularly engaging in binge drinking (Autti-Ramo et al., 2005; Goransson, Magnusson, Bergman, Rydberg, & Heilig, 2003; Health Canada, 2000). However, other studies have found that at least half of all pregnancies are unplanned (Elliott et al., 2008; Nanson, 1997), increasing the risk of alcohol use prior to awareness of pregnancy.

Numerous studies around the world have found that high-risk substance use occurs more frequently in groups that are marginalized and oppressed in society due to racism, poverty, isolation, and social discrimination (Abel, 1995; Larkby & Day, 1997; May, 2011). As it pertains to Canada in particular, Philp (2000) speculates, "there are pockets in the country—destitute neighbourhoods and remote alcohol-plagued native reserves—where estimates peg the incidence at nearly one in five" (p. A16). Reported statistics of FASD in First Nations populations include 10.9 per 1,000 in Yukon and British Columbia (Sandor et al., 1981), 190 per 1,000 on a British Columbia reserve (Robinson et al., 1987), and a 7.2 per 1,000 incidence rate in Thompson, Manitoba (Williams, Odaibo, & McGee, 1999). Prevalence statistics stemming from First Nations communities have perpetuated the myth that FASD is an Aboriginal problem (Van Bibber, 1993).

Generally, only children with the most severe expression of FASD (FAS and pFAS) are the focus of most population-wide prevalence studies, as these are the conditions that are easiest to diagnose with some degree of consistency in diagnostic criteria. May et al. (2009) found that some children who had been diagnosed as a result of broad, thorough screening processes did not present with the severe physical, behavioural, and intellectual deficits that most often lead to detection and referral for assessment.

One of the biggest challenges in establishing prevalence rates of FASD is ensuring that cases of FASD are detected and diagnosed (Warren & Foudin, 2001). The Canadian Guidelines for the Diagnosis of FASD (Chudley, Conry, Loock, Rosales, & LeBlanc, 2005) propose diagnostic criteria for the determination of FAS, pFAS, and ARND. The absence of any other diagnosis and evidence of prenatal alcohol exposure are foundational criteria required for the diagnosis of any FASD. FAS is characterized by a) a distinct dysmorphology, including facial features such as a flattened area between the upper lip and nose, thin upper lip, epicanthal folds, and a narrow palpebral fissure (the length of space between the margins of the eyelids); b) a constellation of central nervous system effects; and c) evidence of significant pre- or post-natal growth impairment (less than the tenth percentile). Partial FAS is characterized by the same criteria, with fewer facial anomalies and no growth impairment. ARND is diagnosed on the basis of three central nervous system effects, without the facial dysmorphology or growth impairment. With alcohol-related birth defects (ARBD) covering an even broader range of alcohol-effect conditions than ARND, the Canadian guidelines suggest using the diagnosis of ARBD with caution due to the challenges in defining clear diagnostic criteria.

While classic FAS is indicated by distinctive facial features, these features may not be noticeable until after the child has reached the age of two years (Larkby & Day, 1997) and may be less evident once the child has reached adolescence (Clarren & Lutke, 2008; Larkby & Day, 1997; Streissguth et al., 1991). Additionally, there may be variations in facial features that have cultural origins, with no relationship whatsoever to prenatal alcohol exposure, which complicates accurate diagnosis of FAS (Aase, 1994). Further, according to Chudley (2008), since children with ARND do not have facial dysmorphology, they are the least visible and therefore the least likely to be identified as having a condition related to prenatal alcohol exposure. Many children and youth receive a wide range of different diagnoses, obscuring the prevalence of FASD (Chudley, 2008; Thomas et al., 2010). This has a profound impact on determining the prevalence of FASD, as Chudley (2008) estimates that "for every child with full blown FAS, there are three or four who have ARND" (p. 721). Conversely, Pacey (2009) cautions that ARND may be subject to overdiagnosis because the effects of ARND are not as specific as FAS.

Diagnosis of FASD in the Tri-Provincial Study:
Alberta, Manitoba, and Ontario

In 2013, there were twenty-one FASD assessment and diagnostic clinics in Alberta, conducting more than four hundred diagnostic assessments annually of children, youth, and adults (although not all clinics have the capacity to assess adults). Clinics may be overseen by community agencies or by government programs and are located in all regions of the province: Calgary (three), Edmonton (five), Lakeland (one), MacKenzie (two), Northeast (one), Northwest (two), Northwest Central (one), East Central (one), Southeast (two), South (two), and Central (one).

Manitoba continues to have only one FASD diagnostic clinic in the province. The Manitoba FASD Centre was established in 2009, a descendent of the former Clinic for Alcohol & Drug Exposed Children (CADEC) that had existed since 1999. The new clinic expanded its services to include assessments of youth and plans to incorporate assessments of adults in the future. Physicians and other health care professionals, child welfare practitioners, school personnel, and other community professionals can make referrals. There are eleven FASD diagnostic coordinators in five health regions throughout the province that assist with coordinating assessments for children and youth in either Winnipeg or Thompson (where the Manitoba FASD Centre also conducts diagnostic assessments).

In 2013, twelve diagnostic clinics operated in Ontario, with at least one clinic in the regions of Kingston, London, Peel, and Sudbury. The Durham region has two clinics and Toronto has six. The Peel region clinic only provides assessments for children between the ages of 0–6 years. Diagnostic clinics network through the Fetal Alcohol Spectrum Disorder Ontario Network of Expertise (FASD ONE).

Although there is consistency across Canadian diagnostic clinics in following the criteria set out by the Canadian guidelines, access to diagnostic services and waitlists affect the process of diagnosis and therefore the number of affected individuals who have been diagnosed. Clarren, Lutke, and Sherbuck (2011) estimated that a seventeenfold increase in FASD diagnostic capacity across Canada is needed to meet the need for diagnostic services.

Overview of the Tri-Provincial FASD Prevalence Project (2010–2014) Methods and Results Study Methodology

The Tri-Province FASD Prevalence Project builds on the research into FASD affecting children in care that was conducted in Manitoba under the Prairie Child Welfare Consortium by the authors, beginning in 2004. The high proportion of children with FASD in child welfare care has been described in Manitoba (Fuchs et al., 2005): 11 per cent of 5,500 children in care had been diagnosed with FASD and a further 6 per cent were in the process of being tested for the condition, considered to be an underestimation of the actual prevalence within this population due to the stringent criteria used to confirm diagnosis in this study. Additional Manitoba studies have examined the needs and experiences of children and youth with FASD, describing their life trajectories in care (Fuchs et al., 2007), their need for placement stability in adolescence when foster homes tend to break down as behavioural challenges increase (Fuchs, Burnside, Marchenski, & Mudry, 2008a), the higher costs incurred to provide for their care (Fuchs et al., 2008b), their higher utilization and costs of health care services and prescription medications (Fuchs et al., 2009), and their needs as they reach adulthood and are transitioning from child welfare care (Fuchs, Burnside, Reinink, & Marchenski, 2010).

The three-year Tri-Province FASD Prevalence Project began in 2011. The aims of the project were to estimate the prevalence of FASD affecting children in the care of mandated child welfare authorities in Alberta, Manitoba, and Ontario and to set the stage for future measures of FASD prevalence affecting children in care at a national level.

Specific research into the prevalence of FASD affecting the child-in-care population is at a beginning stage. As noted above, one approach to measuring prevalence is known as active case ascertainment, which focuses on a small, specific population considered to be at high risk for FASD, such as children in care. This approach yields the highest prevalence rates of FASD but risks the assumption that FASD is a serious issue for only the high-risk group, not the general population.

The Fuchs et al. (2005) study of children in care with disabilities (including FASD) used an active case ascertainment methodology to gather data that involved research associates going to each child welfare agency office throughout Manitoba and reviewing paper files of children in care with disabilities as identified by case managers, according to standardized definitions. At the conclusion of the study, Manitoba's Child and Family Services Information System (CFSIS) was updated to include data fields that allowed for the entry of data pertaining to children's disabilities. These data fields did not exist in the CFSIS prior to the study, so there was no electronic way to capture information about FASD or other types of disability.

Eventually, the data collected from the 2005 study was entered into the new windows and data fields developed in the CFSIS, providing the opportunity for ongoing updating and new entries to better track information about FASD and other medical conditions affecting children in care. The majority of the authors' subsequent FASD studies made use of this new information in the database to identify samples of children with FASD and examine their service trajectories while in care (Fuchs et al., 2007), placement patterns in adolescence (Fuchs et al., 2008a), the cost of providing for their care (Fuchs et al., 2008b), and the utilization and costs of health care services and educational experiences (Fuchs et al., 2009). The utilization study was a partnership with the Manitoba Centre for Health Policy that linked data from the CFSIS with data from other provincial services held in a centralized data repository.

The (years or ongoing) tri-provincial study also used an active case ascertainment approach, in that it focused on the high-risk group of children in care and actively sought out information on those children in care who had been affected by FASD. However, unlike the 2005 study, the Tri-Province FASD Prevalence Project did not have the staff or time resources to travel to every child welfare agency in each province to gather data from paper files. Further, with advances in technology, the availability of electronic databases provides an advantageous avenue for data collection. Consequently, the (years or ongoing) study explored the inclusion of the passive surveillance approach to data collection through the use of existing administrative data collection systems for the child welfare authorities in each participating province.

Increasingly, child welfare administrative databases are utilized for research, outcome measurement, and quality assurance (Drake & Jonson-Reid, 1999). In particular, maintaining detailed and accurate administrative databases in child welfare is promoted as a means to enhance practice (North Carolina Division of Social Services and the Family and Children's Resource Program, 2004), ensure oversight (United States General Accounting Office, 2004), and strengthen accountability (National Technical Assistance and Evaluation Center, 2010). The advantages of using existing administrative databases include time efficiencies and lower study costs, as data is collected during the conduct of normal service provision (Brownell & Jutte, 2013); larger datasets in order to track trends longitudinally (Fallon et al., 2010); and there is the possibility of linking child welfare databases to other public services such as health care (O'Donnell et al., 2010).

However, it is important to note that there are also important limitations in utilizing existing administrative child welfare databases. Administrative databases are not necessarily adaptable to research questions, as they are set up for other purposes and may not capture variables of research interest or importance (Brownell & Jutte, 2013; Drake & Jonson-Reid, 1999; Trocmé et al., 2009). Waldfogel (2000) asserts that child welfare databases only tell part of the story, as the insights gained from children involved with child welfare are limited if we do not also understand the experience of children in the general population in terms of the factors that lead to maltreatment and how children fare after they have received child welfare services. Finally, although each province and territory in Canada maintains administrative data concerning the children and families receiving child welfare services, differences in definitions, terminology, and measurement strategies create challenges for comparisons of data across jurisdictions (Fallon et al., 2010).

As noted above, the present study utilized an active case ascertainment approach (focusing on a population at high risk for FASD). In order to explore the feasibility of utilizing existing child welfare databases to achieve time and cost efficiencies, as well as ensure inclusion of all children in care in each jurisdiction (that is, features of the passive surveillance approach to prevalence estimation), consultations were held with government representatives and other practitioners in each province. Both Alberta and Manitoba have provincial child welfare databases that are utilized (with some limitations) by all child and family services agencies. Ontario does not yet have a centralized provincial child-welfare database, although individual children's aid societies use administrative databases and submit various reports and data to the provincial government, but not including consistent information with regard to FASD.

After the consultation process to determine the feasibility of utilizing the status of provincial child welfare databases was complete, researchers worked with provincial representatives to develop a "Data Dictionary" to identify child welfare terminology and definitions for the relevant variables for this study, the capacity of these variables to be tracked through child welfare databases, and the universal availability of data for each variable throughout the respective databases. The study variables included:

- definition of a "child in care";
- gender;
- date of birth;
- cultural status;
- authority of service;
- legal status;
- primary reason for admission to care;
- placement type;
- diagnosed FASD;
- suspected FASD.

Neither of the existing provincial child welfare databases in Alberta or Manitoba had current FASD data entered into the system for extraction at the start of the study, necessitating the engagement of case managers in updating their respective databases (or providing data through a standardized data collection instrument in communities where the centralized database was not employed). The reader may want to consult the final report of the Tri-Province FASD Prevalence Project (Fuchs & Burnside, 2014) for more details on the methods used to collect valid and reliable data in three different provincial jurisdictions.

Although the specific data collection approaches varied in each province, it is important to note here that engaging front-line staff from each jurisdiction in providing updated information about children in care with FASD on their caseloads was advantageous to ensuring the reliability of study data. It helped to ensure that all social workers across the three provinces used the same definition of diagnosed or suspected FASD to enhance the opportunity to compare prevalence rates across the three jurisdictions. The definitions utilized were consistent with the definitions used in the Fuchs et al. (2005) study.

- A child who has been *diagnosed* with FASD is one who has received the diagnosis by a recognized practitioner qualified to make FASD diagnoses.
- A child who is *suspected* of having FASD is one who is currently awaiting assessment by a qualified practitioner, or has been assessed but a formal diagnosis is not possible due to the inability to confirm maternal substance use during pregnancy.

The (years) tri-provincial prevalence study examined the prevalence of FASD affecting children in care in Alberta, Manitoba, and Ontario, using a common definition of "diagnosed" and "suspected" FASD. The research also endeavoured to follow a similar methodology in each province by utilizing existing centralized databases to take advantage of demographic data collected by the jurisdiction on a routine basis. For Alberta and Manitoba, which each have centralized child welfare information systems used by all agencies, the methodology mainly involved asking case managers to update the client records for each client who had diagnosed or suspected FASD according to the study definitions. For Ontario, which does not yet have a centralized child welfare database, the Ontario Looking After Children (ONLAC) process provided a common data submission process that involved all Ontario children's aid societies. It could be sampled, accompanied by asking case managers to also complete a brief supplement for those children who had diagnosed or suspected FASD as per the study definitions.

What Did the Study Find?

The methodology employed in the study aimed to identify common variables (for example, children in care, their ages, legal status, and placement status) and common definitions (such as the definitions of diagnosed and suspected FASD) to estimate the prevalence of FASD affecting children in care in Alberta, Manitoba, and Ontario. Although the methodology in Alberta and Manitoba utilized existing, electronic child welfare databases, the approaches in all three provinces relied on the data submitted by social workers regarding children in care on their caseloads that had been diagnosed with FASD or met the definition of a child with suspected FASD. Despite the efforts to create a common foundation for the estimation of the prevalence of FASD in all three provinces, comparisons in prevalence rates across the provinces are not possible due to different contextual factors in each province that affect both child welfare service delivery and FASD diagnostic capacity and processes.

In Alberta, the total number of children ages 0–17 who met the study criteria as per the Intervention Services Information System (ISIS) query conducted on August 1, 2013, was 6,767. About 52 per cent of the group was male, and there were more preschool (36.6 per cent) and school-aged (34.4 per cent) children identified than adolescents (28.7 per cent). About 59 per cent of those who met the coded-in study criteria had also been coded as having Aboriginal ancestry.

An analysis of updated ISIS data identified 699 children in care in Alberta out of the total population of 6,767 children who met the study criteria of the ten Child and Family Service regions (CFSA regions were coded as having diagnosed or suspected FASD, according to the definitions framed in this study)—a prevalence rate of 10.3 per cent. A previous study by Alberta Health and Wellness (2000) estimated that up to 29 per cent of children in care were diagnosed with FASD, although definitions and measurements strategies differed from this study. A review of the data used for this study with administrators and regional directors revealed that some regions struggled with updating data in the ISIS due to the migration process from one data system to the other and due to workload challenges during the time frame of this study. Consequently, a complete record of children with FASD receiving services from CFSA regions during the study period was not entered into the ISIS, resulting in an underestimation of the prevalence of FASD.

In Manitoba, the sample of 8,323 children in care ages 0–21 was determined to have 1,021 children and youth who met the study criteria during the study period recorded in the Child and Family Services Information System (CFSIS)—a prevalence rate of 12.3 per cent. As noted above, the sample was based on twenty-two of the twenty-five agencies in the province, as well as the centralized intake agency in Manitoba. The prevalence rate is lower than the 17 per cent identified in the 2005 study of children in care with disabilities (Fuchs et al., 2005). Although both studies used the same definitions of diagnosed and suspected FASD, the first study collected data through a manual review of paper files conducted by research associates, while the present study relied on updates to the centralized information system by case managers. Workload and competing priorities were identified as barriers that prevented social workers from providing updated data for this study. However, it should be noted that the real numbers of children who met the study criteria have increased: 963 children and youth ages 0–21 were identified in 2005, compared to the 1,021 children with FASD identified in the (years) tri-provincial study.

In Ontario, considerable methodological challenges were encountered in attempting to estimate the prevalence of FASD affecting children in care. Without a centralized database or a common approach to data collection across agencies, the strategy was to utilize a uniform process through the Ontario Looking After Children process. A sample of all children requiring an annual assessment review (AAR) between December 1, 2012, and March 31, 2013, presented a more standardized method of data collection. Unfortunately, data was received from a small number of children's aid societies, which greatly restricts the generalizability of the findings. In addition, it is presumed that AARs were not submitted for all children who may have required one, as there is no centralized method to determine how many AARs were expected during the study time frame. Further, as data was received from agencies, there was evidence of some confusion about whether AARs needed to be submitted to the study for those children who did not have FASD, and efforts were made to solicit these missing AARs in retrospect, which may have contributed to the number missing.

Despite these challenges, information was received for 533 children and youth aged 0–21 through this methodology, with fifty-six identified as having diagnosed or suspected FASD according to the study definitions. Consequently, it is difficult to compare the prevalence results from this study to other FASD data from ONLAC studies, as the definitions utilized were not the same. In the (years) tri-provincial study, the prevalence rate was 10.5 per cent. This prevalence rate is also considered to be an underestimation due to many limitations. First, less than one-third of the Ontario children's aid societies participated in the study. Those who did participate volunteered to do so, and therefore did not represent a cross-section of agencies based on size or geographic location. The sample only included children who had attained (or were in the process of attaining) permanent legal status and had been in care for at least one full year, eliminating from the study children from other legal statuses or who had been in care for shorter durations. Finally, it was not possible to determine how many children from the thirteen participating agencies should have had an AAR completed during the study time frame, whether children who had FASD or those who did not (which would confirm the size of the sample with better accuracy in order to establish a prevalence rate with more confidence).

Challenges and Limitations of the (Years) Tri-Provincial Study

Despite the efforts to achieve some uniformity in study methodology across jurisdictions, it is important to refrain from comparisons across the three participating provinces with regard to the prevalence rates derived in this study. Each province has slightly different child welfare legislation, definitions, and practices, which affect which children come to the attention of a given child welfare system, which children are admitted to care, and how their legal and placement histories unfold while in care. Further, although Canadian diagnostic clinics are committed to following the Canadian Guidelines for the Diagnosis of FASD (Chudley et al., 2005; Clarren et al., 2011), it was not possible in this study to assess how the diagnosis of FASD was made for any individual child.

The results of this study are also limited by the availability of relevant data. Diagnostic capacity is not available in some regions of the participating provinces, which may have limited the number of children who would ordinarily be eligible for screening and assessed for having FASD in their communities. Existing child welfare information systems did not have complete FASD data already recorded, necessitating the co-operation of front-line case managers to update their records for those children who had diagnosed or suspected FASD. Finding time to complete additional data entries or submit supplemental paperwork on top of work that is often crisis-oriented can be a formidable challenge, which may have limited the number of children's files that were updated. Finally, the active use of database information systems by social work practitioners is a relatively new phenomenon in casework, which may contribute to reluctance or deprioritization in using the database directly. Consequently, the prevalence rates identified in this study are considered to be an underestimation.

Despite these limitations, the prevalence rates found in this study confirm the necessity for child welfare authorities to plan for the specialized needs of children in care with FASD. Even at the underestimation of 10 per cent of any group of children in care, there are a significant number of children who need skilled caregivers and resources to assist them in their journey to adulthood and aging out of care. While these results point to the responsibilities facing child welfare agencies and funders to plan for the needs of children in care with FASD, the importance of transitioning young people with FASD to adult services after discharge from care must also be emphasized.

Implications for Policy, Programming, and Training in the Prairie Provinces

FASD remains a significant concern affecting children in care. More work is necessary to develop baseline prevalence rates to better understand the full extent of the condition as it affects children in care. The (years) tri-provincial study furthered this work by testing the feasibility of utilizing child welfare information databases to measure the prevalence of FASD in three provinces in Canada. It also demonstrated the importance of using common definitions across jurisdictions to achieve as much consistency in the results as possible.

The efforts of our study to estimate the prevalence of FASD affecting children in care in three provinces point to both the opportunities and challenges in using child welfare information systems as a source of data. The importance of this form of research using administrative databases was identified in the recommendations of the inquiry into the death of Phoenix Sinclair. Justice Ted Hughes (2013), in writing his recommendations in the inquiry report, stated on the subject of administrative databases:

> *Protection of children requires a reliable and up-to-date information management system that tracks not only children in care, but all children receiving protection services; provides comprehensive information about individuals in the system; and allows access to relevant data from other government systems. A new information system will improve the efficiency and effectiveness of workers by providing accurate information, and will reduce administrative workload. It will also allow the Authorities to compile statistical information, which can be used to measure outcomes for children and families. (p. 41–42)*

Administrative databases are current priorities of child welfare systems in Canada and elsewhere. They provide an important resource for understanding the population receiving child welfare services and their needs in order to inform policy and service delivery. Drake and Jonson-Reid (1999) state, "[E]valuating policy changes requires descriptive data and longitudinal tracking of individual service utilization patterns, both of which are major strengths of administrative data. In child welfare, we therefore have a close alignment between the ability to access administrative data and the utility of that data" (p. 313).

However, in order to make appropriate use of information about service users and children in care who are involved with the child welfare system, social workers must see value in maintaining updated, accurate records. Drake and Jonson-Reid (1999) note that "a database is only a collection of inputs from field workers and is therefore dependent upon their conscientiousness. This may be difficult to achieve when workers see no real value in the input work that they do. In this way, administrators and researchers are dependent upon buy-ins from practitioners" (p. 314). Kufeldt, Simard, and Vachon (2000) echo this message in relation to the Ontario Looking After Children data, asserting that management needs to convey to staff exactly how the aggregate results derived from the database are used to generate positive change for children and families. In particular, supervisors are mentioned as key supports to their staff in ensuring that information is collected and updated to facilitate case planning at both the individual and group level.

The results of the (years) tri-provincial study set the stage for future replication following similar methodology, which was also one of the project's goals. With the insights gained through this research, it is recommended that each of the three provinces repeat the study in the near future, attending to some of the barriers that encumbered caseworkers in this iteration of the study to ensure more complete data entry. Variations of the study could also be conducted with samples in each province, complemented by a detailed physical file examination to add credibility to the results derived from the administrative database analysis.

Given that common definitions of FASD are critical in obtaining diagnoses and measuring prevalence consistently, it is also recommended that the administrative databases in each province incorporate the definitions of diagnosed and suspected FASD utilized in this study. This will help to ensure that the data entered in the future will be based on more uniform understandings of what constitutes diagnosed or suspected FASD. Additionally, as Ontario draws nearer to the establishment of its first centralized database, attention should be paid to ensuring that FASD is a variable that can be captured in the information system, again based on the definitions utilized in this study.

Finally, establishing a national perspective on the extent of FASD affecting children in care is an important component of understanding the broader population-level prevalence of FASD and neonatal exposure to alcohol. Prevalence rates must include both the population-level impact of FASD, as well as the higher prevalence rate affecting populations at risk. Both ends of the continuum contribute to researcher, practitioner, and policy-maker understandings of the occurrence of FASD and its impact in different aspects of Canadian society. The responsibilities of child welfare authorities to care for one group who is at higher risk of FASD (that is, children in care) compels child welfare systems to determine the prevalence rates of children in care with FASD and plan/advocate accordingly to meet their specialized needs.

Conclusion

Determining the prevalence of FASD in Canada is a challenge of critical importance (Healthy Child Manitoba, 2012). The costs borne by the individual affected by FASD, by the family members of that individual, and by society at large are significant (Popova, Stade, Lange, Bekmuradov, & Rehm, 2012). In 2013, the Canadian federal government committed to funding a national prevalence project studying elementary school children to investigate the prevalence of FASD at a population level. National prevalence rates will aid in our understanding of the impact of FASD in Canadian society.

While population-level prevalence studies are important, the research is already clear that some groups are at higher risk of FASD than others (Abel, 1995; May, 2011; Philp, 2000). Children in child welfare care, as one of those high-risk populations (Steinhausen, Willms, & Spohr, 1993; Besharov, 1994), place additional demands on child welfare authorities and their ministerial funders that support and oversee their care needs. The transformation of the child welfare system requires accurate estimations of the prevalence of FASD affecting children and youth in care. These data on prevalence are necessary to ensure that child welfare authorities are prepared to meet the needs of children and youth in care (and transitioning out of care) with FASD with appropriate resources, programs, supports to caregivers, training to staff, and policies that facilitate their development into adulthood and emancipation from care.

References

Aase, J. (1994). Clinical recognition of FAS: Difficulties of detection and diagnosis. *Alcohol, Health and Research World, 18*(1), 5–9.

Abel, E. L. (1995). An update on incidence of FAS: FAS is not an equal opportunity birth defect. *Neurotoxicology and Teratology, 17,* 437–443.

Abel, E. L., & Hannigan, J. H. (1995). Maternal risk factors in fetal alcohol syndrome: Provocative and permissive influences. *Neurotoxicology and Teratology, 17,* 445–462.

Alberta Health and Wellness. (2000, January). Health is everyone's business: A snapshot of some of Alberta's wellness initiatives. Edmonton, AB. Retrieved from http://www.health.alberta.ca/documents/Alberta-Wellness-Initiatives-2000.pdf

Aronson, J. E. (2000). Alcohol-related disorders and children adopted from abroad. In R. P. Barth, M. Freundlich, & D. Brodzinsky (Eds.), *Adoption and prenatal alcohol and drug exposure* (pp. 147–169). Washington, DC: Child Welfare League of America.

Autti-Ramo, I., Fagerlund, A., Ervalahti, N., Loimu, L., Korkman, M., & Hoyme, H. E. (2005). Fetal alcohol spectrum disorders in Finland: Clinical delineation of 77 older children and adolescents. *American Journal of Medical Genetics, 140A,* 137–143.

Badry, D., Pelech, W., & Norman, D. (2005). Fetal alcohol spectrum disorder practice standards evaluation project: Final report (Centre for Social Work Research & Development). Calgary, AB: University of Calgary.

Barr, H. M., & Streissguth, A. P. (2001). Identifying maternal self-reported alcohol use associated with fetal alcohol spectrum disorders. *Alcoholism: Clinical and Experimental Research, 25*(2), 283–287.

Besharov, D. (1994). *When drug addicts have children: Rethinking child welfare's response.* Washington, DC: Child Welfare League of America.

Besinger, B. A., Garland, A. F., Litrownik, A. J., & Landsverk, J. A. (1999). Caregiver substance abuse among maltreated children placed in out-of-home care. *Child Welfare, 78*(2), 221–239.

Blackstock, C. (2007). Aboriginal children, families and communities. In the Child Welfare League of Canada (Ed.), *The welfare of Canadian children: It's our business. A collection of resource papers for a healthy future for Canadian children and families* (pp. 83–95). Ottawa, ON: Child Welfare League of Canada.

Blackstock, C., Prakash, T., Loxley, J., & Wien, F. (2005). *Wen:de: We are coming to the light of day.* Ottawa, ON: First Nations Child and Family Caring Society.

Blackstock, C., Trocmé, N., & Bennett, M. (2004). Child maltreatment investigations among Aboriginal and non-Aboriginal families in Canada. *Violence against Women, 10*(8), 901–916.

Brownell, M. D., & Jutte, D. P. (2013). Administrative data linkage as a tool for child maltreatment research. *Child Abuse & Neglect, 37,* 120–124.

Burd, L., Martsolf, J. T., & Klug, M. (1996). Children with fetal alcohol syndrome in North Dakota: A case control study utilizing birth certificate data. *Addiction Biology, 1,* 181–189.

Chasnoff, I. J. (2011). Children prenatally exposed to alcohol: Comments on Astley, O'Brien and Mattson, and O'Connor. *Encyclopedia on Early Childhood Development.* Retrieved from http://www.child-encyclopedia.com/documents/ChasnoffANGxp1.pdf

Chudley, A. E. (2008). Fetal alcohol spectrum disorder: Counting the invisible—Mission impossible? *Archives of Disease in Childhood, 93,* 721–722.

Chudley, A. E., Conry, J. L., Loock, C., Rosales, T., & LeBlanc, N. (2005). Fetal alcohol spectrum disorder: Canadian guidelines for diagnosis. *Canadian Medical Association Journal, 172*(5 Suppl), S2–S21.

Clarke, M., Tough, S. C., Hicks, M., & Clarren, S. (2005). Approaches of Canadian providers to the diagnosis of fetal alcohol spectrum disorders. *Journal of FAS International, 3,* e3.

Clarren, S., & Lutke, J. (2008). Building clinical capacity for fetal alcohol spectrum disorder diagnoses in western and northern Canada. *Canadian Journal of Clinical Pharmocology, 15,* 223–237.

Clarren, S. K., Lutke, J., & Sherbuck, M. (2011). The Canadian guidelines and the interdisciplinary clinical capacity of Canada to diagnose fetal alcohol spectrum disorder. *Journal of Population Therapeutics and Clinical Pharmacology, 18*(3), 494–499.

Coles, C. (1994). Critical periods for prenatal alcohol exposure: Evidence from animal and human studies. *Alcohol Health & Research World, 18,* 22–29.

Curtis, P. A., & McCullough, C. (1993). The impact of alcohol and other drugs on the child welfare system. *Child Welfare, 72*(6), 533–542.

Dore, M., Doris, J. M., & Wright, P. (1995). Identifying substance abuse in maltreating families: A child welfare challenge. *Child Abuse & Neglect, 19,* 531–543.

Drake, B., & Jonson-Reid, M. (1999). Some thoughts on the increasing use of administrative data in child maltreatment research. *Child Maltreatment, 4*(4), 308–315.

Elliott, E. J., Payne, J., Morris, A., Haan, E., & Bower, C. (2008). Fetal alcohol syndrome: A prospective national surveillance study. *Archives of Disease in Childhood, 93,* 732–737.

Fallon, B., Trocmé, N., Fluke, J., MacLaurin, B., Tonmyr, L., & Yuan, Y. (2010). Methodological challenges in measuring child maltreatment. *Child Abuse & Neglect, 34,* 70–79.

Fluke, J. D., Chabot, M., Fallon, B., MacLaurin, B., & Blackstock, C. (2010). Placement decisions and disparities among Aboriginal groups: An application of the decision making ecology through multi-level analysis. *Child Abuse & Neglect, 34,* 57–69.

Fuchs, D., & Burnside, L. (2014, March). *Study on the prevalence of FASD in Canadian child welfare settings: Final report.* Retrieved from http://

fasdchildwelfare.ca/sites/default/files/research/Ap26%20O3b%20%20 PHAC%20FASD%20Prevalence%20Study%20Report%20FINAL%202014.pdf

Fuchs, D., Burnside, L., DeRiviere, L., Brownell, M., Marchenski, S., Mudry, A., & Dahl, M. (2009). *The economic impact of children in care with FASD and parental alcohol issues. Phase II: Costs and service utilization of health care, special education, and child care.* Toronto, ON: Centre of Excellence for Child Welfare.

Fuchs, D., Burnside, L., Marchenski, S., & Mudry, A. (2005). *Children with disabilities receiving services from child welfare agencies in Manitoba.* Retrieved from http://www.cecw-cepb.ca/sites/default/files/publications/en/ DisabilitiesManitobaFinal.pdf

Fuchs, D., Burnside, L., Marchenski, S., & Mudry, A. (2007). *Children with FASD involved with the Manitoba child welfare system.* Retrieved from http://www. cecw-cepb.ca/sites/default/files/publications/en/FASD_Final_Report.pdf

Fuchs, D., Burnside, L., Marchenski, S., & Mudry, A. (2008a). *Transition out-of-care: Issues for youth with FASD.* Retrieved from http://www.cecw-cepb.ca/

Fuchs, D., Burnside, L., Marchenski, S., Mudry, A., & DeRiviere, L. (2008b). *Economic impact of children in care with FASD, phase 1: The cost of children in care with FASD in Manitoba.* Retrieved from http://www.cecw-cepb.ca/ publications/590

Fuchs, D., Burnside, L., Reinink, A., & Marchenski, S. (2010). *Bound by the clock: The voices of Manitoba youth in care with FASD.* Retrieved from http://www. cecw-cepb.ca/publications/2138

Gardner, J. D. (1997). Fetal alcohol syndrome: Recognition and intervention. *American Journal of Maternal and Child Nursing, 22*(6), 318–322.

Goodman, D. (2007). *Evaluating FASD prevalence in an urban children's aid society.* Toronto, ON: Children's Aid Society of Toronto.

Goransson, M., Magnusson, A., Bergman, H., Rydberg, U., & Heilig, M. (2003). Fetus at risk: Prevalence of alcohol consumption during pregnancy estimated with a simple screening method in Swedish antenatal clinics. *Addiction, 98,* 1513–1520.

Guerri, C. (1998). Neuroanatomical and neurophysiological mechanisms involved in central nervous system dysfunctions induced by prenatal alcohol exposure. *Alcoholism: Clinical and Experimental Research, 22,* 304–312.

Health Canada. (1998). *Literature review—National Native Alcohol and Drug Abuse Program (NNADAP): Evaluation strategies in Aboriginal substance abuse programs.* Ottawa, ON: Author.

Health Canada. (2000). *Best practices: Fetal alcohol syndrome/fetal alcohol effects and the effects of other substance use during pregnancy. The Canadian Child and Adolescent Psychiatry Review, 12*(3), 77–80.

Healthy Child Manitoba. (2012). *Position paper: Developing a national prevalence plan for FASD in Canada.* Retrieved from http://www.canfasd.ca/wp-content/ uploads/2013/02/FASD_Prevalence_Position_Paper_final_March2012.pdf

Hughes, T. (2013). The legacy of Phoenix Sinclair: Achieving the best for all our children. Retrieved from http://www.phoenixsinclairinquiry.ca/rulings/ps_volume1.pdf

Kufeldt, K., Simard, M., & Vachon, J. (2000). *Looking after children in Canada: Final report.* Retrieved from http://www.unb.ca/fredericton/arts/centres/mmfc/_resources/pdfs/team2000a.pdf

Lange, S., Shield, K., Rehm, J., & Popova, S. (2013). Prevalence of fetal alcohol spectrum disorders in child care settings: A meta-analysis. *Pediatrics, 132*(4), 980–995.

Larkby, C., & Day, N. (1997). The effects of prenatal alcohol exposure. *Alcohol Health and Research World, 21*(3), 192–197.

May, P. A. (2011). Researching the prevalence and characteristics of FASD in international settings. In E. P. Riley, S. Clarren, J. Weinberg, & E. Jonsson (Eds.), *Fetal alcohol spectrum disorder: Management and policy perspectives of FASD* (pp. 17–25). Weinheim, Germany: Wiley-VCH Verlag & Co.

May, P. A., & Gossage, J. P. (2001). Estimating the prevalence of fetal alcohol syndrome: A summary. *Alcohol Research & Health, 25*(3), 159–167.

May, P. A., Gossage, J. P., Kalberg, W. O., Robinson, L. K., Buckley, D., Manning, M., & Hoyme, H. E. (2009). Prevalence and epidemiologic characteristics of FASD from various research methods with an emphasis on recent in-school studies. *Developmental Disabilities Research Reviews, 15*, 176–192.

McNichol, T., & Tash, C. (2001). Parental substance abuse and the development of children in family foster care. *Child Welfare, 80*(2), 239–256.

Nanson, J. (1997). Binge drinking during pregnancy: Who are the women at risk? *Canadian Medical Association Journal, 156*(6), 807–808.

Nanson, J. (2003). Fetal alcohol syndrome/effect and its impact on psychosocial child development: Comments on Sandra and Joseph Jacobson and Susan Astley. *Encyclopedia of Early Childhood Development, 1*–9. Retrieved from http://www.child-encyclopedia.com/documents/NansonANGxp.pdf

National Technical Assistance and Evaluation Center. (2010). *A closer look: Accountability.* Retrieved from https://www.childwelfare.gov/pubs/acloserlook/accountability/accountability.pdf

Nesbit, W., Philpott, D., Jeffery, G., & Cahill, M. (2004). Fetal alcohol syndrome in First Nations communities: Educational facets. In W. C. Nesbit (Ed.), *Cultural diversity and education: Interface issues* (pp. 139–172). St. John's, NL: Memorial University.

North Carolina Division of Social Services and the Family and Children's Resource Program. (2004, July). Using data to enhance child welfare practice. *Children's Services Practice Notes, 9*(4). Retrieved from http://www.practicenotes.org/vol9_no4.htm

O'Donnell, M., Nassar, N., Leonard, H. M., Mathews, R. P., Patterson, Y. G., & Stanley, F. J. (2010). The use of cross-jurisdictional population data to investigate health indicators of child maltreatment. *The Medical Journal of Australia, 193*(3), 142–145.

Ospina, M., & Dennett, L. (2013). *Systematic review on the prevalence of fetal alcohol spectrum disorders*. Edmonton, AB: Institute of Health Economics.

Pacey, M. (2009). *Fetal alcohol syndrome & fetal alcohol spectrum disorder among Aboriginal peoples: A review of prevalence*. Prince George, BC: National Collaborating Centre for Aboriginal Health.

Philp, M. (2000, November 5). The promise of hope. *Globe and Mail*, pp. A16–A17.

Popova, S., Lange, S., Burd, L., & Rehm, J. (2013). Canadian children and youth in care: The cost of fetal alcohol spectrum disorder. *Journal of Research and Practice in Children's Services, 43*(1), 83–96.

Popova, S., Stade, B., Lange, S., Bekmuradov, D., & Rehm, J. (2012). *Economic impact of fetal alcohol syndrome (FAS) and fetal alcohol spectrum disorders (FASD): A systematic literature review*. Ottawa, ON: Centre for Addiction and Mental Health. Retrieved from http://knowledgex.camh.net/reports/Documents/economic_impact_fas_litreview12.pdf

Robinson, G. C., Conry, J. L., & Conry, R. F. (1987). Clinical profile and prevalence of fetal alcohol syndrome in an isolated community in British Columbia. *Canadian Medical Association Journal, 137*, 203–207.

Sampson, P. D., Streissguth, A. P., Bookstein, F. L., Little, R. E., Clarren, S. K., Dehaene, P.,...Graham, Jr., J. M. (1997). Incidence of fetal alcohol syndrome and prevalence of alcohol-related neurodevelopmental disorder. *Teratology, 56*, 317–326.

Sandor, S., Smith, D., MacLeod, P., Tredwell, S., Wood, B., & Newman, D. E. (1981). Intrinsic defects in the fetal alcohol syndrome: Studies of 76 cases from BC and the Yukon. *Neurobehavioural Toxicology and Teratology, 3*, 145–152.

Semidei, J., Radel, L. F., & Nolan, C. (2001). Substance abuse and child welfare: Clear linkages and promising responses. *Child Welfare, 80*(2), 109–128.

Spohr, H. L., Willms, J., & Steinhausen, H. C. (1994). The fetal alcohol syndrome in adolescence. *Acta Paediatrica, 404*, 19–26.

Steinhausen, H. C., Willms, J., & Spohr, H. L. (1993). Long-term psychopathological and cognitive outcomes of children with fetal alcohol syndrome. *Journal of the American Academy of Child and Adolescent Psychiatry, 32*(5), 990–995.

Streissguth, A. P., Aase, J. M., Clarren, S., Randels, S., LaDue, R. A., & Smith, D. F. (1991). Fetal alcohol syndrome in adolescents and adults. *Journal of the American Medical Association, 265*, 1961–1967.

Streissguth, A. P., Sampson, P. D., Olson, H. C., Bookstein, F. L., Barr, H. M., Scott, M.,...Mirsky, A. F. (1994). Maternal drinking during pregnancy: Attention and short-term memory in 14-year-old offspring. *Alcoholism: Clinical and Experimental Research, 18*, 202–218.

Thomas, J. D., Warren, K. R., & Hewitt, B. G. (2010). Fetal alcohol spectrum disorders: From research to policy. *Alcohol Research & Health, 33*, 118–126.

Trocmé, N., MacLaurin, B., Fallon, B., Shlonsky, A., Mulcahy, M., & Esposito, T. (2009). *National child welfare outcomes indicator matrix (NOM)*. Montreal, QC: McGill University—Centre for Research on Children and Families.

Uban, K. A., Bodnar, T., Butts, K., Sliwowska, J. H., Comeau, W., & Weinberg, J. (2011). Direct and indirect mechanisms of alcohol teratogenesis: Implications for understanding alterations in brain and behavior in FASD. In E. P. Riley, S. Clarren, J. Weinberg, & E. Jonsson (Eds.), *Fetal alcohol spectrum disorder: Management and policy perspectives of FASD* (pp. 73–126). Weinheim, Germany: Wiley-VCH Verlag & Co.

United States General Accounting Office. (2004). *Child and family services reviews: Better use of data and improved guidance could enhance Health and Human Services' oversight of state performance.* Retrieved from http://www.gao.gov/cgi-bin/getrpt?GAO-04-333

Van Bibber, M. (1993). *FAS amongst Aboriginal communities in Canada: A review of existing epidemiological research and current preventative and intervention approaches — An information legacy of the Royal Commission on Aboriginal Peoples.* Ottawa, ON: Libraxus, CD-ROM.

Waldfogel, J. (2000). Child welfare research: How adequate are the data? *Children and Youth Services Review, 22,* 705–741.

Warren, K. R., & Foudin, L. L. (2001). Alcohol-related birth defects — The past, present, and future. *Alcohol Research & Health, 25*(3), 153–158.

Williams, R. J., Odaibo, F. S., & McGee, J. M. (1999). Incidence of fetal alcohol syndrome in northeastern Manitoba. *Canadian Journal of Public Health, 90*(3), 192–194.

Young, N., Gardner, S., & Dennis, K. (1998). *Responding to alcohol and other problems in child welfare.* Washington, DC: CWLA Press.

CHAPTER 8

A Community-Based Research Approach to Developing an HIV Education and Training Module for Child and Family Service Workers in Ontario

Saara Greene, Doe O'Brien-Teengs, Gary Dumbrill, Allyson Ion, Kerrigan Beaver, Megan Porter, and Marisol Desbiens

Introduction

Grounded in community-based research (CBR) principles and an anti-oppression framework, the Positive Parenting Pilot Project (P4) aimed to develop, implement, and evaluate an HIV education and training module that would result in the provision of enhanced support for families affected by HIV and who are at risk of, or involved with, child protection services. A key aspect of our project is to strengthen the ability of child and family service agencies in Ontario to provide anti-oppressive services to families affected by HIV from diverse communities by increasing the capacity of social workers who are currently or who aim to work with children and families to work more effectively with parents living with HIV. Of

Suggested Citation: Greene, S., O'Brien-Teengs, D., Dumbrill, G., Ion, A., Beaver, K., Porter, M., & Desbiens, M. (2016). A community-based research approach to developing an HIV education and training module for child and family service workers in Ontario. In H. Montgomery, D. Badry, D. Fuchs, & D. Kikulwe (Eds.), *Transforming Child Welfare: Interdisciplinary Practices, Field Education, and Research* (pp. 163–185). Regina, SK: University of Regina Press.

equal importance is our goal to develop increased communication within and between the child welfare and HIV service sectors in order to address family needs at societal and structural levels. P4 is an exciting opportunity to forge new collaborative relationships between researchers and service providers from the HIV and child welfare sectors, as well as parents living with HIV from diverse communities. The goal of this project is to provide a framework for developing an anti-oppressive education and training module related to the multiple layers of oppression that are experienced by families living with HIV, including HIV-related stigma and discrimination, racism, sexism, violence, and poverty.

This chapter focuses on our CBR and capacity-building activities and the formative phase of P4, which resulted in establishing and supporting our research team and the subsequent development of the education and training module. This chapter will begin with an overview of the impact of HIV on women and mothers living in Canada, with specific attention to the intersection of HIV and child welfare and the current state of HIV education and training within the social work curriculum. Following this introduction, the chapter will outline our process of developing our research team, with specific attention paid to addressing the capacity-building needs of all team members and the research process that has since guided the development of the HIV education and training module for child and family service workers. We conclude with a presentation of what is included in the training module and our reflections on the importance of working with community stakeholders in developing and providing HIV-specific education to social work students and professionals. The relevance of this work to supporting families affected by HIV within the child welfare system in the Prairies will also be discussed.

Women and HIV in Canada

Since the beginning of the AIDS epidemic, the number of positive HIV tests reported in women in Canada has steadily increased from 11.7 per cent prior to 1999 to 27.8 per cent in 2006 (Public Health Agency of Canada, 2010). Since HIV reporting began in Canada in 1985, a total of 80,469 cases have been reported, of which 24.6 per cent, or approximately 19,700 cases, are known to be female (Public Health Agency of Canada, 2015), with the majority residing in Ontario (Remis, Swantee, Schiedel, Merid, &

Liu, 2006). In Ontario, since the late 1980s, African, Caribbean, and black (ACB) women have increasingly been represented in new HIV diagnoses and accounted for 55 per cent of overall HIV diagnoses from 1980 to 2004 (Liu & Remis, 2007). The proportion of HIV diagnoses among females from countries where HIV is "endemic," which includes ACB women who may be newcomers to Canada, increased steadily, reaching 50–60 per cent after 2001 (Remis & Liu, 2013).

Indigenous women are also overrepresented in the Canadian HIV epidemic, most notably in British Columbia and Saskatchewan. In 2014, Indigenous peoples comprised 11 per cent to 17 per cent of all new HIV diagnoses in British Columbia while comprising approximately 5 per cent of the total provincial population (BC Centre for Disease Control, 2014). Indigenous women under the age of thirty accounted for 93 per cent of the reported female cases of HIV in 2009 (Saskatchewan Ministry of Health, 2010). Importantly, across Canada in 2011, the HIV infection rate was 3.5 times higher among Indigenous people in Canada compared to other ethnicities (Public Health Agency of Canada, 2014).

Our focus on women living with HIV is important to our research and training in the child welfare sector due to the high degree of child welfare involvement in the lives of ACB and Indigenous mothers living with HIV in Canada (Greene, O'Brien-Teengs, Whitebird, & Ion, 2014).

Intersection between Women and Mothers
living with HIV and Child Welfare

Our collective experiences and concerns as service users, practitioners, and researchers in both the HIV and child welfare arena in Ontario inform our commitment to addressing the challenges that mothers living with HIV face in the context of child welfare. While the broader systemic issues that bring mothers living with HIV to the attention of child welfare are not dissimilar to other mothers in Canada (such as poverty and domestic violence), these challenges are exacerbated for ACB and Indigenous mothers living with HIV. These challenges are characterized by their experiences of navigating a web of shelter, housing, immigration, and health and social care systems, while at the same confronting HIV-related stigma within these health and social contexts (Greene et al., 2010; Greene et al., 2014). The stigma confronting mothers living with HIV is not surprising in light of the fact that many people living with HIV around the globe continue to experience HIV-related stigma and discrimination (Alonzo & Reynolds, 1995; Mahajan et al., 2008; Sandelowski, Lambe, & Barroso, 2004). In Canada, HIV-related stigma is exacerbated for Indigenous women, women born outside of Canada, ACB women, and women with lower educational levels in a range of clinical and social care settings (Greene et al., 2010; Greene et al., 2015; Logie, James, Tharao, & Loutfy, 2011; Pooyak & Gomez, 2009; Wagner et al., 2010); this includes circumstances where they share their intentions to become pregnant and to become a mother (Greene et al., 2014; Wagner et al., 2010).

In the child welfare context, past experiences of HIV-related stigma and fears related to the stigmatizing impact of disclosure on their relationship with their social workers are of particular concern to mothers living with HIV (Greene et al., 2010; Greene et al., 2015; Sandelowski & Barroso, 2003). Studies have shown that women view themselves as vulnerable targets of social service agencies simply because of their HIV status (Gilbert, 1999; Greene et al., 2014). The vulnerability of women is due, in part, to the continued presence of HIV-related stigma and the limited amount of research on the interface between people living with HIV and child welfare services. Published studies regarding the intersection of HIV and child welfare date back to the mid-1990s and focus on guardianship arrangements and separation of mother and child prior to HIV disease progression (Blanche et al., 1996; Forehand et al., 1998; Rotheram-Borus, Draimin, Reid, & Murphy, 1997). Yet recent research suggests that the focus should turn to other issues that are more relevant to mothers living with HIV in Canada as a result of the development and success of antiretroviral therapy, undetectable viral loads, and vertical transmission rates of less than 1 per cent in Canada. Consequently, pregnancy and motherhood for women living with HIV has been normalized among some health care providers and women themselves (Chen, Phillips, Kanouse, Collins, & Miu, 2001; Cooper et al., 2002; Forbes et al., 2012; Loutfy et al., 2009). It is important to note, however, that there continues to be barriers to accessing services, including limited transportation, caregiving responsibilities, employment, drug coverage, housing instability, immigration, HIV-related stigma and discrimination, and relationships with multiple providers in multiple locations (Logie, James, Tharao, & Loutfy, 2013; Melchoir et al., 2001; Wood & Tobias, 2004). The current climate of the criminalization of HIV nondisclosure may also complicate women's access to and interaction with health and social services, including HIV testing and HIV care services. Hence, women who are at risk for HIV are also at risk for unplanned pregnancies, which may also increase rates of pregnancy among women living with HIV (St. Lawrence, Snodgrass, Robertson, & Baird-Thomas, 2008). This may result in HIV testing during pregnancy for women who access prenatal care. However, for women who face barriers to care prior to and during pregnancy, there is the potential for HIV diagnosis at the time of birth (Greene et al., in press). These barriers are exacerbated for Positive Aboriginal Women (PAW) in Ontario, Saskatchewan, and British Columbia who have a history of child welfare involvement for reasons not connected to HIV (Greene et al., 2014). However, as our research has shown, mothers living with HIV from across Ontario and Canada are concerned about the possibility of losing their children to child welfare as a result of the multiple consequences of HIV-related stigma and discrimination (Hackl, Somlai, Kelly, & Kalichman, 1997; Greene et al., 2014; Greene et al., in press).

The interaction between people living with HIV and child welfare agencies has received the attention of HIV/AIDS service organizations, including the Teresa Group and the Ontario Aboriginal HIV/AIDS Strategy, also referred to as Oahas. The Teresa Group is an HIV/AIDS service organization that provides services to families and children affected by HIV in the Greater Toronto Area, many of whom are from ACB communities. For example, approximately 25 per cent of families receiving services at the Teresa Group have current or historical involvement with the child welfare system. Research has also shown that although there are multiple reasons for child welfare involvement of parents living with HIV, in some cases, the HIV status of the parent(s) became known after the family became involved with the child welfare agency for other child protection concerns. The disclosure of HIV status led to stigmatizing and discriminatory responses toward parents living with HIV by child welfare workers due to misconceptions and/or misinformation about HIV (Greene et al., 2014).

The lack of attention paid to the intersection of people living with HIV and child welfare and the impact of HIV-related stigma on mothers living with HIV is of equal concern for PAW,[1] particularly in Saskatchewan and

---

1   The acronym "PAW" was coined by Kecia Larkin: "For many Aboriginal or
    Indigenous women, the mother bear and bear paws are powerful cultural...

Manitoba where rates of HIV infection among Indigenous women have
been on the rise (Canadian Aboriginal AIDS Network, 2016a, 2016b). In
2014, Saskatchewan had the highest rate of new HIV diagnosis (per 100,000
population) at 10.8 (the national rate was 5.8 per 100,000) (Public Health
Agency of Canada, 2015). There is also continued overrepresentation of HIV
among Indigenous people in Manitoba, which represent 16.7 per cent of the
population in Manitoba; 38 per cent of new patients in the Manitoba HIV program in 2010 identified as Indigenous (Canadian Aboriginal AIDS Network,
2016b). The disproportionate number of Indigenous families involved with
the child welfare system throughout the country is of particular concern in
light of the history of colonization, assimilation, and child welfare policies
that have failed to recognize Indigenous practices within Canada (Pooyak
& Gomez, 2009; Trocmé, Knoke, & Blackstock, 2004). Although there is no
historical data that speaks to PAW experiences and interactions with the
child welfare system, recent research highlights the presence of HIV-related
stigma and discrimination by child welfare staff in Ontario, and a lack of
knowledge and sensitivity about HIV to provide culturally appropriate care
to PAW mothers (Greene et al., 2014). Given the impact of HIV on Indigenous
families in British Columbia, Saskatchewan, and Manitoba, coupled with
the disproportionate numbers of Indigenous families represented in child
welfare more broadly, there is a significant need for HIV education and
training among social workers who are currently, or who are considering, a
career in child welfare. Circling back to our research team's collective commitment to addressing these challenges, we agree that it is time to address
the absence of HIV content within the Canadian social work education and
training landscape. What follows is our community-based HIV research and
training development process and our recommendations for the future of
HIV education and training within child welfare and beyond.

HIV and Social Work Education

In 2000, the Social Work Manifesto on HIV and AIDS highlighted the importance of social work's contribution to the fight against the HIV epidemic as

---

...symbols of women-centred strength. When consulted, an elder highlighted the
following qualities of the female bear: she is family-oriented, aware of her surroundings, and knowledgeable about the healing properties of nature. These are
qualities that PAW strive to realize in their own lives" (Peltier et al., 2013, p. 87).

a result of its "commitment to social justice, an ability to work in a range of health and social care services, as well as a psychological perspective on people and their issues" (Bywater & Jones, 2007, p. 93). Since that time, the HIV epidemic has continued to expand and shift in terms of the epidemiology of the disease, inequalities in the ways in which treatment is accessed and/or available to people living with HIV globally, and efforts to increase prevention and reduce stigma. In places where treatment, care, and support are more readily accessible, such as in the United Kingdom, the United States, and Canada, for example, the dominant issues have changed from loss and grief to a focus on survival and living with HIV (Strug, Grube, & Beckerman, 2002), which implies an urgent need to attend to social, racial, and economic justice (Bowen, 2013), and ongoing attention to the prevention, treatment, and advocacy of people living with HIV (Rowen & Shears, 2011). Part of meeting these needs involves addressing the ongoing concern and impact of HIV-related stigma and discrimination, since these factors often intersect with other forms of discrimination, including but not limited to sexuality, gender, race and ethnicity, and class and poverty (Parker & Aggleton, 2003). Consequently, we agree with Sogren, Jones, Nathaniel, and Cameron-Padmore (2012) that there is a need to reconfigure social work education in order to ensure that practice is effective in bringing about the requisite social transformation and attitudinal change to reduce stigma and discrimination, to support people living with HIV, and to engender a renewed respect and value for life and living.

This is a tall order given the current invisibility of HIV content in social work education. Although there has and continues to be a strong rationale for the inclusion of HIV education in the social work curriculum, this is not necessarily reflected in social work education programs. As asserted by Natale, Biswas, Urada, and Cheyett (2010), "Despite the tremendous need for social workers imparted with HIV/AIDS knowledge and action skills, the topic appears marginalised in the social work curriculum...HIV/AIDS is often a 'boutique topic' in social work education—a topic worthy of an elective course or at best brief mention in a required course" (p. 42).

Although there is no data available on the representation of HIV-related content in bachelor of social work (B.S.W.) and master of social work (M.S.W.) programs in Canada (where our project took place), discussions with colleagues across the country suggest that HIV and AIDS often only emerge as social justice and practice issues in passing, or in courses that are taught by instructors who have research, practice, or lived experience in the area. Drawing on social work education and HIV research in the United States, Bowen (2013) has observed shifts in both the availability and focus of HIV-related content in the social work curriculum. Bowen (2013) notes that in the first decade of the epidemic there appeared to be a limited amount of HIV/AIDS content in the social work curriculum, with an expansion of HIV content in the following second and third decades. However, based on our review of the literature on the interface between HIV and social work education, it has been observed that in recent years HIV educational content in both B.S.W. and M.S.W. programs is at best marginal (Natale et al., 2010), and, at worst, electives on HIV are disappearing altogether (Rowen & Shears, 2011). While it is unclear why HIV is rarely integrated into the social work curriculum, our research demonstrates the need to address misinformation about HIV to social work students. People living with HIV are members of populations that have been traditionally served by social workers, suggesting that, regardless of their areas of practice, many social workers are very likely to encounter people living with and/or affected by HIV (Koob & Harvan, 2003; Sogren et al., 2012). Through our collective work as researchers, social workers, frontline HIV service workers, and mothers living with HIV in Ontario, Canada, we have found that one area of social work practice that is in dire need of HIV education and training in both academic and organizational settings is in the field of child welfare.

Why HIV Education and Training for Child Welfare Workers?

In Ontario, child welfare social work is typically carried out by social workers practising at children's aid societies (CAS) throughout the province. The CAS is a leading site for social work practice education (field education) and the hiring of new social work graduates. Social workers in Ontario who are employed by the CAS are expected to take a number of training modules and in-service workshops offered and coordinated by the Ontario Association of Children's Aid Societies (OACAS). As part of the OACAS's commitment to lifelong learning within the scope of child welfare practice and education, training modules focus on areas that have been identified as the learning needs of the target groups. The learning needs are identified through regular assessments and consultation with the Ministry of Children and Youth Services and individual CAS agencies. Training is directed to the CAS front-line staff and management, as well as foster, kin, customary care, and adoptive families.

To date, none of the training offered by the OACAS examines the impact of HIV on the families they serve. As highlighted earlier, because HIV education is sparsely available within the B.S.W. and M.S.W. curriculum, most CAS workers will have limited or no up-to-date information on the physical and social aspects of HIV. And yet, given that Ontario continues to account for the highest proportion and number of reported HIV cases across Canada (Public Health Agency of Canada, 2015), it is likely that front-line CAS staff will be working with families affected by HIV at some point in their career. Moreover, mothers living with HIV in Ontario face a myriad of economic and social challenges that may lead to CAS involvement as a result of housing instability, intimate partner violence, and/or HIV-related stigma (Greene et al., 2010). As expressed by mothers living with HIV from ACB communities in Ontario, these challenges sometimes result in concerns about a mother's ability to care for her children, as well as experiences of HIV-related stigma and discrimination. PAW, who continue to experience the long-term impact of colonization, have also highlighted the presence of HIV-related stigma and discrimination by CAS staff, in addition to a lack of knowledge and sensitivity about HIV (Greene et al., 2014). Furthermore, research has highlighted the significant involvement of HIV-affected families with the CAS (Azzopardi et al., 2014; Greene et al., 2014), including 29 per cent of women living with HIV who participated in the HIV Mothering Study in Ontario. This highlights the importance of providing CAS workers and students with the knowledge and skills to support mothers living with HIV. What follows is our response to the mothers who shared their experiences with the CAS and a request that CAS workers become more knowledgeable about how to support families affected by HIV.

Developing Our Team: Our Community-Based Research Approach

Community-based research is a collaborative partnership approach to research that equitably involves community members, organizational representatives, and researchers in all aspects of the research process (Ahmed, 2004). CBR demands that researchers work in collaboration with the community to ensure research questions address community needs and that the results of research reflect the community's vision of social change in social policy and practice arenas (Etowa, Bernard, Oyinsan, & Clow, 2007; Israel, Schulz, Parker, & Becker, 1998). Our use of CBR, with its participatory iterative process that develops knowledge in a reflection and action cycle, facilitated the development of knowledge rooted in the participants' understanding of the community's issues, and has the potential to develop new and improved ways in which the CAS delivers services to the client groups involved in this study.

Building on previous CBR endeavours, community engagement and relationship development had already been established among key stakeholders, including academic researchers, mothers living with HIV, diverse HIV and AIDS service organizations (ASOs), and CAS agencies in Ontario. With these established relationships in place, a full range of stakeholders contributed to the development of the research proposal and the P4 training and education module. The team included mothers living with HIV, ASOs that work with HIV-affected families, and other key stakeholders from the HIV and child welfare sectors. What brought us together was a mutual desire to respond to and share knowledge with current and future CAS staff about the multiple realities facing families affected by HIV.

Based on community partner recommendations, we created two advisory boards. Consequently, this project facilitated the active involvement of parents through leadership and membership on the Positive Parenting Advisory Board (PPAB), as well as the active involvement of representatives from the CAS and ASOs through membership on the Service Provider Advisory Board (SPAB). Importantly, creating an advisory board for parents living with HIV that was separate from the service providers was critical to ensuring the involvement of parents living with HIV who had histories of child welfare involvement. This was a conscious decision that would ensure the confidentiality and safety of parents living with HIV as they shared important personal experiences and, in turn, guidance on what they felt should be included in the training module. With the exception of the co-chair representatives on the PPAB, membership was confidential in order to ensure a space where the members could safely share their thoughts, experiences, and recommendations.

The co-chairs of both advisory boards also held positions on the research team as co-investigators or collaborators. The advisory boards guided the development of data collection tools, data analysis, training module content, and implementation, and will continue to guide our knowledge translation and exchange activities. As highlighted earlier, the PPAB engaged parents living with HIV from diverse communities who have had CAS involvement. This ensured that their perspectives were and will continue to be heard, valued, and reflected in the education and training module. The PPAB is co-chaired by two mothers living with HIV who understand the realities of CAS involvement. The SPAB engaged representatives from CAS and health and social service agencies to ensure front-line worker and care provider perspectives were also incorporated into the education and training module. The advisory boards met separately to focus on data collection and HIV education and training module content specifically from their perspectives. However, to encourage ongoing support and dialogue between the PPAB, the SPAB, and the core research team, the advisory board co-chairs met regularly with the core research team. Members of the core research team met with the PPAB and SPAB two times during the formative phase to enable sufficient time for dialogue, critical reflection, decision making, and finalization of the data collection tools.

Commitment to Service-User Perspectives

A main goal of this project was to have diverse representation of service-user voices within the development, implementation, and evaluation of the HIV education and training module. Our initial goal was to a) provide a space where the PPAB members could share their experiences; b) integrate their experiences into our HIV education and training module; and c) increase their research capacity in developing survey and focus group questions. We discovered, however, that the women involved in the PPAB were less interested in developing research skills than we had initially expected. In the spirit of CBR, the researchers asked the women how they would like to contribute to the overall development of the training in ways that were meaningful to them and that reflected their unique and shared experiences with CAS. Their responses resulted in shifting our focus on building research capacity to a focus on sharing experiences for the purpose of developing "case scenarios" that we could include in our training module. This was an important learning experience for the researchers on the team, as we had to shift our own thinking of what it means to meaningfully involve women living with HIV in research. In this way, the core research team and PPAB members engaged in a process of reciprocal capacity building, where experiential and research knowledge was equally valued and shared. On a practical level, this resulted in opportunities for increasing capacity on issues related to CAS involvement with Indigenous communities; how racism and immigration are experienced by ACB and other racialized communities within the context of CAS; and methodological and procedural aspects of research, including data collection, tool development, and training evaluation. This process also ensured that the education and training module reflected the needs and experiences of mothers living with HIV, which, in the spirit of community-based research and practice, is a critical component of developing an HIV/AIDS social work education curriculum.

Supporting Our Team: Capacity Building for Researchers, Service Providers, and Parents

An integral component that resulted in the development of our CBR team was the inclusion of capacity-building opportunities for all team members, including researchers, service providers, and parents. In the following CBR model, our research process drew heavily on the lived experiences of service users and practice experiences of service providers. In addition, a key aspect of our CBR process was to create opportunities for increasing the research capacity and participation of service users, increase the potential for CAS agency staff to practise more effectively and sensitively with families living with HIV, increase the researchers' capacity to better understand the nuanced ways in which mothers living with HIV experience stigma in the child welfare context, and to draw on service user and service provider knowledge in developing our education module. In this way, our capacity-building process was reciprocal and, therefore, valued, and integrated multiple forms of knowledge from all key stakeholders.

Capacity Building among Service Users and Mothers Living with HIV
A main goal of this project was to increase the capacity of mothers living with HIV to meaningfully contribute to the research process and develop sustainable research and practice skills. This was achieved by involving mothers living with HIV as co-investigators, collaborators, members of the PPAB, and as community research associates (CRAS). Subsequently,

mothers living with HIV actively contributed to the development, facilitation, and evaluation of the HIV education and training module, are an integral part of the training team, and are involved in the knowledge transfer and exchange (KTE) activities that emerged from these processes.

Community Research Associates

Two parents living with HIV were hired and trained as community research associates. The CRAS were responsible for developing and supporting the PPAB in order to ensure a high level of community involvement in developing the education module. In addition, CRAS were highly involved in the data collection and analysis process and the development and implementation of the HIV education and training module. The CRAS were and continue to be supported by a mentor on the core research team as they develop their knowledge of and capacity to do research.

The Positive Parenting Advisory Board

Under the guidance and support of the CRAS, a critical factor in the successful development of the training was the involvement of the PPAB. The purpose of the PPAB was to increase opportunities for the voices of parents living with HIV to contribute to the study design and future KTE activities. Capacity building at this stage focused on supporting the PPAB to lead the development, clarification, and articulation of the important areas of knowledge, attitudes, and skills to be incorporated in the focus groups and surveys (with CAS and student participants) and the HIV education and training module.

Capacity Building among Service Providers, CAS Workers, and Social Work Students

A critical aspect of our CBR process was to create opportunities for knowledge sharing among a diverse group of service providers regarding their varied degree of HIV awareness, knowledge, and experiences of supporting families affected by HIV. This approach supported a process of building capacity in knowledge and practice, as well as the research capacity to support the data collection and tool development processes. Moreover, the completed data collection and training processes were piloted on CAS workers and students, ensuring a process through which participants would increase their capacity to support families affected by HIV.

Capacity Building among Service Providers

Clinical and community-based health and social service providers were invited to participate on the SPAB. The purpose of the SPAB was to increase opportunities for the voices of allies within CAS agencies and service providers based in ASOs, hospitals, community health centres, and other relevant organizations to contribute to the study design, HIV education and training module content, and future KTE activities. We anticipated that members of the SPAB would have varying research capacities. This included the sharing of clinical, biological, and psychosocial knowledge of HIV; colonization, racism, and anti-oppressive practice/ approaches; and child welfare practices and policies and other areas for capacity building as identified by SPAB members. Reflecting our commitment to including the voices of Indigenous and ACB communities within the development, implementation, and evaluation of the HIV education and training module, we recruited a strong presence of service providers working with Indigenous and ACB communities on the SPAB to support capacity-building activities on the unique experiences of these communities, particularly those with or likely to have CAS involvement.

Capacity Building among CAS Staff and Social Work Students

This project has begun to build the capacity of CAS staff and management and students to work more effectively with families affected by HIV. Of particular importance is the increased capacity of front-line CAS staff and students aspiring to work in the field of child welfare to understand the unique issues that families affected by HIV experience, and, in particular, Indigenous families who have had a long and challenging history with child welfare in Canada and ACB families who continue to face racism and other structural barriers. At the time of writing this chapter, the project had completed the pre-training data collection process (surveys and focus groups) with social workers from four CAS agencies (N=67) and students enrolled in child welfare and case management courses from three social work/social service worker programs in Ontario (N=53). As part of the research study, the training has been delivered to seventy-six students and sixty CAS workers. Following the training, we received sixty-five post-training surveys and conducted six post-training focus groups (N=34). We have completed our data collection process; however, due to the popularity of the training module, the training has been provided to an additional forty-five social work students and will be offered on an ongoing basis in two B.S.W. programs in southern Ontario.

Developing the HIV Education and Training Module

The Pre-Training Phase

The purpose of the pre-training phase was to engage in a data collection process that would ensure that the training module not only reflected the interests of the researchers, PPAB, and SPAB but also addressed the learning needs of the participants. The PPAB and SPAB were therefore consulted at the onset of the project to identify key elements and questions for inclusion in our pre-training data collection process. The team agreed to engage in a mixed-method data collection process that included qualitative focus groups and a quantitative, self-report survey measuring knowledge, attitudes, and beliefs of HIV. The HIV-KQ-18 (Carey & Schroder, 2002) scale was used, which models other validated scales that assess knowledge and attitudes of HIV among service providers and the general population. Our data collection activities therefore included:

1. survey and focus group development in consultation with the SPAB and PPAB and overall research team to develop the survey and focus group questions;
2. survey administration to front-line child and family service workers and students;
3. focus groups conducted with front-line child and family service workers and students to contextualize the survey data and enable a deeper discussion and understanding of training interests and needs of child and family service workers; and
4. analysis of data, whereby survey data was entered into a database and analyzed using standard statistical techniques and summarized in aggregate format.

The focus group data was analyzed thematically to increase our understanding of front-line workers' knowledge and attitudes of HIV, experiences of working with families affected by HIV, and their training and education needs. Importantly, members of the core research team met with the PPAB and SPAB multiple times during the formative phase (April

2013 to November 2014) to enable sufficient time for dialogue, critical reflection, decision making, and finalization of the data collection tools and content of the education and training module. This CBR methodological approach to developing the module ensured that the core research team, PPAB, SPAB, and research participants all contributed to finalizing both the process and the content of the HIV education and training module in order that the training accurately reflected gaps in knowledge. The plan is to use post-training survey and focus group data to evaluate the efficacy of the HIV education and training module.

Delivering the Training: The HIV Education Module

The pre-training phase resulted in a three-hour HIV education and training module that was piloted with members of the SPAB and has been conducted by webinar with members of the OACAS. To date, the training module has also been delivered within four CAS agencies (to sixty frontline CAS staff and management), three B.S.W. classes at two different institutions (to ninety-one B.S.W. students), and one social service worker course (a total of six students participated) at a local college. The training was co-facilitated by a researcher, HIV/AIDS educator, social worker, and mother living with HIV. The finalized training module consists of the following components: 1) demystifying HIV with a focus on transmission, treatment, and prevention; 2) HIV, pregnancy, and pre- and postpartum issues and experiences, such as infant feeding and administering antiretroviral therapy to one's baby; 3) social and emotional health, including impact of stigma, psychosocial concerns, and legal issues; and 4) HIV disclosure, privacy, and confidentiality.

The third component of our training includes a presentation by a team member who is a mother living with HIV. This aspect of the module was integral to the CBR approach with its emphasis on the inclusion of service users. The presentation by a mother living with HIV is also an effective aspect of the training because it provokes social workers to have the awareness of their impact on exacerbating or minimizing HIV-related stigma and in connecting mothers living with HIV to appropriate resources. Involving service users also ensured that the content of the training came alive in ways that were meaningful to student social workers and child and family service workers. Another integral component of the training is two to three case scenarios that were developed by the PPAB. The case scenarios reflect the range of challenges that PPAB members have experienced with the CAS and include questions and points for discussion. Similar to the service user's presentation that brought to the fore both challenging and supportive experiences with the CAS, the purpose of the case scenarios is to bring the educational material to life for CAS workers and students. Finally, in addition to the actual education and training module, we also provided participants with a handout that directed participants to additional resources, including ASOs, clinical practice guidelines, and research publications and educational materials available from the Canadian AIDS Treatment Information Exchange (CATIE).

Integrating HIV into Social Work Education and Child Welfare Practice: Reflections on the Process

The evolution of HIV into a chronic illness and advances in clinical and community-based supports for people living with HIV have not found their way into social work education and practice. This raises important concerns for people living with HIV in its broadest sense, and for families affected by HIV more specifically. Consequently, we echo Bowen's (2013) call that "those in the social work profession need to provide an equally progressive response to the psychosocial needs of people living with HIV/AIDS" (p. 274). Moreover, our formative phase, including the pre-training phase with CAS workers and social work students, coincides with Mitchell and Linsk's (2004) suggestion to provide integrated, holistic, and client-centred support with respect to medical management of HIV, and "sexual decision making, legal and human rights, and life course issues" for people and families affected by HIV (Bowen, 2013, p. 274).

There have been various suggestions regarding how to integrate HIV-related practice into social work education. Gilbert and Linsk (2005) argue that the best way of advancing HIV/AIDS social work practice is through continuing education, whereas others suggest that HIV-related education should be a part of the B.S.W./M.S.W. curriculum (Natale et al., 2010). P4 is our attempt to address both these suggestions by developing an HIV education module that can be utilized in both the academy and in the field. We believe that it is imperative that HIV education be accessed in both spaces due to the lack of theoretical and applied research and education in this area locally, nationally, and internationally. Moreover, research and practice in HIV and child welfare (and other areas of social work practice) is dated and thus not relevant to the nature of relationships between practising and burgeoning social workers who may find themselves working with individuals and families affected by and living with HIV. By developing, providing, and evaluating an HIV training module for CAS and for students in social service worker and social work programs, we are at the threshold of advancing knowledge that will shape models of practice and policies in child welfare that reflect the current everyday realities of families living with HIV, and that address the gap in research and practice on the interface between child welfare and HIV.

As per our CBR approach to research and social work education, our ongoing commitment to service-user involvement in research, practice, policy, and education has resulted in the capacity building of all the stakeholders involved in this project. This included mothers living with HIV, CAS staff, and social work educators, all of whom were an integral part of this project. Through participation on the core research team as co-investigators or collaborators and/or members of the PPAB or SPAB, the research capacity of all community stakeholders, including people living with HIV/AIDS, service providers from ASOS, CAS, and allied health and social service organizations, was critical to our process of shaping the development, implementation, and evaluation of the HIV education and training module. In particular, our KTE and mentorship processes provided a strong base from which experiential knowledge and skills were developed, including the research design, data collection, analysis, group facilitation, networking, and partnership building.

Conclusion: Implications for Social Work Practice, Education, and Research

This project has the potential to build the capacity of CAS staff and students to work more effectively with families living with HIV. We have learned that an integral aspect of making this work relevant to parents living with HIV, social workers, social work educators, and social work students is the CBR process itself. The CBR process created a culture of communication between the various stakeholders, in addition to a sustainable research and practice-based relationship that has provided a model for dialogue between CAS agencies and service users. Consequently, this will have a positive impact on the long-term capacity of the CAS and social work students to engage in practice-based research with parents living with HIV and other service-user groups in the future.

Of equal importance was the affirmation of what we already knew—that social work service users have enormous capacity to contribute to the development of policy, practice, and education that will impact their lives (Beresford, 2001; Beresford & Croft, 1992, 2004; Greene et al., 2009). We learned that front-line CAS workers and social work students also have the capacity to contribute to this process and to work in partnership with the very communities they serve. Creating opportunities for the CAS and for social work educators and students more broadly to access this knowledge through this project will ensure that this capacity is tapped. More importantly, we have learned that when parents are involved in shaping HIV and child welfare research, practice, and policy, they are viewed as more than "clients." Rather, parents are viewed as "experts" and as an integral part of the knowledge-to-action process. When lived experience is viewed as an essential requirement for the development of new and more effective strategies for change, social work education and practice has the potential to be transformative.

References

Ahmed, S. M. (2004). Overcoming barriers to effective community based participatory research in U.S. medical schools. *Education for Health: Change in Learning and Practice, 17*(2), 141–151.

Alonzo, A. A., & Reynolds, N. R. (1995). Stigma, HIV and AIDS: An exploration and elaboration of a stigma trajectory. *Social Science and Medicine, 41*(3), 303–315.

Azzopardi, C., Wade, M., Salter, R., Macdougall, G., Shouldice, M., Read, S., & Bitnun, A. (2014). Medical nonadherence in pediatric HIV: Psychosocial risks and intersection with the child protection system for medical neglect. *Child Abuse & Neglect, 38*(11), 1766–1777.

BC Centre for Disease Control. (2014). *HIV annual report, 2014.* Retrieved from http://www.bccdc.ca/health-professionals/data-reports/ annual-surveillance-reports

Beresford, P. (2001). User involvement and participation in social care: Research informing practice. Book review. *International Journal of Social Research Methodology, 4*(3), 254–256.

Beresford, P., & Croft, S. (1992, Autumn). The politics of participation. *Critical Social Policy, 35,* 20–44.

Beresford, P., & Croft, S. (2004). Service users and practitioners reunited: The key component for social work reform. *British Journal of Social Work, 34*(1), 53–68.

Blanche, S., Mayaux, M-J., Veber, F., Landreau, A., Courpotin, C., Vilmer, E.,...HIV Infection in Newborns French Collaborative Study Group. (1996). Separation between HIV-positive women and their children: The French prospective study, 1986 through 1993. *American Journal of Public Health, 83*(3), 376–381.

Bowen, E. A. (2013). AIDS at 30: Implications for social work education. *Journal of Social Work Education, 49*(2), 265–276.

Bywater, J., & Jones, R. (2007). *Sexuality and social work.* Glasgow, Scotland: Learning Matters Ltd.

Canadian Aboriginal AIDS Network. (2016a). Regional factsheets—Saskatchewan. Retrieved from http://www.caan.ca/regional-fact-sheets-/saskatchewan

Canadian Aboriginal AIDS Network. (2016b). Regional factsheets—Manitoba. Retrieved from http://www.caan.ca/regional-fact-sheets/manitoba/

Carey, M. P., & Schroder, K. E. E. (2002). Development and psychometric evaluation of the brief HIV knowledge questionnaire (HIV-KQ-18). *AIDS Education and Prevention, 14*, 174–184.

Chen, H., Phillips, K. A., Kanouse, D. E., Collins, R. L., & Miu, A. (2001). Fertility desires and intentions of HIV positive men and women. *Family Planning Perspectives, 33*(4), 144–152.

Cooper, E. R., Charurat, M., Mofenson, L., Hanson, I. C., Pitt, J., Diaz, C.,... Women and Infants' Transmission Study Group. (2002). Combination antiretroviral strategies for the treatment of pregnant HIV-1-infected women and prevention of perinatal HIV-1 transmission. *Journal of Acquired Immune Deficiency Syndromes, 29*(5), 484–494.

Etowa, J. B., Bernard, W. T., Oyinsan, B., & Clow, B. (2007). Participatory action research (PAR): An approach for improving black women's health in rural and remote communities. *Journal of Transcultural Nursing, 18*(4), 349–357.

Forbes, J. C., Alimenti, A. M., Singer, J., Brophy, J. C., Bitnun, A., Samson, L. M.,... Canadian Pediatric AIDS Research Group (CPARG). (2012). A national review of vertical HIV transmission. *AIDS, 26*(6), 757–763.

Forehand, R., Steele, R., Armistead, L., Morse, E., Simon, P., & Clark, L. (1998). The family health project: Psychosocial adjustment of children whose mothers are HIV infected. *Journal of Consulting and Clinical Psychology, 66*(3), 513–520.

Gilbert, D. (1999). In the best interest of the child: Maintaining family integrity among HIV-positive mothers, children and adolescents. *Journal of HIV/AIDS Prevention and Education for Adolescents and Children, 3*(1–2), 99–117.

Gilbert, D. J., & Linsk, N. L. (2005). The Annual National Conference on Social Work and HIV/AIDS. *Journal of HIV/AIDS & Social Services, 3*(3), 1–4.

Greene, S., Ahluwalia, A., Watson, J., Tucker, R., Rourke, S. B., Koornstra, J.,... Byers, S. (2009). Between skepticism and empowerment: The experiences of peer research assistants in HIV/AIDS, housing and homelessness community-based research. *International Journal of Social Research Methodology, 12*(4), 361–373.

Greene, S., Ion, A., Beaver, K., Nicholson, V., Derry, R., & Loutfy, M. (in press). "Who is there to support our women?" Positive Aboriginal women (PAW) speak out about health and social care experiences and needs during pregnancy, birth and motherhood. *Canadian Journal of Aboriginal Community-Based HIV/AIDS Research*.

Greene, S., Ion, A., Elston, D., Kwaramba, G., Smith, S., & Loutfy, M. (2015). (M)othering with HIV: Resisting and reconstructing experiences of health and social surveillance. In B. Hogeveen & J. Minaker (Eds.), *Criminalized mothers, criminalizing motherhood* (pp. 231–263). Toronto, ON: Demeter Press.

Greene, S., O'Brien-Teengs, D., Whitebird, W., & Ion, A. (2014). How Positive Aboriginal women (PAW) living with HIV talk about their mothering experiences with child and family services in Ontario. *Journal of Public Child Welfare, 8*(5), 467–490.

Greene, S., Tucker, R., Rourke, S. B., Guenter, D., Sobota, M., Monette, L.,… White, P. (2010). "Under my umbrella": The housing experiences of HIV positive parents who live with and care for their children in Ontario. *Archives of Women's Mental Health, 13*(3), 223–232.

Hackl, K. L., Somlai, A. M., Kelly, J. A., & Kalichman, S. C. (1997). Women living with HIV/AIDS: The dual challenge of being a patient and caregiver. *Health & Social Work, 22*(1), 53–62.

Israel, B. A., Schulz, A. J., Parker, E. A., & Becker, A. B. (1998). Review of community-based research: Assessing partnership approaches to improve public health. *Annual Review of Public Health, 19*, 173–202.

Koob, J. J., & Harvan, J. S. (2003). AIDS instruction in U.S. schools of social work: 20 years into the epidemic. *Social Work Education, 22*(3), 309–319.

Liu, J., & Remis, R. (2007). *Race/ethnicity among persons with HIV/AIDS in Ontario, 1981–2004*. Retrieved from http://www.ohemu.utoronto.ca/doc/Ethnicity_report_rev.pdf

Logie, C., James, L., Tharao, W., & Loutfy, M. R. (2011). HIV, gender, race, sexual orientation, and sex work: A qualitative study of intersectional stigma experienced by HIV-positive women in Ontario, Canada. *PLoS medicine, 8*(11), 1475. doi:10.1371/journal.pmed.1001124

Logie, C., James, L., Tharao, W., & Loutfy, M. R. (2013). Associations between HIV-related stigma, racial discrimination, gender discrimination, and depression among HIV-positive African, Caribbean, and black women in Ontario, Canada. *AIDS Patient Care & STDs, 27*(2), 114–122.

Loutfy, M. R., Hart, T. A., Mohammed, S. S., Su, D., Ralph, E. D., Walmsley, S. L.,… Ontario HIV Fertility Research Team. (2009). Fertility desires and intentions of HIV-positive women of reproductive age in Ontario, Canada: A cross-sectional study. *PLoS ONE, 4*(12), e7925. doi:10.1371/journal.pone.0007925

Mahajan, A. P., Sayles, J. N., Patel, V. A., Remien, R. H., Sawires, S. R., Ortiz, D. J.,…Coates, T. J. (2008). Stigma in the HIV/AIDS epidemic: A review of the literature and recommendations for the way forward. *AIDS, 22*(Suppl 2), S67–S79.

Melchior, L. A., Huba, G. J., Gallagher, T., Jean-Louis, E., McDonald, S. S., Smereck, G. A. D.,...Panter, A. T. (2001). Unmet needs in groups of traditionally underserved individuals with HIV/AIDS: Empirical models. *Home Health Care Services Quarterly, 19*(1–2), 29–51.

Mitchell, C. G., & Linsk, N. L. (2004). A multidimensional conceptual framework for understanding HIV/AIDS as a chronic long-term illness. *Social Work, 49*(3), 469–477.

Natale, A. P., Biswas, B., Urada, L., & Cheyett, A. M. (2010). Global HIV and AIDS: Calling all social work educators. *Social Work Education, 29*(1), 27–47.

Parker, R., & Aggleton, P. (2003). HIV and AIDS-related stigma and discrimination: A conceptual framework and implications for action. *Social Science & Medicine, 57,* 13–24.

Peltier, D., Jackson, R., Prentice, T., Masching, R., Monette, L., Fong, M., & Canadian Aboriginal AIDS Networks' Voices of Women (CAAN VOW) Standing Committee. (2013). When women pick up their bundles: HIV prevention and related service needs of Aboriginal women in Canada. In J. Gahagan (Ed.), *HIV prevention and women in Canada* (pp. 85–104). Toronto, ON: Canadian Scholars' Press.

Pooyak, S., & Gomez, Y. (2009). Using a narrative approach to understanding the frontline practices and experiences of Aboriginal and non-Aboriginal child protection workers. *First Peoples Child & Family Review, 4*(2), 10–17.

Public Health Agency of Canada. (2010). *HIV/AIDS epi update – July 2010. Chapter 5: HIV/AIDS among women in Canada.* Retrieved from http://www. phac-aspc.gc.ca/aidssida/publication/epi/2010/5-eng.php

Public Health Agency of Canada. (2014). *HIV/AIDS epi updates. Chapter 8: HIV/ AIDS among Aboriginal people in Canada.* Retrieved from http://www.phac-aspc.gc.ca/aids-sida/publication/epi/2010/pdf/ch8-eng.pdf

Public Health Agency of Canada. (2015). *HIV and AIDS in Canada: Surveillance report to December 31, 2014.* Retrieved from http://www.healthycanadians. gc.ca/publications/diseases-conditions-maladies-affections/hiv-aids-surveillance-2014-vih-sida/index-eng.php

Remis, R., & Liu, J. (2013). *HIV/AIDS in Ontario: Preliminary report, 2011.* Retrieved from http://www.ohemu.utoronto.ca/doc/PHERO2011_report_preliminary.pdf

Remis, R., Swantee, C., Schiedel, L., Merid, M., & Liu, J. (2006). *Report on HIV/ AIDS in Ontario, 2004.* Retrieved from http://www.ohemu.utoronto.ca/ tech%20reports.html

Rotheram-Borus, M. J., Draimin, B. H., Reid, H. M., & Murphy, D. A. (1997). The impact of illness disclosure and custody plans on adolescents whose parents lived with AIDS. *AIDS, 11,* 1159–1164.

Rowen, D., & Shears, J. (2011). HIV/AIDS course content in CSWE-accredited social work programs: A survey of current curricular practices. *Journal of Teaching in Social Work, 31,* 119–130.

Sandelowski, M., & Barroso, J. (2003). Motherhood in the context of maternal HIV infection. *Research in Nursing & Health, 26,* 470–482.

Sandelowski, M., Lambe, C., & Barroso, J. (2004). Stigma in HIV-positive women. *Journal of Nursing Scholarship, 36*(2), 122–128.

Saskatchewan Ministry of Health. (2010). *HIV strategy for Saskatchewan, 2010–2014*. Retrieved from http://www.skhiv.ca

Sogren, M., Jones, A., Nathaniel, K., & Cameron-Padmore, J. (2012). Reconfiguring social work education to fight HIV/AIDS: A model for developmental contexts. *Social Work Education, 31*(7), 880–895.

St. Lawrence, J. S., Snodgrass, C. E., Robertson, A., & Baird-Thomas, C. (2008). Minimizing the risk of pregnancy, sexually transmitted diseases, and HIV among incarcerated adolescent girls: Identifying potential points of intervention. *Criminal Justice and Behavior, 35*(12), 1500–1514.

Strug, D. L., Grube, B. A., & Beckerman, N. L. (2002). Challenges and changing roles in HIV/AIDS social work: Implications for training and education. *Social Work in Health Care, 35*(4), 1–19.

Trocmé, N., Knoke, D., & Blackstock, C. (2004). Pathways to the overrepresentation of Indigenous children in Canada's child welfare system. *Social Service Review, 78*(4), 577–600.

Wagner, A. C., Hart, T. A., Mohammed, S., Ivanova, E., Wong, J., & Loutfy, M. R. (2010). Correlates of HIV stigma in HIV-positive women. *Archives of Women's Mental Health, 13*, 207–214.

Wood, S. A., & Tobias, C. (2004). Barriers to care and unmet needs for HIV-positive women caring for children: Perceptions of women and providers. *Journal of HIV/AIDS & Social Services, 3*(2), 47–65.

CHAPTER 9

Boundaries and Identity: Racialized Child Welfare Workers' Perspectives of Their Histories and Experiences When Working with Diverse Families

Daniel Kikulwe

Introduction

This chapter focuses on one of four broad research questions of my doctoral study completed in 2014. The purpose of my doctoral study was to examine the work processes of racialized child welfare workers within hierarchical institutions, and it involved an understanding of several day-to-day child welfare activities such as case decisions, work training, court attendance, and work with families, as well as with supervisors, co-workers, and collaterals. The inspiration to undertake this study was my own child welfare work experience and the gap in Canadian research on ways racialized workers interact with diverse communities and families when working within the confines of child welfare laws, policies, regulations, and legislation.

Suggested Citation: Kikulwe, D. (2016). Boundaries and identity: Racialized child welfare workers' perspectives of their histories and experiences when working with diverse families. In H. Montgomery, D. Badry, D. Fuchs, & D. Kikulwe (Eds.), *Transforming Child Welfare: Interdisciplinary Practices, Field Education, and Research* (pp. 187–210). Regina, SK: University of Regina Press.

This chapter examines the perspectives of racialized child welfare workers on interventions and interactions with families from diverse backgrounds in Ontario, Canada. My doctoral research was based on a qualitative study. I provide a rich description of the experiences of racialized workers when interacting and intervening with diverse families. The study's use of the term "racialized workers" refers to individuals with racial identities that have social markers (physical characteristics) that result in their marginalization. In Canada, individuals who self-identify as being racialized are both foreign- and Canadian-born, and primarily include South Asian, Southeast Asian, African, and Caribbean women and men.

According to Frankenberg (1993), race and racialization have become associated with marginalized communities. The concepts of race and racialization are not applied to dominant groups because those populations are equated with normality and, as such, have no need to be defined (Solomos, 1995). In this study, I recognize that racialized child welfare workers are not a homogenous group. Gunaratam (2003) argues that all social identities are heterogeneous because there are distinct economic, social, interpersonal, and regional features that make each one of us different, even within the same racial grouping. Intraracial differences are acknowledged in this study.

This chapter is organized into six sections. The first section introduces the chapter. In the second section, I focus on Foucault's theoretical work as a basis for understanding the notion of power and how it is used by racialized workers within child welfare contexts. The third section examines the factors that have contributed to the increasing number of racialized workers in social services in Canada. The study methodology forms the fourth section of the chapter, with a focus on research methods and recruitment of study participants. In the fifth section, I discuss the study findings and examine the shared histories and identities of racialized workers and families within the context of social work. I discuss the social affinities and closeness between service users and workers based on shared experiences, beliefs, and history, as well as the complexities that arise from this closeness. I show that worker sensitivity is heightened when children are removed from families whose history is marked by marginalization and oppression. I also discuss the subtle use of power that racialized workers utilize in order to maintain a gaze on marginalized families and to reinforce the dominant ideas of parenting when protecting children within families they work with. The sixth section of the chapter is about the implications of this study for child welfare practice/education and focuses on the idea that workers' histories and experiences influence their practices with families. I conclude that workers aim to keep racialized and immigrant families intact because of the influences of their histories and experiences.

Theoretical Perspectives

The theoretical underpinning of this chapter is situated in postmodern thinking. The conceptualization of power by postmodern thinkers, like Foucault, helps us understand that the social worker/service user relationship is not symmetrical. In social work interventions, power is regularly used overtly and covertly to create meanings and knowledge about the service users. Analysis of power is central to Foucault's theoretical work. According to Manis and Street (2000), Foucault believed that power is not held or exercised by individuals. Foucault (1979, 1980) conceived of power as spreading through networks of relationships, that power shifts, and that we all act in terms of power relations according to our social locations, which may be based on one or more of the following identities: class, gender, race, sexual orientation, and so on. As I have noted elsewhere (Kikulwe, in press), Foucault has been criticized for his view that power is not held by individuals, which his critics claim neutralizes power and allows no fundamental critique of the power that emerges from those in dominant positions (Grimshaw, 1993). While my study acknowledges that power resides with those in dominant positions, it also raises awareness that racialized workers, who historically have been in marginal social positions, are now beginning to exercise power in their child welfare roles as delegated state agents. The recruitment of racialized workers in child protection has to do with the governability of minority communities and reflects Foucault's idea of a "regime of normalization" (Lewis, 2000, p. 34). The term "normalization" refers to the correction of behaviour that ensures that members of society conform to norms (Kikulwe, in press). Both governability and normalization cannot be ruled out in the work of racialized child welfare workers because child protection interventions with families have the inherent element of legitimized state surveillance. Foucault used the panopticon, or prison, as an illustration of the operations of power and how surveillance is organized in various modern institutions (Farrell, 2005), in which I include child welfare organizations.

I argue that the increased participation of racialized workers in child welfare has placed them in a position of surveillance of families, particularly those in racialized communities. Five factors have been noted in academic literature regarding the increased involvement of racialized workers in child welfare services. These factors include: 1) the continuing negative perceptions of families receiving child welfare services; 2) higher rates of immigration; 3) rising numbers of racialized children in foster care; 4) growing social work educational opportunities; 5) the availability of employment equity programs.

Contributing Factors behind the Rise of Racialized Social Workers in Canada

Societal Perceptions of Child Welfare Families

In general, social work has historically been regarded as a nonracialized profession (Proctor & Rosen, 1981; Rossiter, 2005). Since the inception of child protection work in the early twentieth century, middle-class white women have been the primary providers of child welfare services in Canada (Swift, 1995). Fallon, MacLaurin, Trocmé, and Felstiner (2003) claim that 80 per cent of child welfare workers are female and that 97 per cent use English as the primary language. One can say that the child welfare profession has been traditionally female-dominated (Strega & Carrière, 2008). According to Chambers (1986), child protection/social service work has historically been undervalued because it deals with disadvantaged segments of the population. Perceptions existed, and still exist today, that social services work mirrored the negative societal expectations that women should assume responsibility for caring for the disadvantaged population, including parents receiving child welfare services. Several scholars have described how mothers receiving child welfare services became scapegoats, being held responsible for all sorts of ills: teenage motherhood, delinquent children, juvenile crime, a crisis in masculinity, and social and educational failure in fatherless boys (Brown, 2006; Carabine, 2001; Dominelli, Strega, Callahan, & Rutman, 2005; Scourfield, 2001a, 2001b; Swift, 1995). Negative perceptions of mothers involved with the child welfare system, particularly poor or lone mothers, can influence responses to this population and can result in practices that may not be objective. Although available research is dated, Bernard, Lucas-White, and Moore (1993) noted that there is a perception that the "undeserving" mother may be best served by racialized social workers who have moved into middle-class occupations in the social services and whose primary responsibilities are within minority communities. This perception is reinforced by the unspoken expectation that racialized workers represent their communities and that they are the experts who must have all the answers when it comes to their communities.

Immigration

With the increased immigration of families from non-European countries, particularly in the 1970s and '80s, there has been a need to control and regulate immigrant parents (Lewis, 1997; Williams, 1996). Stubbs (1984) asserted that in the 1970s, a shift from a discourse of "race/immigration problematic" to a discourse of "race/crime problematic" occurred in Britain. Crucially, the shift from an immigration problem to a crime problem meant immigrants were seen to represent a threat to society. Racialized families have become pathologized within the profession of child welfare, which had heretofore been operationalized by middle-class, white, Canadian workers. Others hold the view that expanded child protection services were designed to extend services to new populations that had been unsuccessful in accessing services (Wakefield, 1998).

Grossberg (2002) has succinctly written that Americans have been torn between a fear *for* children and a fear *of* children (as cited in Lee, 2008). For Americans, the safety and future of children have been of public concern, as they are viewed as a resource and the future leaders of the country. There is no doubt that at the core of the interventions to protect children in poor families are child safety concerns that are used by child welfare authorities to justify a public fear *for* children. At the same time, there has always been a fear of underprivileged youth and what will happen to them if they are not given a proper upbringing. The fear is that children in households with inadequate resources will remain poor and drain public resources, leading to their criminality and a repetition of the cycle of abuse, including the mistreatment of their own children. The result is increasing anxiety among the privileged about the behaviour of the urban poor, leading to perceptions that these "dangerous classes" are criminals,

vicious, indolent, and intemperate (Lee, 2008, p. 50). The need to manage and control the increasing numbers of deviant immigrant families has
necessitated the recruitment of racialized workers to act as conduits to
diverse communities.

Available American, British, and Canadian research also indicates that
most racialized workers are in front-line positions as interpreters and activists, engaging in cultural connections between the social workers and families involved with social services (Barn, 2007; Hutchinson, 1989; Lewis,
1996; Morrel, 2007; Perry & Limb, 2004; Stubbs, 1984; Woldeguiorguis,
2003). Alongside their front-line work duties, racialized workers find
themselves cast into the role of cultural expert, while also exerting power
and authority to manage families and conforming to rules established by
child welfare regulatory policies and practices (Lewis, 2000). This trend
of increasing racialized workers in social services is likely to continue in
Canada because of the perceived need for agencies to remain involved
in diverse communities. Additionally, in some cases, the recruitment of
racialized employees has arisen as a means to provide clients with services
in their native languages. Finally, it was also believed that the entry of
racialized workers in social services would help to expand services within
local minority communities (Dorais, 1994) and address a perceived need to
create or construct ethnically sensitive services (Stubbs, 1984).

Children in Care
Several studies demonstrate that in the United Kingdom, Canada, and the
United States child welfare intervention has had a long-standing, conflict-
ual relationship with racialized communities (Barn, 2007; Graham, 2007;
Humphreys, Atkar, & Baldwin, 1999; Maiter, 2009). Canadian research
confirms that racialized and Aboriginal families are more likely to be
investigated by child welfare agencies than any other families in Canada
(Lavergne, Dufour, Trocmé, & Larrivée, 2008). It has also been demonstrated that poverty is a factor in the involvement of child welfare services
with racialized families. Child welfare researchers, like Swift and Callahan
(2009) and Blackstock, Trocmé, and Bennett (2004), have insisted that the
overrepresentation of racialized and Aboriginal children in foster care is
unacceptable and report that no viable plan has yet been established that
could lead to a change in this trend. The discussion of racialized children
in care is connected to workers from diverse backgrounds who have been

recruited by social service agencies to intervene in families from increasingly diverse communities in Canada, Britain, and the United States (Bernard et al., 1993; Proctor & Davis, 1994; Rooney, 1984; Stubbs, 1984).

Educational Opportunities

Correspondingly, social work education has been transformed, resulting in more racialized individuals entering the profession (Razack & Badwall, 2006). Williams and Villemez (1993) describe the trend of men, particularly from black and ethnic communities, transitioning into what they call nontraditional occupations (e.g., social work) because of barriers to employment in other fields as a result of discrimination (as cited in Christie, 2006). Among some racialized groups, job openings in social work represent an opportunity for education and employment. Racialized social workers, and women recruited to work within public institutions, tend to be placed in front-line or liaison jobs that link social service agencies to diverse communities (Bernard et al., 1993; Collins, 1990; Jones, 1986). These authors go on to suggest that the recruitment of racialized workers is common in institutions like corrections or social welfare agencies, which generally serve diverse communities.

Employment Equity Programs

Political pressure has been put on publicly funded social services to develop a workforce that is more reflective of contemporary Canadian society. For example, in Canada, employment equity legislation at the federal level encourages the development and implementation of equity hiring practices at the organizational level (Dorais, 1994). Similarly, in the United Kingdom, employment opportunity policies emerged to meet the needs of racialized individuals who were believed to have limited employment opportunities (Stubbs, 1984). The United States has similar affirmative action policies with the intended purpose of creating employment equity (Holzer & Neumark, 2000). Employment equity programs are laden with assumptions about equalizing job opportunities and expanding the labour force to allow entry of marginalized groups. While many racialized people have benefitted from these policies, such initiatives are not without their critics, as there has been a lack of commitment by both government and involved agencies to implement the Employment Equity Act (Yee, 2007). A relative weakness in employment equity legislation exists because of the lack of popular support for stronger equity-based policies and employers' focus on the corporate bottom line, as well as poor implementation and enforcement of the programs (Shalla & Clement, 2007).

To summarize, one of the recurring themes in academic literature is that child protection work was primarily carried out by middle-class women, and that the recipients of the services were women. In the recent past, these roles and responsibilities have also been assumed by racialized workers, particularly in Canadian urban centres, which will be further discussed in this chapter. I will now turn to the discussion of the study's methodology.

Methodology

For the study upon which this chapter is based, I utilized a qualitative research methodology to understand the work processes of racialized child welfare workers. My study focused on day-to-day child welfare activities, such as case decision making, work training, court attendance, and working with families, as well as factors relating to supervisors, co-workers, and collaterals. My study also involved a review and analysis of the policies and procedures that guide the Ontario children's aid societies' standards regarding child protection work. My review of these documents was part of my initial work to establish the context for the provision of child welfare services in Ontario. In qualitative research, the use of secondary data or information collected by someone else can be valuable to help illuminate new research questions (Colby, 1982). In my study, I demonstrated how racialized workers are implicated in child welfare work processes that require assessment of families that have deviated from established Canadian parenting norms.

The second source of data for my study consisted of semi-structured interviews with individuals. I conducted fifteen individual interviews for primary data generation from October 2011 to February 2012. The participants worked in three main urban centres. Three of them lived in the suburbs and were interviewed outside of an urban centre. The interviews lasted from one-and-a-half to two hours. The individual interviews helped me to develop rapport and trust with participants and assisted me in identifying others who would be willing to participate in the subsequent focus group phase of my study.

My invitation to individual interviewees was deliberate and guided by my desire to understand varying perspectives held within discrete sectors of child welfare service delivery. The cohort of participants who were individually interviewed included four racialized supervisors and eleven racialized front-line child welfare workers. All the participants were practising in mainstream child protection services at the time of the interviews and were over thirty years old, with work experiences ranging from three to eleven years. Twelve of the fifteen participants were born outside of Canada. Gender balance in terms of female and male representation was also considered. Gender difference raises the importance of including participants who could provide perspectives of work experiences based on gender. Twelve research participants were women and three were men, a balance that is generally consistent with the male/female ratio in the social work profession. Eleven of the fifteen participants were parents (three fathers and eight mothers).

I utilized one focus group as a third data source for my study. The combined collection of data using individual interviews and a focus group is a common practice in qualitative research. For my research, the focus group was intended to help explore the range of key issues, concerns, and questions that were generated by the individual interviews. The participants in the individual interviews were not part of the focus group. The focus group for this study consisted of six participants. Of the six focus group participants, one was Canadian-born and five were immigrants. They were all women who were comfortable with each other in terms of the topics discussed for this study. The focus group participants had four to ten years of work experience in child welfare. Three of the focus group participants were mothers. An informed consent form was provided to all invited research participants.

For this chapter, the names of the research participants have been changed to protect their identities. In the sections that follow, I have included quotations that reflect select elements of these participants' stories and perspectives.

Findings

The findings discussed in this chapter are only one part of my doctoral research and focus on racialized worker intervention in and interactions with families. Three specific themes came to light. First, the participants described their social affinities with families based on shared identities, histories, and immigration experiences. Second, the findings showed the workers' commitment to keeping racialized families intact during child welfare intervention. Third, the study results revealed the workers' perceptions of the Canadianizing of immigrant parents.

Social Affinities with Families

A number of participants reported that their child welfare employers expressed concern about their becoming close to families and/or thought that they were identifying too closely with clients based on shared histories and culture. Some participants indicated that they felt an irresistible social affinity with racialized families, particularly with marginalized immigrant families. The participants also noted that they developed close worker/client relationships because families often faced multiple problems and because they wanted to work with the entire family—mother, father, children, and extended family—which took a lot of time. Participants believed that building relationships with families was paramount to keeping children safe. They also noted that relationship building did not mean compromising child welfare laws to ensure the safety of children. For participant Eric, the correct balance between social affinity with families and ensuring that child welfare laws were obeyed occurred when workers were able to recognize that the well-being and safety of the child was not being compromised, despite a worker having cultural similarities with service-using families.

According to participants, their social affinity with families was more than part of their daily work routine. Close relationships with families were also about understanding their marginalization and powerlessness. Implicit in the participants' descriptions of their social affinities with families was an understanding of the vulnerability that families experienced but without the worker excusing inappropriate parenting behaviours. However, such closeness to families raises several issues: 1) How does the worker know when not to overidentify with the family? 2) What does being too close to a family mean? 3) Would being close to the family be of concern if it was a nonracialized worker and a white family?

The question of how the worker knows when not to overidentify with the family is important in child welfare and other social work settings.

Participant Susan noted that closeness to the family could result in the worker minimizing the risks to the child, making relationship building ineffective. Others added that overidentification with families could be problematic because the worker might not insist that parents make the required changes, even though they recognized the problems facing the family. Failing to challenge parents could result in child welfare being involved with the family for a longer time. Viewed from this angle, it is necessary to recognize that children also have rights under Canadian law that need to be protected and that all child welfare workers play a role in maintaining safe home environments for children. Child welfare interventions require a balance between fairness to parents and ensuring the protection of children. Trotter (2002) and Dumbrill (2006) argued that children were better protected when workers balanced investigatory and helping practices. Susan aptly stated that once the worker could no longer maintain that balance, it was reasonable for the worker to seek collegial support, that is, supervision. The problem was whether workers could recognize when to seek support once they had developed a close relationship with a family.

The second question can be addressed from a theoretical perspective. Does "being too close to the family" imply a gaze on race? Dora, a racialized supervisor, noted how she was "perceived by a nonracialized worker as taking up for a racialized family." A worker's closeness to a family can shift the gaze from child protection issues to race in cases where there is a shared racial identity between the worker and the family. Another participant, Patricia, noted that "when the worker's closeness to the family is based on nonmajority racial similarities, white supervisors may feel the need to use their power to control case management and planning." Part of this problem relates to overidentifying with families when racialized workers are expected to use dominant ways of assessing families. This expectation is problematic when a worker's upbringing and values are similar to the families they are working with. The shared histories and experiences of the worker and the family can cause concerns in mainstream institutions where racialized workers come to be mistrusted, as expressed by Patricia. Perceptions of worker bias and misplaced objectivity may lead to intensification in the use of power by child welfare agencies through increased supervision of the racialized worker or the transfer of the file to another worker.

Similarly, racialized worker affinity with families that share racial similarities also reveals the hidden assumption in social work that it is the
professional worker who is always positioned to intervene with lower-class
parents. This social work assumption does not quite fit the picture of the
racialized worker's relationships with families of colour, because both the
social worker and the parents have historically been socially positioned as
nonprivileged. In the white worker/white family dyad, however, the worker/
client relationship appears to be the norm because the power dynamic is
based on class differences rather than race. It is arguable that these social
affinities could also be a concern when a white worker provides services to a
poor white family. However, as the history of social work demonstrates, historically, people of privilege helped those from low socio-economic classes,
the work of the early Charity Organization Society and the Settlement
House Movement being examples of this (Hick, 2009). Therefore, the white
professional/white low-class family dyad is not perceived as a compromise
to objectivity. For nonracialized workers, using tools that are Eurocentric
puts them in a position to assess the other (the poor, single parent and
the marginalized). As a result, questions of overidentification with the family do not even become an issue because professionalism, objectivity, and
appropriate work boundaries are assumed and expected as a norm.

The struggle for racialized workers regarding closeness to families
with similar racial backgrounds also reflects some of the concerns that
are discussed in research on the supervisor/supervisee work relationship.
For example, Pendry (2012) noted that there has been a lack of meaningful discussion of race in the supervisor/supervisee relationship in family
therapy settings. According to Pendry, these supervisor/supervisee work
relationships should involve discussions of race, the fear and anxiety
related to this subject, as well as engage workers in conversations about
their work with families, that is, racialized parents.

Institutional expectations of not becoming too close to families can create ambiguities for workers. On the one hand, engagement with families
is encouraged, but, on the other hand, the professional, clinical judgment
of the worker is questioned when an inappropriate work relationship
with the family is suspected. The need to engage families but not to get
too close to parents poignantly symbolizes the dilemma of working with
families and having limitations on the work relationship. In her doctoral
work, Lee (2008) found that caseworkers were either replaced or fired for

being "too close to the families" (p. 176), and in one cited instance, a case-worker was dismissed from a case for advocating against a court finding that the mother was neglectful. However, Lee noted that many mothers found those caseworkers to be valuable sources of support and that these mothers were pleased with the workers' services.

Other participants stated that their work with families mattered for them because they saw themselves as caregivers. When the focus group participants were asked about closeness to families, Samantha openly stated: "I think it is the cultural background. It is our nature. We feel like we are the caregivers. You just feel that you need to care about the people. You need to embrace everybody." This notion of the caregiver is interesting because it ties into the gendered assumptions that it is women who do social service work. Brown (2006) argues that these societal assumptions shape and reinforce the social processes that determine what women's paid work should or should not be. Again, the dilemma for the focus group participants was that they were not only workers but also mothers who were caught in a contradictory position of being caring service providers while at the same time having to meet expectations regarding being seen as professional and maintaining professional boundaries.

Keeping Families Intact

Research participants emphasized the protection of racialized children within their families of origin in different ways. They drew parallels between punishment meted out on slaves and the use of physical punishment by some black families involved with child welfare services. Dora remarked, "[I]f a black family came into the child welfare system, you would know that it is because of physical punishment, and this could be because of the impact of slavery, meaning that this was the way to punish in slavery—the master used physical punishment. So, that form of discipline moves from generation to generation." Dora's comments indicate that the disciplinary methods used by some black families increasingly led to child welfare involvement and investigation of child abuse. However, according to the participants, the problem of child discipline was rooted in historical practices. Participants did not argue that slavery justified the physical abuse of black children by their parents but that workers should be aware of it throughout family interventions. That the participants saw physical discipline in some racialized families as growing out of slavery is no surprise; Foucault himself believed that history was always alive. In the case of black disciplinary practices, history was perceived as manifested in the current "inappropriate" forms of child discipline that some participants connected to problematic power relations, tragedies, and practices of slavery. In his work *Dark Secrets*, Robinson (2012) also draws parallels between contemporary instability within black families (school dropouts, intimate violence, criminality, and poverty) and American slavery, with its harsh and violent practices. Robinson goes further and argues that training a child to be obedient and physical discipline is interwoven into black child-rearing practices that predate slavery and can be traced to West Africa. The author concludes that both slavery and the legacy of West African child-rearing practices cannot be ignored in our understanding of the contemporary child disciplinary practices used in black families.

The notion of history staying alive was also clear in Eric's discussion of absentee fathers: "[D]uring slavery the husband did not belong to the family. If they [husbands] disobeyed the master they could be sold somewhere and never to be seen again." The participants' beliefs referenced the regularity of excluding fathers in child welfare work and surveillance of the mother, who in most cases was held responsible for the family's ills (see Scourfield, 2001a). For Eric, the phenomenon of the absent father in black families not only showed the connections to Euro-American slavery but it was also a dysfunction that was borne by single black mothers who continued to be accused of poor parenting by child welfare.

Other participants acknowledged the sensitivities involved when removing children from the family and that they were heightened because of their knowledge and awareness of the impact of slavery. As Brittany commented, "[D]uring slavery children were ripped from their families. Slaves were not allowed to develop that attachment because they [children] were not yours [did not legally belong to you]." Drawing on the complex historical events of slavery, some participants perceived child removal as reflecting those historical experiences that disadvantaged many marginalized families and communities. In separate interviews, Brittany and Eric discussed the systematic functioning of slavery in relation to breaking up families and the need for workers to be aware of its pernicious effects in present practices, which often result in the removal of children from homes.

Canada also has a history of separating immigrant families (Dua, 1999). Asian men who came to work in Canada were not allowed to sponsor their wives and children to come join them. Dua also provided the example of Caribbean women coming to Canada as domestic help and mothering Canadian children at the expense of their own families that are left behind in their home countries. Dua concluded that Canadian policies governing families in Asian Canadian and Caribbean Canadian communities were remarkably similar in terms of how they separated family members. These sociohistorical events lie at the heart of why participants wanted to protect children within families and avoid repeating the history of separating families through systematic state policies.

Some of the participants had been separated from their own families because of immigration delays and the restrictions of family sponsorship for biological children and spouses. Donna stated, "I understand that to have supports means having to [make new] friends because as immigrants you are leaving your social network back in the old homeland." These experiences of family separation point to reasons why participants felt that children should be raised by parents and that families consisted of extended kin relations. Donna added that within many immigrant families, children were considered a "family asset"; relationships with sons and daughters are close and become the most significant relationships that parents may have in their new world, where there are limited social networks for them. Donna also indicated that children were an asset in the family's immigration and integration, contributing in meaningful ways, for example, interpreting for their parents, who had limited English skills. Chand and Thoburn (2005), as well as others like Maiter and Stalker (2011), question the appropriateness of using children as interpreters in child protection cases. Maiter and Stalker identify several problems with using children as interpreters: a child's lack of linguistic knowledge to accurately interpret; possible longer-term repercussions of a child being privy to adult issues and concerns; and a disruption of the normal family hierarchy. However, in this study the question is not so much about children acting as interpreters in cases of child protection. Rather, the focus for Donna was on English- or French-speaking children who help their parents make social connections to their ethnic groups and the wider community. Children's ability to speak one of the official Canadian languages contributes significantly to the integration of non-English/French-speaking families in their new home country. Patricia stated, "[W]hen children attend programs that workers have suggested, parents are drawn in as well and take up the responsibility of being part of the activities." Children's roles in immigration and integration are often overlooked because of the focus on the adults, but by focusing on the children, we can see how they contribute to the building of the Canadian state by being the conduits for their families to participate in programs and school activities. Below, I further illustrate the workers' perceptions of integrating newcomers into Canadian society.

The Making of New Canadians

Participants commented that providing newcomer families with information on how to parent in Canada was a necessity, but, at the same time, providing this information was not part of the policy requirements that focused on completing assessments according to timelines. However, what was notable in this research was the idea that workers were actively engaged in educating immigrant parents about Canadian ways of parenting. Several comments were made on the subject of making newcomers learn "parenting in Canada" and the "Canadian parenting law."

It was clear in the study that in their social work practices, racialized workers inadvertently reinforced dominant ways of parenting. Some participants felt that the protection of the child and the family unit was and could be ensured if newcomer parents learned Canadian parenting practices, which meant teaching them that children in Canada are protected under law. In the context of child welfare, making immigrant parents Canadians involved the worker teaching parenting rules. Such education was intended to help children remain safe within their families. In this study, workers were challenged by the high number of racialized children in care—a problem that, in their opinion, should receive public attention—and used their roles as gatekeepers to slow down the admission of children into care. The workers engaged in gatekeeping, particularly when intervening with racialized youth who occasionally threatened to report concerns about their parents. Participants felt that immigrant parents were vulnerable and intimidated when their children threatened to report them to child welfare services. Participants indicated that parents in such situations could not discipline their children for fear of child welfare involvement. In my previous role as a child protection worker, it was not uncommon even in Canadian families for teenagers to threaten to report their parents to child welfare. However, immigrant parents have the added fear that they will lose their control of and right to discipline their children, and, as a result, their children will acculturate to Canadian mainstream values and lose their cultural values and forget their history. Important to note also is the reference by focus group participants that "we are making parents Canadians." This reveals the deeply entrenched role that the state and child welfare institutions play in practices of moralization and normalization that become part of the primary forms of intervention with families that are deemed deficient, including immigrant families. The focus group clarified that helping families learn Canadian parenting rules was not only limited to immigrant families. Canadian-born parents also needed to know the complex court processes related to child protection.

Various academics, including Foucault, who studied the notion of power, have suggested that a liberal state government undertakes a multiplicity of state interventions promoting specific kinds of life (Dean, 1991). According to Foucault and others, modern liberal governments, which emerged in the late eighteenth century, use methods of power, not to punish, but to control through technologies of normalization (Osborne & Rose, 1997). Based on a Foucauldian analysis, one can conclude that racialized child welfare workers have become part of a state dynamic that is charged to implement child protection acts requiring families to learn the discourse of parenting. But, in reality, parenting is about the mother. The mother is under surveillance, and child welfare needs to ensure that she is practising good parenting. The knowledge of how to be a good mother, raise good children, and have a healthy family is legitimated through various practices, policies, and laws that inform society on how we should behave and raise children.

Participants also discussed their role modelling for new immigrant parents who were integrating into Canadian society. Role modelling involved helping families avoid becoming racialized stereotypes (incompetent parents, drug users, violent mothers and fathers). Donna neatly captured these aspects of role modelling: "[A]t the end of the day, if you are to influence and teach families, you need to provide them with tools." She went on to say, "[W]e have to believe in these tools." According to Susan, the tools and teaching were meant to engage parents as she talked to them about alternative forms of discipline, as many of the immigrants involved with child welfare services used physical discipline. From the participants' perspective, families needed different tools to change their behaviours in ways that would promote healthy and positive parenting.

There were other examples of role modelling by racialized workers among the participants. For Eric, who saw himself as having a positive influence on youth behaviour, it was important that racialized youth did not perpetuate stereotypes of negative behaviours (disengagement from school, becoming parents at a young age, and wearing drop-down pants). Samantha, a focus group participant, stated that she had helped with the hair care of racialized foster children. Jacobs (2006) argued that a child's hair and skin care may seem trivial, but appearance can adversely impact a youth's self-esteem, which has long-lasting effects, such as insecurity and lack of confidence. These examples illustrate some of the day-to-day concerns of participants who felt they were role models for racialized children in care. The participants' comments on role modelling demonstrate the subtle message that workers are experts from whom parents can learn how to address the challenges that are present in their lives.

Implications for Child Welfare Practice and Education

In this section, I discuss two unrecognized dimensions within Canadian child welfare practices that racialized workers voiced. First, it is apparent through my research that racialized workers wanted to ensure that their histories, knowledge, and experiences were not considered separate from their child welfare practices with families. The way in which the workers' histories and experiences influenced their interventions in families is noteworthy because the current standardization of child welfare practices is intended to ensure that all child protection workers operate the same way. The standardization of child welfare work can be problematic because such proceduralization and routinization does not regularly take into account the multiple problems and challenges that face child welfare families. Nimmagadda and Cowger (1999) insist that social work practice cannot be acultural and ahistorical, meaning that social workers routinely rely on their tacit cultural knowledge when intervening with families. Yan and Wong (2005) come to the same conclusion: social workers bring their own values and beliefs into the relationship with their clients.

The concept of "family" dominated my research. As such, the parental care for children under state law was important for the participants. However, for participants, it was not the duty of the state to parent the children through permanency plans like Crown wardship and adoption.

Participants' stories reflected the ongoing struggle to make their practices conform to existing policies. The participants engaged in balancing state objectives of protecting children with respecting their own cultural histories and alternative ways of knowing in regard to the place of the child in the family. Participants operated within the child welfare mandate, but they also functioned in ways that were outside of the prescribed parameters of child protection, especially when the policies contradicted their experiences and beliefs regarding families or could be used to support their beliefs and values in relation to families. By functioning outside of the policies, I mean that workers questioned the guidelines and found other ways to practise with families that minimized apprehensions or the removal of children from their homes. They conformed to the laws to maintain the safety of children while, at the same time, they created opportunities to create social affinities with parents and educate families, as well as be role models for them. Taken together, these ways of interacting with and intervening in families were used by study participants to ensure that immigrant parents safely raised the children within their homes. Participants revealed that they had been responsible for only a few children entering foster care over the course of their work. Part of the reason for fewer than average child admissions to care was due to their engagement with families, which often took longer than prescribed child welfare standards allowed, but the process led to early permanency for children, meaning that children stayed with their parents or relatives.

The second dimension of racialized workers' interaction with and intervention in families links to the idea of the best interest of the child. Across Canada, most provincial and territorial child welfare legislation emphasizes the best interest of the child as foundational to practice. In this vein, I argue that the legal system should be holding child welfare workers accountable in terms of the promotion of the concept of family in its broad sense. In this study, the broader family means extended family and not simply nuclear households that are regularly the focus of child welfare practices. Similarly, as noted in the Saskatchewan Child Welfare Review Panel report completed by Pringle, Cameron, Durocher, and Skelton (2010), the Indigenous view of family places the child within kinship systems, clan, band, and tribal membership. Children are cared for within a cultural community with grandparents, aunts, uncles, and older cousins, all having responsibilities in child rearing. Similarly, in most non-Western cultures, children are inextricably linked to extended families and communities. In these cultural world views, notions of interdependence and communalism are basic and highly valued. As illustrated by Chipungu and Goodley (2004), many racialized communities place significant emphasis on communalism, collective values, and responsibility to extended family. These traditions of connection with the extended family and the larger community conflict with American family values, which have emphasized and normalized independence, self-reliance, and autonomy. The authors go on to say that this difference in cultural values can create developmental confusion, where a child is unable to develop a positive social identity. Canadian research by Gough (2006) and Cuddeback (2004) also emphasized the importance of children maintaining family relationships while other permanency options are being considered for them.

Conclusion

As my concluding remarks, I contend that the focus cannot continue to be on the best interest of the child outside of their families and histories. In my view, even when removed from their homes, children can have meaningful access to their families, which can result in a sense of belonging and hence further the best interests of the child. Wensley (2006) has highlighted the importance of not treating children's cultural and family backgrounds as abstract concepts, meaning that any good outcomes for children in care should include their cultural and community connections. The less abstract the cultural/family background is for workers, the greater the opportunity there is to change their individual practices and knowledge to ensure better outcomes for children. Wensley (2006) also noted that a child's connection to their community is not in conflict with their best interest. The question that needs broader attention is how to ensure and enhance child safety within their families and communities.

References

Barn, R. (2007). Race, ethnicity and child welfare: A fine balancing act. *British Journal of Social Work, 37*(8), 1425–1434.

Bernard, W. T., Lucas-White, L., & Moore, D. E. (1993). Triple jeopardy: Assessing life experiences of black Nova Scotian women from a social work perspective. *Canadian Social Work Review, 10*(8), 256–273.

Blackstock, C., Trocmé, N., & Bennett, M. (2004). Child maltreatment investigations among Aboriginal and non-Aboriginal families in Canada. *Violence against Women, 10*(8), 901–916.

Brown, D. (2006). Working the system: Re-thinking the institutionally organized role of mothers and the reduction of "risk" in child protection work. *Social Problems, 53*(3), 353–370.

Carabine, J. (2001). Unmarried motherhood 1830–1990: A genealogical analysis. In S. Yates & M. Wetherall (Eds.), *Discourse as data: A guide for analysis* (pp. 268–310). London, United Kingdom: Sage.

Chambers, A. (1986). Women in the creation of the profession of social work. *The Social Service Review, 60*(1), 1–33.

Chand, A., & Thoburn, J. (2005). Child and family support services with minority ethnic families: What can we learn from research? *Child and Family Social Work, 2*(10), 169–178.

Chipungu, S., & Goodley, T. (2004). Meeting the challenges of contemporary foster care. *The future of children, 14*(1), 75–93.

Christie, A. (2006). Negotiating the uncomfortable intersections between gender and professional identities in social work. *Critical Social Policy, 26*(2), 390–411.

Colby, A. (1982). The use of secondary analysis in the study of women and social change. *Journal of Social Issues, 38*(1), 119–123.

Collins, P. H. (1990). *Black feminist thought: Knowledge, consciousness and the politics of empowerment.* Cambridge, MA: Unwin Hyman Inc.

Cuddeback, S. (2004). Kinship family foster care: A methodological and substantive synthesis of research. *Children and Youth Services Review, 26*(7), 623–639.

Dean, M. (1991). *The constitution of poverty: Towards a genealogy of liberal governance.* London, United Kingdom: Routledge.

Dominelli, L., Strega, S., Callahan, M., & Rutman, D. (2005). Endangered children: Experiencing and surviving the state as failed parent and grandparent. *British Journal of Social Work, 35*(7), 1123–1144.

Dorais, A. (1994). Management of cultural diversity and the public service in Canada. *Optimum, 24*(4), 49–57.

Dua, E. (1999). Beyond diversity. In E. Dua & A. Robertson (Eds.), *Scratching the surface: Canadian anti-racist feminist thought* (pp. 237–259). Toronto, ON: Women's Press.

Dumbrill, G. (Ed.). (2005, July). *Child welfare in Ontario: Developing a collaborative intervention model.* A position paper submitted by the Provincial Project Committee on Enhancing Positive Worker Interventions with Children and Their Families in Protection Services: Best Practices and Required Skills, Toronto, Ontario.

Fallon, B., MacLaurin, B., Trocmé, N., & Felstiner, C. (2003). The Canadian incidence study of child abuse and neglect: A profile of a national sample of child protection workers. In K. Kufeldt & B. MacKenzie (Eds.), *Child welfare: Connecting research, policy and practice* (pp. 41–52). Waterloo, ON: Wilfred Laurier University Press.

Farrell, C. (2005). *Michel Foucault*. London, United Kingdom: Sage.

Foucault, M. (1979). *Discipline and punish: The birth of the prison* (A. Bouchard & S. Sheridan, Trans.). New York, NY: Vintage Books.

Foucault, M. (1980). *Power/knowledge*. Brighton, United Kingdom: Harvester Press.

Frankenberg, R. (1993). *White women, race matters: The social construction of whiteness*. Minneapolis, MN: University of Minnesota Press.

Gough, P. (2006). *Kinship care*. Centre of Excellence for Child Welfare. Retrieved from http://www.cecw-cepb.ca/sites/default/files/publications/en/ KinshipCare42E.pdf

Graham, M. (2007). *Black issues in social work and social care*. London, United Kingdom: British Association of Social Workers.

Grimshaw, J. (1993). Practices of freedom. In C. Ramazanoglu (Ed.), *Up against Foucault: Explorations of some tensions between Foucault and feminism* (pp. 51–72). London, United Kingdom: Routledge.

Grossberg, M. (2002). Changing conceptions of child welfare in the United States, 1820–1935. In M. Rosenheim, F. Zimring, D. Tanenhaus, & B. Dohrn (Eds.), *A century of juvenile justice* (pp. 3–41). Chicago, IL: University of Chicago Press.

Gunaratam, Y. (2003). *Researching race and ethnicity: Methods, knowledge and power*. London, United Kingdom: Sage Publications.

Hick, S. (2009). *Social work in Canada: An introduction* (3rd ed.). Toronto, ON: Thompson Educational Publishing Inc.

Holzer, H., & Neumark, D. (2000). What does affirmative action do? *Industrial and Labor Relations Review, 53*(2), 240–271.

Humphreys, C., Atkar, S., & Baldwin, N. (1999). Discrimination in child protection work: Recurring themes in work with Asian families. *Child and Family Social Work, 4*(4), 283–291.

Hutchinson, M. (1989). And for those of us who are black? Black politics in social work. In M. Langan & P. Lee (Eds.), *Radical social work today* (pp. 165–177). London, United Kingdom: Uwin Hyman Ltd.

Jacobs, D. (2006). The national association of black social workers comes to Montreal. In W. Bernard (Ed.), *Fighting for change: Black social workers in Nova Scotia* (pp. 12–17). Lawrencetown, NS: Pottersfield Press.

Jones, E. W. (1986). Black managers: Dreams unrealized. *Harvard Business Review, 64*(3), 84–93.

Kikulwe, D. (in press). Theorizing race: Examining experiences of racialized families in the child welfare system. In M. Jacobs & L. Visano (Eds.), *"Righting" humanity: In our time*. Toronto, ON: APF Press.

Lavergne, C., Dufour, S., Trocmé, N., & Larrivée, M. (2008). Visible minority, Aboriginal and Caucasian children investigated by Canadian protective services. *Child Welfare League of America, 82*(2), 59–76.

Lee, T. (2008). *Stratified reproduction and definitions of child neglect: State practices and parents' responses* (Unpublished doctoral dissertation). City University of New York, New York.

Lewis, G. (1996, Summer). Black women's experience and social work: Speaking out: Researching and representing women. *Feminist Review, 53*, 24–56.

Lewis, G. (1997). *Living the difference. Ethnicity, gender and social work* (Unpublished doctoral dissertation). Open University, Milton Keynes, United Kingdom.

Lewis, G. (2000). *Race, gender and social welfare. Encounters in postcolonial society*. Cambridge, United Kingdom: Polity Press.

Maiter, S. (2009). Race matters: Social justice not assimilation or cultural competence. In S. Strega & J. Carriere (Eds.), *Walking this path together: Anti-racism and anti-oppressive practice* (pp. 62–77). Halifax, NS: Fernwood Publishing.

Maiter, S., & Stalker, C. (2011). South Asian immigrants' experience of child protection services: Are we recognizing strengths and resilience? *Child and Family Social Work, 16*(2), 138–148.

Manis, E., & Street, A. (2000). Possibilities for critical social theory and Foucault's work: A tool box approach. *Nursing Inquiry, 7*(1), 50–60.

Morrel, P. (2007). Power and status contradictions. In D. Mandell (Ed.), *Revisiting the use of self: Questioning professional identities* (pp. 71–86). Toronto, ON: Canadian Scholars Press Inc.

Nimmagadda, J., & Cowger, C. (1999). Cross cultural practice: Social worker ingenuity in the indigenization of practice knowledge. *International Social Work, 42*(3), 261–276.

Osborne, T., & Rose, N. (1997). In the name of society, or three theses on the history of social thought. *History of Human Sciences, 10*(3), 87–104.

Pendry, N. (2012). Race, racism and systemic supervision. *Journal of Family Therapy, 34*(4), 403–418.

Perry, R., & Limb, G. (2004). Ethnic/racial matching of clients and social workers in public child welfare. *Children and Youth Services Review, 26*(10), 965–979.

Pringle, B., Cameron, H., Durocher, A., & Skelton, C. (2010). *For the good of our children and youth: A new vision, a new direction* (Saskatchewan Child Welfare Review Panel). Retrieved from http://saskchildwelfarereview.ca/CWR-panel-report.pdf

Proctor, E., & Davis, L. (1994). The challenge of racial difference: Skills for clinical practice. *Social Work, 39*(3), 314–323.

Proctor, E., & Rosen, A. (1981). Expectations and preferences for counselor race and their relation to intermediate treatment outcome. *Journal of Counseling Psychology, 28*(1), 40–46.

Razack, N., & Badwall, H. (2006). Regional perspectives from North America: Challenges from the North American context. Globalization and anti-oppression. *International Social Work, 49*(5), 661–666.

Robinson, R. (2012). Dark secrets: Obedience training, rigid physical violence, black parenting, and reassessing the origins of instability in the black family through a re-reading of Fox Butterfield's *All God's children*. *Howard Law Journal, 55*(2), 283–291.

Rooney, B. (1984). Black social workers in white departments. In J. Cheetham (Ed.), *Social work and ethnicity*. London, United Kingdom: National Institute Social Services Library.

Rossiter, A. (2005). Discourse analysis in social work: From apology to question. *Critical Social Work, 6*(1). Retrieved from http://www1.uwindsor.ca/criticalsocialwork/2005-volume-6-no-1

Scourfield, J. (2001a). Constructing men in child protection work. *Men and Masculinities, 4*(1), 70–89.

Scourfield, J. (2001b). Constructing women in child protection work. *Child and Family Social Work, 6*(1), 77–87.

Shalla, V., & Clement, W. (2007). *Work in tumultuous times: Critical perspectives.* Montreal, QC: McGill-Queen's University Press.

Solomos, J. (1995). Marxism, racism and ethnicity. *American Behavorial Scientist, 38*(3), 407–420.

Strega, S., & Carrière, J. (2008). *Walking this path together: Anti-racist and anti-oppressive child welfare practice.* Halifax, NS: Fernwood Publishing.

Stubbs, P. (1984). The employment of black social workers: From ethnic sensitivity to anti-racism? *Critical Social Policy, 4*(12), 6–27.

Swift, K. (1995). *Manufacturing "bad mothers": A critical perspective on child neglect.* Toronto, ON: University of Toronto Press.

Swift, K., & Callahan, M. (2009). *At risk: Social justice in child welfare and other human services.* Toronto, ON: University of Toronto Press.

Trotter, C. (2002). Worker skill and client outcome in child protection. *Child Abuse Review, 11*(1), 38–50.

Wakefield, J. (1998). Foucauldian fallacies: An essay review of Leslie Margolin's *Under the Cover of Kindness. Social Service Review, 74*(4), 545–587.

Wensley, H. K. (2006). *Aboriginal children and child welfare. An overview of recent changes.* Retrieved from http://www.docstoc.com/docs/32965766/Aboriginal-Children-and-Child-Welfare

Williams, F. (1996). Race, welfare and community care: A historical perspective. In W. Ahmad & K. Atkin (Eds.), *Race and community care* (pp. 15–28). Maidenhead, United Kingdom: Open University Press.

Williams, L. S., & Villemez, W. J. (1993). Seekers and finders: Male entry and exit into female-dominated jobs. In C. L. William (Ed.), *Doing "women's work": Men in non-traditional occupations* (pp. 64–90). Newbury Park, CA: Sage.

Woldeguiorguis, M. (2003). Racism and sexism in child welfare: Effects on women of color as mothers and practitioners. *Child Welfare, 82*(2), 273–288.

Yan, M. C., & Wong, Y. L. R. (2005). Rethinking self-awareness in cultural competence: Towards a dialogic self in cross-cultural social work. *Families in Society, 86*(2), 181–188.

Yee, J. (2007). *Examining system and individual barriers experienced by visible-minority social workers in mainstream social services agencies.* Toronto, ON: CERIS.

CHAPTER 10

Pathways: Community-Engaged Research with Youth Transitioning to Adult In(ter)dependence from Government Care

Marie Lovrod, Darlene Domshy, and Stephanie Bustamante

Introduction

Considerable evidence accumulated over decades of social research demonstrates that diverse young people in and from government care and custody share experiential conditions that can contribute to lower educational attainments (Collins & Clay, 2009; Moffat & Vincent, 2009; Flynn & Tessier, 2011; Kirk & Day, 2011; Ferguson & Wolkow, 2012; Stott, 2013; Courtney, Flynn, & Beaupré, 2013) and arduous transitions to adult citizenship (Burnside & Fuchs, 2013; Bender, Yang, Ferguson, & Thompson, 2015; Butler & Benoit, 2015). Challenges arising from uneven care placement experiences affect the life trajectories of youth transitioning from foster care (Geenan & Powers, 2007; Jones, 2011; Cunningham & Diversi, 2013; Batsche et al., 2014) and those being released from custody (Stephens & Arnette, 2000; Woodall, 2007; Corrado, Freedman, & Blatier, 2011; Beal, 2014) in distinct but related ways. To honour the unique effects

Suggested Citation: Lovrod, M., Domshy, D., & Bustamante, S. (2016). Pathways: Community-engaged research with youth transitioning to adult in(ter)dependence from government care. In H. Montgomery, D. Badry, D. Fuchs, & D. Kikulwe (Eds.), *Transforming Child Welfare: Interdisciplinary Practices, Field Education, and Research* (pp. 211–239). Regina, SK: University of Regina Press.

on life chances faced by young people growing up in systems care, both positive and difficult, we follow Butler and Benoit (2015) by referring to youth currently involved or recently aged out of foster care and/or custody as *youth-with-care-experiences*, or occasionally as *systems youth*, when differentiating systems backgrounds from those of nonsystems peers. Frequently, youth-with-care-experiences are overlooked by adults as potential contributors to, and primary stakeholders in, their own development and communities (Saskatchewan Youth in Care and Custody Network [SYICCN], 2014). Yet, given the opportunity, young people have much to offer in ongoing conversations about best practices, sound policies, and the factors that can enhance or impede their successes (Lovrod & Domshy, 2011).

This chapter draws upon a distinctive, community-engaged research partnership with the SYICCN. Our research examines the opportunities that youth networks provide for youth participants and their adult supports (network leaders, social workers, adult caregivers, advocates, former systems youth mentors, researchers, all with police background checks) to interact within and across identity groups in productive ways that can improve service delivery and ease transitions within and from care (Lovrod & Domshy, 2011). A consistent objective is to build social inclusion, working with diverse stakeholders to moderate care deficits and facilitate extended conversations with and among young people who have lived some or most of their early lives in government care systems. Our research partnership engages and supports youth participants in co-designing constructive, future-oriented, evidence-based, knowledge-building strategies about growing up in care. The approach serves as a bridge to personal and social development and as a way to bring youth voice and perspectives to the structures and issues that affect their well-being and lives.

The SYICCN is a youth-led, provincial, nonprofit organization, dedicated to improving the lives of young people, aged fourteen to twenty-four, in or from government care and/or custody. Like other provincial networks, the SYICCN provides opportunities for participating youth to develop peer relationships based on mutual respect and reciprocal knowledge sharing. The network also provides public education to raise awareness about issues that affect youth-with-care-experience among caregivers and the professionals who work with them. The SYICCN is mandated by its youth leaders and through its arms-length provincial funding to help set up local youth-in-care networks throughout Saskatchewan and to develop strategies that empower youth-with-care-experiences. Rather than concentrating network activities exclusively in urban centres, the SYICCN emphasizes distributed access. This model includes experiences of youth in care from far-flung and northern communities, and reveals regional differences in resources available to youth networks. If more young people were advised of their right to participate in the SYICCN, including youth who may miss opportunities to join existing networks or to build local ones among reserve communities, for example, the benefits of youth networking could be extended. Meanwhile, the provincial network strives to ensure that local network members have a voice in their lives and communities.

Two recent research projects, including a longitudinal study of youth networking practices, *Our Dream, Our Right, Our Future*, completed in 2011, and a provincially funded, youth-centred, transitional needs assessment, *Youth in Transit: Growing Out of Care*, completed in 2014, drew on participatory action research (PAR) and youth-friendly creative methodologies to construct welcoming spaces where youth could help build public knowledge about ways to improve their experiences in and transitioning from government care and custody. Focused on strengths and capacities (Peterson & Seligman, 2004), both projects mobilize and invigorate participating networks by supporting skill enhancement and social learning among members. The studies build on cumulative results (Greig, Taylor, & MacKay, 2007) in a continuous learning process where knowledge is shared with participants who have a vested interest in the information generated and method design improvements (Koshy, 2005). For both projects, the academic researcher, network staff, and participating youth gathered original data together, building on principles of local knowledge development through iterative combinations of evidence-based practice and practice-based evidence (Children and Youth in Challenging Contexts Network [CYCC], 2013). In the first project, youth and adult supports worked with the researcher to co-design noninvasive, age-appropriate instruments for documenting the impact of networking among youth-with-care-experiences in Saskatchewan over the previous fifteen-year period. For the second project, youth generated requests and ideas for a comprehensive transition training tool that they could use on their own, together, or with a supportive adult to begin planning their transitions from care. These projects are presented together because they provide a narrative of cumulative shared skill development among youth and also for the researcher and SYICCN staff, who have become more adept at co-creating with young people knowledge projects that are safe, fun, and informative, at every stage.

Both projects generate and theorize new ways of engaging youth in and from government care and custody networks in collective self-programming for better experiences in care, and for more successful transitions. Both emphasize the vital relationship between emerging adult independence and constructive social interdependence while exposing youth participants to advanced educational and/or training opportunities. We use the term *in(ter)dependence* to clarify that adult independence is never achieved in isolation, and to emphasize the importance of supporting social development for more successful transitions within and from government care (see Burnside & Fuchs, 2013; Cunningham & Diversi, 2013; Blakeslee, 2015). One of the many important lessons arising from this research is that government care solutions can be made more effective by engaging youth-with-care-experiences in designing safe, youth-friendly networking strategies and tools through collaborative knowledge building. Below, we provide a brief overview of some of the historical forces and contemporary conditions that have shaped the evolution of child welfare systems in Canada, as they inform our research approaches.

Literature Review: Historical Background and Contemporary Contexts

Government care and related policy and practice emerged in North America in the context of colonial nation building (Strong-Boag, 2011). Prevailing attitudes about race, class, gender, ability, religion, and sexuality have influenced Canadian child welfare systems from the beginning. Early efforts linked un- and underpaid female labour to the needs of the state, providing low-cost, out-of-home care to apprehended children and youth through orphanages, kinship, and foster care. Youth judicial custody, on the other hand, relied more heavily on male purveyors of law and order (Alvi, 2012). Normative in-home care was modelled on hetero-parented families who could rely on higher male incomes, as distributed by race and class (Strong-Boag, 2011). While social attitudes have changed with time, historical legacies inform some of the challenges facing government care in Canada today, such as the overrepresentation of Indigenous, Métis, and Inuit youth,[1] and the devaluation of caring work that sometimes still characterizes care provision. Overcrowding, limited supports for caregivers, and negative media attention have led to a decline in available foster parents, a rise in group home placements (which work better for some youth than others), and the emergency housing of children and youth in hotels.[2] Attending to the particular needs of girls, boys, Aboriginal youth, children and youth with disabilities, queer youth, newcomers, those growing up in rural and urban contexts, those in trouble with the law, or street-involved and homeless youth are all key concerns of contemporary child welfare systems. As the CYCC (2013) argues:

> *Vulnerable children and youth are not all the same; they differ in terms of their experiences, contexts, and cultures. They face common threats to their mental health that come from constraints and challenges built into their community and societal structures. No young person or population of young people is inherently more vulnerable than another. It is the contexts in which they reside that make them more vulnerable. (p. 4)*

The complicated and often challenging positions of youth-with-care-experiences reflect the complex lives of their families and communities, who may not be able to provide care for a number of reasons related to prevailing inequitable social conditions. These include, but are not limited to, structurally reproduced forms of poverty, limited public attention to and investments in rural communities, the insidious effects of social prejudice, undervaluing the voice and agency of subordinated groups, and inequitable resource distribution. Dealing with so many disparities while attending to diversities can be a daunting task for government care systems.

Canada currently has no national advocate for children and youth in government care and custody. The Canadian Council of Child and Youth

---

1 Indigenous cultural assimilation through residential schools and the Sixties Scoop in Saskatchewan influence high numbers of Aboriginal youth in care and custody systems. "First Nations children are 15 times more likely to be removed from their families and placed in foster care than their non-Aboriginal peers" (Blackstock, 2006/2007, p. 8).

2 For a recent news story on these issues, see Cowan (2015).

Advocates do meet regularly to discuss mutual concerns. However, delegating social care and development to provinces, territories, and local communities can contribute to national knowledge gaps (Courtney et al., 2013). While there is certainly merit in supporting locally directed resources, limited national data on child protection hinders attempts to work across sectors and regions to improve service delivery for diverse youth-with-care-experiences.

Under-resourced services, such as those found in remote and Indigenous communities (which may include low staffing, high turnover, insufficient training, and small budgets), have been linked with higher care placement rates (Chabot et al., 2013). Underfunded agencies also tend to rely on standardized theoretical approaches that cannot adequately account for diverse cultural norms among Indigenous and newcomer communities, or for the unique experiences of minoritized subgroups, including LGBTQ+ youth or young people with disabilities (to name just a few distinctive experiences that may be subsumed under the generic term, *youth*). For example, Richardson and Nelson (2007) point out that attachment theory may not account for the full range of relational dynamics in Indigenous communities with traditions of extended, intergenerational care. Understanding the limitations of one-size-fits-all solutions is essential in learning to respond to the particular needs of distinct subgroups of youth in need of care.

Young people can find themselves on the receiving end of unintended structural biases when care policies emphasize protection. While the United Nations Convention on the Rights of the Child endorses provision, protection, *and* participation rights (Howe & Covell, 2007), complex societal power structures may perpetuate disparities in access to meaningful citizenship for youth-with-care-experiences. Because government care emerged in paternalistic state-building conditions, as a vulnerable population, affected youth may still be denied appropriate avenues to public visibility and voice, purportedly for their own good. The problem is that protection without opportunities for participation leave youth-with-care-experiences less visible as knowledgeable agents in their own lives. Butler and Benoit (2015) suggest that much more needs to be understood about how youth-with-care-experiences, forced to negotiate with the "state as parent" (p. 26), practise citizenship. Experiential gaps that emerge even in later years between systems youth and their peers, who have limited understanding of what it means to grow up in out-of-home care (see Stewart, Kum, Barth, & Duncan, 2014), further obscure the contributions that systems youth can make in their communities.

Positive future orientation may also be more difficult as youth-with-care-experiences navigate pressing circumstances, sometimes acquiring defensive social habits in response to restricted personal agency (Metzger, 2008; Brown & Wilderson, 2010; Howse, Diehl, & Trivette, 2010; Ahrens, Katon, McCarty, and Richardsom, 2012). Stott (2013) argues, "in order to more fully address the needs of youth transitioning from foster care, child welfare policies and practices need to focus more attention on relational and social development of youth while in foster care" (p. 218). Certainly, positive service experiences (Sanders, Munford, Liebenberg, & Ungar, 2014) combined with good peer interactions (Melkman, Refaeli, Bibi, & Benbenishty, 2015), acquired through extracurricular and educational activities, support prosocial behaviour and optimism (Flynn, Beaulac, & Vinograd, 2006; Moffat & Vincent, 2009).

However, the education of youth-with-care-experiences may not be a top priority for overburdened agencies or public school boards (Moffat & Vincent, 2009, p. 135; Ferguson & Wolkow, 2012). Systems youth may also be excluded from post-secondary education by narrow interpretations of policy in relation to their in-care status, including definitions of kinship care, permanent, long-term, and temporary wards, extended supports (to age twenty-one), and early emancipation (for sixteen- to seventeen-year-olds). Lack of permanency planning can lead to multiple placements, which exacerbates lower rates of high school completion and reduces social connections in the crucial period immediately following transition from care (Jones, 2011; Tracey & Hanham, 2015). Long-term consequences can include underemployment, poverty, and homelessness (both urban and rural; see Skott-Myhre, Raby, & Nikolaou, 2008), as well as higher rates of systems dependence, offending behaviour, and recidivism among youth transitioning from custody (Griffiths, Dandurand, & Murdoch, 2007).

In response to these challenges, the SYICCN supports more positive future orientation by bringing youth together with supportive adults in constructive purpose and play. As a result, youth-with-care-experiences learn that they are not alone, and that they have allies in striving together for better futures. Cindy Blackstock (2006/2007) affirms that Indigenous cultures, once so harshly devalued by the colonial state, have much to teach Canadians about mutual care, sustainability, and including children and youth in public decision making:

> *Aboriginal societies in Canada are very culturally diverse, represent-*
> *ing over 50 distinct language groups. And yet they share a common*
> *value for the interdependence of all life and land, a strong sense of*
> *responsibility to the generations to follow, and a value for spiritual-*
> *ity. Children were amongst the most valued citizens in society in that*
> *they represented the future of the society and brought a different*
> *and valued perspective to community life. Many Aboriginal deci-*
> *sion-making processes include children as key contributors. (p. 7)*

Recognizing that children and youth in and from care *can* contribute to their communities is an important structural insight when seeking more promising practices of service delivery and better outcomes for young people transitioning to, within, and from government care and custody.

Despite substantial child welfare literature, peer-reviewed studies on youth-centred analyses of the broad determinants of systems youth health and resiliencies are rare (Hannah-Moffat & Maurutto, 2003; Daining & DePanfilis, 2007; Scannapieco, Connell-Carrick, & Painter, 2007; Kaplan, Skolnik, & Turnbull, 2009; Leve, Fisher, & Chamberlain, 2009). Much of the resiliency literature focuses on normative success, which does not account for the detours that can arise through care and custody experiences. Recognition that resiliency is culturally conditioned has emerged only recently (Ungar et al., 2008; Filbert & Flynn, 2010), yet youth are empowered through opportunities to define resilience, in(ter)dependence, and success, themselves.

Introducing Youth in Government Care and Custody as Research Collaborators

Youth in care and custody do not like to be labelled *at risk* (Lovrod & Domshy, 2011). While teenagers are natural risk-takers, youth-with-care-experiences do not choose the societal risks to which they are exposed, resulting in care placements and related challenges in achieving full adult citizenship (Bernstein, 2009; Saskatchewan Child Welfare Review Panel Report,

2010). Social stigmas that reflect public ignorance about diverse experiences of government care create both external and internalized barriers to self-actualization. Because youth can learn from systems experiences to be wary, unaware, or misinformed about existing or new conditions and opportunities (Courtney, Piliavin, Grogan-Kaylor, & Nesmith, 2001; Gilligan, 2005; Unrau, Seita, & Putney, 2008; Casey, Reid, & Trout, 2010; Healey & Fisher, 2011), promising chances to expand their horizons of possibility may be missed, and resilience compromised. No wonder, then, that a study conducted in greater Victoria, British Columbia, found that youth-with-care-experiences approach social citizenship with levels of ambivalence and alienation, ranging from feeling primarily self-responsible to reluctant and dissenting (Butler & Benoit, 2015). Although most young people in care and custody, whatever their social position, are too busy navigating complex life circumstances to pay full attention to the structures that place them at risk, most recognize that something important is amiss.

Sometimes on the road of life, things are not always clear.[3]

---

3   This photo-voice image and its caption were created by a youth participant as part of our longitudinal study of networking impacts. While only a few samples can be presented here, systems youth consistently generate moving and informative documentation of their feelings and experiences in government care.

Today, youth in care and custody come from a wide variety of social locations. When decision-making processes do not include a commitment to take their perspectives into account, peer-to-peer attachments may serve as the most readily available resource for young people seeking to cope with their experiences in, and transitioning from, care. Through the SYICCN, young people and adult supports have identified networking as both a learned skill and a healing practice that can eventually extend to communities of origin and the wider public (Lovrod & Domshy, 2011). Even under trying conditions, youth-with-care-experiences can learn to mobilize caring relations among themselves. As one youth pointed out during our longitudinal study (Lovrod & Domshy, 2011) on the impact of networking in the lives of young people: "It doesn't matter, your race, your age, your sex, your sexuality....We all need to be loved and we all need to belong. And with the Network, we do belong. There's someone from every background here" (p. 8). Clearly, provincial and national networks, including Youth in Care Canada, work hard to provide affirmative environments for constructive meaning-making among diverse youth in and from government care (Collins & Clay, 2009; Charette, 2012; Jackson & Cameron, 2012).

Co-labouring with young people in and from care during some of their most critical developmental years, approximately half of the SYICCN's work goes into formal and informal supports for young people experiencing transition issues. Although relevant support programs are available in some centres, many young people do not know about them, a widespread phenomenon among youth-with-care-experiences. Social location, relational context, and structural biases limit equitable access to appropriate supports.

In efforts to understand the spectrum of barriers to achieving successful adult in(ter)dependence among youth-with-care-experiences, it is important to recognize that "child welfare involvement...can weaken or disrupt natural support relationships, while introducing service-oriented relationships that are not intended to last into adulthood" (Blakeslee, 2015, p. 123). As such, more or less inevitable relational disruptions can reduce access to a host of communally sustained opportunities that youth who are not involved in government care can take for granted. Where positive opportunity structures may be elusive for youth-with-care-experiences, the supportive peer attachments sustained by local, provincial, and national networks by youth for youth help produce practical sites for shared reflection and planning, and therefore more hopeful, strategic interpretations of even difficult transitions.

Difficult transitions within care predict challenging transitions out of care. Multiple disruptions in living arrangements produce chaotic learning pathways and interrupt life skills acquisition. For example, evidence shows that youth with work experience prior to the age of eighteen have longer-term employment success (Stewart et al., 2014). However, achieving the necessary suite of skills and habits required to undertake youth employment can be difficult for youth in care, and even more so for those in custody. Youth-with-care-experiences may lack natural mentors (Greeson, Usher, & Grinstein-Weiss, 2010, p. 565) and role models, or extended support networks, including culturally appropriate, recreational, and social connections (Fraser et al., 2012; Courtney et al., 2013; Jager et al., 2009). For those placed at a distance from home communities, as may occur with Inuit and Indigenous children, for example, cultural re-entry can be difficult if sustained connections are not well supported (Fraser et al., 2012). Similar problems occur for youth transitioning from custody and for crossover youth with experiences of both foster/group care and youth justice systems, each of which constitutes a distinct subgroup among transitioning youth (Byrne et al., 2014, p. 307).

Passing from one very specific environmental context to another can create stressful periods of "disorientation and reorientation" (Bateman & Neal, 2015, p. 2). Steinberg, Chung, and Little (2004) argue, for example, that involvement with the criminal justice system *arrests* development, with implications for psychosocial adaptation upon emancipation. Coupled with the fact that "a minimum of 30% to 50% of youth involved in juvenile crimes have special needs" (Osher et al., 2002, p. 3), including cognitive, emotional, and behavioural disabilities with which staff are not trained to engage constructively, Hocking's (2014) point that "young people who offend are in every sense *children* in need" (p. 192) is even more compelling. Taking a closer look "at the factors that bring youth to become juvenile offenders and what can lead them to re-offend" (Torres, 2015, p. 3) is a vital task in a crowded provincial criminal justice system where, nevertheless, youth-friendly transition spaces have faced closure.[4] This has led

---

4   The Yarrow Youth Farm near Saskatoon was closed recently despite concerns raised from many quarters (Lagaden, 2015).

to more frequent moves and increased restrictions in open custody cases, reducing rehabilitative opportunities as youth are held in modified spaces within secure facilities (Saskatchewan Advocate for Children and Youth, 2015, p. 33). Community or open custody agreements that tie youth to social networks through active engagements reduce recidivism, whereas closed custody, with limited or no social or community connections, starts the process of institutionalization, leading to more system dependence, higher recidivism, and self-harm. Where victims are amenable, restorative and reparative justice models (Rodriguez, 2007; Tomporowske, Manon, Bargen, & Binder, 2011) may be helpful in healing community connections involving juveniles.

Understanding that no one achieves success entirely on their own is vital to young people removed from families and communities of origin. Appreciating interdependence is also an important condition for working with service providers who experience competitive funding environments and may lack helpful guidelines for interacting constructively across pro-fession-specific systems constraints (Ferguson & Wolkow, 2012, p. 1146). Because in a "restrictive fiscal environment, states have looked for ways to reduce the number of children entering care and to speed their exit from care" (Freundlich, 2010, cited in Courtney et al., 2013, p. 166), youth nav-igate a complex terrain of policy and practice, in which those "who are at the age of majority without extended care and maintenance are sym-bolically and literally dumped out of the system" (Youth in Care Canada, 2005, p. 1). Harrowing experiences are frequently described to the SYICCN staff by youth-with-care-experiences. Four days to come up with rent and providing a young person with the number for social assistance intakes are both examples of some of the unacceptable transition plans that youth have shared.

Poor transition planning is a symptom of overburdened social and com-munity services, and can undermine the good work accomplished through the SYICCN. As one staff member commented in an oral history for *Our Dream, Our Right, Our Future*: "We watch youth who have made such good progress lose that in transition—they have no foster family, no supports, except maybe those which are not best for them. That is so hard!" (2011, p. 26). High aspirations cultivated in care can fall away when survival needs become paramount (Ferguson & Wolkow, 2012, p. 1145). Similarly, most youth transitioning from custody are at different stages of voluntary desistance from offending activities (Lussier, McCuish, & Corrado, 2015, p. 87). However, the need for relief from relentless transition challenges may lead to poor decisions. Young people may also exit care too early—assuming or having been ill advised that adulthood is constituted by self-reliant independence from community and government supports, which non-system youth often learn to rely upon. If their voices and opinions have been discounted in past service contacts, there is strong incentive for youth-with-care-experiences to emancipate, or simply break and run.

Many youth approaching transition struggle with the practical contradictions of growing up in care. On the one hand, under state protection, they may have limited or interrupted opportunities to learn how to build community-engaged self-determination, and on the other, they are expected suddenly to step into full-blown autonomy when they reach the age of majority (Geenen & Powers, 2007; McCoy, McMillen, & Spitznagel, 2008; Burnside & Fuchs, 2013; Courtney et al., 2013). In part, this paradox of underpreparation for compulsory independence reflects messages that circulate in patriarchal culture; the heroic self-made individual who pulls themselves up by their so-called bootstraps is not expected to account for all of the forces that supported them along the way. Youth in care and custody are particularly vulnerable to such disempowering messages, owing to internal and external pressures to exit government care as soon as possible.

This pressure is endured by youth in care and custody at a time when both systems and nonsystems youth are experiencing longer transitions to adult interdependence. Some provinces have now extended care supports to accommodate this new social reality. However, reaching the age of majority is often an entirely different experience for youth transitioning from care. Youth-with-care-experiences are required to complete the task of identity formation "at an earlier age than their peers" (Burnside & Fuchs, 2013, p. 43). Hiles, Moss, Thorne, Wright, and Dallos (2014) argue that for transitioning youth, the task of developing an adult identity occurs "in the midst of an unstable environment which often serve[s] to undermine their journey" (p. 1). Unfortunately, due to poor transition preparation, many youth exiting care become reliant on adult government programs rather than becoming confident, self-reliant citizens. Youth need education and employment, with functional rather than "superficial" (Hocking, 2014, p. 192) supports, to get there.

Research Overview and Design

Saskatchewan is uniquely situated for youth-centred research on child welfare transitions, owing, in part, to the active presence of the SYICCN, and to the diverse demographic pressures that shape child welfare provincially and nationally. Saskatchewan's high incidence of Indigenous youth in government care, its diverse urban and rural development patterns, its investments in northern resource development, and its pro-immigration policies provide an important context for investigating the conditions that shape experiences informing youth-centred research about government care on the Prairies and in Canada.

This chapter draws on two projects that engaged youth from government care networks in collaborative research design, using age-appropriate, participatory, process-oriented, community-based qualitative methods that affirm youth access to public voice, without compromising anonymity, confidentiality, or life chances. Both projects are founded on the principle that "young people share power with adults in the design, implementation and evaluation of the programs that serve them" (CYCC, 2013, p. 7). For youth who may grow up feeling isolated by their difficult life situations, or by relocation to unfamiliar cultural and community contexts (Chandler & Lalonde, 1998; Davis & Baena, 2001; Ungar et al., 2008; Filbert & Flynn, 2010; Walls & Whitbeck, 2012; Anderson & Linares, 2012; Zinga, 2012), interacting with other youth from care and custody is an important opportunity to normalize their experiences. Participating in research development together adds to this potential for a sense of belonging by promoting transferable skill development while demonstrating that autonomy and social connection are interwoven. Mitchell, Jones, and Renema (2014) affirm that youth in transition can be "meaningfully engaged and empowered through the research process" (p. 291), which offers meaning-making space that responds to structural adversity with creativity, naming the issues, and finding workable solutions that build resilience, confidence, and leadership capacity. Constructive relations with peers, researchers, and other adult supporters can become a significant resource in preparing for adult in(ter)dependence.

Networking among youth in government care and custody is based on the premise that social relationships matter in supporting individual successes. All research projects conducted in partnership with the

SYICCN are overseen by a project-specific group of stakeholders, themselves involved in relevant relational networks. This approach reflects in(ter)dependence as an important value in all network collaborations. Stakeholders for the projects we describe here have included young people from provincial networks and other youth-serving organizations; representatives from the ministries of Social Services, Healthcare, Education, and Justice; Aboriginal Family Services; the Federation of Saskatchewan Indian Nations; Saskatchewan First Nations Family and Community Institute; the Saskatchewan Advocate for Children and Youth; and the Saskatchewan Foster Families Association.

Ethics approval was sought for both projects from the University of Saskatchewan Research Services and Ethics Office, which operates in compliance with tricouncil agency requirements for ethical research involving children and youth, and with respect for First Nations guidelines for ownership, control, access, and possession (OCAP). All of the questions or approaches, which were developed in co-operation with staff and youth leaders at the SYICCN, were designed to be respectful and non-invasive, inviting participants to provide future-oriented perspectives and opinions. Participants were provided with consent forms outlining the goals of the research, risks involved (deemed minimal), and their right to withdraw. The researcher and SYICCN staff reviewed the forms with participants and answered any questions prior to research activities. Those aged sixteen and over signed their own consent forms. For youth participants, ages 14–16, guardian or worker consent was obtained.

Our first project, named by youth—*Our Dream, Our Right, Our Future*—used collaboratively designed surveys, photo-voice, oral histories, and focus groups to evaluate the impact of networking in the lives of 106 participating youth in and from government care, together with twenty-one adult supports. Our second project, *Youth in Transit: Growing Out of Care*, engaged ninety-five youth and thirty-one adults, province-wide, in stakeholder meetings and focus group design and delivery of a transition planning program provided through the provincial network. In addition, 115 more young people from care, five Elders, and fifteen additional adult supports took part in our Knowledge Sharing Days, undertaken in co-operation with the Saskatchewan First Nations Family and Community Institute (SFNFCI). Both organizations were mutual stakeholders in efforts to create transition resources for young people from government care and First Nations child and family service workers, respectively. The Knowledge Sharing Days events were conducted in April and May 2015, in Regina, Saskatoon, Yorkton, Moose Jaw, and Prince Albert, with final data analysis and youth and stakeholder consultations completed in October.

Youth and adult supports involved in knowledge gathering and sharing events participated in generating new information through focus group activities and in data analysis, offering their perspectives in co-creative documentation projects and summarizing their views in final wrap-up sessions. Participants completed evaluation forms and provided comments about what they liked and learned during their time together, including ideas for future research. SYICCN staff, youth leaders, and the researcher compiled this evaluative information, together with any materials generated in focus groups, such as flip-chart discussion summaries, photo-voice pages, or creative-mapping projects, in order to identify themes and articulate outcomes. Themes and summaries were brought back to youth members for confirmation, wherever possible. Since all SYICCN research projects also develop youth-friendly reports and information tools, which are vetted by youth members and project stakeholders, participants and members of the public who access these resources benefit directly from the research.

Youth-Friendly Participatory Action Methods: Putting Learning into Practice

Participatory research begins with the recognition that youth need to be honoured as agents in their own lives. This means the projects we develop together take a forward-looking, aspirational approach to the ethical issues of working with youth in care. We do not dwell in stigma or ask youth about painful experiences. Rather, we focus on creative expression and interactive processes that concentrate on positive actions youth can take to support their own futures, building what Lee and Berrick (2014) have termed "identity capital" (p. 78), arising from their own knowledge and experiences.

For example, our *Youth in Transit: Growing Out of Care* study used a combination of community and body mapping to chart healthy ways for growing out of care. In initial focus groups, where youth were encouraged to identify their transition needs and best approaches to meeting them, we invited participants to document what they consider to be the most important resources available to them on a large, shared, community map. Young people ultimately identified ten issues of primary concern, together with places to find relevant information and support: identification; general life skills; health and well-being; education; employment; housing and healthy living; financial education and money management; social supports and healthy relationships; parenting; and youth justice. Youth readily cited local community resources or opportunities for improvements. Young mothers, for example, accustomed to pushing strollers, worked as budding urban planners, articulating the need for walkable neighborhoods with sidewalks in good repair, adequate signage, and traffic management. Indigenous youth identified resources specific to their cultural needs and, in northern communities, nature was recognized as a resource in moderating difficult emotions. Participants who self-identified as queer, as youth with disabilities, and newcomers indicated that social conditions may play out differently for them in urban versus rural communities. Community maps were also an important aspect of the five Knowledge Sharing Days held across the province with the SFNFCI. At each of these events, Indigenous Elders and youth-with-care-experiences opened day-long meetings, where both organizations shared the results of their respective research on youth transitions. Participants found the workshops informative and stimulating, and many commented that they had not been aware of all of the local resources that resonated with youth.

As indicated, we keep all of our community maps, focus group flip-chart pages, or photo-voice pages summarizing data for future meetings scheduled with youth and for thematic analysis. As a result, youth at the SYICCN's recent biennial provincial conference could compare resources identified in different locations around the province. Sometimes, the contrasts in resources identified by different generations in different places were stark. More youth than adults are likely to identify a skateboarding park as a resource, for example. At other times, there was considerable overlap. Just seeing the lists generated by others helped inspire new ideas. Working in small groups with representatives from across the province, youth built shared maps that pooled resource ideas drawn from many communities.

Once community maps were completed, again working in small groups, youth applied what they had learned to collaborative body maps through which they identified individual qualities and strengths that would enhance transition success. In each group, one youth or adult support volunteered to have their body traced by one or two of their co-group members as a way to represent the many important individual qualities that young people can bring to their transition plans. Each small group participant was asked to add at least one significant personal quality or strength that they could bring to their own transition to the space inside the body traced on large sheets of paper that would later be posted for review by all participating groups. Then we invited youth to surround the body they had filled with their own capacities and ideas by available community resources drawn from previous mapping exercises, emphasizing their personal agency in accessing available supports. Thus, we created a positive space where youth addressed gaps in transition readiness with information and learning to prepare.

Creative mapping projects, at both the provincial conference and Knowledge Sharing Days, were followed by a transitional case-planning project. Participants were presented with a composite, fictional, young person with an invented name, Rae, who was preparing for transition. Imagined as a young Indigenous woman in foster care, Rae was described as having maintained ties to her community through an aunt who could not take her in because she has multiple sclerosis. Youth, then, whatever their own background, knew that Rae was familiar with her cultural heritage and why that matters. They could also consider the impacts of living with a chronic disability (see Young et al., 2009, and Whitehouse, 2015). We reminded youth that even if Rae, like many young people in care, was not familiar with the SYICCN, numerous caring people would be ready to help, if only they knew how or had the chance to do so. Helping to build confidence that it is possible to find such invaluable community connections is part of the positive impact of the research project.

Based on information provided about Rae's interests, her dreams, and what she did and did not know about transition, participants broke into groups, each organized around one of the transition training modules that young people themselves had helped to prepare, in order to build what turned out to be a remarkably workable transition plan for Rae. During the Knowledge Sharing Days, every participating community constructed a different transition plan for Rae, based on the resources available. It was clear that different futures would open up for her as a result. One lesson stood out in this planning exercise. If every young person leaving government care had a thoughtful team like the young people who helped generate strategic and informed plans for Rae, youth-with-care-experiences would have sound, context-specific, and forward-looking transition plans with a higher potential for improved outcomes.

Results and Recommendations: Lessons Learned

During the course of both research projects, youth learned about healthy responses to systems experiences together. Supportive adults learned a great deal from participating youth as well. We all learned together how better to honour differences when planning for healthier transitions to adult in(ter)dependence. While the *Our Dream, Our Right, Our Future* project investigated the effects of networking among youth in care and custody, and provided summary recommendations, the *Youth in Transit* project confirmed a strong need for specific transition planning resources, such as those created by the SYICCN and the SFNFCI. Drawing on information gathered throughout both projects, SYICCN staff recommended that transition planning begin as early as possible, by the age of thirteen to fourteen, if not before. Below, we summarize primary themes that emerged through focus group discussions, our community mapping exercises, as well as anonymous written commentary gathered in evaluation forms completed by seventy-three participants during our Knowledge Sharing Days.

Youth in Transit participants agreed that every transition plan should keep youth voice at its core and that, clearly, youth can benefit from working on transition plans with each other and supported by adults. At the same time, participants recognized that every young person has unique gifts and challenges, so transition planning must also be individualized. Through the community mapping exercise, participants were convinced that all transition plans need to recognize and engage available community supports and that strong youth programs are needed in all communities. Well-trained transition-planning social workers and adult allies, who understand the full spectrum of factors that can influence a young person's well-being, are urgently needed in public school and post-secondary systems, as well as in care and custody services. Current topics workshops that address emergent youth career interests, health, and lifestyle trends are a must for adult workers, foster parents, and allies. Youth also need more focused information on career development and options. One respondent commented that, as a start, "First Aid and CPR Training, as well as Young Worker Readiness certificates should be made available for all youth in government care. Domestic violence intervention training would also be beneficial."

Beyond consensus on extending supports past the age of twenty-one in Saskatchewan, focus group discussions identified a need for more transitional housing, with specific, culturally appropriate supports for Indigenous youth, newcomers, youth with disabilities, queer and questioning youth, and youth transitioning from custody. Increased supports for teen parents and expectant young mothers were endorsed for their ability to reduce intergenerational cycles of systems involvement. Youth and workers from northern Saskatchewan's more isolated and remote communities urgently advocated for more community resources. Those familiar with kinship care, where less training and resources are provided, asserted that family support should *not* be seen as a cost-saving measure. Young people in care with siblings indicated that it is usually preferable to keep siblings together and, where separation is necessary, in frequent and regular contact, as much as possible. Respondents agreed that more collaboration among relevant ministries and with community-based organizations would benefit youth transitions. Government ministries, schools, health institutions, and private, public, and community organizations need to work together to revise policies and practices that

impede successes among systems youth. One evaluator mentioned the hesitancy to rent to former youth-with-care-experiences as a housing barrier that could be addressed through public education. Responsive mental health resources were also identified as essential for young people who have experienced childhood maltreatment, and for those who are navigating barriers and gaps that target specific social and needs-based groups.

Conclusion: Communities Need Transition Plans, Too

Community interest and investment in youth transitions is an important part of preparing youth for adult citizenship. Youth in government care rub shoulders every day with community members who may have very limited awareness of the challenges they navigate in life. Educating adults and communities about youth-with-care-experiences is an important part of the SYICCN's work. For example, when we co-developed SYICCN policy for evaluating potential research partnerships with the network, it became clear that young research collaborators can quickly gauge whether assessments of their own best interests will be respected by adult researchers. Once they have developed more trusting relationships with adult supports and researchers who maintain network relationships between active initiatives, youth include them in their teasing, projecting their own status as network "lifers." Their sometimes warm, sometimes macabre, humour outlines the affective borderlands where our shared aspirations for inclusive voice and social justice meet.

Finally, when they have a chance to work together with caring adults, youth learn to appreciate that public service employees may be overextended, and that social workers often deal with heavy caseloads. As one participant indicated during data gathering for *Our Dream, Our Right, Our Future,*

> *Another stand-out experience is the awesome adult support. Now the thing I will say is that there was, like, just a handful of people. Adults, social workers, have neither enough opportunity, nor the time to put into the Network to support these young people. That's sad because we could learn so much, and could make new ways of doing things. (Lovrod & Domshy, 2011, p. 20)*

Young research collaborators in these projects have achieved exactly that—new ways of doing things. Our longitudinal study of network impacts helped solidify more sustained funding for the SYICCN, and the resulting research report was one of a handful of documents cited by the Youth Services Legislative task team for the recent Saskatchewan Child Welfare Legislation review. Both provincial universities have extended scholarships to youth from government care, a practice that is emerging in other provinces as well. Drawing on evidence developed in our research, the SYICCN has collaborated with the Ministry of Social Services to establish Child and Youth in Care Week to remind the general public that when young people enter care, it is neither their fault nor their choice, and that youth-with-care-experiences are developing new skills and capacities all the time.

In terms of future research, it would be worthwhile to follow up on how young people are using the transition modules developed through the *Youth in Transit* project and to evaluate how their transition support networks are evolving in terms of "size, composition, density and...actual support provision through identified relationships" (Blakeslee, 2015, p. 123). It would also be useful to note any gaps in "appraisal and instrumental support" (Berzin, Singer, & Hokanson, 2014, p. 2110), and the impact of being forced to rely on impermanent relationships during transition. Given tensions between the goal of "self-sufficiency" and the practical need to maintain and create supportive social connections (Curry & Abrams, 2014, p. 143), charting pathways to natural mentors (Greeson, 2013; Burnside & Fuchs, 2013) and to stronger educational outcomes would help operationalize lessons learned so far. Murray and Goddard (2014) argue that there are "strong social justice reasons for extending research into the older adult lives of such young people" (p. 102). A long-term study of successful youth transitions (ten, fifteen, twenty years down the road after leaving care) could provide role models for transitioning youth and help to outline primary factors in sustained resilience.

On the edge of the future, young people are full of promise. This is also true for youth-with-care-experiences, even when they have endured the difficult circumstances and social disparities that have brought them into care, and even when they must make transitions to adulthood that are often more difficult than for nonsystems youth, who can usually rely on more lasting connections with home and community. After our most recent provincial conference, a group of young people walked along the edge of the lake where the event was held, looking for evidence of history. They found buffalo teeth, quartz, sage, and various artifacts from past lives. Their exchanges were full of banter, ease, and curiosity. They had been asking for research and resources for better transitions for a long time. As they encountered the history of the region through traces left on the edge of a human-made lake, their voices echoed with renewed hope and faith in themselves and one another.

Authors' Note

The co-authors would like to thank the University of Saskatchewan President's SSHRC and Conference Funds adjudicators, the Community Initiatives Fund, and the Saskatoon Health Region Foundation for their support. Our sincere appreciation goes to the Ministry of Social Services for providing extended financial support for the SYICCN's research coordinator position. We would also like to thank the young people from government care and custody who contributed to this research, stakeholders, adult supports, and community partners. Both Candace Fairley, as the SYICCN's provincial outreach coordinator, and her predecessor, Jessica McFarlane, have made invaluable contributions to our participatory research. We deeply appreciate the opportunity to work together with the Saskatchewan First Nations Family and Community Institute (www.sfnfci.ca), and are grateful for the helpful comments provided by reviewers. Copies of the *Youth in Transit* handbook are available through the SYICCN (syiccn.ca).

References

Ahrens, K. R., Katon, W., McCarty, C., & Richardson, L. P. (2012). Association between childhood sexual abuse and transactional sex in youth aging out of foster care. *Child Abuse and Neglect, 36,* 75–80.

Alvi, S. (2012). *Youth criminal justice policy in Canada: A critical introduction.* New York, NY: Springer-Verlag. doi:10.1007/978-1-4419-0273-3

Anderson, M., & Linares, L. O. (2012). The role of cultural dissimilarity factors on child adjustment following foster placement. *Children and Youth Services Review, 34,* 597–601.

Bateman, T., & Neal, H. (2015). *Beyond Youth Custody: Custody to Community: How Young People Cope with Release.* Retrieved from http://www. beyondyouthcustody.net/wp-content/uploads/BYC-Custody-to-community-How-young-people-cope-with-release.pdf

Batsche, C., Hart, S., Ort, R., Armstrong, M., Strozier, A., & Hummer, V. (2014). Post-secondary transitions of youth emancipated from foster care. *Child & Family Social Work, 19*(2), 174–184. doi:10.1111/j.1365-2206.2012.00891.x

Beal, C. (2014). Insider accounts of the move to the outside: Two young people talk about their transitions from secure institutions. *Youth Justice, 14*(1), 63–76. doi:10.1177/1473225413520362

Bender, K., Yang, J., Ferguson, K., & Thompson, S. (2015). Experiences and needs of homeless youth with a history of foster care. *Children and Youth Services Review, 55,* 222–231. doi:10.1016/j.childyouth.2015.06.007

Bernstein, M. (2009). *A breach of trust: An investigation into foster home overcrowding in the Saskatoon service centre.* Saskatoon, SK: Saskatchewan Children's Advocate Office. Retrieved from http://cwrp.ca/sites/default/files/publications/en/SK-BreachTrustReport.pdf

Berzin, S. C., Singer, E., & Hokanson, K. (2014). Emerging versus emancipating: The transition to adulthood for youth in foster care. *Journal of Adolescent Research, 29*(5), 616–638. doi:10.1177/0743558414528977

Blackstock, C. (2006/2007). Building on the multi-generational strength of First Nations communities. *Transition, 36*(4), 7–10.

Blakeslee, J. E. (2015). Measuring the support networks of transition-age foster youth: Preliminary validation of a social network assessment for research and practice. *Children and Youth Services Review, 52,* 123–134. doi:10.1016/j.childyouth.2015.03.014

Brown, S., & Wilderson, D. (2010). Homelessness prevention for former foster youth: Utilization of transitional housing program. *Children and Youth Services Review, 32,* 1464–1472.

Burnside, L., & Fuchs, D. (2013). Bound by the clock: The experiences of youth with FASD transitioning to adulthood from child welfare care. *First Peoples Child and Family Review, 8*(1), 41–62.

Butler, K., & Benoit, C. (2015). Citizenship practices among youth who have experienced government care. *Canadian Journal of Sociology/Cahiers canadiens de sociologie, 40*(1), 25–49.

Byrne, T., Stephen, M., Kim, M., Culhane, D. P., Moreno, M., Toros, H., and Stevens, M. (2014). Public assistance receipt among older youth exiting foster care. *Children and Youth Services Review, 44,* 307–316. doi:10.1016/j.childyouth.2014.06.023

Casey, K. J., Reid, R., and Trout, A. I. (2010). The transition status of youth departing residential care. *Child Youth Care Forum, 39,* 323–340.

Chabot, M., Fallon, B., Tonmyr, L., MacLaurin, B., Fluke, J., & Blackstock, C. (2013). Exploring alternate specifications to explain agency-level effects in placement decisions regarding Aboriginal children: Further analysis of the Canadian Incidence Study of Reported Child Abuse and Neglect Part B. *Child Abuse and Neglect, 37,* 61–76.

Chandler, M. J., & Lalonde, C. (1998). Cultural continuity as a hedge against suicide in Canada's First Nations. *Transcultural Psychiatry, 35*(2), 191–219.

Charette, R. (2012). Remembering the self-actualizing tendency: Lessons from a child and youth care student's first attempt at independent research. *Relational Child and Youth Care Practice, 25*(3), 62–70.

Children and Youth in Challenging Contexts Network (CYCC). (2013). *Youth engagement: Empowering youth voices to improve services, programs, and policy.* Retrieved from http://cyccnetwork.org/en/engagement

Collins, M. E., and Clay, C. (2009). Influencing policy for youth transitioning from care: Defining problems, crafting solutions, and assessing politics. *Children and Youth Services Review, 31*(7), 743–751.

Corrado, R., Freedman, L., & Blatier, C. (2011). The over-representation of children in care in the youth criminal justice system in British Columbia: Theory and policy issues. *International Journal of Child, Youth and Family Studies, 1 & 2*, 99–118.

Courtney, M., Flynn, R. J., & Beaupré, J. (2013). Overview of out of home care in the USA and Canada. *Psychosocial Intervention, 22*, 163–173.

Courtney, M., Piliavin, I., Grogan-Kaylor, A., & Nesmith, A. (2001). Foster youth transitions to adulthood: A longitudinal view of leaving care. *Child Welfare, 80*(6), 685–717.

Cowan, M. (2015, September 18). Foster parent worried current system can damage kids. *CBCNews.* Retrieved from http://www.cbc.ca/news/canada/saskatchewan/foster-parent-worried-current-system-can-damage-kids-1.3232822

Cunningham, M. J., & Diversi, M. (2013). Aging out: Youths' perspectives on foster care and the transition to independence. *Qualitative Social Work, 12*(5), 587–602. doi:10.1177/1473325012445833

Curry, S. R., & Abrams, L. S. (2014). Housing and social support for youth aging out of foster care: State of the research literature and directions for future inquiry. *Child and Adolescent Social Work Journal, 32*(2), 143–153. doi:10.1007/s10560-014-0346-4

Daining, C., and DePanfilis, D. (2007). Resilience of youth in transition from out-of-home care to adulthood. *Children and Youth Services Review, 29*(9), 1158–1178.

Davis, R. G., & Baena, R. (Eds.). (2001). *Small worlds: Transcultural visions of childhood*. Pamplona, Spain: Ediciones Universidad de Navarra (EUNSA).

Ferguson, H. B., & Wolkow, K. (2012). Educating children and youth in care: A review of barriers to school progress and strategies for change. *Children and Youth Services Review, 34*, 1143–1149.

Filbert, K. M., & Flynn, R. J. (2010). Developmental and cultural assets and resilient outcomes in First Nations young people in care: An initial test of an explanatory model. *Children and Youth Services Review, 32*(4), 560–564.

Flynn, R. J., Beaulac, J., & Vinograd, J. (2006). Participation in structured voluntary activities, substance use, and psychological outcomes in out-of-home care. In R. J. Flynn, P. M. Dudding, & J. G. Barber (Eds.), *Promoting resilience in child welfare* (pp. 216–230). Ottawa, ON: University of Ottawa Press.

Flynn, R. J. & Tessier, N. G. (2011). Promotive and risk factors as concurrent predictors of educational outcomes in supported transitional living: Extended care and maintenance in Ontario. *Children and Youth Services Review, 33*(12), 2498–2503.

Fraser, S. L., Vachon, M., Arauz, M. J., Rousseau, C., & Kirmayer, L. J. (2012). Inuit youth transitioning out of residential care: Obstacles to re-integration and challenges to wellness. *First Peoples Child and Family Review, 7*(1), 52–75.

Geenen, S., & Powers, L. E. (2007). "Tomorrow is another problem": The experiences of youth in foster care during their transition into adulthood. *Children and Youth Services Review, 29*, 1085–1101.

Gilligan. R. (2005). Promoting resilience and permanence in child welfare. In
    R. J. Flynn, P. M. Dudding, & J. G. Barber (Eds.), *Promoting resilience in child
    welfare* (pp. 3–17). Ottawa, ON: University of Ottawa Press.

Greeson, J. K. P. (2013). Foster youth and the transition to adulthood: The theoretical
    and conceptual basis for natural mentoring. *Emerging Adulthood, 1*(1), 40–51.

Greeson, J. K. P., Usher, L., & Grinstein-Weiss, M. (2010). One adult who is crazy
    about you: Can natural mentoring relationships increase assets among young
    adults with and without foster care experience? *Child and Youth Services
    Review, 32*(4), 565–577. doi:10.1016/j.childyouth.2009.12.003

Greig, A., Taylor, W., & MacKay, T. (2007). *Doing research with children*. London,
    United Kingdom: Sage.

Griffiths, C. T., Dandurand, Y., & Murdoch, D. (2007). *The social reintegration
    of offenders and crime prevention*. Ottawa, ON: The International Centre for
    Criminal Law Reform and Criminal Justice Policy (ICCLR).

Hannah-Moffat, K., & Maurutto, P. (2003). *Youth risk/needs assessment: An
    overview of issues and practices*. Ottawa, ON: Research and Statistics Division,
    Department of Justice Canada.

Healey, C. V., & Fisher, P. A. (2011). Young children in foster care and the
    development of favorable outcomes. *Children and Youth Service Review, 33*,
    1822–1830.

Hiles, D., Moss, D., Thorne, L., Wright, J., & Dallos, R. (2014). "So what am I?"
    Multiple perspectives on young people's experience of leaving care. *Children
    and Youth Services Review, 41*(1), 1–15. doi:10.1016/j.childyouth.2014.03.007

Hocking, S. (2014). (Re) Settlement? Transitions from custody to community for
    socially excluded children and young people. *Plymouth Law and Criminal
    Justice Review, 1*, 192–213.

Howe, B., & Covell, K. (Eds.). (2007). *Children's rights in Canada: A question of
    commitment*. Waterloo, ON: Wilfred Laurier University Press.

Howse, R. B., Diehl, D. C., & Trivette, C. M. (2010). An asset-based approach to
    facilitating positive youth development and adoption. *Child Welfare, 38*(4),
    101–116.

Jackson, S., & Cameron, C. (2012). Leaving care: Looking ahead and aiming
    higher. *Children and Youth Services Review, 34*, 1107–1114.

Jager, K. B., Bak, J., Barber, A., Bozek, K., Bocknek, E. L., & Weir, G. (2009).
    Qualitative inquiry and family therapist identity construction through
    community-based child welfare practice. *Journal of Feminist Family Therapy,
    21*, 39–57.

Jones, L. (2011). The first three years after foster care: A longitudinal look at the
    adaptation of 16 youth to emerging adulthood. *Children and Youth Services
    Review, 33*(10), 1919–1929. doi:10.1016./j.childyouth.2011.05.018

Kaplan, S. J., Skolnik, L., & Turnbull, A. (2009). Enhancing the empowerment of
    youth in foster care: Supportive services. *Child Welfare, 88*(1), 133–161.

Kirk, R., & Day, A. (2011). Increasing college access for youth aging out of foster
    care: Evaluation of a summer camp program for foster youth transitioning
    from high school to college. *Children and Youth Services Review, 33*, 1173–1180.

Koshy, V. (2005). *Action research for improving practice*. London, United Kingdom: Sage.

Lagaden, C. (2015, January 28). Youth correctional facilities in Saskatoon and Yorkton shutting down. *CBC News*. Retrieved from http://www.cbc.ca/news/canada/saskatoon/youth-correctional-facilities-in-saskatoon-and-yorkton-shutting-down-1.2934339

Lee, C., & Berrick, J. D. (2014). Experiences of youth who transition to adulthood out of care: Developing a theoretical framework. *Children and Youth Services Review, 46*, 78–84. doi:10.1016/j.childyouth.2014.08.005

Leve, L. D., Fisher, P. A., & Chamberlain, P. (2009). Multidimensional treatment foster care as a preventive intervention to promote resiliency among youth in the child welfare system. *Journal of Personality, 77*(6), 1869–1902.

Lovrod, M., & Domshy, D. (2011). *Our dream, our right, our future: Voices from Saskatchewan's Youth in Care and Custody Network*. Regina, SK: SYICCN. Retrieved from http://www.syiccn.ca/documents/SYICCN%20-%20Our%20Dream%20Our%20Right%20Our%20Future.pdf

Lussier, P., McCuish, E., & Corrado, R. R. (2015). The adolescence–adulthood transition and desistance from crime: Examining the underlying structure of desistance. *Journal of Developmental Life Course Criminology, 1*, 87–117. doi:10.1007/s40865-015-0007-0

McCoy, H., McMillen, J. C., & Spitznagel, E. L. (2008). Older youth leaving the foster care system: Who, what, when, where, and why? *Children and Youth Services Review, 30*(9), 735–745.

Melkman, E., Refaeli, T., Bibi, B., & Benbenishty, R. (2015, March). Readiness for independent living among youth on the verge of leaving juvenile correctional facilities. *International Journal of Offender Therapy and Comparative Criminology*, 1–17.

Metzger, J. (2008). Resiliency in children and youth in kinship care and family foster care. *Child Welfare, 87*(6), 115–140.

Mitchell, M. B., Jones, T., & Renema, S. (2014). Will I make it on my own? Voices and visions of 17-year-old youth in transition. *Child Adolescent Social Work Journal, 32*, 291–300. doi:10.1007/s10560-014-0364-2

Moffat, S., & Vincent, C. (2009). Emergent literacy and childhood literacy-promoting activities for children in the Ontario Child Welfare System. *Vulnerable Children and Youth Studies, 4*(2), 135–141.

Murray, S., & Goddard, J. (2014). Life after growing up in care: Informing policy and practice through research. *Australian Social Work, 67*(1), 102–117. doi:10.1080/0312407X.2013.868010

Osher, D., Magee Quinn, M., Kendziora, K., & Woodruff, D. (2002). Addressing invisible barriers: Improving outcomes for youth with disabilities in the juvenile justice system. Washington, DC: Center for Effective Collaboration and Practice at the American Institutes for Research, Office of Juvenile Justice and Delinquency Prevention.

Peterson, C., & Seligman, M. E. P. (2004). *Character strengths and virtues: A handbook and classification*. New York, NY: American Psychological Association & Oxford University Press.

Richardson, C., & Nelson, B. (2007). A change of residence: Government schools and foster homes as sites of forced Aboriginal assimilation – A paper designed to provoke thought and systemic change. *First Peoples Child and Family Review, 3*(2), 75–83.

Rodriguez, N. (2007). Restorative justice at work: Examining the impact of restorative justice resolutions on juvenile recidivism. *Crime & Delinquency, 53*(3), 355–379.

Sanders, J., Munford, R., Liebenberg, L., & Ungar, M. (2014). Multiple service use: The impact of consistency in service quality for vulnerable youth. *Child Abuse and Neglect, 38*(4), 687–697. doi:10.1016/j.chiabu.2013.10.024

Saskatchewan Advocate for Children and Youth. (2015). *Annual Report*. Saskatoon, SK: Author. Retrieved from http://www.saskadvocate.ca/sites/default/files/u11/ACY%20ANNUAL%20REPORT%202015%20FINAL.pdf

Saskatchewan Child Welfare Review Panel Report. (2010). *For the good of our children and youth: A new vision, a new direction*. Retrieved from http://cwrp.ca/sites/default/files/publications/en/SK_ChildWelfareReview_panelreport.pdf

Saskatchewan Youth in Care and Custody Network (SYICCN). (2014). *Child welfare review 2014*. Retrieved from http://www.syiccn.ca/documents/CWR2014.pdf

Scannapieco, M., Connell-Carrick, K., & Painter, K. (2007). In their own words: Challenges facing youth aging out of foster care. *Child and Adolescent Social Work Journal, 24*, 423–435.

Skott-Myhre, H. A., Raby, R., & Nikolaou, J. (2008). Towards a delivery system of services for rural homeless youth: A literature review and case study. *Child Youth Care Forum, 37*, 87–102.

Steinberg, L., Chung, H. L., & Little, M. (2004). Re-entry of young offenders from the justice system: A developmental perspective. *Youth Violence Juvenile Justice, 2*(1), 1–16. doi:10.1177/1541204003260045

Stephens, R., & Arnette, J. (2000, February). From the courthouse to the schoolhouse: Making successful transitions. *Juvenile Justice Bulletin*. Washington, DC: Office of Juvenile Justice and Delinquency Prevention.

Stewart, C. J., Kum, H., Barth, R. P., & Duncan, D. F. (2014). Former foster youth: Employment outcomes up to age 30. *Children and Youth Services Review, 36*, 220–229. doi:10.1016/j.childyouth.2013.11.024

Stott, T. (2013). Transitioning youth: Policies and outcomes. *Children and Youth Services Review, 35*, 218–227.

Strong-Boag, V. (2011). *Fostering nation? Canada confronts its history of childhood disadvantage*. Waterloo, ON: Wilfrid Laurier University Press.

Tomporowske, B., Manon, B., Bargen, C., & Binder, V. (2011). Reflections on the past, present and future of restorative justice in Canada. *Alberta Law Review, 48*(4), 815–829.

Torres, G. (2015). South Los Angeles Youth Offender Re-Entry Program: A grant proposal. California State University, Long Beach, CA.

Tracey, D., & Hanham, J. (2015, June). Applying positive psychology to illuminate the needs of adolescent males transitioning out of juvenile detention. *International Journal of Offender Therapy and Comparative Criminology*, 1–16.

Ungar, M., Liebenberg, L., Boothroyd, R., Kwong, W. M., Lee, T. Y., Leblanc, J.,...Makhnach, A. (2008). The study of youth resilience across cultures: Lessons from a pilot study of measurement development. *Research in Human Development, 5*(3), 166–180.

Unrau, Y. A., Seita, J. R., & Putney, K. S. (2008). Former foster youth remember multiple placement moves: A journey of loss and hope. *Children and Youth Services Review, 30*, 1256–1266.

Walls, M. L., & Whitbeck, L. B. (2012). The intergenerational effect of relocation policies on Indigenous families. *Journal of Family Issues, 33*(9), 1272–1293.

Whitehouse, S. (2015). When chronic care youth age out: Transition planning. BC *Medical Journal, 57*(2), 70–71.

Woodall, J. (2007). Barriers to positive mental health in a young offenders institution: A qualitative study. *Health Education Journal, 66*(2), 132–140. doi:10.1177/0017896907076752

Young, N. L., Barden, W. S., Mills, W. A., Burke, T. A., Law, M., & Boydell, K. (2009). Transition to adult-oriented health care: Perspectives of youth and adults with complex physical disabilities. *Physical and Occupational Therapy in Pediatrics, 29*(4), 345–361.

Youth in Care Canada. (2005). Leaving care. *Primer Fact Sheets*. Retrieved from http://unpub.ecloud-eclipse.websplanetdemo.com/var/ m_1/16/166/5679/136916-Emancipation(1).pdf?t=1421862903

Zinga, D. (2012). Journeying with youth: Re-centering Indigeneity in child and youth care. *Child and Youth Services, 33*, 258–280.

CHAPTER 11

Narrative Threads in the Accounts of Women with Learning Difficulties Who Have Been Criminalized

Elly Park, David McConnell, Vera Caine, and Joanne Minaker

Determination

It's really hard
I want my kids to be bright and vivacious
Personality shine through

Have you thought about adoption?
How can you take care of your baby?
Are you having withdrawal?
Will you use again?

I gave my kids to their dad
    because I started using
wanted them to be safe
wanted to use more
I lost all my parental rights

Suggested Citation: Park, E., McConnell, D., Caine, V., & Minaker, J. (2016). Narrative threads in the accounts of women with learning difficulties who have been criminalized. In H. Montgomery, D. Badry, D. Fuchs, & D. Kikulwe (Eds.), *Transforming Child Welfare: Interdisciplinary Practices, Field Education, and Research* (pp. 241–268). Regina, SK: University of Regina Press.

No one will believe you –
you're a crackhead
you can't take your kids

> I will never abuse them
> I will never put a guy before my kids
> *I am going to win. They are going to win*

Carla[1] is one of four women living in Alberta, Canada, who took part in a narrative inquiry with young women with learning difficulties who have been involved in the criminal justice system. This found poem[2] (Lahman et al., 2011) was created from transcripts of conversations I had with Carla.[3] This poem describes Carla's experiences of facing abuse, judgment, and discrimination, as well as her desire of providing a different experience for her children. She was told by her sons' father that "no one would believe [her]," because "[she's] a crackhead." When she was using drugs, she voluntarily gave up custody, and he would not let her see her sons. Now, she takes her sons on the weekends and school breaks and they stay with her. She also has another baby, Jake, who lives with her.

Over a period of eight to eighteen months, I met regularly with each of the four women. Sometimes we would talk over coffee or a meal. Other times, our conversations were part of other activities, such as looking for an apartment, going to the food bank, or meeting with a probation officer. To help me understand, the women talked about their childhood experiences, including their exposure to abuse and neglect and difficulties with learning at school; their relationships with professionals, parents, partners, and (in the case of three of the four women) their children; as well as their daily lives, including but not limited to their ongoing struggles with substance use. The stories of the four women contribute to a body

---

1   All names and identifiers used in this chapter have been changed.
2   Poetry has been used by researchers in various ways and is referred to as "found poetry" or "data poems," where the participants' words are used to create poetry to present in research settings.
3   "I" is used in reference to the first listed author of this chapter, who carried out the fieldwork. The three remaining co-authors were involved in the conceptualization of the project, the data analysis, as well as the writing of the chapter manuscript. Given the relational aspect of the fieldwork, a choice was made to preserve the first-person account in the writing.

of feminist criminology and disability studies research that challenges "monolithic representations" of women in the criminal justice system and women with learning difficulties.[4]

My research puzzle[5] was based on the following questions: What are the life stories of young women with learning difficulties, and how do they experience the criminal justice system (CJS)? What kind of impact do their experiences in the CJS have on their present and future stories? In what ways have their stories contributed to how the participants see themselves and how they relate with others? The stories the participants shared were often implicitly connected to their involvement in the CJS and confirmed the need to hear about experiences from their perspective.

Background

The postmodern feminist viewpoint in particular is foundational to this study. Several feminist scholars have discussed this perspective in relation to criminology (Balfour & Comack, 2014; Burgess-Proctor, 2006; Daly & Chesney-Lind, 1988; Harding, 1991; Minaker, 2001). Such scholars note that the direction of feminist criminology has shifted as a result of postmodern influences, and rather than looking at *why* women are involved in the criminal justice system, postmodern feminists look at *how* certain forms of "governance (in a number of different sites) work to contain, control or exclude those who are marginalized in society" (Comack, 2014, p. 33). Likewise, "postmodern feminists reject fixed categories and universal concepts," recognizing the potential for multiple truths (Burgess-Proctor, 2006, p. 29). Instead of establishing "grand narratives of the social world," there is an emphasis on multiplicity within women's lives (Comack, 2014, p. 32; Smart, 1990).

The book *Razor Wire Women* by Lawston and Lucas (2011) is composed of contributions from women who have been or are incarcerated. Pieces of

---

4 In this inquiry, the term "learning difficulties" is defined as mild cognitive impairment presented as significant challenges in learning.

5 A "research puzzle" refers to the research questions that influence the inquiry. "Problems carry with them qualities of clear definability and the expectation of solutions, but narrative inquiry carries more of a sense for a search...a sense of continual reformulation" (Clandinin & Connelly, 2000, p. 124).

writing and art from the women illustrate and emphasize the importance of their perspectives and aspirations, which can help us move beyond harmful stereotypes to progress toward a world where "dignity and respect are fostered for all human beings" (Lawston & Lucas, 2011, p. 15). This book provides an opportunity for women to share their experiences in a respectful way through validating and prioritizing their experiential knowledge. Furthermore, women who are criminalized have been categorized as being "out of control, drug addicted, unruly, and sexually promiscuous, and often these stereotypes reach beyond incarcerated women to their families, children and communities" (Lawston & Lucas, 2011, p. 7). The women share their thoughts about the direct effects of being misrepresented and the impact on their lives, as well as the lives of others who are important to them.

Similarly, feminist disability studies scholars have discussed the way certain constructs of disability promote the marginalization of women with disabilities by distinguishing and focusing on what they *cannot* do (Morris, 1993, 2001). Mayes, Llewellyn, and McConnell (2006) offer an example of challenging stereotypes in a study with pregnant women who have intellectual disabilities. In contrast to the societal view that women with intellectual disabilities would not and/or should not want to have children, the women in this study show their desire and capability to be loving mothers. Namely, the women are active in shaping their social connections and show a sense of agency that seems to contradict pervasive societal perceptions. Mayes et al. (2006) highlight the importance in hearing the experiences from the women themselves, and that failing to do so would possibly silence "the gendered experiences of women with intellectual disabilities as women and as mothers" (p. 121).

Johnson and Traustadóttir (2000) illustrate the diverse experiences of women with intellectual disabilities in their book, *Women with Intellectual Disabilities: Finding a Place in the World*. The book focuses specifically on experiences of women with intellectual disabilities because they have been dually ignored in feminist literature and in disability studies discourse, leading to an absence in their voices in both areas of research. The book not only considers the challenges but also looks at achievements for women with intellectual disabilities in different communities. For example, although some stories are about women with intellectual disabilities being excluded from families and being inhibited from forming relationships and/or having families of their own, other women "are central figures in their families of origin; others have become lovers and parents; still others have achieved creative and fulfilling careers and many make a contribution to the disability movement and to their own wider communities" (Johnson & Traustadóttir, 2000, p. 16).

Women with learning difficulties are thought to be overrepresented in the criminal justice system, although specific rates have not been determined (Hayes, 2007). A small number of studies have investigated the prevalence of learning difficulties in predominantly male prison populations. These studies report prevalence rates typically ranging from 30 to 60 per cent, depending on how learning difficulties are operationally defined (Hayes, Shackell, Mottram, & Lancaster, 2007; Loucks, 2007; Morris & Morris, 2006; Oshima, Huang, Jonson-Reid, & Drake, 2010; Shelton, 2006). The reasons or "causes" for the presumed high rate of incarceration remain poorly understood. However, researchers have observed that women with learning difficulties are more likely to be exposed to adversities that heighten the risk of involvement with the criminal justice system, such as childhood abuse, low educational attainment, unemployment, poverty, and low social support (Hayes, 2007; Morris, 1993). Further, researchers have also observed that once "caught," persons with learning difficulties are more likely to be convicted and incarcerated because the criminal justice system does not accommodate their special needs and circumstances (Covington, 2003; Hayes, 2007; Jones & Talbot, 2010).

Among adults in the criminal justice system, the proportion of women has steadily increased over the past twenty years (Balfour & Comack, 2014). Being in the CJS may involve arrest, charges laid, sentencing in court, being held in custody, and probation, and, although widely varying experiences, all of these can lead to a criminal record. Little is known about the experiences of women with learning difficulties who have been arrested, sentenced, and incarcerated. A recent metasynthesis reviewed literature pertaining to experiences of people with learning disabilities in the CJS, not surprisingly with a largely male representation (Hyun, Hahn, & McConnell, 2014). In the four studies reviewed, Hyun and her colleagues found that people with learning disabilities in custody and those making the transition back into the community were filled with anxiety and uncertainty about the future. They were afraid and unsure about where to go or who to turn to when they were trying to resist reverting to drugs and alcohol use because of fear of judgment and stigma (Hagner, Malloy, Mazzone, & Cormier, 2008; Unruh & Bullis, 2005). The studies reviewed all described a need for more or different support for people who have learning disabilities in the CJS (Hyun et al., 2014). The metasynthesis review pointed to a clear need for more research that considers the experiences of women, with a focus on the interactions between the women and other people in their lives, as well as broad systems in place for support and rehabilitation.

Inquiring into the experiences of women with learning difficulties can provide opportunities to share stories that challenge stereotypes and can offer examples of struggles and obstacles but also determination to rise above the challenges. With the growing interest in feminist perspectives, both in criminology and in disability disciplines, there is a need for more explicit research inquiring into the experiences of women, including women with learning difficulties, in the criminal justice system to fill the gaps in knowledge.

Research Method

Narrative inquiry is a relational research methodology that aims to understand experiences (Clandinin & Connelly, 2000). Feminist criminology and feminist disability scholars have noted the paucity of research that looks explicitly at experiences to better understand women's experiences in the criminal justice system and experiences with having disabilities (Balfour & Comack, 2014; Johnson & Traustadóttir, 2000).

Temporality, sociality, and place make up the three-dimensional narrative inquiry space (Clandinin & Caine, 2013; Clandinin & Connelly, 2000). Temporality includes the interactions with participants that take place over an extended period of time, as well as reflections of earlier experiences that are shared and co-composed as part of the narrative accounts. In addition, narratives show the continuous nature of experiences (Clandinin & Connelly, 2000). Sociality attends to the inward "thoughts, emotions, and moral responses and outward to events and actions" of the participants and researchers (Clandinin & Caine, 2013, p. 167). Place refers to the physical places, as well as the social and cultural context, where the inquiry process unfolds. In addition, past, present, and future stories are situated within certain contexts.

In narrative inquiry, "field text" is a term used to describe the data gathered during the initial stage of the research (Clandinin & Connelly, 2000). In this study, field texts, which included transcripts of audio-recorded conversations, field notes I wrote, and personal journal writings the participants shared with me were used to create their narrative accounts, also referred to as "interim text." The participants and I discussed and negotiated what to include and found poetry was part of their narrative accounts. As an iterative process with ongoing negotiation, the participants were heavily involved, from composing field texts to shaping final research texts. Across the narrative accounts, significant resonances across stories are described as narrative threads (Clandinin & Connelly, 2000). The purpose of this narrative inquiry was to understand the experiences of women with learning difficulties who have been involved in the Canadian CJS. Furthermore, I explored the narrative threads while considering possibilities to shape policy and practice.

Research Process

From January 2013 to June 2014, I met with four young women: Tasha, Carla, Caris, and Lina (pseudonyms to protect confidentiality). The relationships we formed allowed opportunities to have conversations about their experiences as women with learning difficulties in the CJS. After receiving ethics approval,[6] I went to two community organizations I knew through past volunteering experiences. The agencies supported me in recruiting participants. Each of the participants had been involved in the criminal justice process and had self-identified as having learning difficulties.

The participants and I met 15–25 times, about once every two weeks over a period of eight to eighteen months. We met in different settings, and our relationships developed over time. We often sat and talked over a meal or in a participant's home, but I also went places with them. Our shared experiences became another way to understand their experiences. We would go to the food bank, spend time with family members, meet a probation officer or social worker, and go to buy groceries together. Our interactions became a reflection of our lives in relation to one another. I

---

6   The project received ethics approval from the University of Alberta Research Ethics Board.

was open with participants and shared some of my own related experiences. I knew that our relationship needed time and space to build mutual respect and trust.

Participants

The participants were 20–28 years old. Two of the women were Aboriginal,[7] one was of German descent, and one of French descent; all of them were born in Canada. In Alberta, Aboriginal women in custody in 2009–2010 were overrepresented (Mahoney, 2011). Three of the women were mothers with two or three children. None of them were married or in common law relationships at the time I met them; two of them were initially living with boyfriends but did not stay in the relationships because they were being abused. All of them identified as heterosexual. The participants had been arrested and charged at least once. Their charges were for shoplifting, theft, and violating administration of justice conditions (failure to appear in court, probation breaches, etc.), which was representative of the most common offences for women according to Canadian statistics from 2009 to 2010 (Mahoney, 2011). Two of the women had a criminal record, and two had their records expunged under the Youth Criminal Justice Act. Three of the women had been detained in custody for at least a week, with the longest single period being two months. Two of the women mentioned they had been "in the system" since they were thirteen years old, having had many interactions with police officers and being familiar with CJS procedures. One participant stated that she was categorized as a "high-risk" case and assigned a specialized caseworker.

Each participant identified herself as having learning difficulties; these difficulties were described as having trouble keeping up in class and possibly related to specific challenges with learning. One of the participants completed high school with additional support from teachers, and the other three women did not complete high school. Two participants left school in Grade 10, and one left in Grade 7. Although all of the women had received a clinical diagnosis—attention deficit hyperactive disorder/attention deficit disorder (ADHD/ADD), general anxiety disorder, fetal alcohol

---

7 Aboriginal peoples include First Nations, Métis, and Inuit people as defined
   by Statistics Canada (Mahoney, 2011).

spectrum disorder (FASD), and learning disabilities in math and reading – their experiences as women with learning difficulties, rather than their specific diagnoses, were the focus of the study.

Tasha

> *I like school, it makes me feel smart, and I am so proud of myself. I feel more confident in myself and more independent. And I just can't wait to get my education rolling so I can go on. Right now, it's just English and computers. I still have to do my math probably next year. I am going to try to get into full time in September....But if you mess it up, you have to wait four years. And you have to go every day. If you miss 5 days at school, then you get kicked out. If you get kicked out, you can't go back. It is stressful now because what if I don't get child care for February?* (Tasha, January 17, 2014)

At twenty years old, Tasha had returned to formal education, or school, after leaving when she was in Grade 7, when she was thirteen. She began taking classes three months after we first met to upgrade so she could take her GED (high school equivalency exam). School is empowering for Tasha; she is eager to pursue a career. She had to find child care, apply for a subsidy to pay for daycare, and figure out transportation and scheduling so she could get to her classes and pick her son Kobi up on time, as well as find time to complete her homework each day. Tasha returned to school after seven years and has begun the long process toward her goal, despite all the hurdles she faces to continue and succeed.

When Tasha left school at age thirteen, she was living with her mom but would run away and go to different group homes. She said her mom did not make her go to school, so she just stopped going. She began drinking with friends and would shoplift to survive and pay for the alcohol.

> *I started drinking when I was 13, and I would drink all the time. The first time I drank I blacked out. I dunno why I drank, I think it was because I always felt sad and neglected. And I didn't know how to deal with my feelings. And now I am learning. I think it's just like, being a mom, I don't want to be like my mom. Like I remember I used to always cry for my mom, all the time.* (Tasha, March 28, 2014)

Tasha has two young sons, Kurt and Kobi. When Kurt was taken from her, Tasha drank even more. She felt such a deep sense of defeat, and she did not know how to deal with it. In the midst of this pain, she could not imagine having a baby and possibly losing custody of another child. She was eighteen.

> When I found out I was pregnant, that's when I put myself into treatment. I wasn't even going to have [Kobi]. Just 'cause Kurt was in the hospital; I didn't have custody of him. I felt like I couldn't take care of him or myself. I dunno I was just tired. And then I felt really guilty...I even went to the abortion clinic....But I am so happy I didn't. I don't think I would ever get an abortion, either. And then I am happy I went to treatment. I thought with him, I thought it was my second chance to be a mom. And then everyone I see who was there, relapsing. I think I am the only one who got sober. (Tasha, February 2014)

Tasha is Aboriginal. Her childhood stories included a cultural context; her grandparents raised her in an Aboriginal community until she was thirteen, and she talked about living close to her aunts, uncles, and cousins. However, she said that as an adult she did not feel connected to her culture. She told me about a recent experience at the grocery store when a stranger called her racist names.

> My mom was parked in front, and then I had a shopping basket and I bought some groceries. And there was a guy beside us, and I put my basket down, and then we drove away because he honked at us to leave. And then later he came up beside us and starting yelling at us because we left the basket there. And he was an old white man and he was calling us racist slurs and stuff. And then I felt real bad after, and then my sister in law went in [to the store], and he was trying to accuse her of shoplifting....Yeah, before he came to yell at us he said that he went inside to report her for shop lifting. (Tasha, December 2013)

She feels like being Aboriginal is an added barrier in certain ways because of the discrimination she has experienced when trying to get a job or find a place to live: *"That's my big problem, well, not a big problem, but that's how I feel when I go to job interviews, or when I have a hard time finding a place. I just like feel like...I don't know. Cause some people think badly of us"* (Tasha, January 17, 2014).

Providing her with long-term support, Tasha's social worker Karrie has been instrumental during the past four years of her life, helping her get an apartment, a job, funding for school, and advocating for her. *"I had everything I needed, my social worker, [Karrie], would give me vouchers, but I rarely had money"* (Tasha, March 2014). Karrie was the first person Tasha would call if she was in trouble, and she knew Karrie was there for support.

Tasha wants to be a role model. She wants to be someone that other women can look up to. She said she doesn't feel sorry for herself. She does not try to excuse her past, but, rather, she is looking ahead. She wants to have a career. She realizes there is much more to be done, but she is just taking it day by day, to reach her goals. *"I think I just want to be a successful person that people want to be. It just feels like such a slow process. But I know I will get there eventually. I'm still 20"* (Tasha, March 2014).

Carla

I got so many different sides to me. I have like so many different personalities or whatever. Like I am dark, or whatever, I like dark things, and gothic, and I am bubbly and I like vibrant and bright. I like being mellow and quiet sometimes, and then loud. (Carla, July 2013)

I have been able to see the different sides to Carla with each meeting and each conversation we have had. When I first met Carla, she was quiet. However, after meeting a few times, she was much more talkative and able to laugh at herself. There were times when she would feel depressed and want to stay in her apartment. She would express loneliness and frustration with living at the recovery house. Six months after we had first met, she admitted she was anxious that day. I thought she was shy, but after getting to know her, I realized my first impression of her was not accurate.

I was quiet because I was assessing the situation, like when I was in the drug scene, you just sit there and you don't say anything around certain people, you sit there and learn and get a feel for what kind

of people they are, and see how much you can open up and be a
dork. Like people wouldn't suspect that I was the way I am, like
now I am joking around and obnoxious. Oh, now I am in everyone's
face all the time, cracking jokes, making fun of everybody. (Carla,
July 2013)

I understood what Carla meant when she said people would not suspect that she likes to make fun of others and joke around. I only saw this
playful side of Carla after meeting with her several times. She was confident enough in herself and comfortable enough with me to admit that she
was a "dork," and we were able to laugh about it together.

Carla has three boys and her youngest, Jake, was only one month old
when we first met. Her two older boys lived with their father, but stay with
her on weekends and breaks. She spoke candidly about her experiences
selling drugs and being addicted to the drug crystal methamphetamine
for five years. She told me a story about having to hide from certain gang
members because her mom had spent some of the money she was supposed to give. She also told me about giving up her apartment and all her
possessions to pay for drugs. Her reason for quitting drugs was to have a
place to live for Jake. She had been couch surfing when she found out she
was pregnant with Jake, and she knew she would not be able to keep him if
she did not have a home. She was able to get into a program that included
subsidized housing at a recovery house, as long as she stayed clean.

Carla's experiences with child protective services began when she was
a child and she would call them for help:

Child services was involved lots. I remember calling children ser-
vices when I was younger; my mom just beat up my brother and
me really bad, and I called and said if you don't get me out of this
house I am going to kill myself. And they were like, can you wait
until tomorrow? We will see you at school. And I was like, ok. (Carla,
March 7, 2013)

Now, as a mother, she has had to deal with child protective services
again. Carla was worried that she was experiencing depression and not
being as affectionate as she should be with Jake. With a doctor's referral, she went to see a postpartum specialist. Rather than giving Carla

suggestions to address her concerns, the counsellor suggested putting her son up for adoption. She then contacted child protective services, telling them that Carla might be at risk of relapsing or endangering her son. For several weeks, Carla received visits from a child welfare worker. Carla had reached out for guidance from the post-partum specialist, but her response was, "How can you take care of your baby?"

Carla was physically abused as a child. Her determination to be a different kind of mother to her kids was evident in our conversations. When she was involved with gangs and heavily using drugs, she gave her boys to their father as a way of keeping them safe; she did it out of a sense of responsibility and love.

> *My mom was abusive. So I will never abuse them, I don't like spanking my kids, there are other ways of doing it. I just have to be stern to my kids. I will just take them into the bedroom; I will take him by the arm. I will not spank my kids. I remember I did it once and I felt so bad. I said sorry, and then I think I bought him something....And I will never put a guy before my kids. If a guy doesn't like my kids, he can leave. My mom let guys kick me out of the house or whatever. She always put guys before us.* (Carla, December 2013)

Carla seemed to have few role models in her life growing up. I asked Carla who the most significant person was in her childhood, the person who stood out the most for her. Carla told me that she really loved having a youth worker and felt a connection with her. Even though their time together was brief – less than a year – the relationship left a lasting impression on Carla.

> *So at 13, I had to have a youth worker. And she would take me to do things and stuff like that. I was the only kid that they ever allowed...like my worker was allowed to take me anywhere and whenever she wanted. She'd teach me how to draw pot leaves and stuff like that. And Kenny from South Park. She was really cool.* (Carla, March 28, 2013)

The found poem at the beginning of this chapter is Carla's expression of determination, an example of how Carla's experiences have shaped her identity. She knew she was "different," but rather than embrace her uniqueness, she tried to "fit in" so she would not have to endure judgment. However, she wants her children to be able to be themselves. She is determined to give them opportunities she never had. Her devotion to her children, as well as her resolve to be a mother to them, is a significant part of her identity.

Caris

Caris was diagnosed with FASD at twenty-two, when she was incarcerated. She said she was relieved to finally have an explanation for why she behaved in certain ways that had caused problems for her in the past, like being extremely forgetful and acting out with aggression. She said that knowing she has FASD has changed the way she sees her behaviour. In junior high and high school, she had a difficult time academically and socially. She left school when she was in Grade 10. She has thought about going back to school to take her GED tests and get her high school equivalency diploma, but she said it would not be for awhile.

Caris started drinking as a teenager, and she spoke about her struggle with alcohol addictions. She said she went to treatment several times but only completed the program twice.

> I would listen to the people talk and listen to like little things that they would say and at first I was like, I am just doing it for court, I was like, aww I don't really need this, and blah blah, but then I was just gonna go and drink again, but slowly then things started changing and my life started changing and I started seeing how like sobriety can be a better way of living and stuff like that, and not be so hectic all the time because growing up I was used to it being hectic all the time...and so to me like that was normal, but actually, like living like a sober life has taught me, you can have a stable life, you know, instead of a hectic life, and it's less stressful and stuff like that. Like it must have been hard for my mom cause she had four kids and we were all really bad kids. (Caris, February 28, 2013)

Caris identifies with being Aboriginal. She talked about wanting to attend ceremonies but being unable to for a long time. Recently, she had started to reconnect with her Aboriginal community. Anne, the community worker who introduced us, is a mentor for Caris and often invited her to attend different cultural events. Her sister, a significant source of encouragement for Caris, used to go to sweats or powwows with her in the past. She said she hoped to participate in ceremonies with her sister and Anne soon.

Caris has two children. When I first met her, she had just been released from jail. She was completing all the conditions set out by the court so she could regain custody of her two-year-old son Josh. A week later, they were together. At the time, she was living at a shelter, and I helped her move into subsidized housing. She talked about how important Josh was to her, and how he helped her stay on track. He was an anchor in her life that kept her grounded. She had a routine, and she was trying to get a job or work toward going back to school. After we met for about six months, I could not reach Caris. I was able to reconnect with her through Anne, who told me that Caris had gone through a rough time. I was glad to hear that Anne still heard from her regularly. She relapsed badly, and over the winter she and Josh were homeless. She gave him over to child services because she was worried about his health and safety. When I met with Caris, she did not want to talk about the past few months, but she was quite upset about having to give Josh up. I asked her why she did not call me for help. She said that when she was going through tough times, she kept to herself and did not like to depend on others. Although I was able to show her the narrative account and we talked about it, the lapse in time created a noticeable shift in our relationship.

Lina

Lina and I began our relationship with a connection through our shared experiences with eating disorders, which she would always refer to as "ED." I could relate on some level with her struggles, and we were able to talk openly about them. *"It gives you a rush, it's an escape and I feel like it is more socially acceptable than doing drugs. I feel like they would not be as mad [as if] I was overdosing on drugs"* (Lina, October 16, 2013). Although we found similarities in our challenges with addictions and eating disorders, our experiences were different because of the circumstances and relationships in each of our lives. After meeting Lina for eight months, she shared some of her writing with me. Her powerful words expressed just how much she struggled to get through each day.

My life begins with ED (eating disorders)

1 in 4 they say,
I am that 1 in 4.
Statistics are shocking,
Every time I am in a group
I feel that number staring me down...telling me I am the fuck-up, I
am the crazy mental one. I will suffer for the rest of my life. I become
anti-social, low confident, unable to breathe around social situa-
tions because ED (eating disorders) has his grip around me, all
the time. 'Breaking Free' seems like a joke, have the therapists and
doctors really experienced ED (eating disorders)? NO. The mental
workout every day, I want to be in a different body a different world,
a different life where there are NO statistics, Judgments, thoughts,
Just peace. Drugs were my 'place' to escape its only temporary....
Just like my life.

Lina's school stories differed from the other participants. She was able to find support and to work with her teachers to overcome specific challenges. Lina's Grade 6 teacher recognized the symptoms Lina had presented because her own child had ADHD, and Lina was assessed and diagnosed. Her experiences included staying after school and receiving one-on-one instruction. She spoke fondly about her relationship with one teacher who was patient with her and kept her motivated.

But they would sit with me, I remember that. Mrs. Richmond, I loved
her. She knew I had a problem with math, she would sit there and
she would correct it and correct it. And in high school, they would
help me too. They would hide it under the cover, but they were really
nice....I always felt that people can grasp things, and for me it takes
a little longer, and it's a bummer, but I don't let it. I just...And I just
know it takes a little longer to get things, so whatever. (Lina, March
17, 2014)

Lina was caught shoplifting for the first time when she was twelve years old. Her dad taught her how to steal. She got caught several more times, with the most recent being an arrest for shoplifting and assaulting a peace officer a week before we first met. Many of the times she would get a warning, but a couple times she had to go to court.

> *Yep. I spent a night downtown at the police station—that was when I was 16. That was a scare tactic. It didn't work though. They put me in a cell. Yeah, but see, I didn't even learn from it. Oh the second time it was more for, well it was for shoplifting but my friends had drugs on them too, so...Yeah. 'Cause they can't really do anything when you are under 18, right. And I went to court and all that.* (Lina, March 27, 2014)

In terms of feeling judged or discriminated against, Lina felt like people were staring and expecting her to steal after she had stopped shoplifting: "*I noticed people would look at me in stores, and I know I'm not going to do anything, but...I don't feel like a criminal. I want to blend in. I am trying to just be part of society*" (Lina, March 28, 2014).

Although Lina wanted to be accepted by others, she realized that she needed to focus on her health and happiness. Her closest relationships were stressful for her, and she expressed that she wanted to be more autonomous, rather than depending on her friends and family for support. She wanted to be stronger so she would not be so deeply affected by what others said to her. "*That's why I don't want to date right now. I don't know what I want. I am just thinking about my future and I am like, well, who would I want to be with*" (Lina, January 3, 2014).

Lina has been especially affected by her mother's disapproving judgments about Lina's appearance, her relationships, and her addictions.

> *She wants us to live the life she didn't live. She would prefer if I do everything right now, but do it her way. She needs to move on, she can't hold onto the past. And I need to move on too, or I will get sick. Really sick....That's what she says, I will love you when you are better...and healthy and don't look like the way you look now....I know and it hurts.* (Lina, February 13, 2014)

Whenever I met with Lina, she would be doing extremely well, in terms of relationships and work, or she would be deeply depressed. Some of our conversations were filled with hope and Lina was motivated to take care of herself. She felt healthy and eager to pursue a career. Other times, Lina was suicidal and did not want to talk. She felt alone, and she said she could not be honest with her family or friends. Her circumstances and her aspirations changed and fluctuated throughout the time we met, and her hopefulness seemed to ebb and flow like a changing tide.

Narrative Threads as Plot Lines

Narrative threads (Clandinin & Connelly, 2000) are resonances across narrative accounts. The narrative threads contribute to the understanding about the participants' experiences, as well as the social, cultural, and political landscapes where the stories are situated (Clandinin & Raymond, 2006). In this study, four threads resonated across the narrative accounts: uncertainty and instability in circumstances, having someone to turn to, enduring judgment and stigma, and mothering and being mothered.

Thread 1: Uncertainty and Instability in Circumstances
Each of the women went through a number of transitions, facing many obstacles and challenges throughout the time I was meeting with them. Tasha and Carla were both trying to pass their GED exams, but they needed to take some classes, which meant arranging child care, getting financial aid, and finding time to study. Tasha had not been in school for seven years, so she felt physical and mental strain when she started to attend classes again. Caris needed a place to live in order to keep her son once she had gained custody. She asked me to help her look for an apartment. We went out a few times but could not find a place that did not require a criminal record check. She was able to get into a subsidized apartment, but she stayed there for only three months and then moved in with her boyfriend. Two months later, she was living at a shelter for abused women and I lost touch with her. Her living situation had changed several times throughout our relationship.

Lina had difficulties in her relationships with the people closest to her, including her mom, dad, sister, and boyfriends. During the time we met, she moved from a subsidized apartment into her mom's basement as a way to save money but expressed that she wanted to get out because she was feeling extremely depressed and mentally unstable. Carla was living in a "recovery house," and she noted, *"Living here, really I feel like I am crippled, I don't feel like a whole person. I dunno – it's hard to explain"* (Carla, February 10, 2014). She was looking for a new place to live, but she could not find an apartment within her price range. She eventually received subsidized housing when the recovery house was shut down. Maintaining a place to call home was a challenge for Caris, Lina, and Carla. The women seemed to be in a constant state of change.

The uncertainty in circumstances was important to consider when understanding how the women formed and sustained relationships, as well as in thinking about their hopes for the future. Similar to the findings in Hyun et al. (2014), the participants in this narrative inquiry felt anxious and uncertain about their futures. In addition, they were often worried about how they would meet daily needs, such as a place to sleep and food to eat. Although they expressed the need for support, what they perceived as beneficial seemed to change based on their circumstances.

Thread 2: Having Someone to Turn to

Each of the women had someone they could turn to who provided them with a sense of stability and support. Tasha had Karrie, her social worker, Carla had a youth worker in Grade 6, Caris had Anne, a parenting program facilitator who became a mentor to her, and Lina had Mrs. Richmond when she was in high school. The way that these relationships had an obvious and lasting impact on each of the participants is significant because they did not fill a particular role, and it was not necessarily "part of the job." Rather, the support was based on a strong connection and appreciation for the women as individuals, deserving of attention and affection. Tasha admitted that initially she simply called on Karrie when she needed food vouchers and she did not open up. However, during our conversations, I noticed that Tasha often spoke about Karrie and their relationship. Caris had several "workers," including a social worker, a FASD worker, a probation officer, and others. However, she noted that Anne did much more for her than any of her workers who got paid. She met Anne years ago when she took a parenting program, and they maintained a relationship after the program ended. Anne had initially introduced me to Caris.

For Carla and Lina, the significant relationships were shorter and came at an earlier point in their lives, but both women expressed the impact these relationships had. They felt empowered and more positive about themselves as a result of having someone who believed in them and focused on their strengths. Carla said that her youth worker was the most significant person from her childhood, and Lina talked about how Mrs. Richmond played a critical role in helping her successfully complete high school. Each of the participants' lives included a person who they could turn to, and the relationships they had, although sometimes initiated through being assigned, stood out above the others.

Thread 3: Enduring Judgment and Stigma

Participants shared private stories embedded in broad social and institutional systems, such as school, the criminal justice system, and child protective services. In school, Carla and Lina talked about being treated poorly by others. They were teased and bullied for being different. Being labelled by others was a substantial part of the participants' stories, not only through explicit experiences of discrimination but also the way they internalized the labels, leading to their fear of being judged. Some of their challenges were due to prejudice in the form of uninvited and unnecessary involvement from others. Other times, they did not get the assistance they needed because they were afraid to ask for help. Feeling judged and stigmatized was a part of their lives and influenced how they perceived professionals and workers who were in positions to provide assistance and support.

Tasha had several experiences of racial discrimination that made it difficult for her to pursue her goals, such as finding an apartment or getting a job. She heard hurtful remarks from strangers at grocery stores, which affected her self-esteem and confidence. She said she wanted to be a role model for other women and implied that she wanted to show others that she could be successful and have a career. Tasha's desire to be a role model was one way she was able to retell her story in a way that fit with how she perceived herself now and hoped for in the future.

Carla had an open file with child protective services[8] for six weeks because of the judgment she faced from a postpartum counsellor. It was

---

8   Child protective services fall under a branch of the government of Alberta
    called Alberta Human Services. It ensures that the children are receiving an...

stressful for her because she felt she was being judged by the caseworker, who was evaluating her parenting abilities. She was able to show the worker her competency at mothering during home visits by talking about the strategies she used in caring for Jake, such as setting up alarms on her phone for evening baths and feedings. She created a monthly budget to cover basic necessities such as formula and diapers. She told me that the caseworker was surprised at how much she had done to care for Jake.

As was previously mentioned, Caris received a FASD diagnosis at a correctional centre when she was twenty-two. Before she had been diagnosed, she struggled to understand her behaviours and the choices she made. Now, she knew that certain areas of her brain had been affected and some of the challenges she had faced, such as anger outbursts and impulsive actions, were not simply due to a lack of control. She said she hoped to educate herself and find opportunities to talk about FASD to help reduce the stigma associated with it, as well as improve awareness for professionals working with people who have FASD. Lina had difficulty opening up to professionals about her eating disorder because she did not think they would understand and would judge her based on her illness. She felt she could not be completely honest with anyone. She wanted to blend in and be an accepted part of society, and she was afraid of judgment from her family and close friends. Lina was unable to reconcile what she wanted with her actual experiences, and she would fluctuate between trying to say and do what she thought others wanted and trying to be herself.

The stories presented here show glimpses of resilience in the women. Tasha went back to school and expressed her desire to be a role model to other young women. Carla was able to impress the caseworker with her ability to care for Jake. Caris saw an opportunity to educate others about FASD and made a video for the judge. At times, it was difficult to stand up against stigma and they would become cynical and cautious about who to trust. Lina felt like she could not be herself without disappointing her mom and sister. Yet they wanted to be perceived as more than the labels other people had placed on them. The professionals who were part of their lives, from teachers to doctors, had to earn the women's respect because of the negative experiences they had as children and continued to have as

...appropriate level of supervision in the home and are kept safe (Government of Alberta, 2015). Similar services are found in all other provinces of Canada.

adults. They seemed to expect to be judged by others, and some of their stories were about conforming so they could avoid being judged. As Carla put it, *"I used to be different, now I am not like that"* (Carla, July 2013).

The participants' experiences with learning difficulties began when they were children, but they became part of their experiences as women living in poverty, trying to go back to school while caring for their own children. They had to find ways to survive while trying to resist the discrimination they faced as women who were criminalized. Like in the studies by Hagner et al. (2008) and Unruh and Bullis (2005), the participants in this narrative inquiry felt judged and discriminated against by the people who were supposed to provide support, making it difficult to trust or depend on others.

Thread 4: Mothering and Being Mothered

Three of the participants are mothers, and their own needs were often an extension of their children's needs and trying to ensure they were being cared for. Tasha put herself into treatment when she found out she was pregnant because she thought she was getting a second chance to be a mom. She stayed sober for the rest of her pregnancy and was able to rent an apartment for her and her son. Carla stated that she quit using drugs so she could have a place to live and keep her son. She made sure his needs were met and, in doing so, was able to meet her own needs. She was especially adamant about putting her kids before romantic relationships and not using physical force as a form of discipline. Her experiences of mothering were heavily based on her experiences as a child. Caris was motivated to attend parenting programs because she knew it increased her likelihood of regaining custody of Josh. She was aware of how the programs could be helpful for her and her kids, but her reason for attending was her fear of losing Josh. Eleven months after we first met, Caris lost custody of Josh again and she was determined to get him back. She said it was the only thing she was living for. She realized that when Josh was with her, she was more responsible, and she had established a routine that "kept her out of trouble." Her desire to stay sober and maintain a healthy lifestyle was based on her desire to get Josh back.

Lina did not have any children. Her narrative account contrasted with the other participants in the sense that she did not have a person or people who motivated her or anchored her in quite the same way. Lina said she wanted to be single and learn about herself again. She thought of this time in her life as a new beginning. She did not seem to be driven to maintain a close connection to others, but, rather, she saw a potential for growth by being on her own and being more independent. Her stories contrasted with the other three participants because she did not have an explicit and tangible need to stay out of jail or quit using drugs.

Being mothered and mothering were central to three of the participants' stories. They spoke about trying to give their children different experiences from the ones they had as children. The participants were all abused by their mothers, emotionally and/or physically. Yet each of them had an ongoing relationship with their mothers, who are an active part of their present lives. They had feelings of resentment for what had happened in the past, but they still loved their mothers and wanted to stay connected to them. Tasha, Carla, and Caris each felt a sense of purpose from being a mother and having the responsibility to care for their children. They saw themselves as mothers despite the negative way others perceived them, seeing them as criminals and drug addicts. They expressed determination to mother their children differently from the way they were mothered, and they were able to look into the future with hope.

Implications

The individual stories were situated within a lifetime of experiences of women living at the margins of, and within, political, social, and institutional systems. In the present, surviving each day entailed challenges that were ongoing and dynamic, including meeting their basic needs of housing and food in the midst of uncertainty, their desire for support without judgment and stigma, and their commitment to mothering their children. They talked about having to face neglect and rejection as children from their parents, especially their mothers. Their relationships and circumstances changed throughout the time we met, which directly impacted their needs. Having someone to turn to, who was reliable and trustworthy, had a significant impact on the participants at various times in their lives.

The participants' desire for individualized support was based on specific situations, the need for a relational space where stories could be told and retold in different ways, and attentiveness to diverse experiences within the women's lives. Care professionals, including social workers, nurses, and occupational therapists who work with women in correctional centres and transitioning into the community from prison settings, can offer support for women by creating a relational space and fostering relationships emphasizing trust and respect (e.g., Eggers, Muñoz, Sciulli, & Crist, 2006; Farnworth & Muñoz, 2009; Parsons & Warner-Robbins, 2002; Peternelj-Taylor, 2004; Visher & Travis, 2003). Moreover, relationships are not only based on listening to the women's stories but also on welcoming and embracing stories as experiential knowledge (Belenky, Clinchy, Goldberger, & Tarule, 1986; Bruner, 1986). To recognize the women as experts in their experiences shows the significance of their stories. All four participants talked about the expectation of failure, based on the stigma they experienced, associated with using illicit substances and being labelled a criminal. Lawston and Lucas (2011) identify that stereotypes often affect women's sense of identity, as well as aspirations for their children. For example, Carla wanted her kids to have the freedom to be themselves without having to fight pressures to conform as she had to do. Sharing experiences made it possible to move past the stereotypes that labelled them.

Through a postmodern feminist lens, the rationale for inquiring into women's experiences is the knowledge they offer that challenges or re-evaluates normative viewpoints, including stereotypes and assumptions, about criminology and disability (Comack, 1996; Johnson & Traustadóttir, 2000; Morris, 1993). Rather than categorizing the women based on specific characteristics, hearing about individual experiences was necessary to understand how the women perceived themselves and the world around them. As previous research has shown, the women in this narrative inquiry were survivors of emotional and physical violence, mothers at risk of losing their children, and women in the lowest income bracket (Balfour & Comack, 2014; Hayes, 2007; Minaker, 2001; Minaker & Hogeveen, 2015). They faced discrimination and felt the stigma associated with having a criminal record, being Aboriginal, and having addictions and learning difficulties. Marginalization in the form of exclusion and limitations was a part of their stories, and focusing on *how* rather than *why* they experienced marginalization was important to understanding how best to support them (Comack, 2014).

Limitations

It is critical to note how I selected certain stories among many. I chose pieces that I thought reflected some of the significant experiences in their lives, but these depictions are only a glimpse of the women I came to know. The stories underscore how important it is to enter into relationships aware of preconceptions or assumptions about certain experiences and to be awake to the possibilities that are within reach once we become aware of them. My hope is that the reader will see how the participants' lives continue to evolve, and that I entered and exited in the midst of lives being lived (Clandinin, Murphy, Huber, & Orr, 2009).

Conclusion

The stories the participants shared were based on individual experiences and circumstances. The stories show the complexity and multiplicity of lives that can enhance our understanding of the diversity of women with learning difficulties in the criminal justice system. At the same time, the narrative threads point out the consistencies that resonate across stories, which are important to recognize. The threads in this narrative inquiry were uncertainty and instability in circumstances, having someone to turn to, enduring judgment and stigma, and mothering as well as being mothered. Returning to the research puzzle, I wonder how professionals who work with women involved in the criminal justice system could offer meaningful, lasting support in the midst of tumultuous circumstances based on the findings of this narrative inquiry. Building relationships and including the women who are receiving services in the decision-making process to determine what they need and want to focus on are two possible ways to attend.

References

Balfour, G., & Comack, E. (2014). *Criminalizing women* (2nd ed.). Halifax, NS: Fernwood Press.

Belenky, M. F., Clinchy, B. M., Goldberger, N. R., & Tarule, J. M. (1986). *Women's ways of knowing: The development of self, voice, and mind*. New York, NY: Basic Books.

Bruner, J. S. (1986). *Actual minds, possible worlds*. Cambridge, MA: Harvard University Press.

Burgess-Proctor, A. (2006). Intersections of race, class, gender, and crime: Future directions for feminist criminology. *Feminist Criminology, 1*(1), 27–47. doi:10.1177/1557085105282899

Clandinin, D. J., & Caine, V. (2013). Narrative inquiry. In A. Trainor & E. Graue (Eds.), *Reviewing qualitative research in the social sciences* (pp. 166–179). New York, NY: Taylor and Francis/Routledge.

Clandinin, D. J., & Connelly, F. M. (2000). *Narrative inquiry: Experience and story in qualitative research*. San Francisco, CA: Josey-Bass.

Clandinin, D. J., Murphy, M. S., Huber, J., & Orr, A. M. (2009). Negotiating narrative inquiries: Living in a tension-filled midst. *The Journal of Educational Research, 103*(2), 81–90.

Clandinin, D. J., & Raymond, H. (2006). Note on narrating disability. *Equity & Excellence in Education, 39*(2), 101–104.

Comack, E. (1996). *Women in trouble: Connecting women's law violations to their histories of abuse*. Halifax, NS: Fernwood Publishing.

Comack, E. (2014). The feminist engagement with criminology. In G. Balfour & E. Comack (Eds.), *Criminalizing women: Gender and (in)justice in neo-liberal times* (2nd ed., pp. 12–46). Halifax, NS: Fernwood Publishing.

Covington, S. (2003). A woman's journey home: Challenges for female offenders. In J. Travis & M. Waul (Eds.), *From prisoners once removed: The impact of incarceration and reentry on children, families, and communities* (pp. 67–103). Washington, DC: Urban Institute Press.

Daly, K., & Chesney-Lind, M. (1988). Feminism and criminology. *Justice Quarterly, 5*(4), 497–538.

Eggers, M., Muñoz, J. P., Sciulli, J., & Crist, P. A. H. (2006). The community reintegration project: Occupational therapy at work in a county jail. *Occupational Therapy in Health Care, 20*(1), 17–37. doi: 10.1300/J003v20n01_02

Farnworth, L., & Muñoz, J. P. (2009). An occupational and rehabilitation perspective for institutional practice. *Psychiatric Rehabilitation Journal, 32*(3), 192–198.

Government of Alberta. (2015). *Child protective services*. Retrieved from http://humanservices.alberta.ca/abuse-bullying/17182.html

Hagner, D., Malloy, J. M., Mazzone, M. W., & Cormier, G. M. (2008). Youth with disabilities in the criminal justice system: Considerations for transition and rehabilitation planning. *Journal of Emotional and Behavioral Disorders, 16*(4), 240–247.

Harding, S. G. (1991). *Whose science? Whose knowledge? Thinking from women's lives*. New York, NY: Cornell University Press.

Hayes, S. C. (2007). Women with learning disabilities who offend: What do we know? *British Journal of Learning Disabilities, 35*(3), 187–191. doi:10.1111/j.1468-3156.2007.00462.x

Hayes, S., Shackell, P., Mottram, P., & Lancaster, R. (2007). The prevalence of intellectual disability in a major UK prison. *British Journal of Learning Disabilities, 35*(3), 162–167.

Hyun, E., Hahn, L., & McConnell, D. (2014). Experiences of people with learning disabilities in the criminal justice system. *British Journal of Learning Disabilities, 42*(4), 308–314.

Johnson, K., & Traustadóttir, R. (2000). *Women with intellectual disabilities: Finding a place in the world*. London, United Kingdom: Jessica Kingsley Publishers.

Jones, G., & Talbot, J. (2010). No one knows: The bewildering passage of offenders with learning disability and learning difficulty through the criminal justice system. *Criminal Behaviour and Mental Health, 20*(1), 1–7.

Lahman, M. K. E., Rodriguez, K. L., Richard, V. M., Geist, M. R., Schendel, R. K., & Graglia, P. E. (2011). (Re)forming research poetry. *Qualitative Inquiry, 17*(9), 887–896. doi:10.1177/1077800411423219

Lawston, J. M., & Lucas, A. E. (2011). *Razor wire women: Prisoners, activists, scholars, and artists*. Albany, NY: State University of New York Press.

Loucks, N. (2007). *Prisoners with learning difficulties and learning disabilities – Review of prevalence and associated needs*. London, United Kingdom: Prison Reform Trust.

Mahoney, T. H. (2011, April). Women and the criminal justice system. In *Women in Canada: A gender-based statistical report* (Component of Statistics Canada Catalogue no. 89-503-X). Ottawa, ON: Minister of Industry. Retrieved from http://www.statcan.gc.ca/pub/89-503-x/2010001/article/11416-eng.pdf

Mayes, R., Llewellyn, G., & McConnell, D. (2006). Misconception: The experience of pregnancy for women with intellectual disabilities. *Scandinavian Journal of Disability Research, 8*(2–3), 120–131.

Minaker, J. C. (2001). Evaluating criminal justice responses to intimate abuse through the lens of women's needs. *Canadian Journal of Women and the Law, 13,* 74–106.

Minaker, J. C., & Hogeveen, B. R. (2015). *Criminalized mothers, criminalizing mothering*. Bradford, ON: Demeter Press.

Morris, J. (1993, March). Feminism and disability. *Feminist Review, 43,* 57–70. doi:10.1057/fr.1993.4

Morris, J. (2001). Impairment and disability: Constructing an ethics of care that promotes human rights. *Hypatia, 16*(4), 1–16.

Morris, K. A., & Morris, R. J. (2006). Disability and juvenile delinquency: Issues and trends. *Disability & Society, 21*(6), 613–627.

Oshima, K. M. M., Huang, J., Jonson-Reid, M., & Drake, B. (2010). Children with disabilities in poor households: Association with juvenile and adult offending. *Social Work Research, 34*(2), 102–113.

Parsons, M. L., & Warner-Robbins, C. (2002). Factors that support women's successful transition to the community following jail/prison. *Health Care for Women International, 23*(1), 6–18.

Peternelj-Taylor, C. (2004). An exploration of othering in forensic psychiatric and correctional nursing. *Canadian Journal of Nursing Research, 36*(4), 130–146.

Shelton, D. (2006). A study of young offenders with learning disabilities. *Journal of Correctional Health Care, 12*(1), 36–44.

Smart, C. (1990). Feminist approaches to criminology or postmodern woman meets atavistic man. In L. Gelsthorpe & A. Morris (Eds.), *Feminist perspectives in criminology* (pp. 70–84). Philadelphia, PA: Open University Press.

Unruh, D., & Bullis, M. (2005). Facility-to-community transition needs for adjudicated youth with disabilities. *Career Development for Exceptional Individuals, 28*(2), 67–79.

Visher, C. A., & Travis, J. (2003, August). Transitions from prison to community: Understanding individual pathways. *Annual Review of Sociology, 29*, 89–113.

PART IV

Teaching

The Caregiver Curriculum on FASD: Transforming Practice through Knowledge and Education

Dorothy Badry, Deborah Goodman, and Jamie Hickey

Introduction: Fetal Alcohol Spectrum Disorder as a Public Health Issue

The need has always existed to provide care for children who cannot remain with their family in the child welfare system. Approximately sixty-seven thousand children are in care in Canada, with recent research suggesting that out-of-home placements have increased dramatically over fifteen years from 5.7 out of one thousand in 1992 to 9.2 out of one thousand in 2007 (Mulcahy & Trocmé, 2010). While prior estimates were that about 6 per cent (sixty out of one thousand) of children in child welfare care had fetal alcohol syndrome (FAS), a recent study reports that approximately 16.9 per cent (169 out of one thousand) had a condition along the spectrum of FAS disorder (FASD) (Lange, Shield, Rehm, & Popova, 2013). The combination of the increase in placements required coupled with the fact that FASD is a disability that has been identified as having significant social, health, and

Suggested Citation: Badry, D., Goodman, D., & Hickey, J. (2016). The caregiver curriculum on FASD: Transforming practice through knowledge and education. In H. Montgomery, D. Badry, D. Fuchs, & D. Kikulwe (Eds.), *Transforming Child Welfare: Interdisciplinary Practices, Field Education, and Research* (pp. 271–294). Regina, SK: University of Regina Press.

economic costs to society as a result of prenatal exposure to alcohol (Popova, Lange, Burd, & Rehm, 2014) means there are considerable pressures on the child welfare system and the caregivers who provide care to these complex youth. Children with FASD often end up in care, and the prevalence rate of child welfare involvement continues to climb, as alcohol-exposed pregnancies remain a substantial concern in Canada (Tough, 2009). In short, a compelling need exists to provide caregivers with information and education about FASD in order to effectively support children and families.

The focus of this chapter is on the development of the Caregiver Curriculum on Fetal Alcohol Spectrum Disorder (FASD), which resulted from a research project entitled, *A Tri-Province Initiative to Expand Understanding of Costs, Services & Prevention of a Public Health Issue: Fetal Alcohol Spectrum Disorder & Children/Youth in Care [2010–2014]* (Goodman, Badry, Fuchs, Long, & Pelech, 2014). This project involved team members from three provinces and included the Child Welfare Institute at the Children's Aid Society of Toronto as the lead agency, the University of Calgary, Faculty of Social Work, and the University of Manitoba. The four main goals of the research project were to: 1) create a community of practice website (www.FASDchildwelfare.ca); 2) to conduct a review of the prevalence of children in care with FASD across the three participating provinces; 3) to identify resources and develop inventories of FASD-related services across all the provinces and territories of Canada; and 4) to create a curriculum in FASD for caregivers. An analysis of the standardized data on the prevalence of confirmed or suspected FASD in child welfare settings finds that the prevalence rate ranges from 10.3 per cent (Alberta) to 12.3 per cent (Manitoba) to 10.5 per cent (Ontario) (Goodman et al., 2014). In sum, 103–123 per one thousand, which is higher than previous general population estimates of nine per one thousand (Public Health Agency of Canada, 2003). There is an increasing amount of prevalence data as indicated above that points to a growing concern about the demand on the child welfare system to meet the complex needs of children with FASD. In this chapter we contextualize the need for caregiver education through exploring relevant literature, describing the development of the Caregiver Curriculum on FASD, and identifying the utility of this curriculum and discussing its applications for caregiver training and education.

Canada has been viewed as a global leader in its response to FASD, and the Canada FASD Research Network exists to support research across the provinces and territories of Canada in relation to prevention, intervention, and diagnosis (www.canfasd.ca). The concern that FASD is a costly public health issue remains persistent and complex, largely due to the knowledge that this is a preventable disability. In theory, FASD is preventable through alcohol abstention during pregnancy. In reality, children and families where FASD emerges are themselves often struggling with addictions, poverty, marginalization, historical trauma, and mothers often absent from their children's lives (Astley, Bailey, Talbot, & Clarren, 2000). These are well-known factors that contribute to child welfare involvement. O'Malley (2007) has identified that disabilities associated with FASD can include developmental, cognitive, social, emotional, and behavioural effects (p. 29) that are often described as neurobehavioural problems. O'Malley (2007) also indicated that environmental factors including physical, emotional, and sexual abuse and neglect can be additional compounding problems contributing to stress responses and disorders in young children.

It is important to highlight the need to understand·FASD as a disability. Romi (as cited in Nagler, 1990) suggested that when disability is viewed as a phenomenon, it takes into consideration not only the individual with the disability but the social structures that contribute to the concern. FASD is a phenomenon that is concerned with the individual who has the disability, as well as the social/family structures that contribute to the emergence of FASD. The cause—alcohol use during pregnancy—presents a conundrum in relation to prevention, as women's alcohol use in Canada continues to increase (Dowsett Johnston, 2013). The need to look beyond substance use and examine historical trauma where FASD is an outcome takes the onus off the mother and serves to identify the precursors and environmental factors contributing to these circumstances.

When parents are actively engaged in addictions and substance use, their capacity to care for their children is affected, and this is a major factor in child welfare intervention and involvement. Csiernik and Alaggia (2003) stated: "By the time most individuals who are abusing substances are referred to treatment, their alcohol and/or drug use has touched not only themselves but also their entire social and family structure...family is still the primary biological, economic, social, legal and historical unit of our society" (p. 129). Addiction often interferes with the parents' ability to meet the needs of their children. Substance use disorders are often raised as a concern in child protection matters. If substance use interferes with meeting the basic care needs of children, and a referral is made for further assessment or investigation, and these concerns are substantiated, a plan of action is required.

FASD and Caregiving

There are multiple challenges faced by children with FASD across their lifespan, and best practice in caregiving that is specifically focused on child welfare practice is evolving. For example, Alberta Human Services has an ongoing FASD Community of Practice that provides training on FASD to caseworkers and caregivers and this initiative has been going on for over a decade. A chapter on this initiative was written for the last book in the Voices from the Prairies Series (Badry, Pelech, & Milne, 2014).

Caregivers of children with FASD require training and education; support in relation to risks, vulnerabilities, and behavioural concerns; regular caseworker and foster care support contact; respite; and grief and loss support. Further, support that is meaningful, structured, and consistent is required to promote placement stability, including regular caseworker contact (Pelech, Badry, & Daoust, 2013). We know that concerns emerge for children with FASD across different environments and particularly in the transition to adolescence.

The Caregiver Curriculum on FASD was developed in consideration of the need to provide some basic training and knowledge about FASD to caregivers. Understanding the needs of children with FASD for constant supervision, structure, and support requires training, as FASD is a complex disability that is often invisible. Many children in the child welfare system have a FASD diagnosis, and Fuchs et al. (2009) identified the high economic impact of FASD on the child welfare and health care system. There are many risk factors and vulnerabilities associated with disability, and children in care with complex disabilities place high demands on care systems, including the potential of needing services in a child welfare agency (Fuchs, Burnside, Marchenski, & Mudry, 2005; Fuchs, Burnside, Marchenski, Mudry, & DeRiviere, 2008). In Manitoba, Fuchs et al. (2005) determined that one-third of children in care fall within a broad definition of disability and 17 per cent of children in care were affected by, diagnosed with, or suspected of having, FASD.

In a survey of over 1,100 human service professionals, including foster parents, Caley et al. (2008) indicated that over 70 per cent of the participants stated they did not feel prepared to care for or feel confident in managing cases where children had FASD. Participants indicated that approximately 43 per cent had taken some training on FASD and the effects of alcohol exposure. In contrast, over 80 per cent of participants indicated they had no training and knowledge about interventions, making referrals, and assisting clients. In part, this study, along with other literature reviewed, identified the need for accessible FASD training and learning resources.

Walls and Pei (2013) explored the systems of care as perceived by caregivers, primarily foster parents of children with an FASD diagnosis. In a qualitative study with eight caregivers, three main themes emerged: 1) caregiver considerations; 2) challenges identified in program delivery; and 3) building on identified strengths. Further, Walls and Pei focused on caregiver experience in responding to the needs of children with FASD, which included "seeking, reflecting, collaborating and planning" (p. 88). The *seeking* stage was identified by caregivers as trying to figure things out and collecting as much information as possible regarding the needs of the child. Gathering the information was viewed as an important phase in the caregivers' involvement with the child and helped to facilitate a sense that the information gained would help guide their care, especially when the child was perceived to have complex needs. In the *reflecting* stage, caregivers identified feelings of self-doubt in their capacity to meet the needs of the child—and not quite understanding why this was such a challenging experience. In the *collaborating* stage, it was recognized by caregivers that adaptation in response to the child's needs was an ongoing process. Caregivers also recognized that they were extending themselves by making accommodations in their lifestyle around the needs of the child. The need to make accommodations for children with complex needs by caregivers often evolves over time and its impact is not fully realized or appreciated. A number of caregivers identified the concern that, due to the complex needs of the child, and behavioural concerns in particular, the family had at times withdrawn from social activities they previously enjoyed. The last element, the *planning* stage, was reflected in developing an understanding of the child, their needs, and recognition of issues related to grief and loss. Caregivers need to be able to express their challenges with the child as part of the process of moving forward, with some strength and a sense of renewed perspective. Challenges that foster parents faced in providing care for children with FASD include the multiple demands of a service system that is cross-disciplinary and not generally centralized. The basic need for information (training) on FASD and its developmental trajectory over the child's lifespan are critical learning activities that do make a difference in outcomes for children and families. The need for training on FASD is critical for caregivers and provides a foundation to understanding the often-intense needs of children living with this disability.

In previous research, Badry (2009) identified that the transition to adulthood was often a major source of grief and loss for caregivers. Walls and Pei (2013) identified the need that caregivers express for a consistent and continued system of care for children with FASD that supports youth through adulthood. Caregivers are deeply concerned about the vulnerabilities and risks for the youth they have raised, and they experience a sense of loss and grief about the transition to adulthood. The need to align support services and respite was also identified as important in supporting the caregiver. Burnside and Fuchs (2013), in their examination of youth with FASD leaving care, raised concerns about young people who were physically eighteen but in no way prepared for the demands and responsibilities of adult life because of the dismaturity associated with their disability. Caregivers who raise children with FASD are intensely concerned about the transition to adulthood and often become a voice advocating for the young person's needs. In relation to the experiences of grief and loss, Lutke (2013) identified a process of relapsing and remitting cycles of grief that occur for adoptive and foster parents of children with FASD. As an adoptive and foster parent, Lutke's work is original and grounded in many years of experience, and she graciously shared this work in the Caregiver Curriculum on FASD through a special topic module focused on grief and loss. Lutke, along with many foster and adoptive parents, has been a fierce advocate and voice for children, youth, and adults with FASD and these influences have shaped policy and practice in the Canadian context.

In their research, Shannon and Tappan (2011) found that child welfare service providers and caregivers expressed concerns about the prevalence of children with developmental disabilities, the lack of understanding of developmental disabilities, their capacity to identify disabilities, and

training to improve child protective services (CPS) workers' ability to identify children with developmental disabilities. There is a dearth of training
on developmental disabilities in social work degree programs and this
is an issue that warrants attention in post-degree or workforce training
within CPS (Badry, 2013). This is a common problem in child welfare training. Core training in child welfare work does not generally cover the topic
of developmental disability or FASD. However, Alberta has had sustained
workforce development and foster care training on FASD through its FASD
Community of Practice (Badry, 2013, 2014). Further, caregivers such as foster parents rely on the child welfare authorities and their foster care associations to provide training in order to effectively respond to the needs of
children in their care.

Understanding FASD as a disability can provide a meaningful contribution to the types of support and intervention in working with children
and families. Families of children with FASD, foster parents, kinship caregivers, students in the health professions, and interested learners can also
benefit from the information in the online curriculum. The intent of the
curriculum is to provide a user-friendly resource that is balanced between
information about FASD on a variety of topics, as well as practical applications of that information. Training on FASD has increased dramatically
in the past decade and includes provincial, national, and international
conferences. While these educational opportunities are important, they
may not be readily available to the front line and this was part of the driving concern in relation to the need to develop a curriculum on FASD to
support caregivers to engage in FASD-informed practice.

Development Process for the Caregiver Curriculum on FASD

A primary goal of the Caregiver Curriculum on FASD project was to
develop a series of educational resources that could be utilized by parents, grandparents, foster parents, and other caregivers of children with
FASD. There was a particular focus on addressing the needs of caregivers
living in rural areas where formal training programs are less accessible.
The Caregiver Curriculum on FASD was written from a social work lens
with a disability perspective. Across the curriculum, FASD is reflected as
a lifespan disability and emphasis is placed on the changing needs of
individuals with FASD across their lifespans. While the primary intended

audience for the curriculum is caregivers for individuals with FASD, efforts were made to create a curriculum that would be useful to other professionals. To this end, the curriculum was divided into multiple modules to allow the caregiver or professional to tailor the curriculum to their individual learning needs.

The development process for the Caregiver Curriculum on FASD was highly collaborative, involving regular consultation with a stakeholder council that included FASD-informed researchers, caregivers, and other professionals. Additionally, the research team met monthly for the first two years of the project and in the last year bimonthly and received frequent reports and updates on the curriculum development. Additionally, members of the research team also provided feedback to inform the curriculum. The following developmental steps were taken for this project:

- reviewing relevant literature to identify areas of need for the curriculum;
- establishing a curriculum review council;
- reviewing existing FASD curriculums, including those intended for professional audiences;
- collecting potential curriculum resources, including the Alberta FASD learning series videos;
- linking the Alberta FASD learning series videos to relevant topic areas;
- conducting a survey to identify the learning needs of caregivers, including stakeholders such as foster parents, child welfare staff, FASD educators, researchers, and professionals;
- proposing curriculum topics for subsequent discussion and approval by the council;
- reviewing, on an ongoing basis, the curriculum ideas and development within the research team;
- developing individual modules;
- submitting modules to council and selecting stakeholders for feedback and revisions;
- finalizing curriculum modules;
- publishing curriculum modules online at www.fasdchildwelfare.ca.

Brief Results from the Stakeholder Survey

A survey was conducted with twenty-five key stakeholders in 2013 to inform the curriculum and ask the following questions. Some of the most significant responses are included below each question.

- Caregiver education is a focus of this project in relation to children and youth who have an FASD. Are there specific areas that you would recommend for a caregiver curriculum?

    I think it is important for caregivers to realize the different stages in a person's life with FASD. [To recognize] that a lot of the issues do not arise until twelve or thirteen or even later. This is the main area that should be focused on, since we see so many caregivers become overwhelmed at this stage of the FASD-affected individual.

- Considering the often-intensive needs and nature of children/ youth with FASD, what training would you recommend for caregivers around self-care and support?

    [It is important to know] what self-care looks like and how to implement it....it is imperative to keep oneself emotionally, physically and mentally healthy and prioritizing...Knowing that good self-care and the grief and loss piece...are inter-related [helps in] not getting stuck in a negative emotional cycle. Understanding stress and its effects on the body should be part of this [training}...and how to juggle multiple roles, responsibilities; how to prioritize, how to set limits; how to say "no"...how to advocate without being aggressive and/or negative.

- What suggestions would you have for issues related to grief and loss? We know this is an issue that continues to be important for many families and caregivers.

    It is important to find support with others that are living with a person with FASD, such as a parent support group. It is also important to take time for yourself and your relationship, since these individuals are very hard on you and your relationships. It is important...to realize you need to get away, not to just ship off the kids. Kids need stability, so it is better to go away and get someone in to look after them. This way they stay in their own surroundings. They need training in sleep techniques for their children, since sleep is most important for these children and it gives time for yourself and your spouse.

Caregivers have to be taught how to talk to their children. How to advocate for their children, especially those in care, multiple placements can cause much grief. We had to go through a lot of loss and grief in our family....Realizing and accepting the multiple roles a caregiver has in addition to that of caregiver for a child in care; understanding the different ways grief affects different family members....Understanding how to access help and ways to work through the issues....Understanding grief and loss [for] the children [in care]—this never gets talked about and everything gets written off as behaviour or FASD...grief is rarely considered.

- Are you aware of any existing caregiver training or caregiver curriculum materials that are currently available? If yes, and you believe it's a resource we should know about, can you please identify.

   There is absolutely no culturally relevant or accessible curriculum (for foster parents) for some of our Aboriginal communities.

   There are many different FASD curricula, but nothing that is comprehensive and developed specifically for caregivers of children in care.

- Are there special topics that you feel are especially important within a caregiver curriculum?

   All the nuts and bolts—positive and effective advocacy; objective record keeping, note taking and letter writing; how to read

medical and psychological reports and test results and under-
stand them; how to make those things work for the child and the
caregiver; how to develop IEPs [Individual Education Plans];
how to set up and run a meeting; how to make a paper trail...
how to work with different systems; how to work with a therapist,
a teacher, etc.; respect for and working with a birth family and
also an understanding of safety issues related here; how to know
if a child being considered for placement in a home is a good fit
with others already in the home and what to do about this.

It was important to consider the responses from the survey in order
to inform the curriculum, and many conversations and dialogues took
place with various stakeholders and professionals who were interested
and invested in supporting the development of a user-friendly curriculum
on FASD. This information is also helpful in constructing new modules in
the future.

Focus of the Caregiver Curriculum

The purpose of the Caregiver Curriculum on FASD is to provide a venue
for caregivers (including foster parents, kinship care, youth and child care
workers, child welfare services, families, and others) trying to understand
and cope with some of the life challenges presented by children with FASD.
The curriculum was developed with caregivers in mind and is intended
to promote FASD-informed care in foster homes, kinship, and adoptive
homes and in casework practice. Children with FASD have complex needs
and live with a lifelong disability that is not always well understood. The
Caregiver Curriculum on FASD (Badry & Hickey, 2014) is a free resource and
is made available through the website www.fasdchildwelfare.ca, which is
now under the auspices of the Children's Aid Society of Toronto. The modules were designed as a self-study format in PowerPoint, with links and
toggle buttons to navigate through each module. The PowerPoint modules
are also easily downloadable and can be used for presentations on FASD.
While each module has a different learning topic, all the modules have
a consistent format organized under the headings Topic, Introduction,
Learning Objectives, Topic Slides, Recap, and Activity. The topics for the
curriculum are included in Table 12.1 below.

Table 12.1: Caregiver Curriculum on FASD Module Description

Module	Main Topic	Unit Descriptions
	Introduction	• Introduction
1	The Impact of FASD	• Unit 1: The Impact of Alcohol on the Developing Brain • Unit 2: Neurological Effects of FASD • Unit 3: Co-occurring Conditions
2	Understanding FASD as a Disability for Children in Care	• Unit 4: Understanding FASD as a Disability • Unit 5: Viewing FASD as a Lifespan Disability • Unit 6: FASD-Informed Care • Unit 7: FASD and Employment • Unit 8: Reframing FASD from a Strengths-Based Perspective
3	Caregiver Self-Care	• Unit 9: Caring for the Caregiver • Unit 10: Compassion Fatigue
4	FASD and Behaviour	• Unit 11: Behavioural Concerns and FASD • Unit 12: Understanding Dismaturity • Unit 13: Adjusting and Adapting Expectations • Unit 14: Practical Approaches to Behaviour Management
5	Special Topics	• Unit 15: Grief & Loss (I) and (II)
6	Working with Professionals	• Unit 16: The Interprofessional Matrix for FASD

Launching the Caregiver Curriculum on FASD: Considerations

The Caregiver Curriculum on FASD was launched in August 2014 as a result of the tri-provincial project. The goal of the project was to provide families and caregivers for individuals with FASD an informative resource that could be accessed at low or no cost. Key challenges that had to be addressed in the planning process included accessibility, flexibility, and adaptability to caregiver information needs. We wanted the curriculum to be easily accessible through the web, available 24/7, as well as useful and practical to caregivers. With the intention of providing needed resources to rural and under-resourced areas, accessibility issues were discussed early in the project. The original project was developed in PDF and PowerPoint formats to allow for resources to be saved and accessed off-line if needed. Flexibility, not only of delivery options but also timing, was another key area of focus during curriculum development. It was recognized that caregivers often have limited time available and that an effective curriculum would be most useful if broken into short modules while supporting the user to stop, start, pause, and return to the curriculum at their own pace. The module format was also selected as it also allowed the curriculum to be adaptable to caregiver information needs. By offering the curriculum in a series of short, single-topic units divided into six themed modules, caregivers are able to select units and modules based on their current needs. In this spirit, each unit and module was designed to function either as a stand-alone resource or as part of the larger curriculum, depending on caregiver preference.

Module Development and Focus

Six modules make up the curriculum, each with an important focus on an area of care for an individual with FASD. It was important to consider current literature in informing the module development. Below, we provide a brief description of each module, as well as the reasoning behind the inclusion of each module in the curriculum.

Module 1: The Impact of FASD

The first module is centred on providing quality information to caregivers relating to what FASD is, the neurological effects of prenatal alcohol exposure, and a brief overview of co-occurring or co-morbid conditions that commonly impact individuals with FASD. The module contains both introductory and expert-level information. The decision to provide expert-level information to caregivers is congruent with the Prepared Family Caregiver Model described by Houts, Nezu, Nezu, and Bucher (1996). This model suggests caregivers must be supported in developing creativity, optimism, planning, and expert knowledge, emphasizing the role of caregivers within the professional coordinated care plan.

Module 2: Understanding FASD as a Disability for Children in Care

Module two was developed using a disability lens to examine FASD from a lifespan approach. Fetal alcohol spectrum disorder has been identified as a lifelong disability with challenges that arise, evolve, and change based on the individual's stage of life (O'Malley, 2007; Ramsay, 2010; Brintnell,

Bailey, Sawhney, & Kreftin, 2011). Units within this module include under-standing FASD as a disability, understanding FASD across the lifespan, providing FASD-informed care, supporting employment for individuals with FASD, and reframing FASD from a strengths-based perspective. This module encourages caregivers to focus on what the individual can do while still maintaining realistic expectations across the lifespan.

Module 3: Caregiver Self-Care

The importance of caregiver self-care was universally indicated as import-ant in the early stages of developing the curriculum. Research by Acton (2002) found that health-promoting self-care behaviours performed by caregivers acted as a mediator to reduce overall caregiver stress. Lu and Wykle (2007) also found connections between caregiver self-care behaviours, caregiver stress, and functional ability, suggesting that an early-intervention program to promote self-care in response to stress symptoms would be valuable. Within the curriculum, the module on self-care provides education on compassion fatigue, information about pro-cessing grief, and offers suggestions on cognitive reframing as a potential self-care technique.

Module 4: FASD and Behaviour

Managing behaviour concerns when providing care to an individual with FASD can be challenging even for well-resourced caregivers (Sanders & Buck, 2010; Watson, Hayes, Coons, & Radford-Paz, 2013). The module includes information on behavioural concerns in FASD, understanding dismaturity in the context of FASD, adjusting and adapting expectations as a caregiver, and general behaviour management approaches. In devel-oping this module, it was acknowledged that it would be inappropriate to present an online resource as a "complete source" of behaviour manage-ment strategies, as each individual with FASD will present a unique set of behaviours requiring different interventions. Caregivers are therefore advised at multiple points within the units to seek additional professional support for challenges involving extreme or dangerous behaviours.

Module 5: Special Topics

The special topics module within the Caregiver Curriculum on FASD was developed with the intention of future expansion. During the development of the curriculum, a survey was administered to a varied group of stake-holders including professionals in multiple disciplines and caregivers. Survey respondents identified many unique challenges and issues for inclusion in the curriculum over the course of this survey. Currently, the units within this module are limited to grief and loss, but the module may be expanded in the future to contain units on other important topics.

Module 6: Working with Professionals

The final module within the curriculum, "Working with Professionals," was developed to assist caregivers in understanding more about the professionals involved in the care of an individual with FASD and to help caregivers conceptualize the caregiving role in the context of the professional care team. This module contains information on coordinating care for an individual with FASD, advocating for care when necessary, and an interactive "interprofessional matrix" that details the duties and professional focus of various disciplines involved in the care of an individual with FASD. This module is highly compatible with the Houts et al. (1996) Prepared Family Caregiver Model in that it acknowledges the expanded role of a caregiver in the life of a person with FASD, provides a framework through which caregivers can seek information related to care, and supports the empowerment of the caregiver in advocating for care.

Future Directions for the Caregiver Curriculum

Throughout the development of the Caregiver Curriculum on FASD, efforts were made to allow for future expansion and modification. At the time of writing, efforts are underway to further digitize the curriculum into an interactive website that can be accessed at no cost. The updated Caregiver Curriculum will be available online in June 2016. Additional functionalities, including audio and video components, are being evaluated for potential inclusion to enhance caregiver learning. In addition to increased delivery options, much potential exists within the curriculum for potential context area expansion. Special topics, including resources for grandparents and educators, have been suggested, as have units related to specific lifespan challenges, such as human sexuality. While at present efforts are being focused on translating the existing curriculum content into an interactive format, the potential for future expansion remains an exciting possibility. We have inserted a few slides from one module in Appendix A in order to share an example of the curriculum with the reader.

Considerations in Developing an Online Curriculum

Developing the curriculum and the website required engagement (contracting) with a web designer who helped us move the process forward. The technical aspects of designing an online curriculum that was suited for independent study or small group training was a lengthy process, required multiple discussions, and was definitely a steep learning curve for the research team. While we had knowledge about FASD, the pathway to online learning requires the combined expertise and knowledge of a collaborative team. Creating a series of individual modules made it possible to allow for future expansion/updates and additional topics without re-authoring the entire curriculum. The following Table 12.2 has been generated based on our learning through developing the curriculum online.

Table 12.2: Considerations in Developing an Online Curriculum for a Diverse Audience

PowerPoint	PowerPoint was selected as a delivery platform as it is available for both PC and Mac users. It is also reasonably "user-friendly" and downloadable.
Internet Access	Having access to the Internet was identified as potentially problematic for some caregivers, particularly in rural and remote communities. Utilizing PowerPoint enabled the curriculum to be used off-line as well as online.
Online Accessibility	We put the curriculum online to ensure that this resource is free to caregivers, families, students, and anyone interested in learning about FASD.
Asynchronous	The curriculum was also published in PDF after seeking direction from a librarian in relation to user accessibility. Publishing in PDF supports users to download and use/share/ study the curriculum at any time.
Finding Time to Learn	Finding time to study was a major concern for many caregivers. To address this, the curriculum was developed into short modules and a table of contents was incorporated in each module to allow caregivers to work through small sections of the curriculum and to navigate each section easily.

Ease of Accessibility: Literacy and Language	Literacy, particularly in an online forum, was identified as varying among users of the curriculum. To address this, definitions and practical examples were incorporated wherever possible. Efforts were made to ensure a user-friendly, plain-language, informative resource. This resource is useful across a wide audience.
Potential for Creating a Certificate	We have received feedback from users to create a certificate to support continuing education specifically for foster parents. This idea is currently being examined and considered, thanks to the input of people using the curriculum to learn about FASD.
Including a Disclaimer	While every effort was made to produce a sound curriculum, it is recognized that FASD is a complex disability and the information included in the curriculum is not in any way associated with diagnostic or medical concerns. A disclaimer was written to ensure clarity and purpose.
Forthcoming: Modules in French	While the curriculum has been translated word for word into French, as Canada is a bilingual country, additional work is required and underway to mobilize the translation for online publication.

Other Proposed Topics for Modules

Based on feedback from stakeholders and users, other module topics have been suggested (see Table 12.3 below).

Table 12.3: Proposed Modules

Family- and Care-Related Modules	• parenting with FASD (supporting parents in raising children) • FASD and grandparents who provide care or act as guardians • supporting and working with birth mothers of children in care, including mentoring relationships • supporting infants and young children • involvement with child welfare
Additional Topics	• sexual health and supporting individuals with FASD in healthy relationships • advocacy: legal/justice system/child welfare involvement • supporting children with FASD in school • culturally sensitive and culturally relevant materials for Aboriginal communities • lifespan planning, including the transition to adulthood and financial management for individuals with FASD

It is important to consider the value of online learning opportunities and to engage in knowledge translation by sharing the collective wisdom of research and practice-based wisdom in response to FASD.

Conclusion

The Caregiver Curriculum on FASD, published online in 2014, was the result of a research project funded by the Public Health Agency of Canada, and reflects a partnership between the University of Calgary, Faculty of Social Work, University of Manitoba, and the Children's Aid Society of Toronto. The research team included research assistants in each province, including a master of social work student from the University of Calgary who helped develop and co-author the curriculum, which was designed from a social work perspective. It is important to recognize the need for grassroots education on "FASD as a disability" and to strongly identify the need for such initiatives in child welfare training more broadly. It is the child welfare system and the caregivers this system relies upon that most often respond to the needs of children and families where addiction is a problem and children are placed in care. We are encouraged by the response to the curriculum to date. A recent analysis by our web team discovered current use has expanded from 1,200 hits a month in fall 2013, to 3,000 hits a month in spring 2014, to 6,000 hits a month in fall 2014, and, finally, to approximately 12,000 hits a month to the website, most to access the curriculum (including 6,000 downloads) in fall 2015. This self-study training is offered at no cost to the caregiver/professional. A number of foster care agencies across Canada have contacted us and indicated that they are incorporating the curriculum into regular foster parent training, including the Children's Aid Society of Toronto, where the curriculum will be used to enhance face-to-face training. Based on the number of users of the Caregiver Curriculum on FASD, and related feedback, we plan to continue to develop and expand the curriculum as a means to support the care of children with FASD. Additionally, mechanisms for evaluation and feedback related to future modules are underway through the Children's Aid Society of Toronto. There is increasing recognition that FASD is a lifespan disability and the complex needs of individuals who live with FASD require lifelong support. The uptake of the curriculum and feedback from users of the curriculum has been very positive. In fact, we have been told that one province is using the curriculum for all its foster care training on FASD. We have many similar accounts from various individuals and groups and foster parents asking if these modules could be turned into a certificate. We are working on this request, as we know there is a strong desire to engage in FASD-informed practice and care across systems. Interest in FASD and providing effective support is a rapidly evolving area of child welfare, health, and human service practice and we plan to continue to develop new materials based on input from users of the curriculum. Supporting children with FASD to have stable lives means supporting families and caregivers through support, respite, education, and training. We know that FASD-informed practice, sound knowledge grounded in research on FASD, and strengths-based approaches make a positive difference in the lives of children, families, and caregivers.

Appendix A: Curriculum Examples with Selected Slides

The following curriculum example with selected slides (see www.fasd-childwelfare.ca) is intended to provide some insight into the approach and style of the modules. Images are also embedded to enhance the visual appeal of the slides. Theories that are relevant to the module, such as Howard Gardner's (2006) theory of multiple intelligences, are included for users to review and consider and this supports a strengths-based approach. The modules present an invitation to learn and to think differently about the needs of children with FASD while providing practical knowledge and useful information with a goal of offering effective and meaningful support to children and families.

Module Topic: Reframing FASD from a Strengths-Based Perspective and Learning Styles

Slide: Introduction and Topics Covered
- This module covers several topics such as strengths-based approaches, stability, learning styles, and decision making.
- We cover several topics, but these key areas are interrelated.
- When we understand the way a person learns, we can work with their strengths and abilities and this supports informed decision making that is in the best interests of the child.

Slide: What Supports a Strengths-Based Approach?
- Always insist on moving forward by adopting a lifespan perspective and long-term support.
- Advocate for a better life for the individual.
- Consider the physical, mental, emotional, and spiritual nature of the child or youth from a disability lens.
- Remember the blanket of oppression that overlays the lives of individuals with FASD.

Slide: The Language of a Strengths-Based Approach
- Hopes and dreams,
- Vision and clarity,
- Ability, talents, competency, change,
- Believing in the individual,
- These terms stand up against words like incompetent, unable, diagnosis, failure, destructive, and dysfunctional.

Slide: What Is a Strengths-Based Approach?
- Determine the strengths and assets of the individual.
- Find out about past successes.
- Find out where the child struggles and what supports are required in these circumstances.
- Ask questions like: What is he/she good at? What has worked out well in the past? What would we like to see more of? Is there something new that he/she might be good at? What activities and sports does he/she like to do? (Try some out and see what works).
- (Note: These questions are structured to look at the child's experience from a positive lens.)

Slide: Why Is Understanding Learning Styles
Important in Relation to FASD?
- Understanding learning styles helps build self-esteem as it means working with the strengths of the individual.
- It is important to recognize that each person learns in his or her own way.
- Each child has their own gifts.

Slide: The Importance of Caregiving

- Individuals who provide care to children with FASD and other disabilities and needs, such as foster and adoptive parents, know the realities of living with the child — and the day-to-day ups and downs.
- With this in mind, it is important to engage in reflective practice and to have someone you can share your thoughts and ideas with.
- You are encouraged to keep a journal or daily log on the things you notice in caring that work. This also helps you to remember what isn't working. The child's disability of FASD remains the same, and it is up to those in the life of the child to continue to adapt to these needs from a FASD-informed perspective.
- Attend training workshops if you can.
- Complete the questions on the following slide (recap and activity).

Slide: Recap and Activity

- Think about the needs you have in relation to the child you care for. Identify how you define structure and routines for a person with FASD.
- Reflect on the following questions and find a professional involved in the child's life who you can talk with about these concerns:
    1. Identify the most important concern you have for a child/youth with FASD in care.
    2. Identify the most important support you need in caring for your child/youth with FASD.
    3. Identify the most important thing you do for yourself to keep on going.
- The module on *Caring for Yourself: Self-Care* is also helpful to review.

References

Acton, G. J. (2002). Health-promoting self-care in family caregivers. *Western Journal of Nursing Research, 24*(1), 73–86.

Astley, S., Bailey, D., Talbot, C., & Clarren, S. (2000). Fetal alcohol syndrome (FAS) primary prevention through FAS diagnosis: I. Identification of high-risk birth mothers through the diagnosis of their children. *Alcohol & Alcoholism, 35*(5), 499–508.

Badry, D. (2009). Fetal alcohol spectrum disorder standards: Supporting children in the care of children's services. *The First Peoples Child & Family Review, 4*(1), 47–56.

Badry, D. (2013). *The FASD community of practice: Leading from within initiative, advanced case consultations* (Unpublished report, Evaluation Report for Alberta Human Services, Workforce Development). Retrieved from http://fasd. alberta.ca/cop-human-services-report.aspx

Badry, D. (2014). *The FASD community of practice: Leading from within initiative, advanced case consultations* (Unpublished evaluation report for Alberta Human Services, Workforce Development).

Badry, D., & Hickey, J. (2014). The caregiver curriculum on FASD. Retrieved from http://www.fasdchildwelfare.ca/learning/caregivers

Badry, D., Pelech, W., & Milne, D. (2014). The FASD community of practice project: Promising practices for children in care with fetal alcohol spectrum disorder: A model for casework practice. In D. Badry, D. Fuchs, H. M. Montgomery, & S. McKay (Eds.), *Reinvesting in families: Strengthening child welfare practice for a brighter future. Voices from the Prairies* (pp. 21–43). Regina, SK: University of Regina Press.

Brintnell, E. S., Bailey, P. G., Sawhney, A., & Kreftin, L. (2011). Understanding FASD: Disability and social supports for adult offenders. In E. P. Riley, S. Clarren, J. Weinberg, & E. Jonsson (Eds.), *Fetal alcohol spectrum disorder: Management and policy perspectives of FASD* (pp. 233–257). Wienheim, Germany: Wiley-VHC Verlag & Co.

Burnside, L., & Fuchs, D. (2013). Bound by the clock: The experiences of youth with FASD transitioning to adulthood from child welfare care. *First Peoples Child & Family Review, 8*(1), 40–61.

Caley, L., Syms, C., Robinson, L., Cederbaum, J., Henry, M., & Shipkey, N. (2008). What human service professionals know and want to know about fetal alcohol syndrome. *Canadian Journal of Clinical Pharmacology, 15*(1), 117–123.

Csiernik, R., & Alaggia, R. (2003). Going home: Rediscovering the family in addiction treatment in Canada. In R. Csiernik & W. Rowe (Eds.), *Responding to the oppression of addiction: Canadian social work perspectives* (pp. 129–148). Toronto, ON: Canadian Scholars Press Inc.

Dowsett Johnston, A. (2013). *Drink: The intimate relationship between women and alcohol*. New York, NY: Harper Collins.

Fuchs, D., Burnside, L., DeRiviere, L., Brownell, M., Marchenski, S., Mudry, A., & Dahl, M. (2009). *The economic impact of children in care with FASD and parental alcohol issues: Phase 2: Costs and service utilization of health care, special education, and childcare*. Retrieved from http://www.cecw-cepb.ca/publications/1146

Fuchs, D., Burnside, L., Marchenski, S., & Mudry, A. (2005). *Children with disabilities receiving services from child welfare agencies in Manitoba*. Retrieved from http://www.cecwcepb.ca/sites/default/files/publications/en/DisabilitiesManitobaFinal.pdf

Fuchs, D., Burnside, L., Marchenski, S., Mudry, A., & DeRiviere, L. (2008). *Economic impact of children in care with FASD: Phase 1: The cost of children in care with FASD in Manitoba.* Retrieved from http://www.cecw-cepb.ca/publications/590

Gardner, H. (2006). *Multiple intelligences: New horizons.* New York, NY: Basic Books.

Goodman, D., Badry, D., Fuchs, D., Long, S., & Pelech, W. (2014). *A tri-province initiative to expand understanding of costs, services & prevention of a public health issue: FASD and children & youth in care.* Retrieved from http://fasdchildwelfare.ca/content/tri-province-initiative-expand-understanding-costs-services-prevention-public-health-issue

Houts, P. S., Nezu, A. M., Nezu, C. M., & Bucher, J. A. (1996). The prepared family caregiver: A problem-solving approach to family caregiver education. *Patient Education and Counseling, 27*(1), 63–73.

Lange, S., Shield, K., Rehm, J., & Popova, S. (2013). Prevalence of fetal alcohol spectrum disorders in child care settings: A meta-analysis. *Pediatrics, 132*(4), 980–995.

Lu, Y. F. Y., & Wykle, M. (2007). Relationships between caregiver stress and self-care behaviors in response to symptoms. *Clinical Nursing Research, 16*(1), 29–43.

Lutke, J. (2013, October). Anticipating and considering the emotional consequences of a diagnosis of FASD in an adult: Relapsing, remitting grief. Oral presentation to the Canada FASD Research Network Diagnostic Guidelines Meeting, Edmonton, Alberta.

Mulcahy, M., & Trocmé, N. (2010). *Children and youth in out-of-home care in Canada* (Centre of Excellence for Child Welfare [CECW] information sheet #78). Montreal, QC: Centre for Research on Children and Families, McGill University.

Nagler, M. (Ed.). (1990). *Perspectives on disability.* Palo Alto, CA: Health Markets Research.

O'Malley, K. D. (2007). *ADHD and fetal alcohol spectrum disorders (FASD).* New York, NY: Nova Science Publishers.

Pelech, W., Badry, D. E., & Daoust, G. (2013). It takes a team: Improving stability among children and youth with fetal alcohol spectrum disorder in care in Canada. *Children and Youth Services Review, 35*(1), 120–127.

Popova, S., Lange, S., Burd, L., & Rehm, J. (2014). Canadian children and youth in care: The cost of fetal alcohol spectrum disorder. *Child Youth Care Forum, 43*(1), 83–96.

Public Health Agency of Canada. (2003). *Fetal alcohol spectrum disorder (FASD): A framework for action.* Ottawa, ON: Author.

Ramsay, M. (2010). Genetic and epigenetic insights into fetal alcohol spectrum disorders. *Genome Medicine, 2*(4), 27.

Sanders, J. L., & Buck, G. (2010). A long journey: Biological and non-biological parents' experiences raising children with FASD. *Journal of Population Therapeutics and Clinical Pharmacology, 17*(2), 308–322.

Shannon, P., & Tappan, C. (2011). Identification and assessment of children with developmental disabilities in child welfare. *Social Work, 56*(4), 297–305.

Tough, S. (2009, October). Incidence and prevalence of FASD in Alberta and Canada. *Proceedings of the IHE Conference on FASD — Across the Lifespan, Calgary, AB*. Retrieved from http://www.ihe.ca/documents/002-Tough.pdf

Walls, L. J., & Pei, J. (2013). Fetal alcohol spectrum disorder service delivery: Exploring current systems of care from the caregivers' perspective. *The International Journal of Alcohol and Drug Research, 2*(3), 87–92.

Watson, S. L., Hayes, S. A., Coons, K. D., & Radford-Paz, E. (2013). Autism spectrum disorder and fetal alcohol spectrum disorder. Part II: A qualitative comparison of parenting stress. *Journal of Intellectual and Developmental Disability, 38*(2), 105–113.

CHAPTER 13

An Indispensable Tool in the Tool Kit: Distance Delivery in Social Work Education to Support Child Welfare Practice

James Mulvale

Introduction

This chapter can be thought of as an "appreciative inquiry" into the work to date, and the possibilities and challenges ahead, for the Prairie Child Welfare Consortium (PCWC). The PCWC is a collaboration between the social work education programs at four universities in Canada's Prairie provinces, specifically the universities of Manitoba, Regina, and Calgary, and the First Nations University of Canada. The PCWC also includes senior representatives of child welfare service delivery agencies and provincial government officials working in child welfare. It began its development in 1999 (McKay, 2007) and has been continuously meeting and working since then.

Of particular interest in this discussion is the suite of online courses that have comprised the PCWC's e-learning project. Each of these courses is offered by one of the participating universities but is made available to students at all of the universities. Since the courses are all entirely online,

Suggested Citation: Mulvale, J. (2016). An indispensable tool in the tool kit: Distance delivery in Social Work education to support child welfare practice. In H. Montgomery, D. Badry, D. Fuchs, & D. Kikulwe (Eds.), *Transforming Child Welfare: Interdisciplinary Practices, Field Education, and Research* (pp. 295–311). Regina, SK: University of Regina Press.

there is no geographic impediment to students taking courses with a PCWC partner university located far from where they live.

I am taking the perspective of appreciative inquiry (AI) in this chapter. AI is an organizational development tool that "involves...the art and practice of asking questions that strengthen a system's capacity to apprehend, anticipate, and heighten positive potential" (Cooperrider, Kaplin, & Stavros, 2003, p. 319). My modest objective in this chapter is to offer my individual "appreciative inquiry" into the status, challenges, and possibilities of the PCWC, which I see as an exemplar of how to use distance education technology to better equip social workers to deal with the multiple and complex challenges in the child welfare field.

The discussion in this chapter will map out challenges in three areas that pertain to the PCWC's e-learning initiative: administration, curriculum, and pedagogy. It will conclude with some suggestions for future program development and research priorities. This chapter is written from my point of view as an academic administrator in a faculty of social work but also as someone who has been involved in the development and delivery of online university courses. It is premised on the vital imperative for social work academic programs to prepare our students for effective, culturally competent, innovative, and evidenced-based practice in the field of child protection and child welfare.

The chapter makes a case for the usefulness of distance learning pedagogy and technology in meeting the challenges of educating child welfare professionals. It recognizes the work done to date by the e-learning committee of the PCWC, and in particular its development of its suite of online undergraduate social work courses. I argue for extending and enhancing the work of the e-learning committee in order to reach more students, practitioners, and researchers. This work can build on the fruitful collaboration to date between PCWC academics across the Prairie provinces, their respective governments, and their community partners. This educational initiative can continue to be enriched by the PCWC's commitment to child welfare scholarship, including its organization of biennial conferences and its publication of five books to date that draw on the papers and presentations from these conferences.

As a starting point, it is important to briefly underscore the moral and professional imperative we face as social work educators as we strive to improve our reach and effectiveness in preparing future child welfare practitioners.

The field of child welfare is frequently the subject of intense public scrutiny and critiques as a result of harm that comes to children in its care.

Understanding and Meeting the "Crisis" in Child Welfare

There have been daunting challenges facing the child welfare field in the Prairie provinces of Canada over the last several years. These difficulties include the very high proportion of First Nations children in care, challenges in service delivery in First Nations communities, and the lack of support- ive and culturally appropriate alternatives when parental care in a child's home is not an option. The consequences of these difficulties have included the tragic deaths of children in the care of child and family service agencies, which have led to damning indictments of the system in the media (e.g., Adam, 2015; Blaze Carlson, 2014; Wood, 2015; *Globe and Mail*, 2014).

Provincial governments have been called upon to address and remedy the problems in child welfare in the three Prairie provinces. In response to the tragic death of five-year-old Phoenix Sinclair in 2005, the Manitoba govern- ment commissioned an inquiry by Justice Ted Hughes, leading to a report (Hughes, 2014) containing numerous findings and recommendations. In Saskatchewan, the Advocate for Children and Youth (2014, 2015) has focused on service delivery problems in the child welfare system. In Alberta, an exten- sive newspaper investigation (Kleiss & Henton, 2013) found that "145 foster children have died since 1999, nearly triple the 56 deaths revealed in govern- ment annual reports over the same period." This investigation argued that this under-reporting of deaths in the child welfare system was "undermining public accountability and thwarting efforts at prevention and reform."

Given these tragedies and ongoing challenges, the need to rethink inter- vention approaches and reconfigure program delivery in child welfare seems readily apparent. In their journalistic inquiry into deaths of foster children, Kleiss and Henton (2013) recommended "six steps Alberta can take to fix the child welfare system." These steps included action to end the underfunding of Aboriginal child welfare agencies; a commitment to prevention and early intervention; and action to "improve work conditions and raise educational standards for front-line caseworkers." Additionally, the Phoenix Sinclair inquiry (Hughes, 2014) recommended that all those employed in child welfare have a bachelor of social work (B.S.W.) degree, given that they do "demanding work that requires a high level of knowledge, skills, and analytical abilities" (Recommendation 26); that more qualified Aboriginal people be employed in child welfare, as the system "serves an overwhelmingly Aboriginal population, [and] needs the unique insights and perspectives that Aboriginal social workers can bring to their practice" (Recommendation 27); and that "workers be specifically trained on the multigenerational impacts of residential schools and on the role of poverty, poor housing, substance abuse and other social and economic factors in assessments of child neglect" as the "the underlying causes of the conditions that can lead to maltreatment" (Recommendation 29).

All of these calls for change and improvements in child welfare involve extending and intensifying the education that is provided to people working in child welfare. These calls for change thus place a burden of responsibility on university social work programs to "get it right" as we map out our role in education for child welfare. The PCWC and its e-learning project can take specific practical steps and develop general strategies in its ongoing work to educate child welfare professionals who are critical thinkers, culturally competent, and highly skilled in intervention models and techniques.

The PCWC is a rather large and complex undertaking, with many partners and an ambitious agenda. Getting things right in education and research for child welfare are not easy tasks. Some of the challenges facing the PCWC are outlined below.

Administrative Challenges

None of our universities suffer from a paucity of bureaucratic rules and administrative requirements. Given these complexities at the level of a unitary institution, it is no mean feat in the e-learning project to navigate and coordinate these procedures and rules across the institutional players involved—the University of Calgary, the University of Regina (including its federated partner, the First Nations University of Canada), and the University of Manitoba.

Several practical tasks must be accomplished on the administrative front in order to ensure the ongoing success and further development of the e-learning project. These tasks include the following:

- Building a predictable and consistent slate of online PCWC course offerings across the three universities over a two- or three-year cycle so that students can plan their programs in advance and work with the faculty members and student advisors to build their interests and knowledge in child welfare.

- Instituting "bureaucratic streamlining" across the three partner institutions in regard to student registration, advising, recording of grades, transfer credits, and matters to do with student grade appeals and academic discipline. Each university has its somewhat unique requirements and procedures in these areas. Part of the PCWC's agenda is to make each student's registration in pursuit of a course at another partner university as seamless and straightforward as possible.
- Providing adequate administrative and student advising support to e-learning courses (in regard to course development, scheduling, and delivery; student support and assistance; and internal communication and coordination among PCWC partners) to ensure efficient use of scarce resources and maximization of learning outcomes for students.
- Ensuring equity of workload and financial costs across the participating universities so there is approximate reciprocity in investment by and benefit to each partner institution.

Two key elements in meeting the above challenges will be the finalization of a comprehensive and up-to-date memorandum of understanding among the PCWC partners, and an adequate commitment from the governments of the three Prairie provinces to provide financial and in-kind support for the work of the e-learning committee. Such support could ensure both adequate staff support for the project and ongoing and strong communication links among academic, community, and government partners in the PCWC.

Curricular Challenges

The PCWC e-learning initiative presents an exciting possibility for social work students to acquire specialization in the field of child welfare while pursuing a generalist B.S.W. degree. For this potential to be fully realized, some challenges in regard to curriculum must be met, including the following:

- Coordinating program and course planning in the e-learning initiative with the overall B.S.W. program, curriculum development, and class scheduling at the partner universities. One key aspect of this challenge is to ensure that each of the B.S.W. programs at the partner institutions has enough "space" in its degree requirements so students can register for courses offered by the PCWC without having to take more credits than are necessary to complete their degree program, given the differing requirements at the universities of Manitoba, Regina, and Calgary.
- Ensuring that course content draws upon cutting-edge research and service delivery innovation in the child welfare field. The PCWC has had links with research groups and institutes in the child welfare field and should continue to enhance these links to maximize the quality of course content and student learning outcomes. It can also carry out research using the "scholarship of teaching and learning" approach (Hutchings, Huber, & Ciccione, 2011) to assess and enhance pedagogical effectiveness of PCWC courses. Further, instructional skills workshops are currently the focus of a research project at the University of Calgary, and these results can influence the current e-learning initiative.
- Communicating, on an ongoing basis, with practitioners, agencies, and government partners to ensure the relevance of curriculum content to the challenges and opportunities in child welfare practice.
- Securing an adequate number of high-quality field education placements in child welfare settings for students interested in this specialization, including placements in agencies that are serving Indigenous communities and taking innovative approaches to service delivery.
- Working toward "credentialization" of the child welfare specialization in the PCWC partner institutions, including a post-B.S.W. certificate option for those who have already graduated and are practising in the child welfare field.

The current master of social work degree specializing in child welfare being offered at the University of Calgary can serve as a model for similar degrees across the PCWC partner universities.

Pedagogical Challenges

As social work academics, we strive for "continuous quality improvement" in all aspects of our pedagogy. The PCWC e-learning initiative is dedicated to this task as it continues its work to develop pedagogical approaches in delivering courses related to child welfare that are as informative as possible in facilitating student learning and also cost-effective in their use of financial and human resources.

A defining characteristic of distance-learning approaches is that they can improve access to university studies in social work. Such an outcome advances social justice by enabling social work educators to more effectively reach not just geographically remote students but also students from groups that have experienced economic and social disadvantages in their personal lives and local communities. Ensuring better access to professional education in social work through distance delivery is particularly vital for Indigenous communities and Indigenous students. We have an opportunity to prepare future Indigenous leaders in social work who are more likely to work in the territories from which they come, unlike social work graduates from the south or the city who tend to cycle through for short periods of time. Distance education can also help us to decolonize social work education by designing curriculum and delivery methods that are relevant to students located in and committed to their Indigenous territories and cultures. We will turn to this question again below.

Another key component in social work programs is, of course, field education, which presents special challenges with distance students who are not physically proximate to field education staff based at the university where they are registered. New tools provided by information and communications technology can be of particular value in enhancing contact between students and field educators and the learning that students can do during field placements. The use of various synchronous and interactive tools (e.g., audio- and video-conferencing) and asynchronous modalities for students (e.g., online journalling, discussion boards, problem solving via email) can enrich field instruction. Such tools can be effective, particularly when compared to the old days of telephone contact supplemented by an occasional field visit. That being said, however, the use of technology-assisted forms of communication and instruction for students in field education can still be augmented by periodic face-to-face visits by academic staff with individual students and their field supervisors in their practicum settings.

One important challenge in social work distance education is finding the right "fit" between the types of courses being delivered and the specific distance education pedagogical tools that are available. Just as one selects a screwdriver when fastening a screw, rather than a hammer, it is necessary to use the right tools from our varied tool kit of distance education pedagogy that match the type of material being taught and the learning goals established in particular types of social work courses.

For instance, in "content-heavy" social work courses (e.g., mastering research findings and theoretical knowledge, immersion in substantive policy topics, learning about historical aspects of social welfare), the use of asynchronous online and web-based resources, augmented by interactive web-based communication to ensure a thorough and critical understanding of content, may be the most effective approach. Specific asynchronous techniques in this regard could include lecture capture, web-based content modules to be completed by students individually, online quizzes and assignments, discussion boards, and wiki construction by students individually or in groups.

Conversely, in "high-touch" social work courses requiring tutoring and coaching (e.g., courses on enhancing communication skills, applying intervention approaches and techniques in professional practice, and exploring professional ethics and navigating ethical dilemmas), different techniques would likely be required. More reliance would be placed on synchronous and interactive tools for instruction and learning, such as face-to-face instruction with proximate students and video- and audio-conferencing and interactive web-based communication with students at a distance from the instructor. The use of synchronous tools for distant students could include (whenever possible) some face-to-face and co-located instruction or tutoring, such as a short-term residency component that brings students to a main campus in the summer, or instructor "road trips," in which the instructor meets with students on their home turf at points in time during the term.

This need to be discriminating and creative in the use of distance education tools, depending on the type of social work course being taught, is borne out in available academic literature. For example, Coe Regan and Youn (2008) tackle the topic of how to teach clinical skills through web-based learning environments. They identify "generational trends" in the development of distance education, moving over time from print-based materials supported by written communication (such as correspondence courses) on to open broadcast by television or radio. These delivery models have now been superseded by integrated multimedia approaches with learning materials designed for study at a distance, used in conjunction with communication among students, instructors, and third parties using information technology tools.

Coe Regan and Youn (2008) recognize there is continuing debate and resistance among some social work educators to adopting such tools but contend that "a blended/hybrid/multimodal method of combining face-to-face and Web-based learning environments to teach clinical skills is effective." They also point to the "need to develop a coherent body of knowledge to support the teaching of clinical skills in Web-based learning environments for future social work education" (p. 107). They argue that "certain types of Web-based techniques may be effective in ways that do not exist within face-to-face classroom environments," and point to text-based chat rooms and multimedia programs as possible examples of such techniques. Further, they identify the need for "a change from behavioral to cognitive to constructivist learning perspectives in designing Web-based learning environments for teaching clinical skills" (p. 108).

Along the same line, Flynn, Maiden, Smith, Wiley, and Wood (2013) contend that "one can indeed teach practice skills online and it can be done effectively, because technological advances have increased rapidly in the past few years....[O]ne of the most important of these [advances] has been the development of the synchronous, live interactive technology"(pp. 355–356).

Vernon, Vakalalahi, Pierce, Pittman-Munke, and Adkins (2009) review literature on distance education in social work and reach a number of conclusions.

- "[C]omputer-mediated technology effectively facilitates the teaching of advanced clinical skills in working with couples" (p. 264).
- Both "instructivist" and "constructivist" learning approaches can be used in distance education. "The instructivist perspective is useful in presenting Web-based on-demand didactic content through lectures and Web sites, and testing through quizzes and exams. The constructivist perspective (which holds that all knowledge

   is a socially mediated process) finds suitable the use of threaded discussion boards and chat rooms in distance learning" (p. 265).

- "[S]tudents who do not normally contribute in traditional classrooms may find it safe to contribute to the class through electronic posting" (p. 265).
- "[Some research] suggests that practice courses and field practica can be effectively incorporated into distance education, possibly mediated by occasional face-to-face meetings" (p. 274).
- "[E]ducational policies and standards for accreditation will have to address the fact that programs are producing degrees in whole, as well as in part through distance education" (p. 274).
- There is a lack of consensus concerning the teaching of practice courses through distance education, especially online. The most recent studies in this area reported that although differences between online students and traditional students may indeed be present, these might not be significant enough to warrant concern (p. 274).

These findings not only posit the validity of distance and electronic modalities in social work education but they also offer us practical guidance in designing courses and programs.

   Bellefeuille (2006) addresses the teaching of practice competencies for child welfare. Drawing on "formative evaluation" in a course that he taught, he argues for a blended approach that combines "objectivist" computer-mediated learning focused on "traditional knowledge domains and core practice competencies considered essential for basic child welfare practice" and "constructivist" instructional design "which prompted learners to reflect critically on the course materials" (pp. 88–89). He contends, "[L]earning with technology, based on a constructivist design, can actually enhance the learning process and help students in doing, reflecting, deciding, and thinking critically. However, the focus in the learning environment must shift from one of teaching to one of learning" (p. 97).

   Bellefeuille (2006) also cautions that students must have an opportunity to familiarize themselves with the online learning environment before the course begins, and that "the teacher-as-coach needs to work closely with the learners in the early part of the course to teach them the skills of inquiry and personal reflection" (p. 100).

Ayala (2009) focuses on blended learning, arguing that research must go beyond just comparing it with classroom teaching and seek to discover "approaches, tools, technologies, and blends to deliver social work education" (p. 284). It is necessary to discern the optimal characteristics for "blended learning environments [including] instructors and their teaching, students and their learning, and technology-related factors" (p. 284).

Levin, Whitsett, and Wood (2013) conclude that "it is possible to successfully teach practice in an online environment," provided that certain conditions are met. They adopted a format for their graduate, social work, foundation-year practice class that had an even split of teaching and learning time between in-class instruction and online engagement and a variety of synchronous or asynchronous learning activities. They recommend that "synchronous class sessions involve an application or elaboration of concepts presented in the learning activities of the asynchronous components" (p. 411). They emphasize the importance of having blended online courses taught by faculty members who can function with commitment, skill, and adaptability in this environment. They also emphasize that students must stake out private space for themselves for learning, with a reliable Internet connection and appropriate hardware/software. Students should also observe rules of decorum during synchronous, video-linked sessions that are parallel to those that would pertain to university classrooms (e.g., no wearing of pajamas or drinking beer during class). If these conditions are met, Levin et al. contend that the students and instructor can be "socially present" with one another in an online environment. Because of the use of real-time audio and video, students and instructors are able to hear and see emotional expression, vocal inflection, and a full range of verbal and nonverbal communication. Social presence can be greatly increased as a result (p. 411).

Pelech et al. (2013) tackle the question of optimal size for classes in distance delivery courses in social work and conclude that "the available supports and the technologies utilized, as well as the instructional purpose, substantive content, and professional values, will help to determine optimal class size" (p. 399). In larger online classes, they emphasize the need to work "smarter rather than harder" (p. 401), in part through facilitating peer interaction among students (p. 398) and ensuring adequate teaching and marking assistance for the instructor (p. 401). As to the type of social work classes that lend themselves to online learning, they state that "a wide variety of social work courses can be offered effectively online" (p. 402), including the teaching of multicultural competencies and skills, research methods, and social work practice. One of the usual arguments as to why face-to-face teaching is preferable to online delivery is that the latter makes instructor-student interaction difficult. However, Pelech et al. cite evidence that "online learning has been associated with increased interaction when compared to traditional classroom settings" (p. 402).

Beyond specific design and resource questions to do with online education in social work, Reamer (2013) points out the increased accessibility that digital technology provides for those who want to pursue a social work degree but who are too far away from campuses to attend classes in person. At the same time, he points to "complex ethical issues associated with the proliferation of digital and online social work education" (p. 369). These issues include accommodating students with disabilities who have difficulty in an online environment, keeping tuition fees affordable when institutions move toward a cost-recovery model in distance education, managing the logistics of field education, dealing with instances of academic dishonesty, protecting the privacy of students, and generally ensuring the academic quality and integrity of a social work program delivered at a distance.

Montgomery (2012) examines the ways in which social work distance education can be structured to optimize support and success for place-bound Indigenous students. He highlights the need for "identification of the practical and latent resources that exist within [the students'] local communities" (p. 160). He also underlines that students should have "a good sense of their own educational objectives and local resources before entering into a distance education program," including whether they are better off as an individual e-learner or as part of a cohort of peers moving through an academic program together (p. 159). He stresses that "there is no 'typical' Indigenous adult learner, just as there is no 'generic' Aboriginal community in Canada" (p. 158). He also points to the importance of Indigenous communities honouring the accomplishments of their own members who are pursuing a degree through distance education.

Educational institutions offering social work programs at a distance to Indigenous students need to set in place a range of resources to ensure student success and to guard against student isolation. Montgomery (2012) points to supports such as dedicated personnel for student advising, websites that are easily navigable and incorporate multimedia resources for e-learners, and strong IT support for students as they use learning management systems and when they encounter technical problems. He also recommends "culturally sensitive face-to-face orientation for incoming e-learners" (p. 171). Students should also have "spaces within online courses that provide opportunities for the voicing of anti-colonial and anti-oppressive narratives" (p. 171). Recognizing that Indigenous students may come from many different nations, it is also vital that the host university avoid the "privileging of one place-based narrative...over one or more other Indigenous narratives" (p. 170).

Montgomery (2012) concludes on an optimistic note, stating, "[I]nstitutional resources that have been invested in supporting distance learners have led to the creation and implementation of pedagogically appropriate curriculum, technologically current course management tools, and academically sound resource materials" (p. 176).

Looking to the Future

This chapter has mapped out some administrative and curricular challenges in distance education in social work and has surveyed a growing body of research literature that can guide us in our quest for good pedagogical design and strong learning outcomes for students. I will conclude with a brief discussion of future challenges facing the PCWC in regard to program development and potential new research initiatives.

Program Development

Building upon its suite of online courses in child welfare that comprises the current e-learning initiative, the PCWC could work to achieve more ambitious goals in the medium to long run in regard to curriculum and academic program development. Possible goals might include:

- a child and family services concentration as part of the generalist B.S.W. that could be jointly offered by the partner universities at their various sites;
- a post-baccalaureate child welfare certificate for those already employed in the field;
- use of distance technology to provide training and credentials for other workers in the child welfare system, including foster

parents, child and youth care workers, outreach workers, and
community helpers;

- advanced undergraduate- and graduate-level courses for students
  interested in pursuing child welfare topics at advanced levels.

Research on Distance Education in Social Work and Child Welfare

This chapter has outlined research findings to date on distance education in social work. Much of the existing research uses data gathered
from students and instructors and makes straightforward comparisons
between teaching alternative versions of the same course in either a traditional face-to-face fashion or in an online or blended environment.
However, Quinn, Fitch, and Youn (2011) challenge researchers to take a
more sophisticated methodological approach to research on social work
distance education. They argue that we must focus on the "interaction
between four constructs: the student, the setting in which the education
is delivered, the educational content, and the expected educational outcomes" (p. 321). They see significant methodological flaws in research on
distance education and, in particular, in bivariate analysis of distance
compared to face-to-face courses. Most studies do not adequately take
into account other variables besides delivery format, "such as feelings,
attitudes, and influence of instructor"; characteristics of the students
who choose one delivery format or the other; the geographical, physical, and virtual space in which the course is taught; and the content of
the course (e.g., whether the topic relates to research, policy, or practice; whether the course is required or elective; the particular theoretical orientation adopted) (pp. 322, 324–328). Quinn et al. call for "the
development of models that allow for multivariate analysis that consist
of viewing the outcome of learning regressed against several predictor
variables" (p. 323).

Bearing such a challenge in mind, and if the necessary resources
(including research funding) could be obtained, the PCWC could aspire to
evolve into a research hub and dissemination centre for evidence on best
practices in distance education to enhance social work and child welfare
practice. Focal areas for such research could include:

- ongoing review of best pedagogical practices based on research
  evidence in distance education in social work and related fields of

study (following in the wake of studies cited in this chapter, such
as Westhuis, Ouellette, & Pfahler, 2006; Coe Regan & Youn, 2008;
Vernon et al., 2009);

- investigation of models for building and sustaining social
connections among distance students in social work, and
between them and their instructors, such as the Community of
Inquiry model (Garrison, Terry, & Walter, 2010);
- further research on culturally appropriate delivery methods in
social work distance education for Indigenous communities and
newcomer populations;
- research on how to connect evidence-based practice and
competency building in the child welfare field with critical
analysis and systems advocacy to improve and/or shift our service
delivery paradigms in child welfare.

It is absolutely important that we nurture and protect our children,
both within our families and collectively as a society. The child welfare
field of social work has a key role in helping to achieve this goal. The
Prairie Child Welfare Consortium has made important contributions to
date and is poised to continue and extend its work in professional education, advancing knowledge, and reshaping public policy related to the
safety and well-being of children.

References

Adam, B. A. (2015, April 21). Poor casework led to death, Pringle says; missed
opportunities might have saved Lee Bonneau. *Saskatoon StarPhoenix*, p. A1.

Advocate for Children and Youth, Province of Saskatchewan. (2014). *Lost in
the system: Jake's story*. Saskatoon, SK: Author. Retrieved from http://www.
saskadvocate.ca/

Advocate for Children and Youth, Province of Saskatchewan. (2015). *No time for
Mark: The gap between policy and practice*. Saskatoon, SK: Author. Retrieved
from http://www.saskadvocate.ca/

Ayala, J. S. (2009, Spring/Summer). Blended learning as a new approach to social
work education. *Journal of Social Work Education, 45*(2), 277–288.

Bellefeuille, G. L. (2006). Rethinking reflective practice education in social work
education: A blended constructivist and objectivist instructional design
strategy for a web-based child welfare practice course. *Journal of Social Work
Education, 42*(1), 85–103.

Blaze Carlson, K. (2014, November 19). Manitoba revamps child-welfare program: Move to reduce hotel stays for children, boost care-worker numbers comes after death of Tina Fontaine and amid calls for inquiry. *Globe and Mail*, p. A1.

Coe Regan, J. R., & Youn, E. J. (2008). Past, present, and future trends in teaching clinical skills through web-based learning environments. *Journal of Social Work Education, 44*(2), 95–115.

Cooperrider, D. L., Kaplin, D., & Stavros, J. M. (2003). *Appreciative inquiry handbook*. San Francisco, CA: Berrett-Kohler Publishers.

Flynn, M., Maiden, R. P., Smith, W., Wiley, J., & Wood, G. (2013). Launching the virtual academic center: Issues and challenges in innovation. *Journal of Teaching in Social Work, 33*(4), 339–356.

Garrison, D. R., Terry, A., & Walter, A. (2010). The first decade of the community of inquiry framework: A retrospective. *The Internet and Higher Education. Special Issue on the Community of Inquiry Framework: Ten Years Later, 13*(1–2), 5–9.

Hughes, T. (2014). *Inquiry into the circumstances surrounding the death of Phoenix Sinclair* (Vols. 1–3). Winnipeg, MB: Government of Manitoba, Attorney General. Retrieved from http://phoenixsinclairinquiry.ca/index.html

Hutchings, P., Huber, M. T., & Ciccione, A. (2011). *The scholarship of teaching and learning reconsidered: Institutional integration and impact*. San Francisco, CA: Jossey-Bass.

Kleiss, K., & Henton, D. (2013, November 25–30). Fatal care [six-part series]. *Edmonton Journal* and *Calgary Herald*. Retrieved from http://www. edmontonjournal.com/news/children-in-care/index.html

Levin, S., Whitsett, D., & Wood, G. (2013). Teaching MSW social work practice in a blended online learning environment. *Journal of Teaching Social Work, 33*(4–5), 408–420.

McKay, S. (2007). Introduction: Development of the Prairie Child Welfare Consortium and this book. In I. Brown (Ed.), *Putting a human face on child welfare: Voices from the Prairies* (pp. xv–xxxvi). Regina, SK: CPRC Press.

Montgomery, H. (2012). *Discerning the network of supports employed by off-campus Indigenous adult e-learners through an Indigenous methodological lens* (Doctoral dissertation). University of Saskatchewan, Saskatoon, SK. Retrieved from http://ecommons.usask.ca/xmlui/handle/10388/ETD-2012-08-630

Pelech, W., Wulff, D., Perrault, E., Ayala, J., Baynton, M., Williams, M.,...Shankar, J. (2013). Current challenges in social work distance education: Responses from the elluminati. *Journal of Teaching in Social Work, 33*(4–5), 393–407.

Quinn, A., Fitch, D., & Youn, E. (2011). Considering construct validity in distance educational research in social work education: Suggestions for a multivariate approach to researching efficacy. *Journal of Social Work Education, 47*(2), 321–336.

Reamer, F. G. (2013). Distance and online social work education: Novel ethical challenges. *Journal of Teaching in Social Work, 33*(4–5), 369–384.

The native child welfare calamity [editorial]. (2014, August 30). *Globe and Mail*, p. F9.

Vernon, R., Vakalalahi, H., Pierce, D., Pittman-Munke, P., & Adkins, L. F. (2009). Distance education programs in social work: Current and emerging trends. *Journal of Social Work Education, 45*(2), 263–276.

Westhuis, D., Ouellette, P. M., & Pfahler, C. L. (2006). A comparative analysis of on-line and classroom-based instructional formats for teaching social work research. *Advances in Social Work, 7*(2), 74–88.

Wood, J. (2015, September 1). NDP vows reviews of child fatalities; Sabir says government committed to bringing in independent oversight. *Calgary Herald*, p. A5.

Epilogue

Dorothy Badry and Daniel Kikulwe

The Prairie Child Welfare Consortium (PCWC), since 1999, has endeavoured to ensure that voices from the Prairies in relation to child welfare matters are heard. The PCWC conferences have offered a gathering place for the purpose of renewing commitments to best practice in child welfare. The echo of Jordan's Principle, introduced in 2007 at a PCWC conference in Winnipeg, Manitoba, was highlighted by Dr. Cindy Blackstock and collaborators on January 26, 2016, in a press conference announcing the positive outcome of the child welfare human rights case in relation to the care of Aboriginal children in Canada. Jordan's Principle was grounded in the rights of children to live in their home communities, no matter what their challenges or disabilities are, and to receive a standard of care that is universally provided in other jurisdictions in Canada. This historical announcement is a rallying call for rights and social justice for all children in Canada.

This book primarily reflects the voices of social workers and allied health professionals who are committed to child welfare practice and social justice from the front line to research, policy, and practice. The chapters in this book have covered a wide range of critical topics that are diverse and relevant to child welfare practice and reflect a spirit of collaboration among practitioners, educators, and policy-makers. It is recognized that child welfare work is increasingly under review and the learnings from child-in-care death reviews make up a pivotal chapter that highlights the challenges and lessons from these reports. It is through this type of research that front-line child welfare work intersects with social policy, research, and professional practice – this chapter serves to inform us about the learnings from these deeply troubled spaces in our system.

Further, the historical roots of research that have been harmful in First Nations communities are identified by Montgomery and colleagues and re-envisioned as work taken up by Indigenous scholars and allies, whose role is breathing new life into community-based research.

We have an opportunity through the work of the PCWC to raise issues that are incredibly complex because they are about children and families and the way in which child welfare practice unfolds. This book reflects the need for strength-based approaches, harm reduction, deeper understanding of racialized issues in child welfare work in Canada, the voices of youth, practice with diverse populations, supporting children with FASD and disabilities, the need for anti-oppressive HIV training in child welfare, the importance of narrative, shifting child welfare education in social work programs, the value of caregiving, and an overall identification of the need for collaborative work that is cross-disciplinary. The contributions to this book from across Canada offer critical research and practice wisdom reflecting the current state of child welfare practice and issues. The PCWC has worked across Manitoba, Saskatchewan, and Alberta to create cross-listed social work courses offered at the University of Manitoba, the University of Regina, and the University of Calgary, and its books offer important resources for communities, students, professionals, and researchers.

Abstracts

Chapter 1: Honouring the Twenty-Fifth Anniversary of the United Nations Convention on the Rights of the Child: Transforming Child Welfare in Canada into a Stronger Child Rights-Based System
Marvin M. Bernstein

This chapter is based on the Prairie Child Welfare Consortium (PCWC) symposium keynote presentation the author gave in October 2014, on the topic of honouring the twenty-fifth anniversary of the United Nations Convention on the Rights of the Child (hereinafter referred to simply as "the Convention" or the UNCRC). Although UNICEF Canada is based in Ontario, the work of UNICEF Canada transcends provincial boundaries and geographic regions in Canada. UNICEF Canada engages with all levels of government and with other partners to promote the rights of children everywhere in Canada and to advocate for the implementation of the principles set out in the Convention. UNICEF is the only organization named in the UNCRC as a source of expertise for governments. The five key themes addressed in this chapter are: 1) the important functions of the UNCRC in advancing children's rights; 2) the progress made within Canada since the adoption of the Convention by the United Nations General Assembly twenty-five years ago; 3) an overview of the current state of Canada's children; 4) current challenges impeding full implementation of the UNCRC across Canada; and 5) What action steps still need to be taken to fulfill the original vision of the Convention? This chapter highlights the best interests of children through offering unique insight into the ways in which children's rights intersect with child welfare work.

Chapter 2: Forms and Strategies for Integrated Working in Child Welfare
Judy Gillespie

This chapter discusses forms and strategies for interdisciplinary and interprofessional working in child welfare, situating these within an examination of the complexity of child welfare and the range of child welfare interventions. It highlights Canadian legislation, policy, and practice examples and concludes with an examination of the practice, education, and research implications of interdisciplinary and interprofessional working in child welfare within Canadian contexts. The major areas addressed include the complexity of child welfare, the goals of child welfare interventions, and strategies and forms of interdisciplinary and interprofessional working in child welfare. This chapter highlights the value of cross-jurisdictional research and highlights the need for collaborative education that includes university and community agencies.

Chapter 3: Saskatchewan First Nations: Researching Ourselves Back to Life
H. Monty Montgomery, A. J. Felix, Patsy Felix, Margaret Kovach, and Shelley Thomas Prokop

The aim of this chapter is to transcend some of the historic mistrust and missteps that have taken place with respect to child, family, and community research with Indigenous peoples across the Numbered Treaty areas of Canada. This chapter provides an overview of the contemporary relationship that many First Nations have with social science research, the role that an Indigenous Research Advisory Committee can take in guiding ethical research activities, and Elder teachings that speak to the steps that individuals can take to initiate and conduct research in a respectful, good way. This chapter is presented in a spirit of generosity and with no aim of casting aspersions among those who are truly interested in helping, healing, and decolonizing child welfare across Canada.

Chapter 4: Child Protection Inquiries: What Are They Teaching Us? A Canadian Perspective
Peter Choate

When a child dies or is seriously injured while involved with child protection services (CPS) there is often outrage in the media. Even in situations where the case has not received media scrutiny, several provinces, particularly in Western Canada, have legislation that child and youth advocates shall investigate these cases. To varying degrees, the results of those investigations are then made public. In other cases, the outrage reaches intensity, either through the extent of media coverage or as a result of the "horror" of the case, and large-scale inquiries might be held. This chapter offers a qualitative analysis of ninety-two published reports from 1985 to 2015. Results indicate that there are repeating practice errors that warrant a higher profile in social work education and child protection training. There are also systemic issues that require a public policy response. Recommendations are made for educators, practice professionals, and policy-makers.

Chapter 5: Strengthening Children's Capacity to Cope with Separation, Loss, and Uncertain Futures: Action Steps for Front-Line Child Welfare Practice
Sharon McKay

This chapter emphasizes children as rights holders as set out in the United Nations Convention on the Rights of the Child and draws upon literature relevant to children's rights to be heard and to have voice. The primary question identified in this chapter is: How does the language of the law, of bureaucracy, and of professional education and training influence how we communicate with children and youth in the child welfare system? Caring for the long-term health and well-being of children and youth caught in circumstances largely out of their control requires concerted attention to daily needs for safety and psychological and physical sta-bility, and diligent regard for hearing what the child has to say about their own needs, hopes, and worries. This chapter calls attention to cultural, professional, and linguistic barriers to good practice and presents principles, guidelines, and action steps for improving, strengthening, and transforming existing services to safeguard the child's rights to voice.

Chapter 6: Aligning Practice, Ethics, and Policy: Adopting a Harm Reduction Approach in Working with High-Risk Children and Youth
Peter Smyth

This chapter will examine the application of a harm reduction approach in child welfare practice with high-risk children and youth. It will address questions about how and why this approach can help engage and empower such a challenging pop-ulation. This chapter defines harm reduction through drawing on contemporary literature that is relevant to child protection and highlights the High Risk Youth Initiative in Edmonton, Alberta. This chapter offers a case example that supports the unique application of a harm reduction approach to a traditionally risk-averse system. This chapter offers a sound argument for harm reduction approaches as a foundation for strengths-based approaches with high-risk youth. Further, this chapter recognizes this work is challenging and identifies that a social justice framework is a driving force that compels this work forward in the best interests of children and youth.

Chapter 7: Prioritizing Children in Care with FASD: Why Prevalence Matters
Don Fuchs and Linda Burnside

Children and youth with a diagnosis of fetal alcohol spectrum disorder (FASD) present in child welfare agencies with an array of complex and variable needs as a consequence of a range of neurodevelopmental disorders. This chapter will define what prevalence is and discuss why it is important to study the prevalence of chil-dren and youth with FASD in the care of the child welfare system. To illustrate the benefits of studying prevalence of children in care with FASD, this chapter reports on the major findings of a tri-provincial study of the prevalence of FASD among children in care in Alberta, Manitoba, and Ontario. It examines the implications of these findings for policy, programming, and training in the Prairie provinces. In addition, it illustrates the importance of using administrative databases for FASD prevalence research. Finally it identifies some important directions for fur-ther research using data gathered regularly and consistently from administrative databases for evidence-based approaches to the examination of the outcomes of prevention and intervention programs.

Chapter 8: A Community-Based Research Approach to Developing an HIV Education and Training Module for Child and Family Service Workers in Ontario

Saara Greene, Doe O'Brien-Teengs, Gary Dumbrill, Allyson Ion, Kerrigan Beaver, Megan Porter, and Marisol Desbiens

This chapter focuses on our community-based research and capacity-building activities, development of the research team, and the subsequent development of the education and training module. This chapter begins with an overview of the impact of HIV on women and mothers living in Canada, with specific attention to the intersection of HIV and child welfare and the current state of HIV education and training within the social work curriculum. The chapter outlines our process of developing our research team, with specific attention paid to addressing the capacity-building needs of all team members and the research process that has since guided the development of the HIV education and training module for child and family service workers. We conclude with a presentation of what is included in the training module and our reflections on the importance of working with community stakeholders in developing and providing HIV-specific education to social work students and professionals. The relevance of this work to supporting families affected by HIV within the child welfare system in the Prairies will also be discussed.

Chapter 9: Boundaries and Identity: Racialized Child Welfare Workers' Perspectives of Their Histories and Experiences When Working with Diverse Families

Daniel Kikulwe

This chapter focuses on one of the four broad research questions of the author's doctoral study. The question discussed herein examines racialized child welfare workers' perspectives on the interventions and interactions with families from diverse backgrounds in Ontario, Canada. This chapter presents qualitative research on the experiences of racialized workers when interacting and intervening with diverse families. The study's use of the term "racialized workers" refers to groups with racial identities that have social markers (physical characteristics) that result in conditions of their marginalization. In Canada, individuals who self-identify as having racialized backgrounds are both foreign- and Canadian-born and primarily include South Asian, Southeast Asian, African, and Caribbean workers. This chapter concludes that the work of racialized child welfare workers has largely remained invisible and unacknowledged in the Canadian child welfare field.

Chapter 10: Pathways: Community-Engaged Research with Youth Transitioning to Adult In(ter)dependence from Government Care

Marie Lovrod, Darlene Domshy, and Stephanie Bustamante

The two related projects described in this chapter engage Saskatchewan youth from local and provincial government care and custody networks in collaborative research design, with an emphasis on finding constructive ways to create better outcomes, together. Using age-appropriate, process-oriented, community-based qualitative and creative methods, our research affirms the importance of supporting youth access to public voice, without compromising anonymity, confidentiality, or life chances. While we attend to broad determinants of youth well-being, including historical and contemporary conditions, a consistent objective is to build social inclusion, working with diverse stakeholders to facilitate extended conversations about care experiences through co-operative knowledge-building partnerships with youth. Province-wide youth project teams have identified ten specific areas where transition training is needed: health and well-being; education; employment; housing and healthy living; financial education and money management; social supports and healthy relationships; identification; general life skills; parenting; and youth justice. Inviting youth to build evidence-based resources and constructive recommendations for program, practice, and policy changes is a productive way to address some of the challenges they face in care and custody systems while modelling transferable learning and social skills. Our analysis recognizes that community engagement with youth in transition is an important factor in empowering youth to achieve adult "in(ter)dependence," a term we use to emphasize autonomous functioning within constructive relational networks.

Chapter 11: Narrative Threads in the Accounts of Women with Learning Difficulties Who Have Been Criminalized

Elly Park, David McConnell, Vera Caine, and Joanne Minaker

Little qualitative research looks at women who have learning difficulties and have been involved with the criminal justice system (CJS), with fewer studies including their experiences or life stories. Using a narrative inquiry approach, the first author met with four participants over eighteen months. Prolonged relationships offered time and space to understand their experiences and the ongoing dynamics of their lives. The stories showed resistance, not as insolence or defiance but as a kind of determination to preserve a sense of identity and overcome challenges. Four threads resonated across the four narrative accounts: uncertainty and ambiguity in circumstances, having someone to turn to, enduring judgment and stigma, and being mothered as well as mothering. The narrative threads pointed out a need for individualized support based on specific challenges and obstacles and a re-evaluation of current programs and services. Forming meaningful relationships and including the women receiving services in the decision-making process are two possible ways to address what the women in this narrative inquiry expressed as what they need and want to focus on.

Chapter 12: The Caregiver Curriculum on FASD: Transforming Practice through Knowledge and Education
Dorothy Badry, Deborah Goodman, and Jamie Hickey

The Caregiver Curriculum on Fetal Alcohol Spectrum Disorder emerged from a three-year research project funded by the Public Health Agency of Canada and was developed to mobilize knowledge directly related to caring for children with this complex disability. Many children in the child welfare system have a diagnosis of FASD. The concern about FASD as a public health issue remains persistent and complex, despite knowledge that this is a preventable disability. The cause – alcohol use during pregnancy – presents a conundrum in relation to prevention. The challenge for parents with substance use problems often relates to their capacity to care for their children while actively struggling with addictions. This chapter reviews the curriculum and its contribution to FASD-informed practice and care.

Chapter 13: An Indispensable Tool in the Tool Kit: Distance Delivery in Social Work Education to Support Child Welfare Practice
James Mulvale

This chapter is written from the position of an academic administrator in social work who has also developed and delivered online courses. It is premised on the vital imperative for social work academic programs to prepare students for effective, innovative, culturally competent, and evidenced-based practice in the field of child protection and child welfare. This imperative is grounded in the problems facing the child welfare field in the Prairie provinces. These difficulties include the very high proportion of First Nations children in care, the inability of the system to keep (especially Indigenous) children from coming to harm, the lack of supportive and culturally appropriate alternatives when parental care is not an option, and a series of deaths of children in care that have led to damning indictments of the system. This chapter makes a case for the usefulness of distance learning pedagogy and technology in meeting the challenges of educating child welfare professionals. It recognizes and examines the work done to date by the e-learning committee of the PCWC; proposes extending and enhancing this work to reach more students, practitioners, and researchers; and maps out challenges in regard to administration, curriculum, and pedagogy in the PCWC's e-learning courses offered jointly by partnered universities in Alberta, Saskatchewan, and Manitoba.

Contributors

Dorothy Badry is an associate professor in social work and has long-standing front line and research involvement with the child welfare system in Alberta. She is a member of the Prairie Child Welfare Consortium (PCWC) steering committee and the co-chair of the Education and Training Council in Alberta under the umbrella of the FASD (fetal alcohol spectrum disorder) Cross-Ministry Committee of Alberta Human Services. Dorothy has focused on FASD-related research, particularly in relation to children and families. She also teaches a course on FASD and child welfare practice online for students in the PCWC collaborative university course offerings at the University of Calgary, University of Regina, and University of Manitoba. Her interests lie in excellence in practice for children and families involved in the child welfare system.

Kerrigan Beaver is a 2-Spirited mother who resides in Toronto, Ontario, with her family. She currently works at PASAN (Prisoners' HIV/AIDS Support Action Network) as its Aboriginal program coordinator. She is also a peer research associate for the Women's College Research Initiative and McMaster University. Kerrigan sits on many advisory committees and is chair of VOW (Voices of Women's) and the Aboriginal Leadership Standing Committee for the Canadian Aboriginal AIDS Network. She also holds the women-at-large seat on the board of directors for the Canadian Aboriginal AIDS Network and is currently the president of the 2-Spirited People of the 1st Nations board of directors.

Marvin M. Bernstein is the chief policy advisor for UNICEF Canada, a position he assumed in September 2010 after serving as Saskatchewan's second Children's Advocate from 2005 to 2010. Prior to coming to Saskatchewan, Marv spent twenty-eight years as a lawyer and senior professional within Ontario's child welfare system. He has written extensively on a variety of child welfare and children's rights topics. Marv is a member of the board of directors of the Children's Aid Society of Toronto and the chair of the national Children's Law Committee of the Canadian Bar Association. Marv has been awarded both the Saskatchewan Centennial Medal and the Queen Elizabeth II Diamond Jubilee Medal, has been recognized as a distinguished alumnus by New College at the University of Toronto, and is the recipient of both the Child Welfare League of Canada Advocacy Award and the North American Council on Adoptable Children Adoption Activist Award.

Linda Burnside is a social worker and certified counsellor (with the Canadian Counselling Association) who obtained her bachelor of social work, post-baccalaureate certificate in educational psychology, and master of education in counselling degrees from the University of Manitoba. She holds a doctorate in social work at the University of Manitoba. Much of her work experience is in the field of child welfare, having worked as a child protection social worker, a therapist in sexual abuse treatment, as the assistant program manager with Winnipeg Child and Family Services, and as Authority Relations of Disability Programs with Manitoba Family Services and Housing.

Stephanie Bustamante is the executive director of the Saskatchewan Youth in Care and Custody Network and a collaborator in the joint research project, *Youth in Transit: Growing Out of Care*. She brings a background in advocacy, community engagement, human rights, anti-poverty work, the youth criminal justice custody system, restorative justice, and in domestic violence prevention and response. She also serves as chairperson or member-at-large on several boards involving community and the child welfare system.

Vera Caine is an associate professor in the Faculty of Nursing at the University of Alberta. Her research reflects her interest in cross-disciplinary work and health equity in the areas of Indigenous health and HIV infections. Since joining the faculty in 2009, Vera has held numerous operating grants and in 2013 received a New Investigator Award from the Canadian Institutes of Health Research. She maintains close relationships with community organizations such as the Boyle McCauley Health Centre, the Mustard Seed, Streetworks, and HIV Edmonton. Her research has made significant contributions to narrative inquiry, a qualitative research methodology. She has also worked in supervisory roles with post-doctoral fellows and undergraduate and graduate students in the faculties of nursing, medicine, education, and anthropology.

Peter W. Choate is a registered social worker and member of the Clinical Registry, Approved Clinical Supervisor for the Alberta College of Registered Social Workers. He is an assistant professor of social work at Mount Royal University. He also teaches professional development programs through the University of Calgary. Peter has been engaged in clinical private counselling and an assessment practice with an emphasis on addictions, domestic violence, and child protection matters. He has been qualified as an expert witness on more than 150 occasions in the Provincial Court of Alberta (Family and Youth Division) in Calgary, Red Deer, and Edmonton, as well as the Court of Queen's Bench (Calgary and Medicine Hat). His particular emphasis is on child and adolescent mental health, including maltreatment, neglect and abuse (physical, sexual, emotional), and these issues within family systems. His areas of research are related to assessment of parenting for child protection, as well as practice errors in child protection related to deaths of children.

Marisol Desbiens is a peer research associate and volunteer. She has been working in the HIV community for the past eight years. Some of the organizations she has worked for include the Ontario AIDS Network, Committee for Accessible AIDS Treatment, Ontario HIV Treatment Network, Fife House, Women's College Hospital, and McMaster University. She has also volunteered at the Toronto People with AIDS Foundation in the Speaker's Bureau and Ontario HIV and Substance Use Training Program. Marisol is very engaged in working in different HIV settings and enjoys working with people living with HIV from diverse communities.

Darlene Domshy is the research coordinator and former executive director of the Saskatchewan Youth in Care and Custody Network and a collaborator in the joint research projects, *Our Dream, Our Right, Our Future* and *Youth in Transit: Growing Out of Care*. A previous background in cultural studies, and as an advocate for youth voice, has led her to a strong interest in the health and well-being of youth-with-care-experiences and in exploring the broad social determinants of health through her training as a registered nurse.

Gary Dumbrill is interested in child welfare and anti-racist/anti-oppressive practice. Most of his work focuses on the intersection of these areas; on the ways child welfare can be undertaken from an anti-racist/anti-oppressive perspective. This interest emerges from the twelve years Gary has spent working in British and Canadian child protection systems. He uses mostly participatory action and in-depth qualitative (particularly Grounded Theory) methodologies and has recently explored photo-voice and photojournalistic methods.

Elders A. J. and Patsy Felix are from the Sturgeon Lake First Nation in Saskatchewan and have contributed decades of effort in support of First Nations-administered child and family services agencies as cultural advisors on community activities and research.

Don Fuchs is a full professor in the Faculty of Social Work at the University of Manitoba. He has conducted extensive research on FASD and children in care in the province of Manitoba. Don is a founding member of the Prairie Child Welfare Consortium. He currently chairs PCWC's steering and e-learning committees and has co-edited all four books emerging from the biennial conferences held in Alberta, Saskatchewan, and Manitoba. His current program of research focuses on establishing the prevalence of children with disabilities in care and examining the determinants that result in children with disabilities (particularly FASD) coming into care and their experiences while in care.

Judy Gillespie is an associate professor in the School of Social Work at the University of British Columbia's Okanagan campus. Prior to obtaining her Ph.D., she worked for many years in children's services in northwestern Alberta. Her research interests encompass the role of communities in the welfare of children, with a particular focus on policy frameworks that strengthen the community-level social, physical, and political infrastructures that support children. She is also interested in the development of knowledge to support interprofessional practice in child welfare.

Deborah Goodman is the director of the Child Welfare Institute (CWI) at the Children's Aid Society of Toronto. She has worked, taught, and conducted research in the Ontario child and family, child welfare, and children's mental health fields for over thirty years. She and her CWI team currently provide training on a multitude of topics to thousands of human service and helping professionals each year. As well, Deborah is actively involved in over thirty research, agency, or community-based evaluations of practice. She was the lead on the three-year, $700,000, Public Health Agency of Canada Tri-Province Study on FASD completed in 2014. In 2007, she received the Outstanding Achievement in Research and Evaluation Award from the Child Welfare League of Canada.

Saara Greene is an associate professor and the chair of undergraduate studies in the School of Social Work at McMaster University. She is involved in a number of community-based HIV/AIDS research studies funded by Canadian Institutes of Health Research and the Ontario HIV Treatment Network. Her main activist and research activities are focused on highlighting the experiences and needs of women living with HIV. She is particularly interested in engaging in research that can lead to positive shifts in practice and policy arenas. Her most recent research projects include the Positive Parenting Pilot Project and Women under Surveillance: Mapping Criminalization's Creep into the Health and Social Care of Women Living with HIV (WATCH). Saara is a board member of the Teresa Group, a HIV service organization in Toronto, Ontario, that provides support for families affected by HIV.

Jamie Hickey is a graduate of the University of Calgary and a registered social worker. She worked as a research assistant with Dorothy Badry to produce the Caregiver Curriculum on FASD while completing her masters in social work. She has worked extensively in the areas of education and violence prevention and has research interests in the areas of child and adolescent mental health, practitioner professional development, curriculum development, and FASD.

Allyson Ion is a Ph.D. student in social work at McMaster University. Prior to starting her Ph.D., she was a research coordinator and community-based educator in the area of women and HIV and has participated in the HIV movement since 2001. Allyson's research focuses on the perinatal health care experiences of women living with HIV. More specifically, her dissertation research is concerned with how and why health care is organized the way that it is, and it aims to uncover how the organization of health systems that women interface with during the perinatal period produces certain conditions and experiences for women living with HIV.

Daniel Kikulwe is an assistant professor at the University of Regina, Faculty of Social Work. His areas of academic interest are in families, immigration, and child welfare practices and policies. The United Nations Convention on the Rights of the Child and its applicability to the global south, as well as kinship care trends in Canada, are an important focus of his work.

Margaret Kovach is of Plains Cree and Saulteaux ancestry. She holds an interdisciplinary Ph.D. in education and social work. She is currently an associate professor in the Department of Educational Foundations, College of Education, at the University of Saskatchewan.

Marie Lovrod is the coordinator of Women's and Gender Studies at the University of Saskatchewan. Combining humanities and social science frameworks, she researches youth trauma and resiliency, mobilizing institutional resources to help heal the diverse lived effects of social violence. She values communities of practice that respect research, learning, and social environments as inclusive spaces.

David McConnell trained at the University of Sydney in Australia. He is currently a professor and the director of the Family and Disability Studies Initiative in the Faculty of Rehabilitation Medicine at the University of Alberta. His research interests include social inclusion, supported parenting, and sustainable family caregiving. David is an international leader in the field of parents and parenting with intellectual disability. The work of his research group in Australia, spanning two decades, led to the world's first national strategy to build system's capacity to support parents with intellectual disabilities and promote a healthy start to life for their children. He is currently the chair of the International Association for the Scientific Study of Intellectual and Developmental Disabilities, Special Interest Research Group on Parents and Parenting.

Sharon McKay is professor emerita in the Faculty of Social Work at the University of Regina. Prior to beginning her teaching career at Lakehead University (1975–1990), she worked full-time and part-time in the fields of child and family services and mental health. She served as dean of social work at the University of Regina (1990–2000) and is a founding member of the Prairie Child Welfare Consortium, serving as steering committee chair from 1999 to 2011 and as a co-editor of the first four PCWC books. She served as the president of the Canadian Association of Schools of Social Work from 2002 to 2004 and served as the president of the

Ontario Association of Professional Social Workers (now the OASW) from 1985 to 1987. Now retired, she lives in Dundas, Ontario, where she continues to be active in the community in a variety of capacities.

Brad McKenzie is professor emeritus at the Faculty of Social Work at the University of Manitoba. He has conducted a number of evaluation research projects in the child and family welfare field and published several books and articles on child welfare and social policy. His most recent book is the fourth edition of *Connecting Policy to Practice in the Human Services* (co-author Brian Wharf, now deceased) in 2016.

Joanne Minaker is an associate professor in the Department of Sociology at MacEwan University. An engaged mother of three and a socially conscious academic, her life/work is rooted deeply in her commitment to family, social justice, and the power of meaningful connections. She is an award-winning educator and author/editor of *Criminalized Mothers, Criminalizing Mothering and Youth, Crime, and Society: Issues of Power and Justice*. Joanne studies care, human connection, and social in/justice, including publications on domestic violence, criminalized girls and women, youth justice, and parenting. With a Ph.D. in socio-legal studies from Queen's University (2003), she has devoted almost two decades to critical reflection and social engagement for social justice for the most vulnerable and marginalized. Her latest quest is leading Cared Humanity, a care-based community encouraging mutual support for the fundamental human tasks of care (caredhumanity.com). She speaks passionately about the transformative power of caring and inspires people to be change agents, radically restructuring the landscape of care in bold and powerful ways.

H. Monty Montgomery has been working in collaboration with the Prairie Child Welfare Consortium since 2008, initially as executive director of the Saskatchewan First Nations Family and Community Institute and—since 2009—as an assistant professor in the Faculty of Social Work at the University of Regina Saskatoon campus. Monty was the lead organizer for the PCWC symposium 2014.

James Mulvale is dean of the Faculty of Social Work at the University of Manitoba. Previous to this appointment, he spent fourteen years at the University of Regina in the Department of Justice Studies and the Faculty of Social Work. His academic interests include poverty reduction, basic or guaranteed income, and the historical and theoretical foundations of social work. He is vice-chair of the Basic Income Canada Network and a member of the Social Policy Interest Group of the Canadian Association of Social Workers. Before embarking on his academic career, he worked in community development positions in the fields of developmental disability and community mental health in southwestern Ontario.

Doe O'Brien-Teengs is a Cree-Irish Canadian storyteller, writer, scholar, and activist. Although she grew up in Northern Ontario, she currently lives in southern Ontario with her wife and their two children. She developed connections with the Toronto Indigenous community when she worked for 2-Spirited People of the 1st Nations for seven years and the Ontario Aboriginal HIV/AIDS Strategy for fourteen years. Doe is currently working on her Ph.D. in education through Lakehead University. She is also engaged in a number of community-based research projects that involve Indigenous communities and various HIV issues in Ontario and nationally.

Elly Park holds a Ph.D. from the Faculty of Rehabilitation Medicine at the University of Alberta. Her doctoral work focused on using a narrative inquiry approach to understand experiences of young women with learning difficulties involved in the Canadian criminal justice system. Her research interests include young people involved in the criminal justice system, social justice, and restorative justice practices. She volunteers for different community organizations that work with marginalized populations, including the Youth Restorative Action Project (YRAP) and the Elizabeth Fry Society, and she hopes to bridge her research with social policies and community initiatives.

Megan Porter has worked as a community-based social worker since graduation and spent more than ten years working with children and families affected by HIV at the Teresa Group in Toronto, Ontario. With experience in case management, counselling children and family members, and running groups with children and parents living with HIV, as well as family members affected by HIV, she has had the privilege of learning from and with the people she works alongside.

Peter Smyth is currently with Alberta Human Services, Edmonton Region Child and Youth Services Division, overseeing the High Risk Youth Initiative. From 2005 to 2012, he was the supervisor of the High Risk Youth Unit. He developed a practice framework and philosophy incorporating nontraditional intervention methods to better meet the needs of this challenging population. Prior to this, he supervised the Inner City Connections partnership between government and inner city agencies. Peter has been a social worker for twenty-seven years. He is a co-founder of the Old Strathcona Youth Society in Edmonton, Alberta, which has served homeless and disadvantaged youth since 1998. He has written about issues confronting youth and provides consultation, training, and workshops on engaging and working with youth and understanding youth through an attachment, trauma, and brain development lens. Peter is a sessional instructor at the University of Calgary, Faculty of Social Work, Central and Northern Alberta Region.

Shelley Thomas Prokop is a Cree from Beardy's & Okemasis First Nation, north of Saskatoon. She has been involved with First Nations child welfare for much of her career, teaching in the faculty of social work and doing research and evaluation with First Nations in Saskatchewan and across Canada. Currently, she works as a policy analyst at the Saskatchewan First Nations Family & Community Institute and is excited to be part of a growing organization that focuses on professional development and research based on First Nations culture, tradition, and knowledge.

Subject Index

Author Index